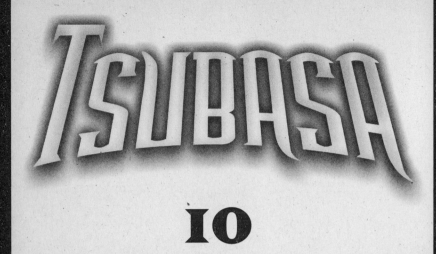

10

CLAMP

TRANSLATED AND ADAPTED BY
William Flanagan

LETTERED BY
Dana Hayward

BALLANTINE BOOKS · NEW YORK

Tsubasa volume 10 is a work of fiction. Names, characters, places, and incidents are the products of the author's imagination or are used fictitiously. Any resemblance to actual events, locales, or persons, living or dead, is entirely coincidental.

A Del Rey Trade Paperback Original

Published in the United States by Del Rey Books, an imprint of The Random House Publishing Group, a division of Random House, Inc., New York.

Publication rights arranged through Kodansha, Ltd.

First published in Japan in 2005 by Kodansha, Ltd., Tokyo

ISBN 0-345-48430-4

Printed in the United States of America

www.delreymanga.com

9 8 7 6 5 4 3

Lettered by Dana Hayward

Translation and adaptation by William Flanagan

Contents

Tsubasa crosses over with *xxxHOLiC*. Although it isn't necessary to read *xxxHOLiC* to understand the events in *Tsubasa*, you'll get to see the same events from different perspectives if you read both!

Honorifics Explained

Throughout the Del Rey Manga books, you will find Japanese honorifics left intact in the translations. For those not familiar with how the Japanese use honorifics and, more important, how they differ from American honorifics, we present this brief overview.

Politeness has always been a critical facet of Japanese culture. Ever since the feudal era, when Japan was a highly stratified society, use of honorifics — which can be defined as polite speech that indicates relationship or status — has played an essential role in the Japanese language. When addressing someone in Japanese, an honorific usually takes the form of a suffix attached to one's name (example: "Asuna-san"), or as a title at the end of one's name or in place of the name itself (example: "Negi-sensei," or simply "Sensei!").

Honorifics can be expressions of respect or endearment. In the context of manga and anime, honorifics give insight into the nature of the relationship between characters. Many translations into English leave out these important honorifics, and therefore distort the "feel" of the original Japanese. Because Japanese honorifics contain nuances that English honorifics lack, it is our policy at Del Rey not to translate them. Here, instead, is a guide to some of the honorifics you may encounter in Del Rey Manga.

-san: This is the most common honorific, and is equivalent to Mr., Miss, Ms., Mrs., etc. It is the all-purpose honorific and can be used in any situation where politeness is required.

-sama: This is one level higher than "-san." It is used to confer great respect.

-dono: This comes from the word "tono," which means "lord." It is an even higher level than "-sama" and confers utmost respect.

-kun: This suffix is used at the end of boys' names to express familiarity or endearment. It is also sometimes used by men among friends, or when addressing someone younger or of a lower station.

-chan: This is used to express endearment, mostly toward girls. It is also used for little boys, pets, and even among lovers. It gives a sense of childish cuteness.

Bozu: This is an informal way to refer to a boy, similar to the English term "kid" or "squirt."

Sempai/senpai: This title suggests that the addressee is one's senior in a group or organization. It is most often used in a school setting, where underclassmen refer to their upperclassmen as "sempai." It can also be used in the workplace, such as when a newer employee addresses an employee who has seniority in the company.

Kohai: This is the opposite of "sempai," and is used toward underclassmen in school or newcomers in the workplace. It connotes that the addressee is of a lower station.

Sensei: Literally meaning "one who has come before," this title is used for teachers, doctors, or masters of any profession or art.

-[blank]: Usually forgotten in these lists, but perhaps the most significant difference between Japanese and English. The lack of honorific means that the speaker has permission to address the person in a very intimate way. Usually, only family, spouses, or very close friends have this kind of permission. Known as *yobisute*, it can be gratifying when someone who has earned the intimacy starts to call one by one's name without an honorific. But when that intimacy hasn't been earned, it can also be very insulting.

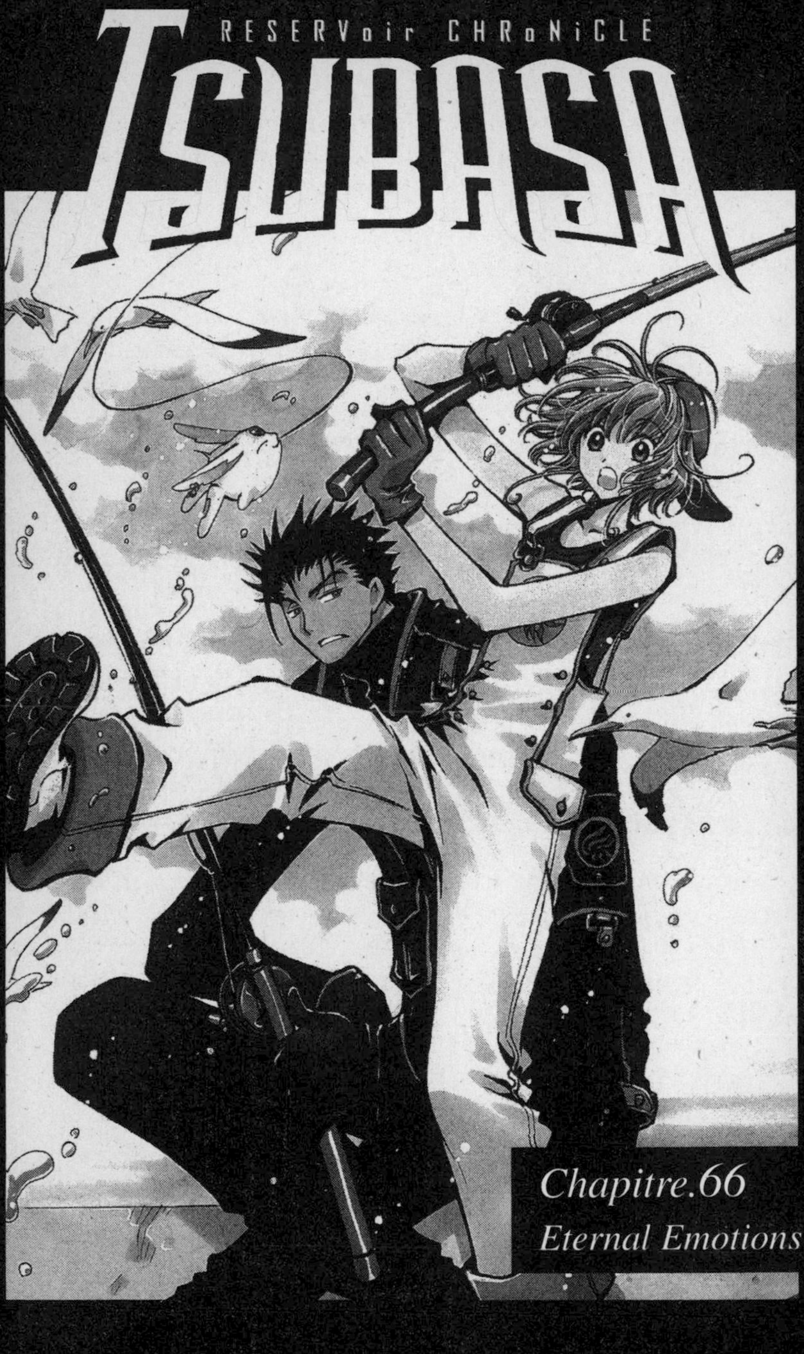
RESERVoir CHRoNiCLE
TSUBASA
Chapitre.66
Eternal Emotions

ツバサ

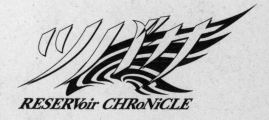

RESERVoir CHRoNiCLE

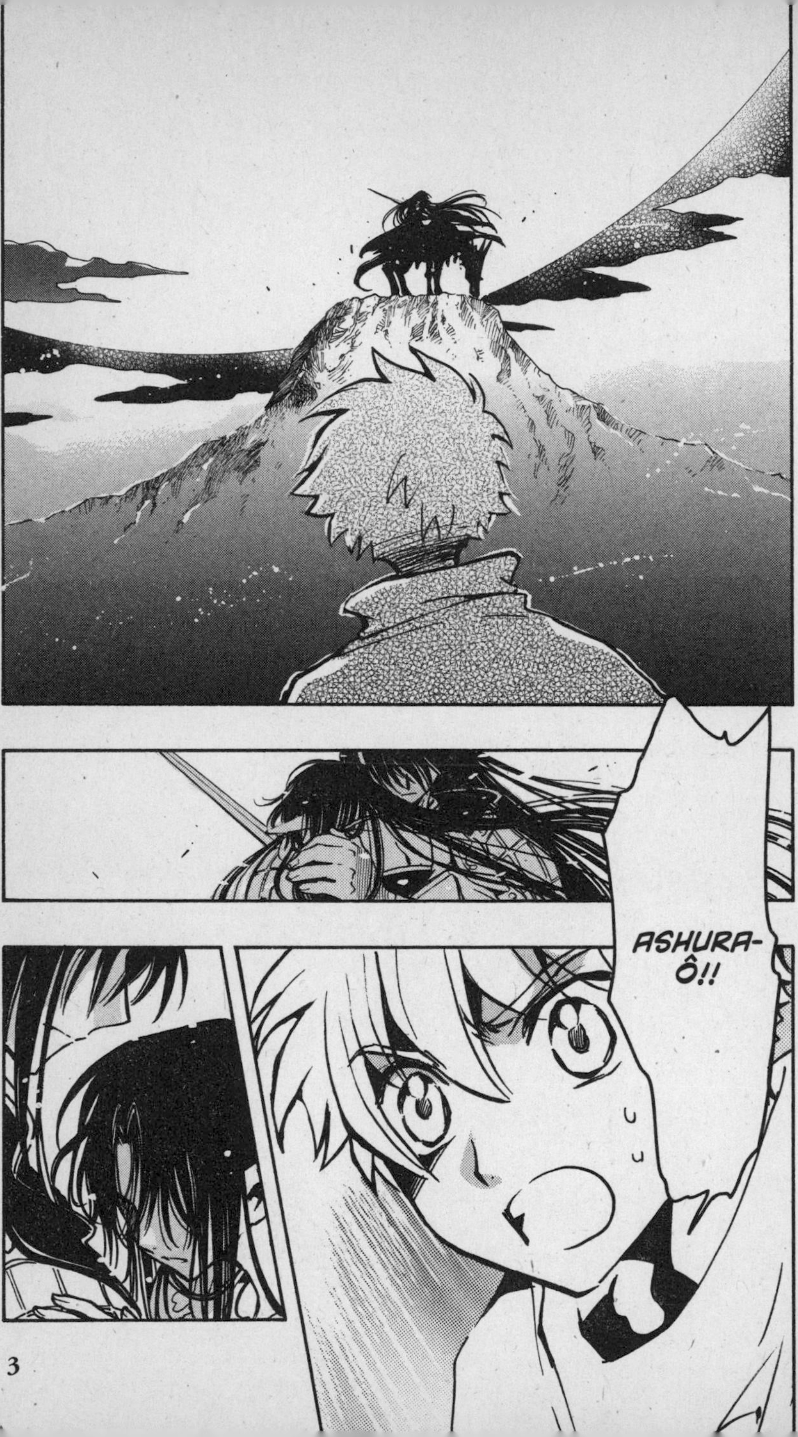
ASHURA-
Ô!!

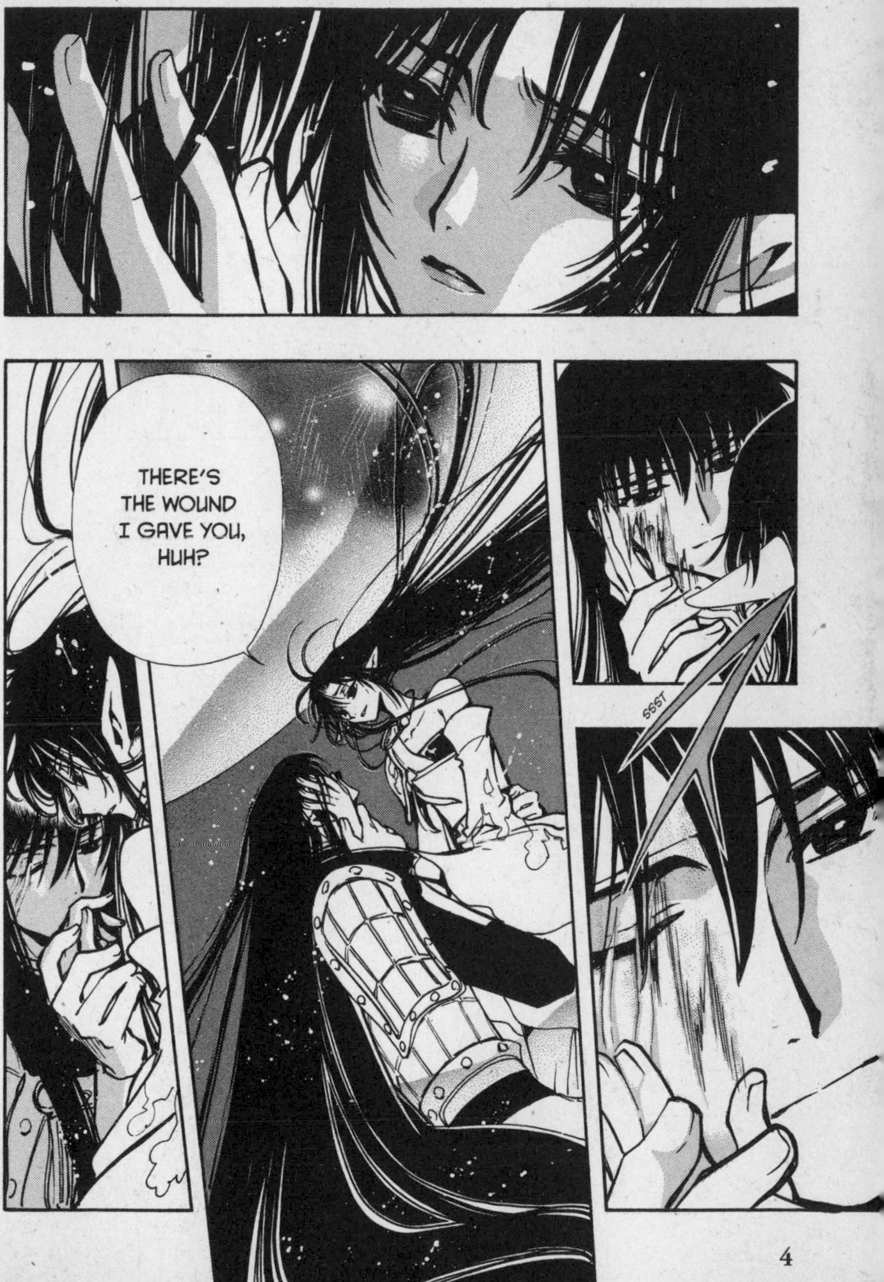
THERE'S THE WOUND I GAVE YOU, HUH?
SSST

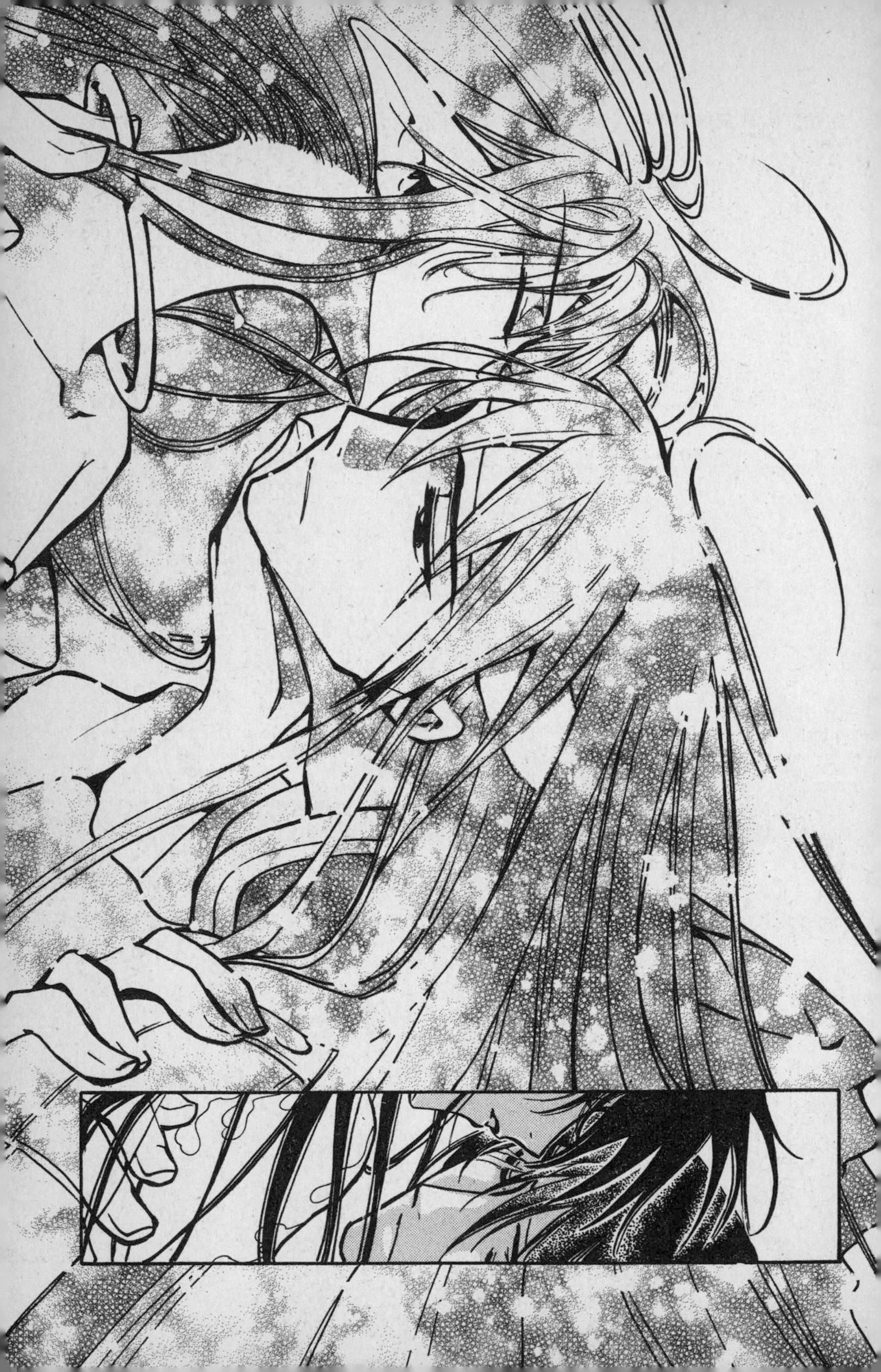

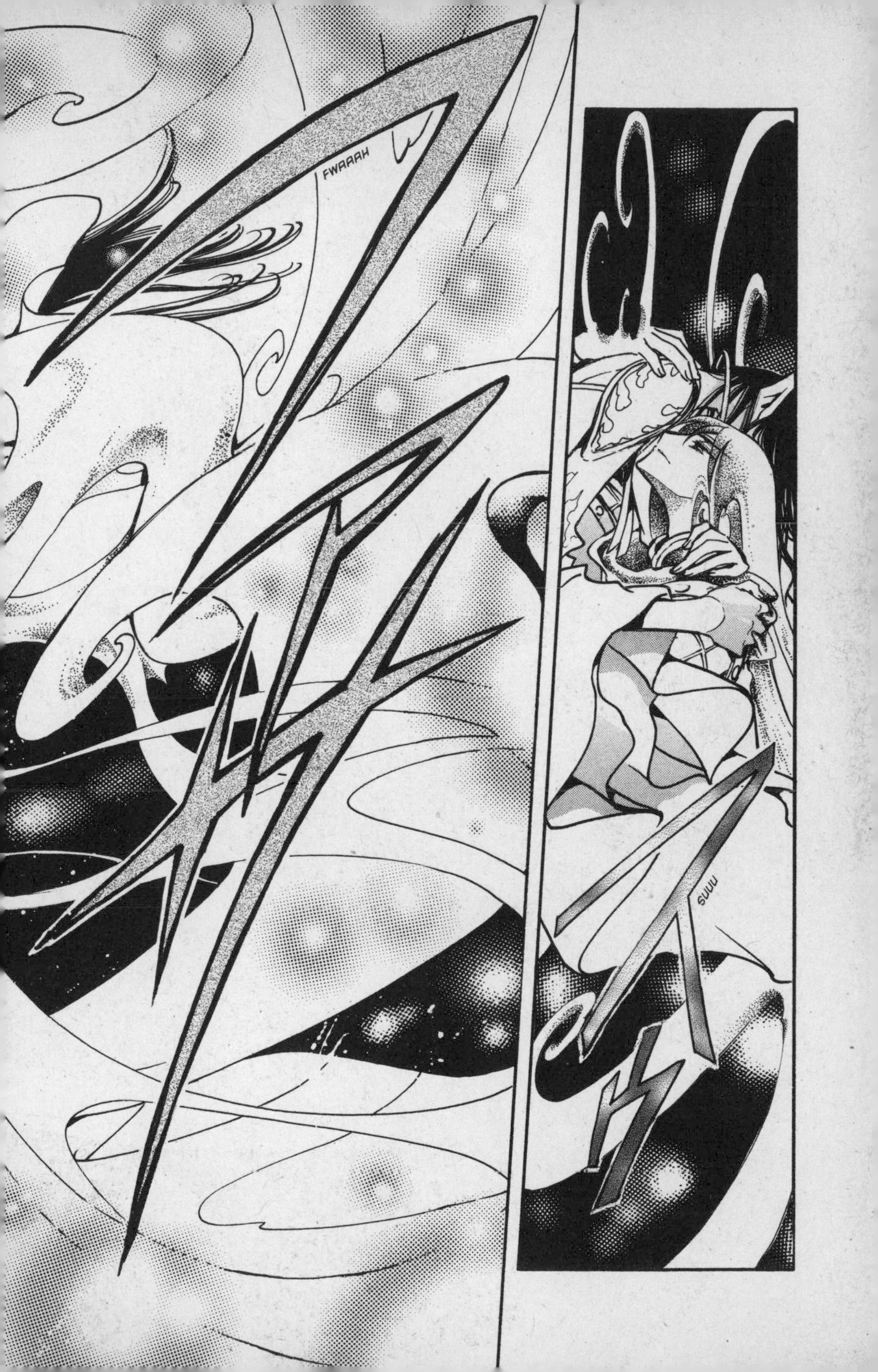
SUUU
FWAAAH

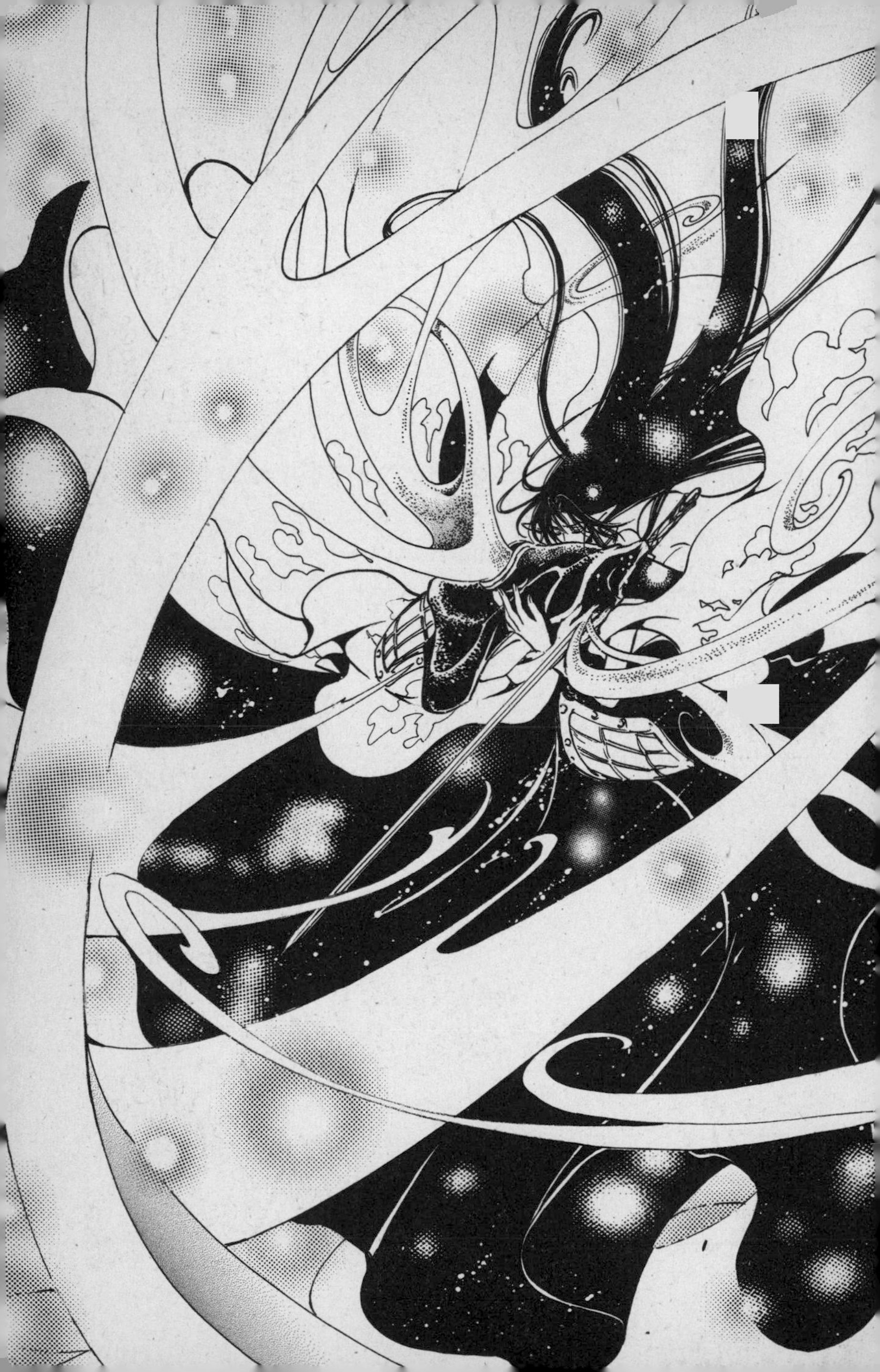

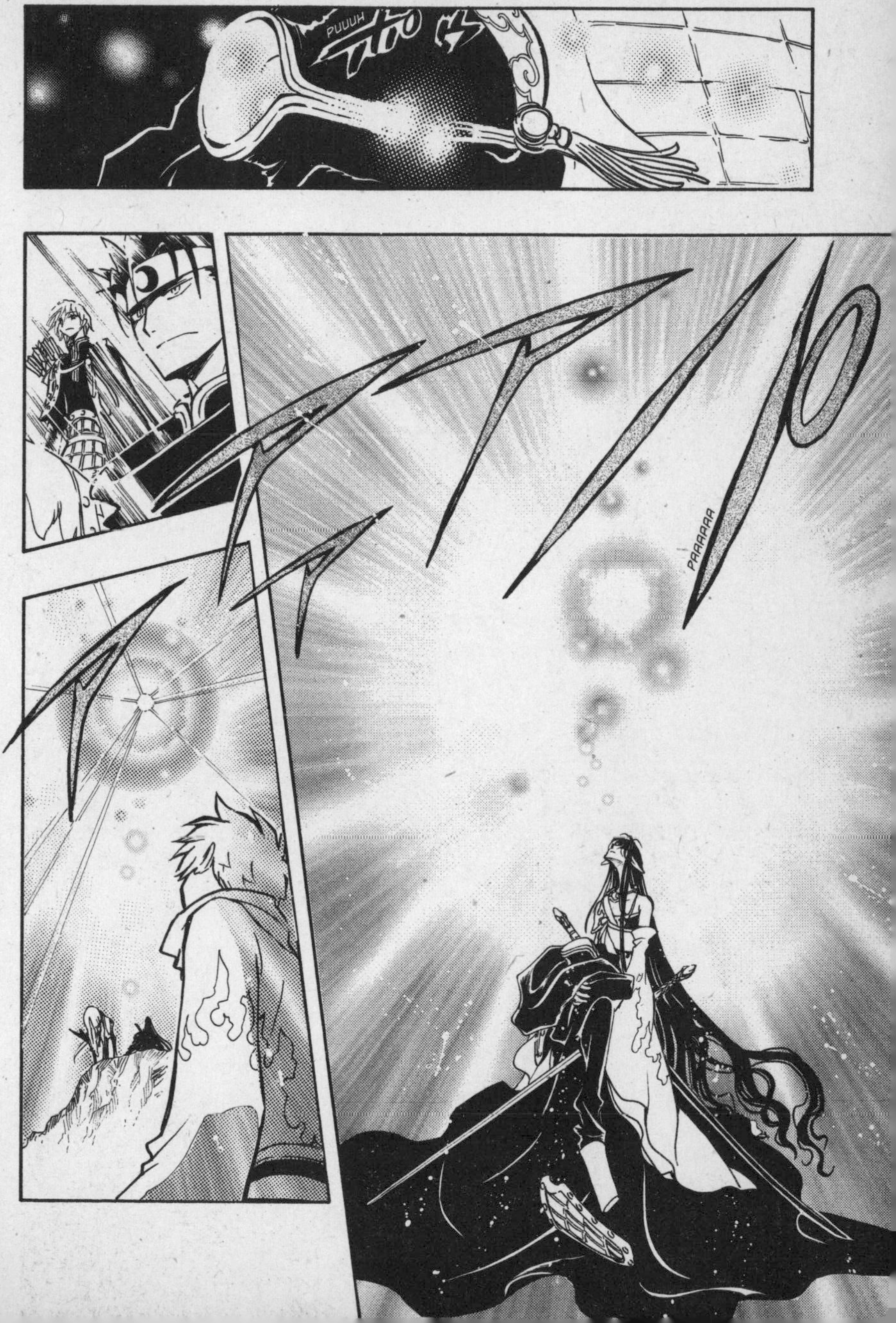
PUUUH
PAAAAAA

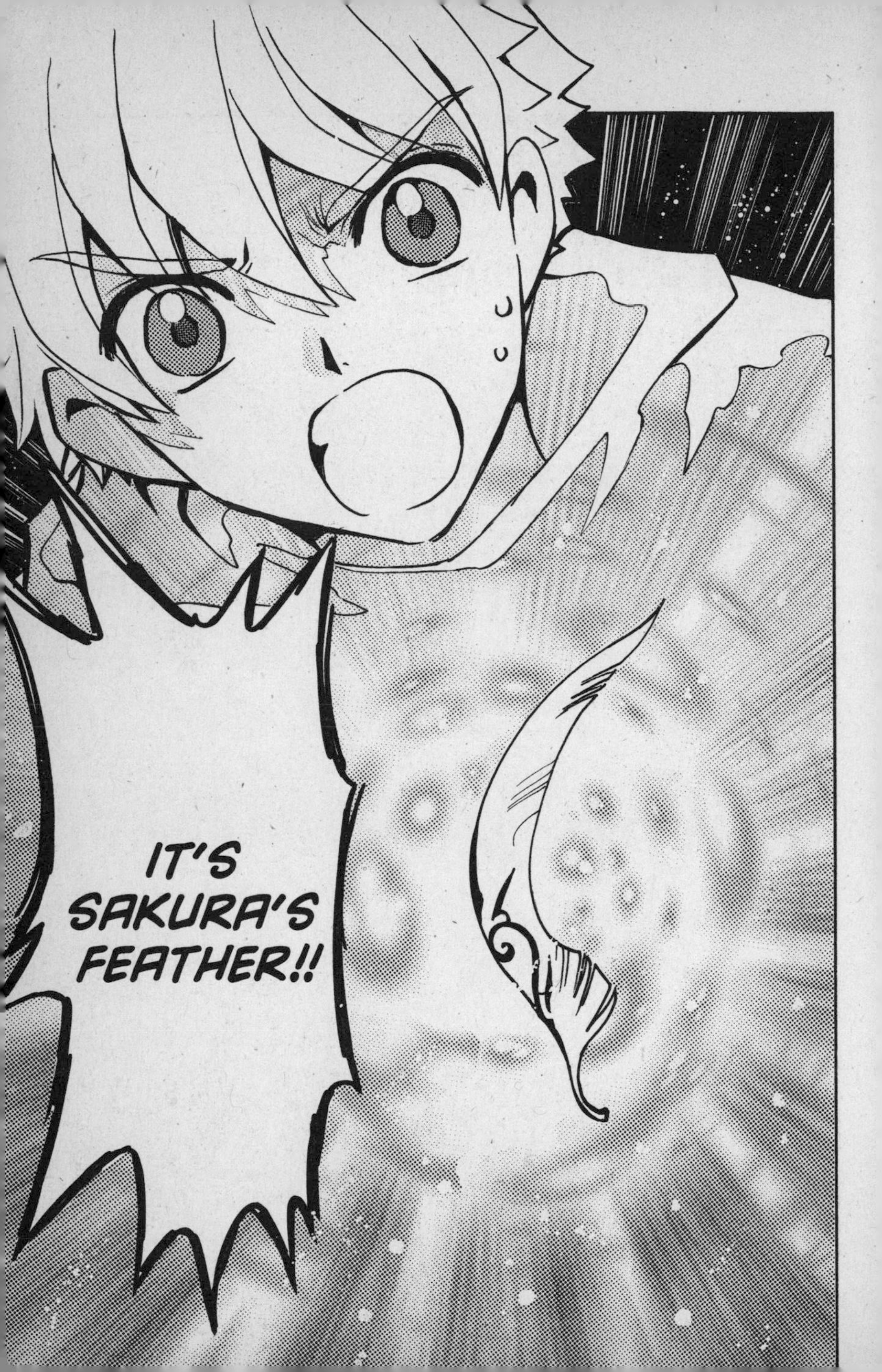
IT'S SAKURA'S FEATHER!!

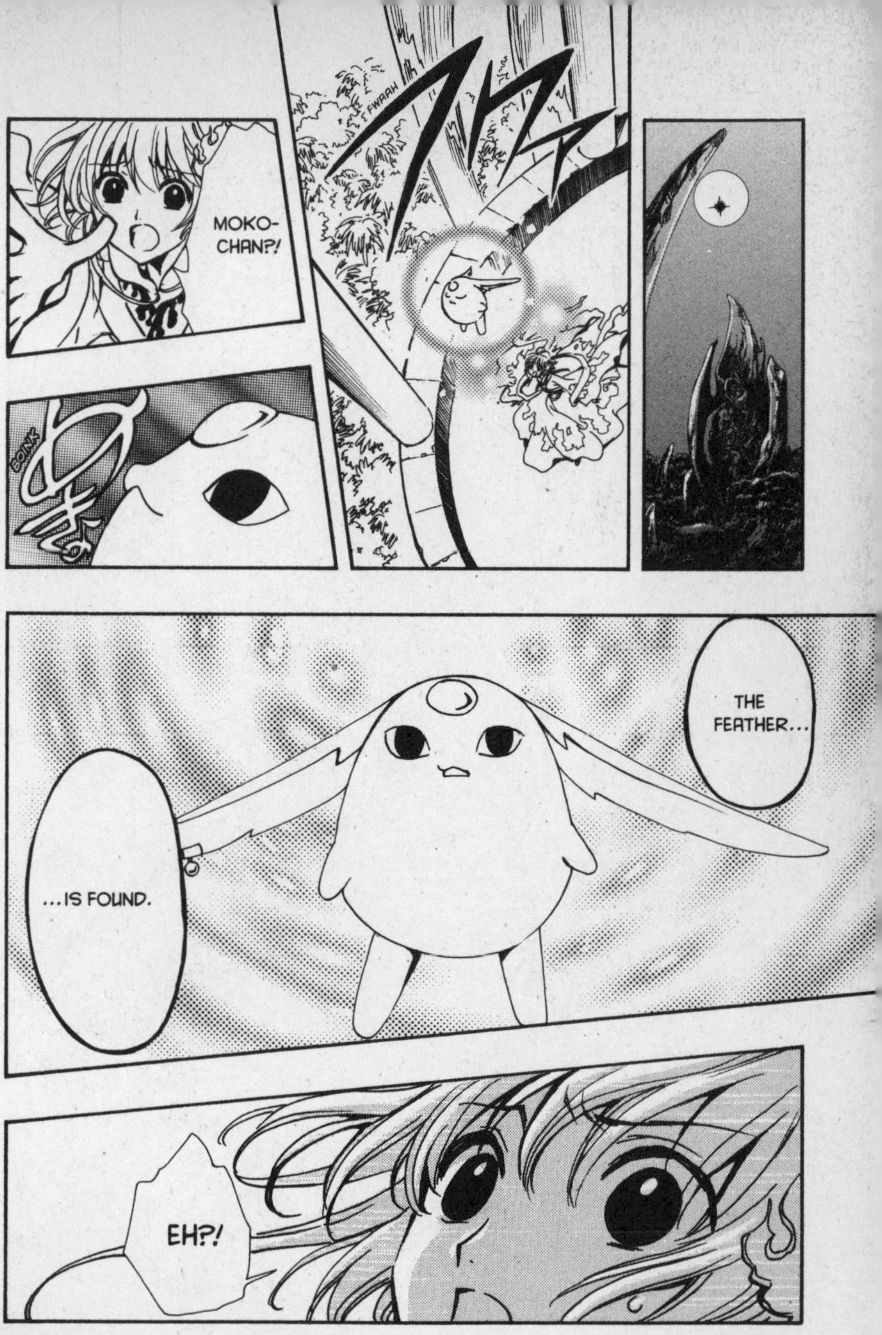
FWAAH
MOKO-CHAN?!
BOINK
THE FEATHER...
...IS FOUND.
EH?!

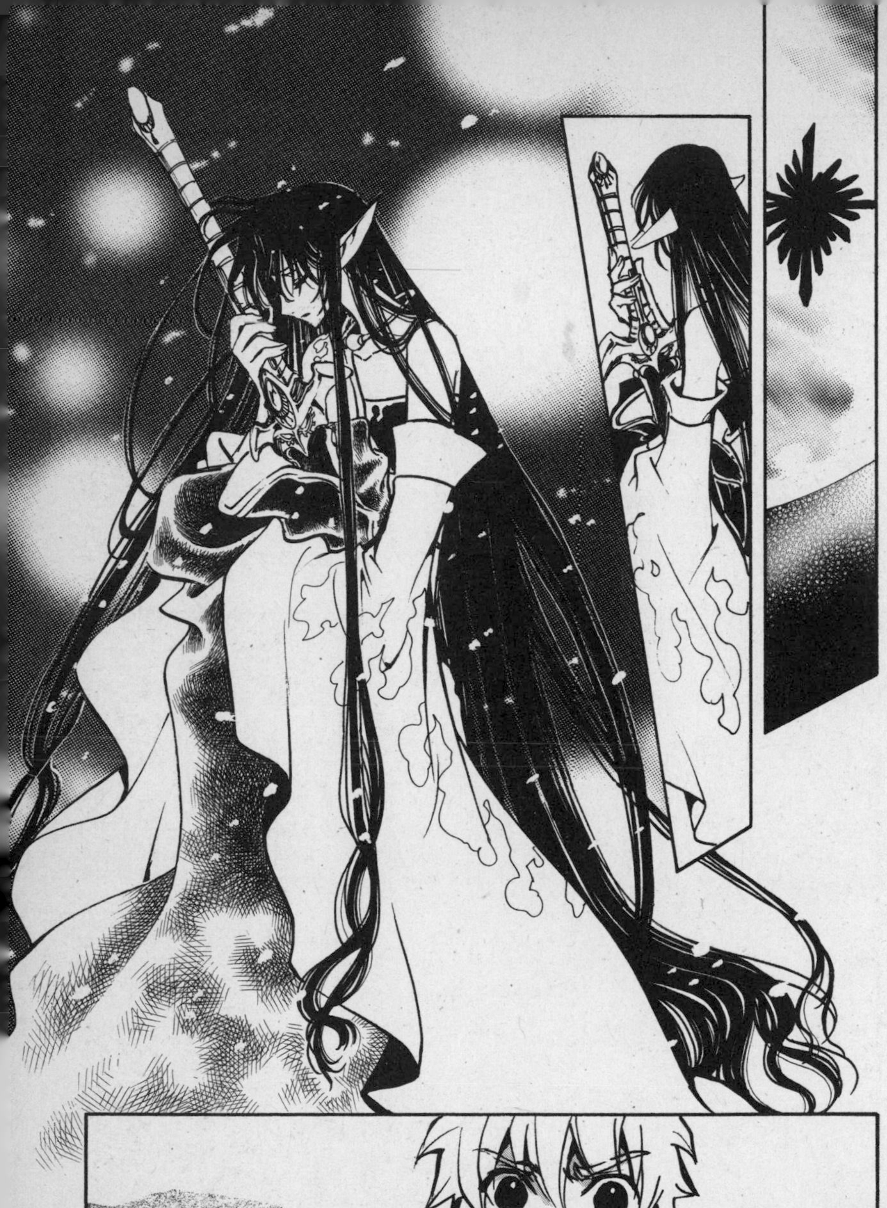

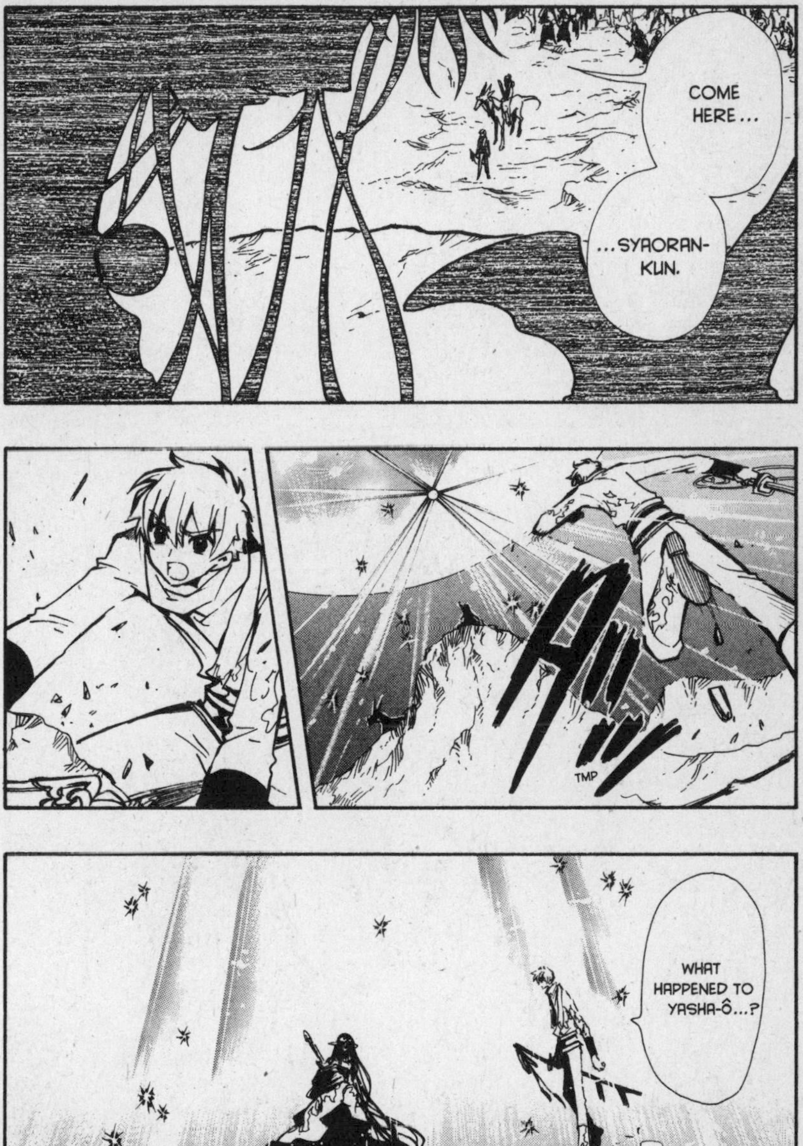
COME HERE...
...SYAORAN-KUN.
TMP
WHAT HAPPENED TO YASHA-Ô...?

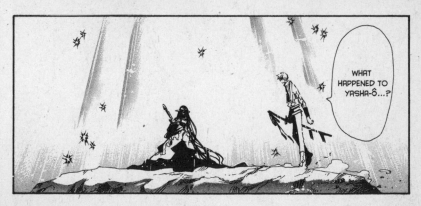

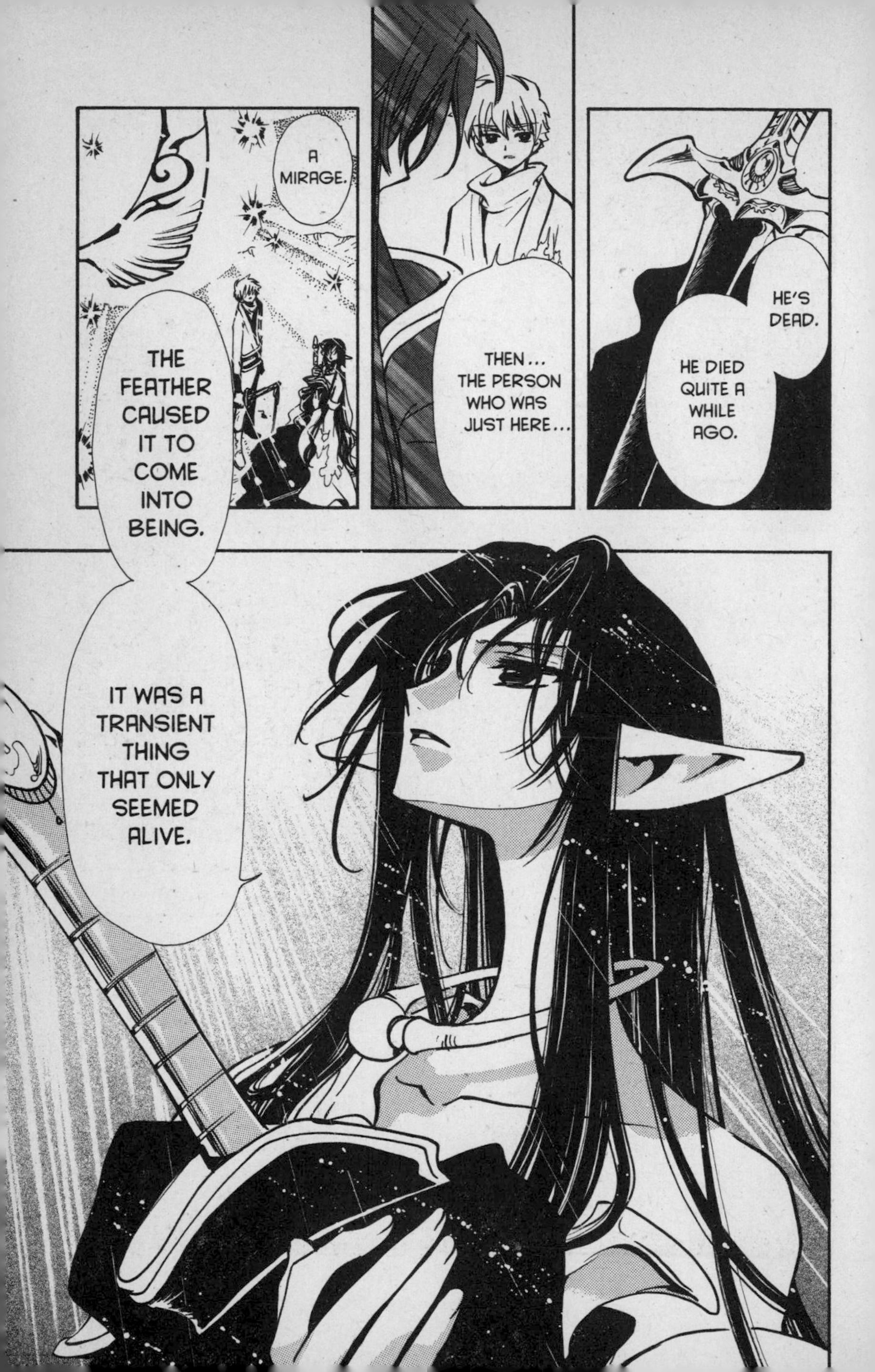
HE'S DEAD.
HE DIED QUITE A WHILE AGO.
THEN... THE PERSON WHO WAS JUST HERE...
A MIRAGE.
THE FEATHER CAUSED IT TO COME INTO BEING.
IT WAS A TRANSIENT THING THAT ONLY SEEMED ALIVE.

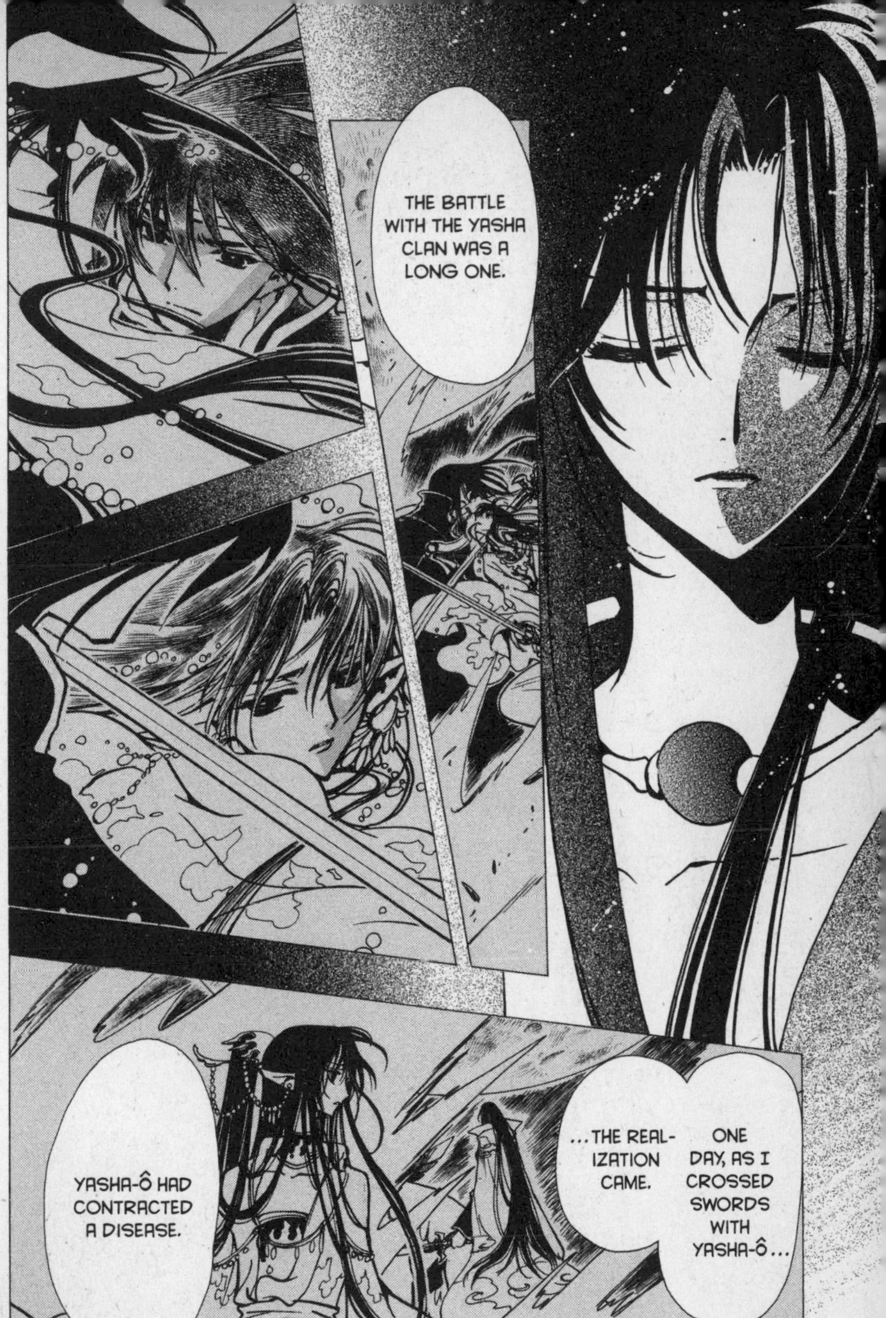
THE BATTLE WITH THE YASHA CLAN WAS A LONG ONE.
ONE DAY, AS I CROSSED SWORDS WITH YASHA-Ô...
...THE REAL-IZATION CAME.
YASHA-Ô HAD CONTRACTED A DISEASE.

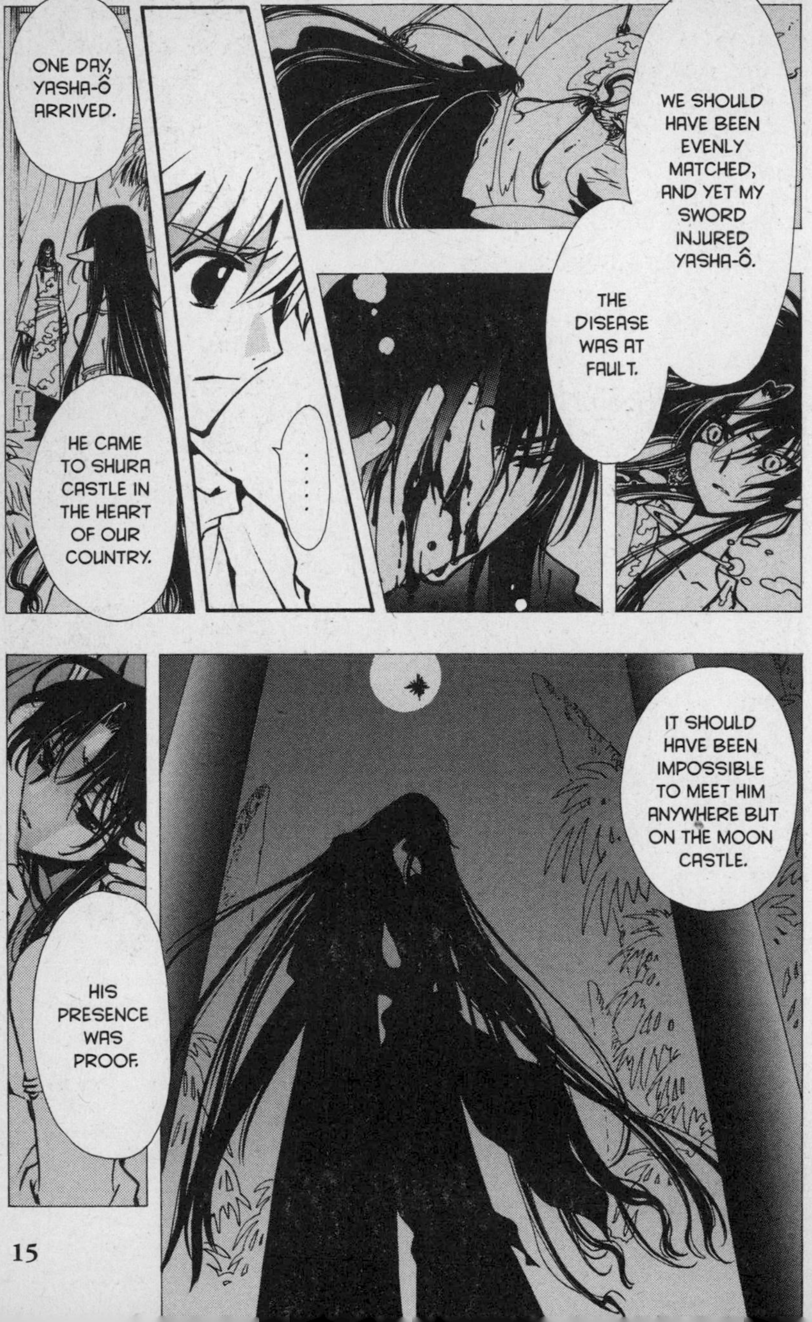
WE SHOULD HAVE BEEN EVENLY MATCHED, AND YET MY SWORD INJURED YASHA-Ô.
THE DISEASE WAS AT FAULT.
......
ONE DAY, YASHA-Ô ARRIVED.
HE CAME TO SHURA CASTLE IN THE HEART OF OUR COUNTRY.
IT SHOULD HAVE BEEN IMPOSSIBLE TO MEET HIM ANYWHERE BUT ON THE MOON CASTLE.
HIS PRESENCE WAS PROOF.

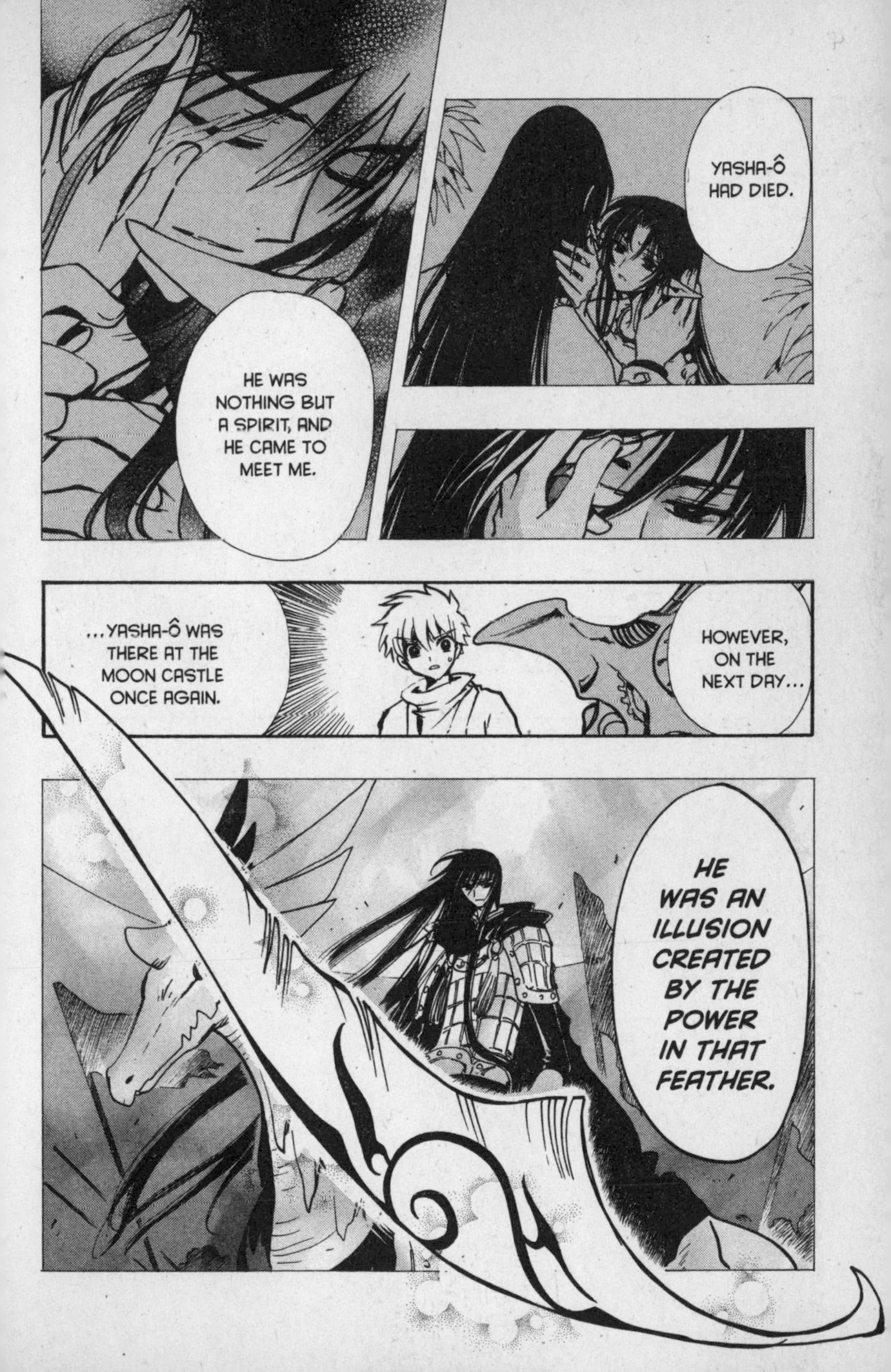
YASHA-Ô HAD DIED.
HE WAS NOTHING BUT A SPIRIT, AND HE CAME TO MEET ME.
HOWEVER, ON THE NEXT DAY...
...YASHA-Ô WAS THERE AT THE MOON CASTLE ONCE AGAIN.
HE WAS AN ILLUSION CREATED BY THE POWER IN THAT FEATHER.

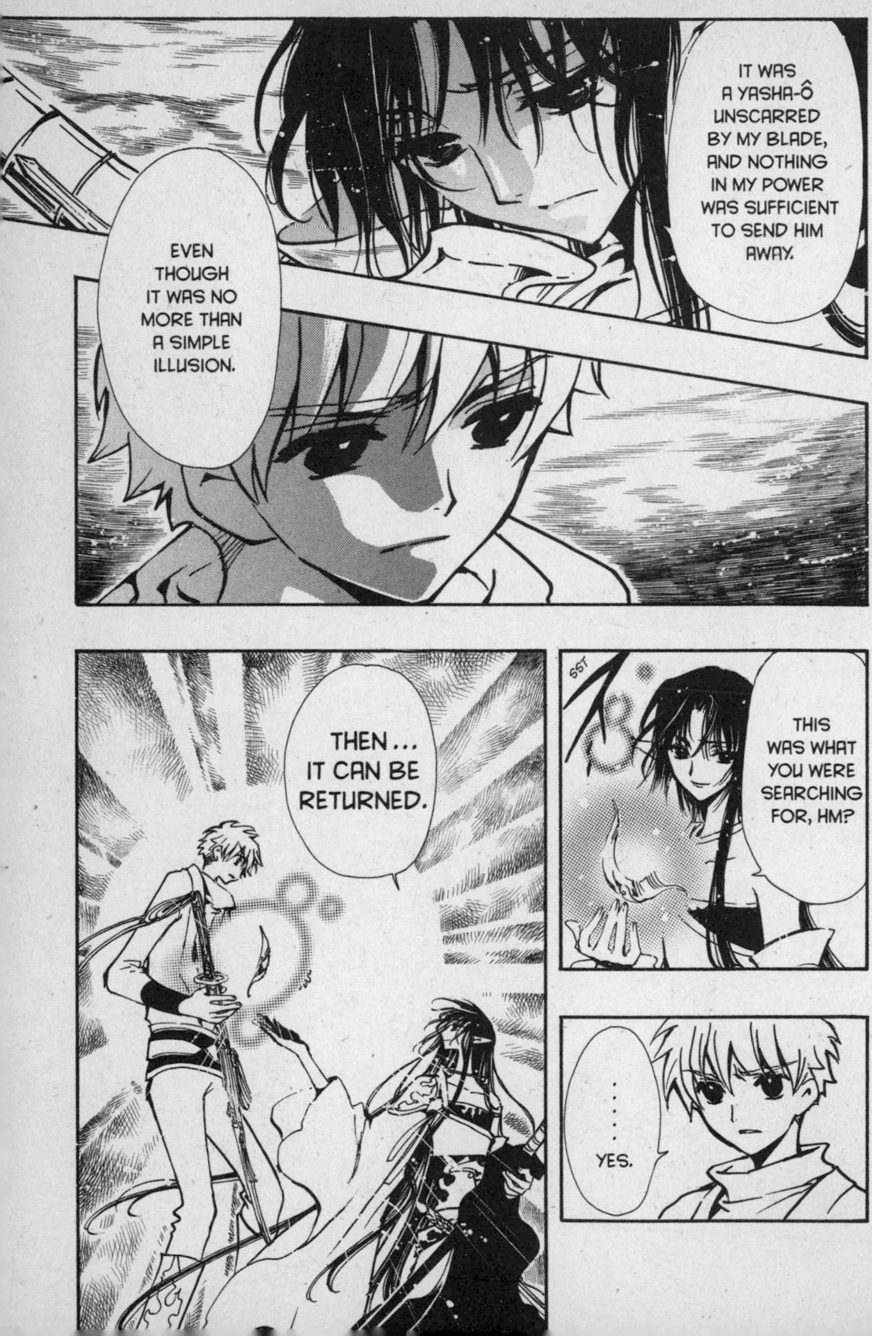
IT WAS A YASHA-Ô UNSCARRED BY MY BLADE, AND NOTHING IN MY POWER WAS SUFFICIENT TO SEND HIM AWAY.
EVEN THOUGH IT WAS NO MORE THAN A SIMPLE ILLUSION.
SST
THIS WAS WHAT YOU WERE SEARCHING FOR, HM?
...... YES.
THEN... IT CAN BE RETURNED.

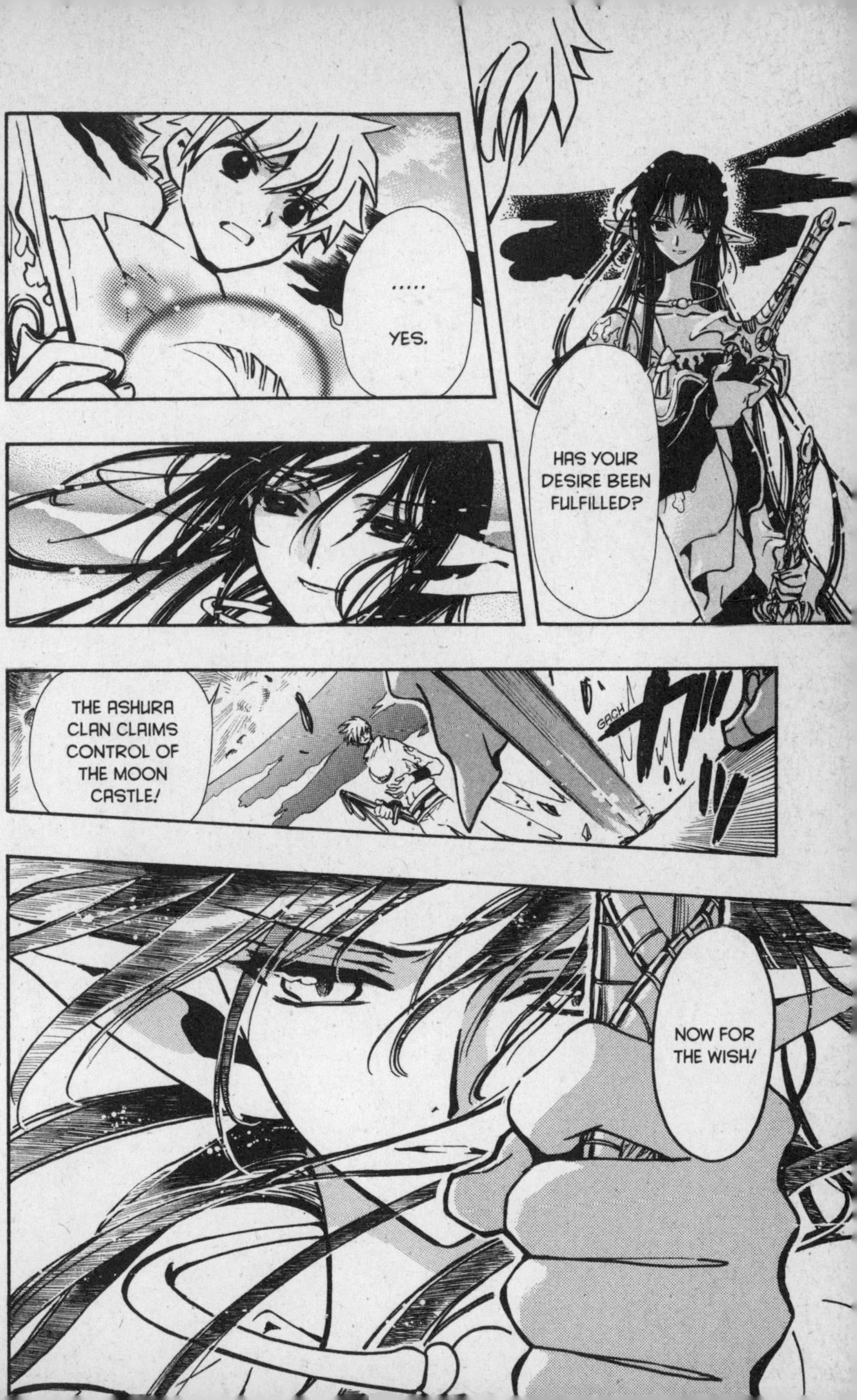
HAS YOUR DESIRE BEEN FULFILLED?
..... YES.
GACH
THE ASHURA CLAN CLAIMS CONTROL OF THE MOON CASTLE!
NOW FOR THE WISH!

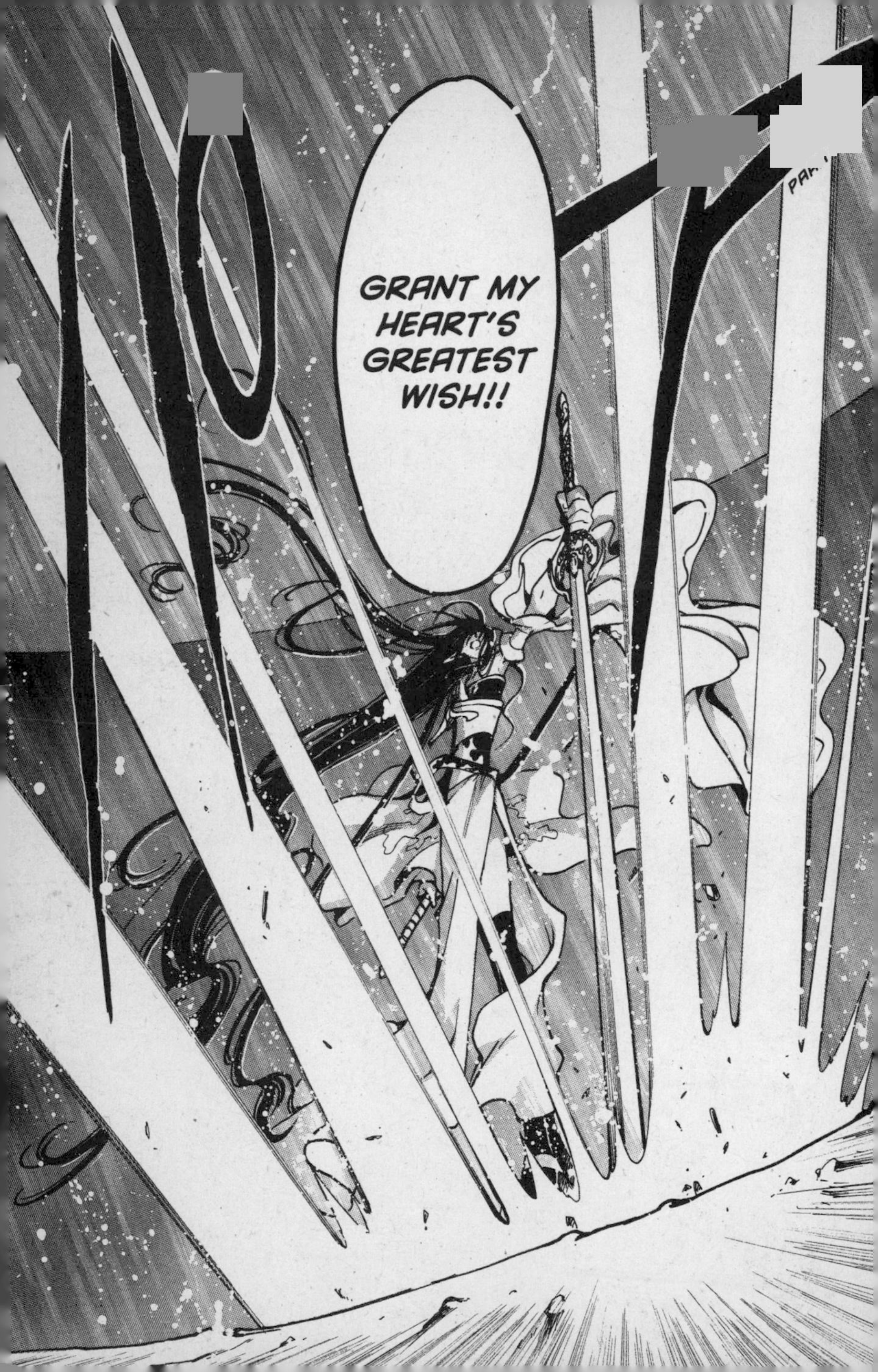
GRANT MY HEART'S GREATEST WISH!!

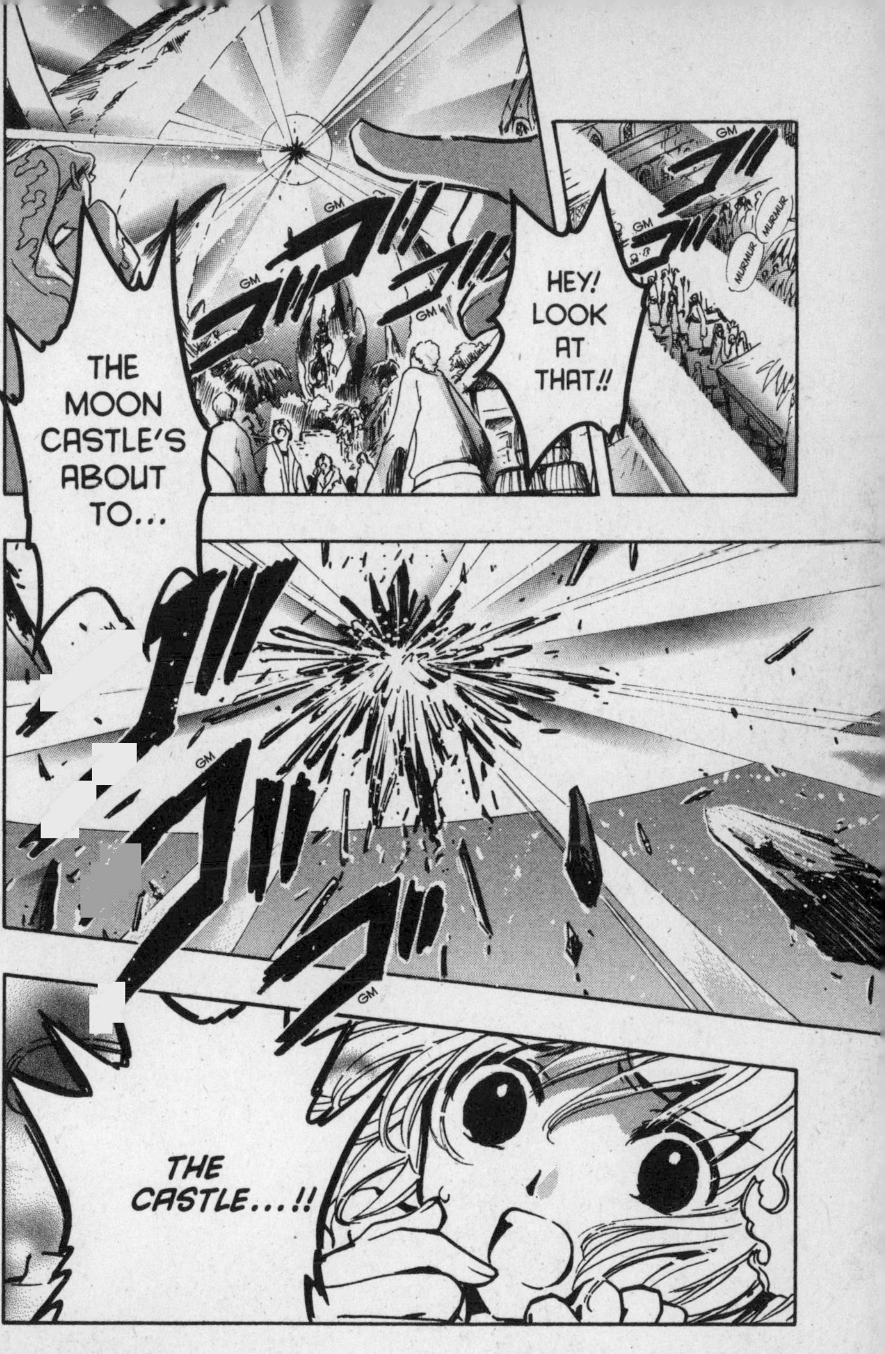
GM
GM
MURMUR
MURMUR
HEY! LOOK AT THAT!!
GM
GM
GM
THE MOON CASTLE'S ABOUT TO...
GM
GM
THE CASTLE...!!

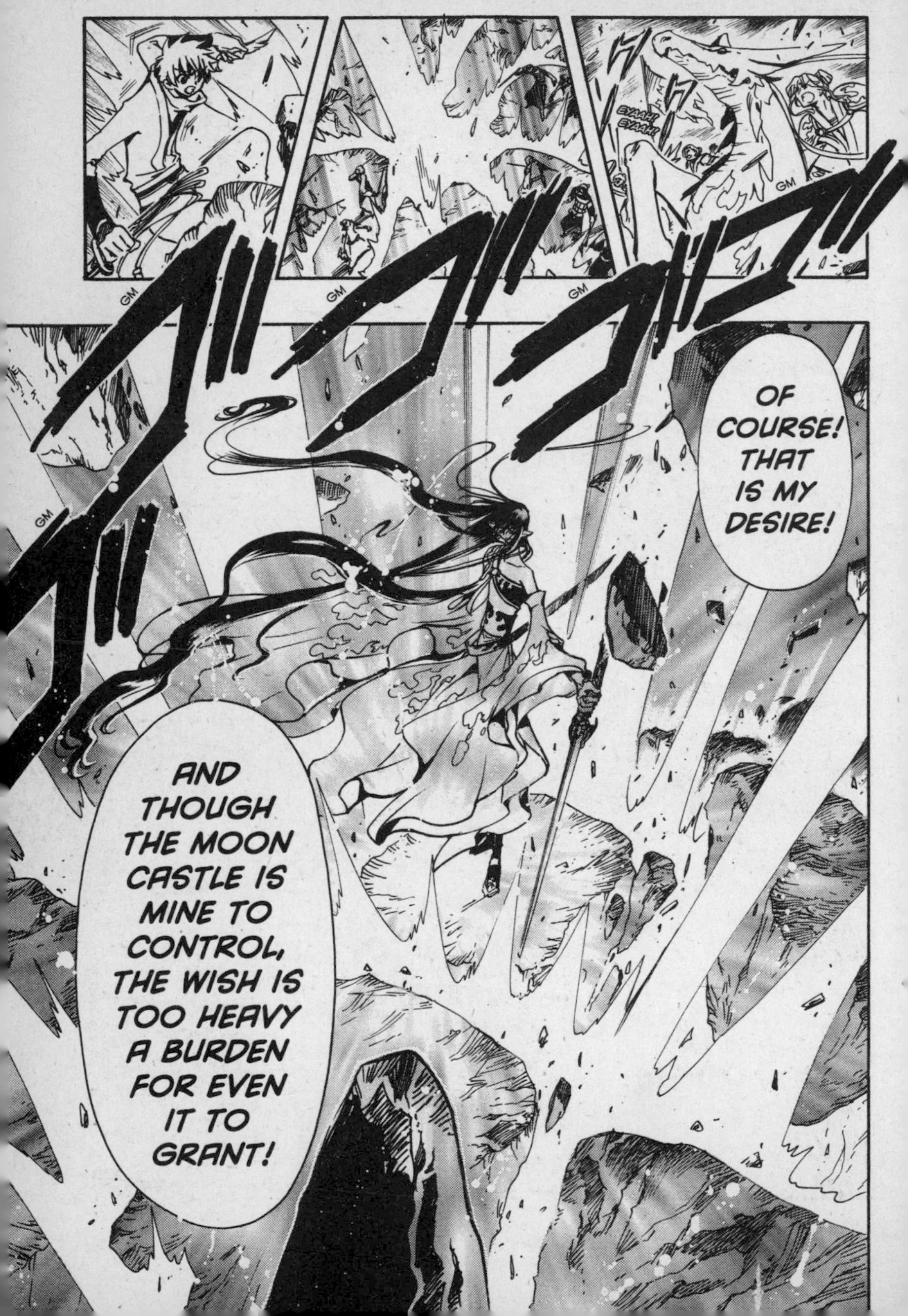
EYAAH!
EYAAH!
GM
GM
GM
GM
GM
OF COURSE! THAT IS MY DESIRE!
AND THOUGH THE MOON CASTLE IS MINE TO CONTROL, THE WISH IS TOO HEAVY A BURDEN FOR EVEN IT TO GRANT!

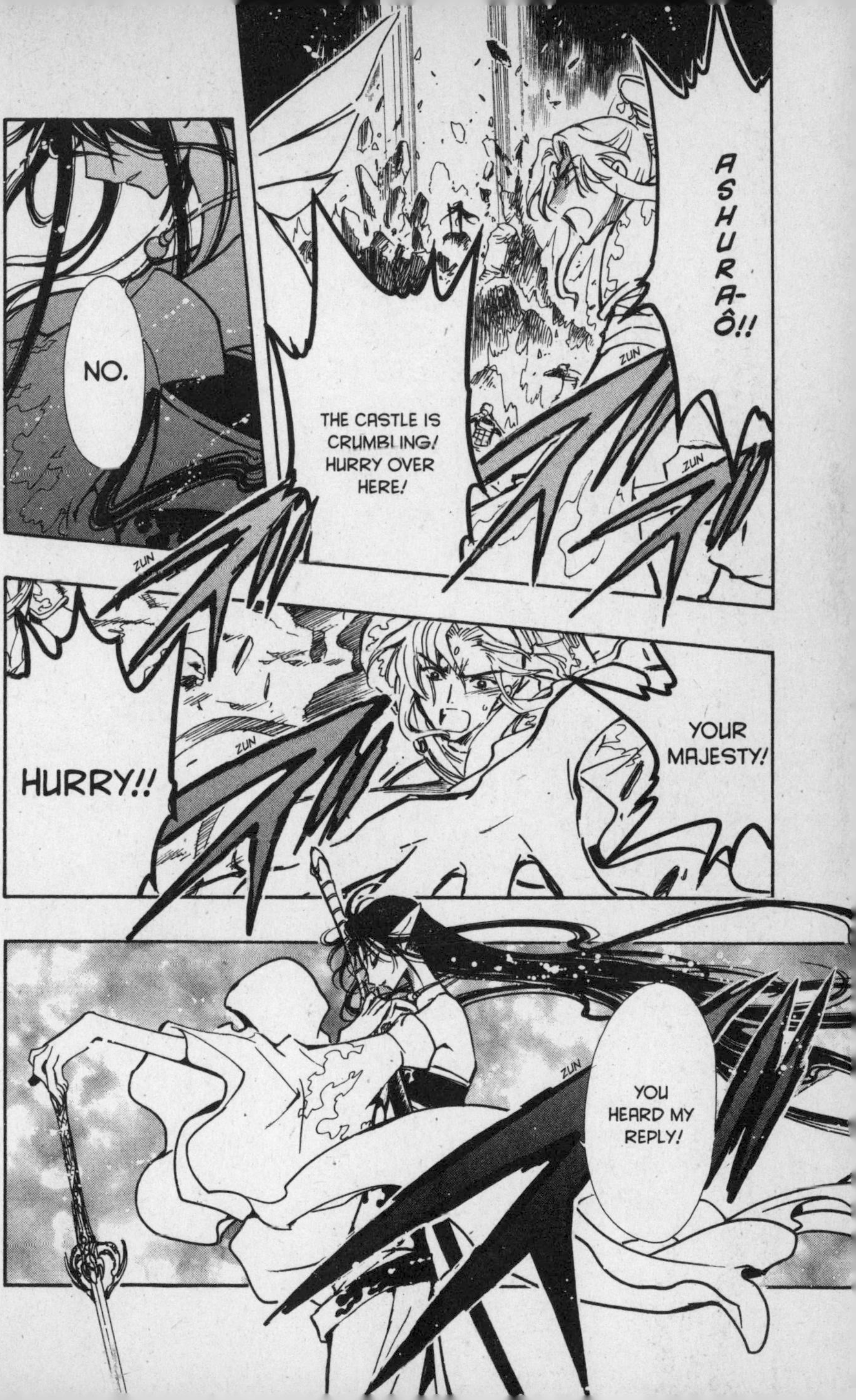
ASHURA-Ô!!
ZUN
ZUN
THE CASTLE IS CRUMBLING! HURRY OVER HERE!
NO.
ZUN
YOUR MAJESTY!
ZUN
HURRY!!
ZUN
YOU HEARD MY REPLY!

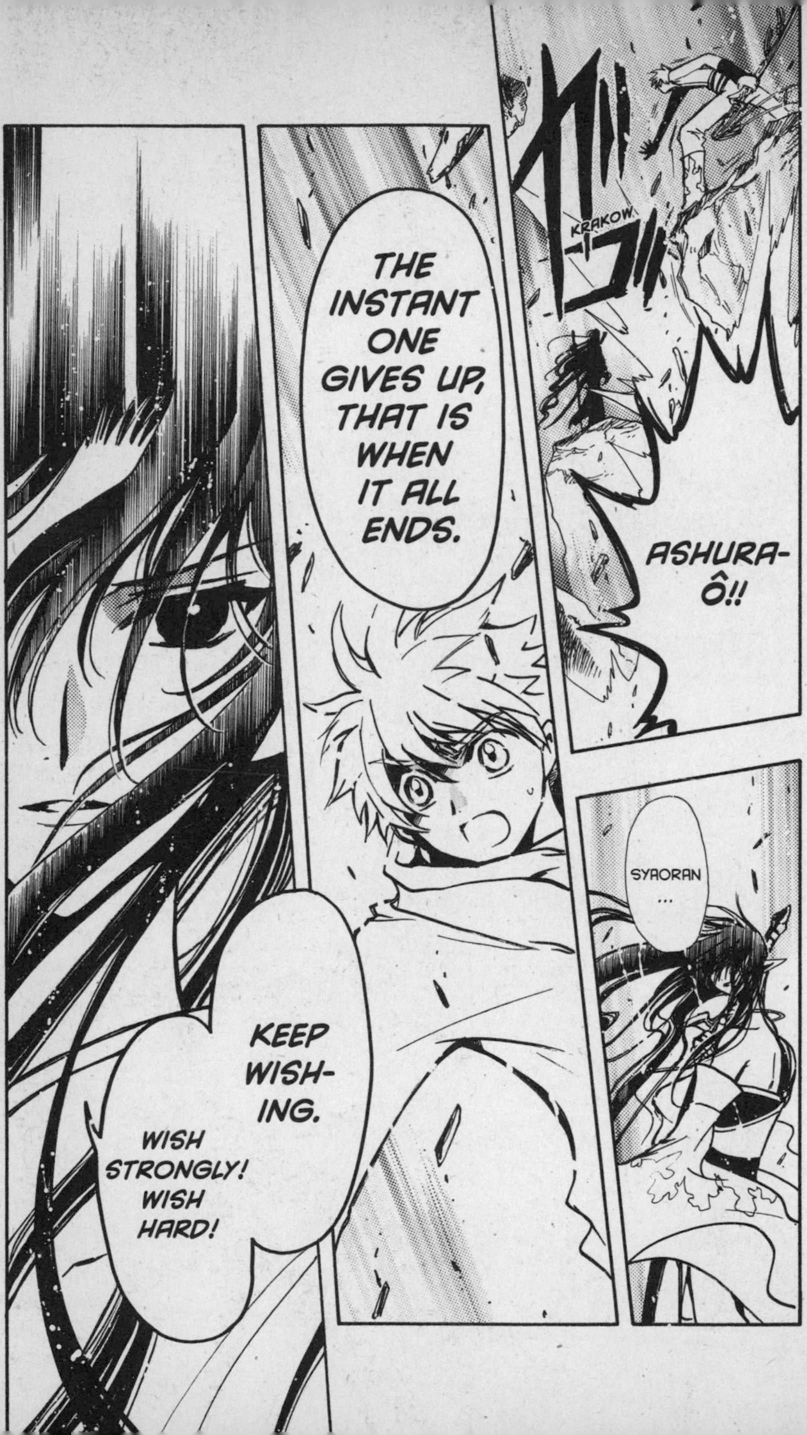
KRAKOW
ASHURA-Ô!!
SYAORAN ...
THE INSTANT ONE GIVES UP, THAT IS WHEN IT ALL ENDS.
KEEP WISH-ING.
WISH STRONGLY! WISH HARD!

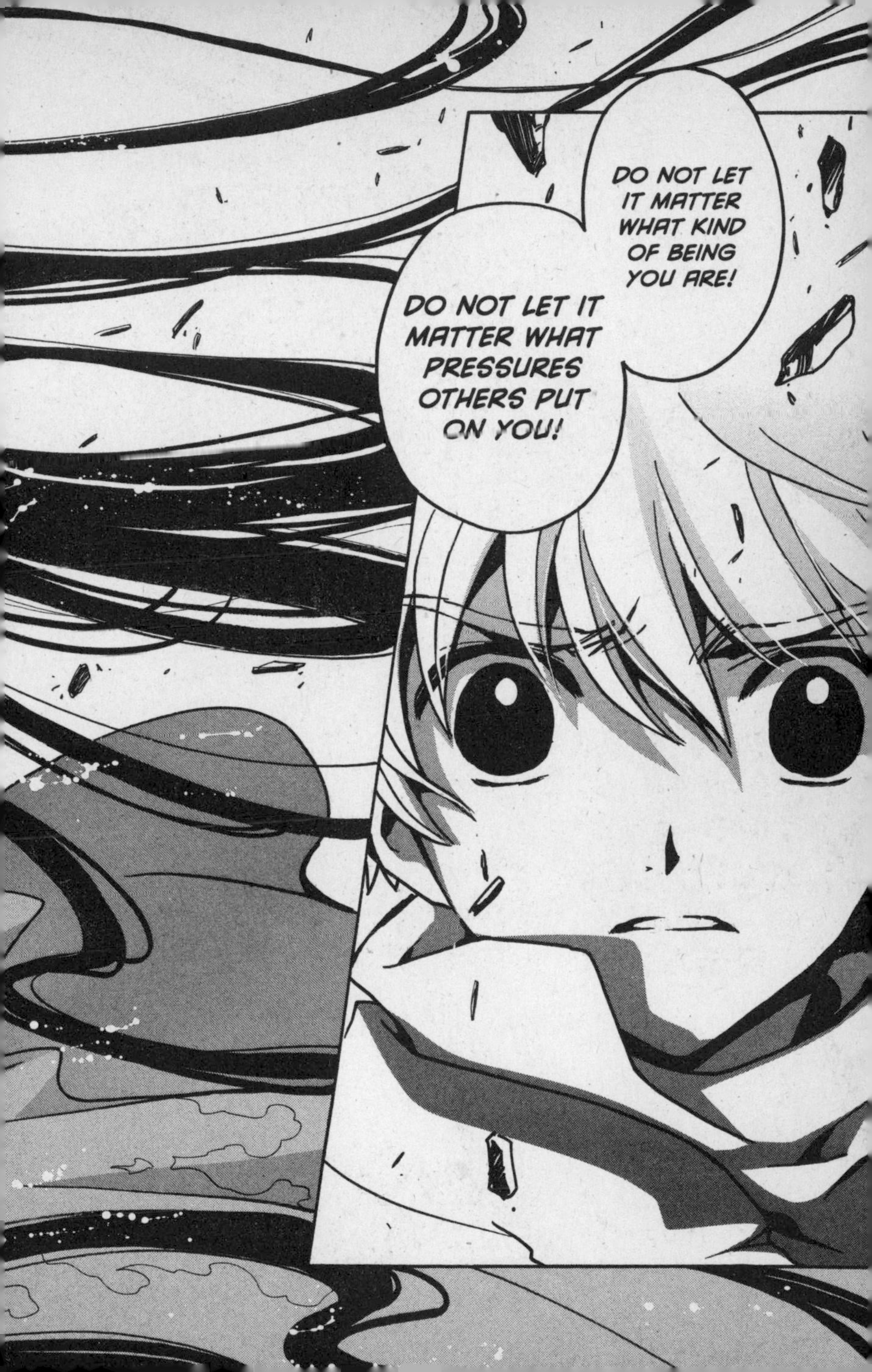
DO NOT LET IT MATTER WHAT KIND OF BEING YOU ARE!
DO NOT LET IT MATTER WHAT PRESSURES OTHERS PUT ON YOU!

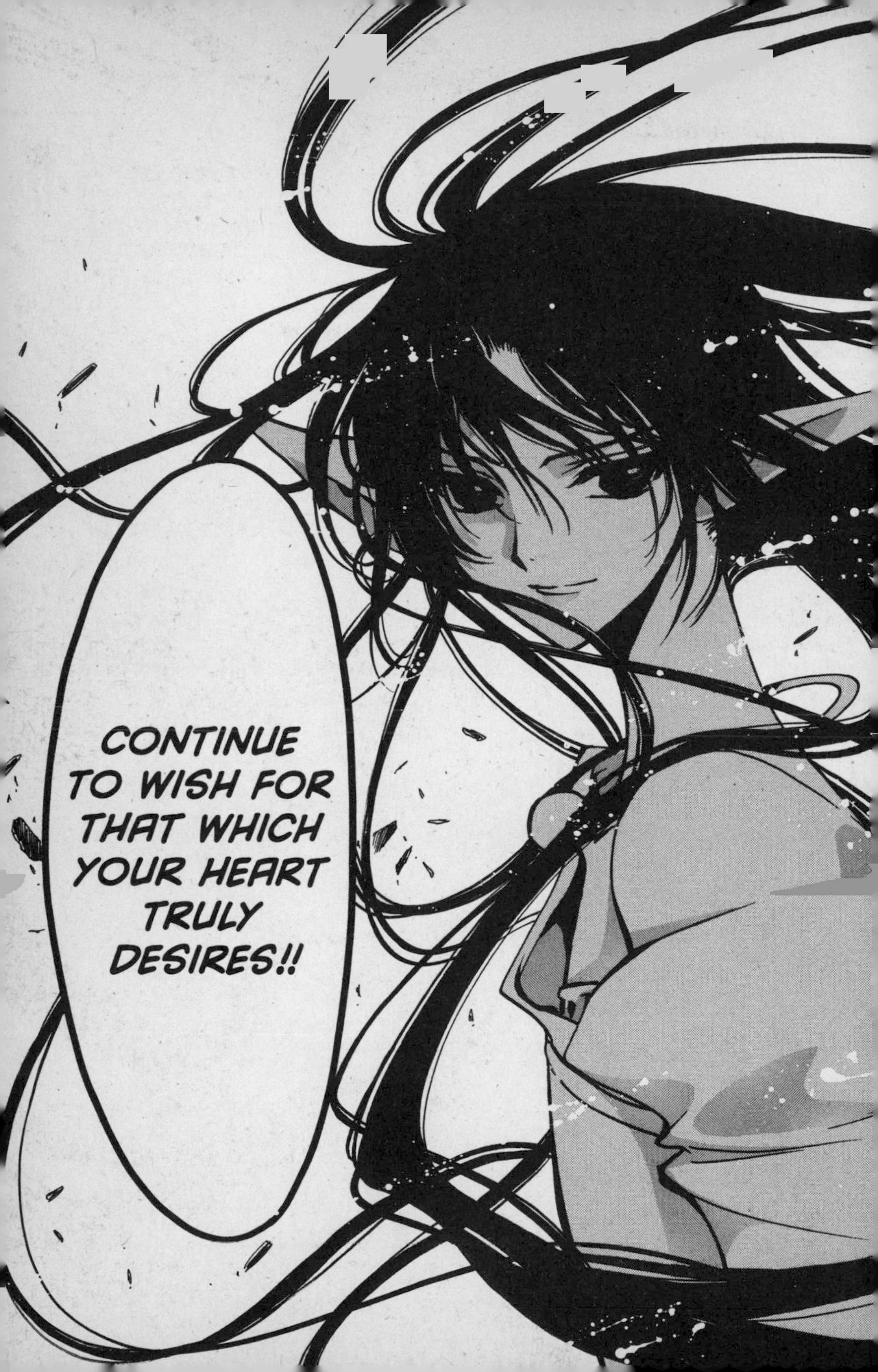
CONTINUE TO WISH FOR THAT WHICH YOUR HEART TRULY DESIRES!!

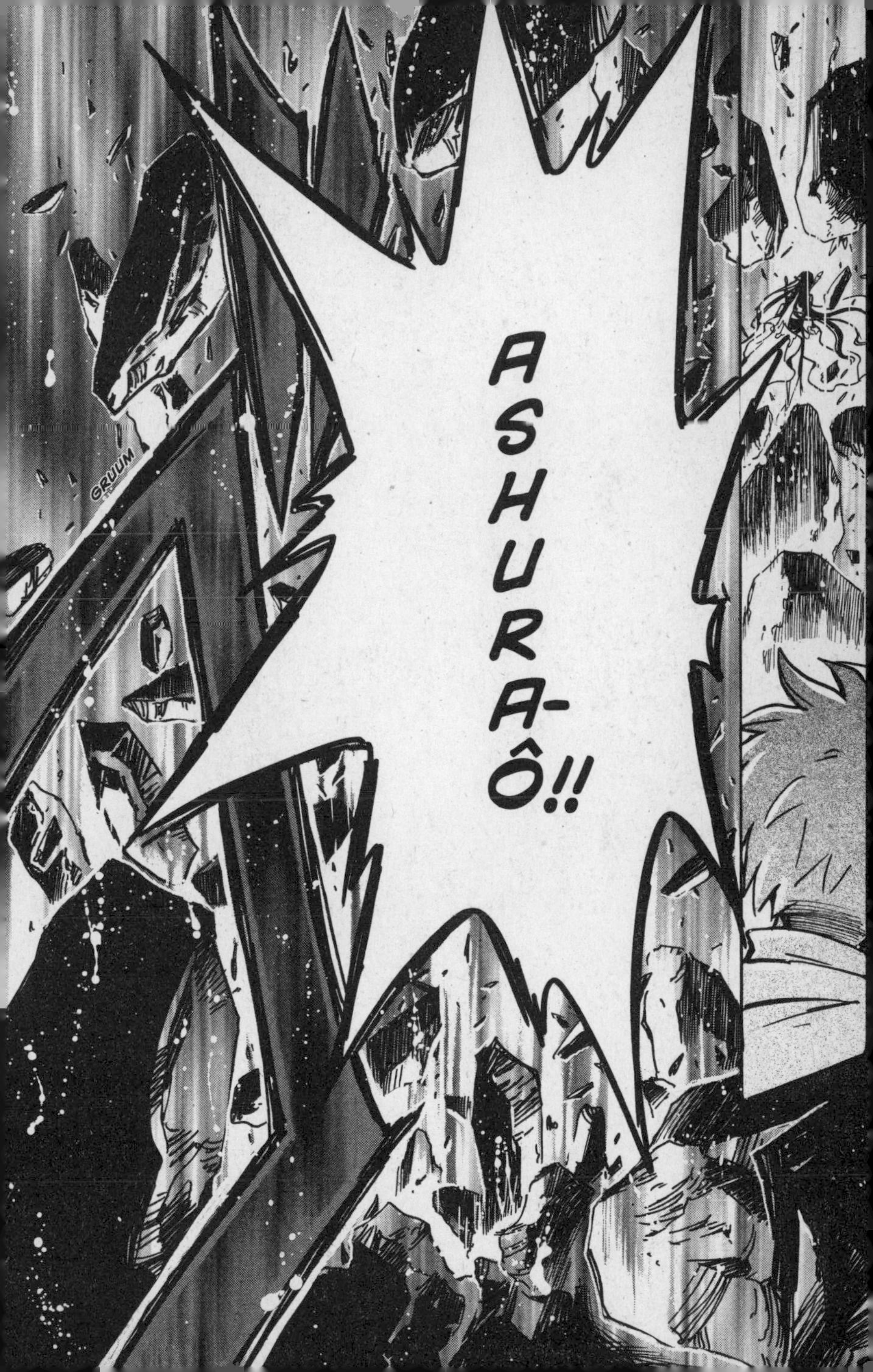
ASHURA-Ô!!
GRUUM

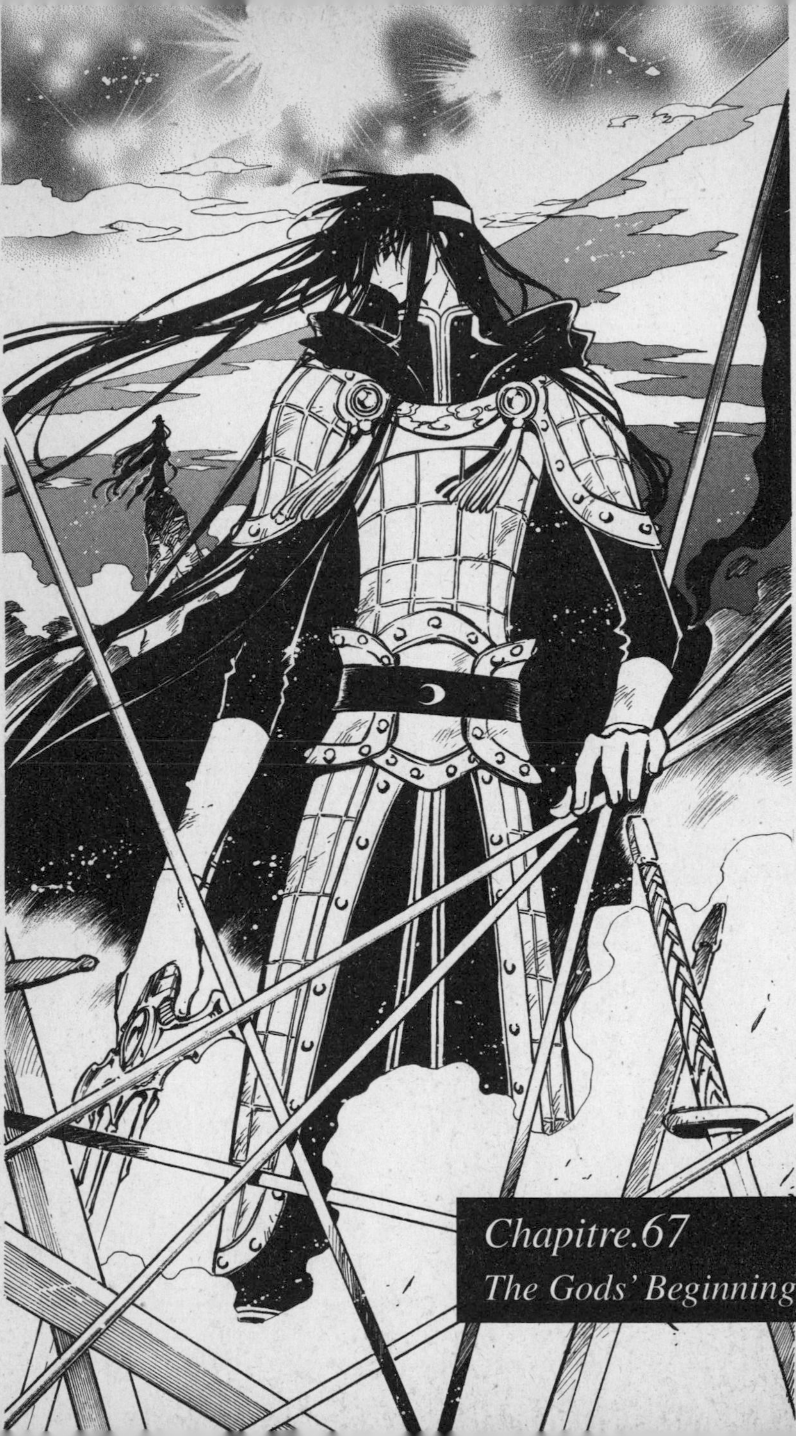
Chapitre.67
The Gods' Beginning

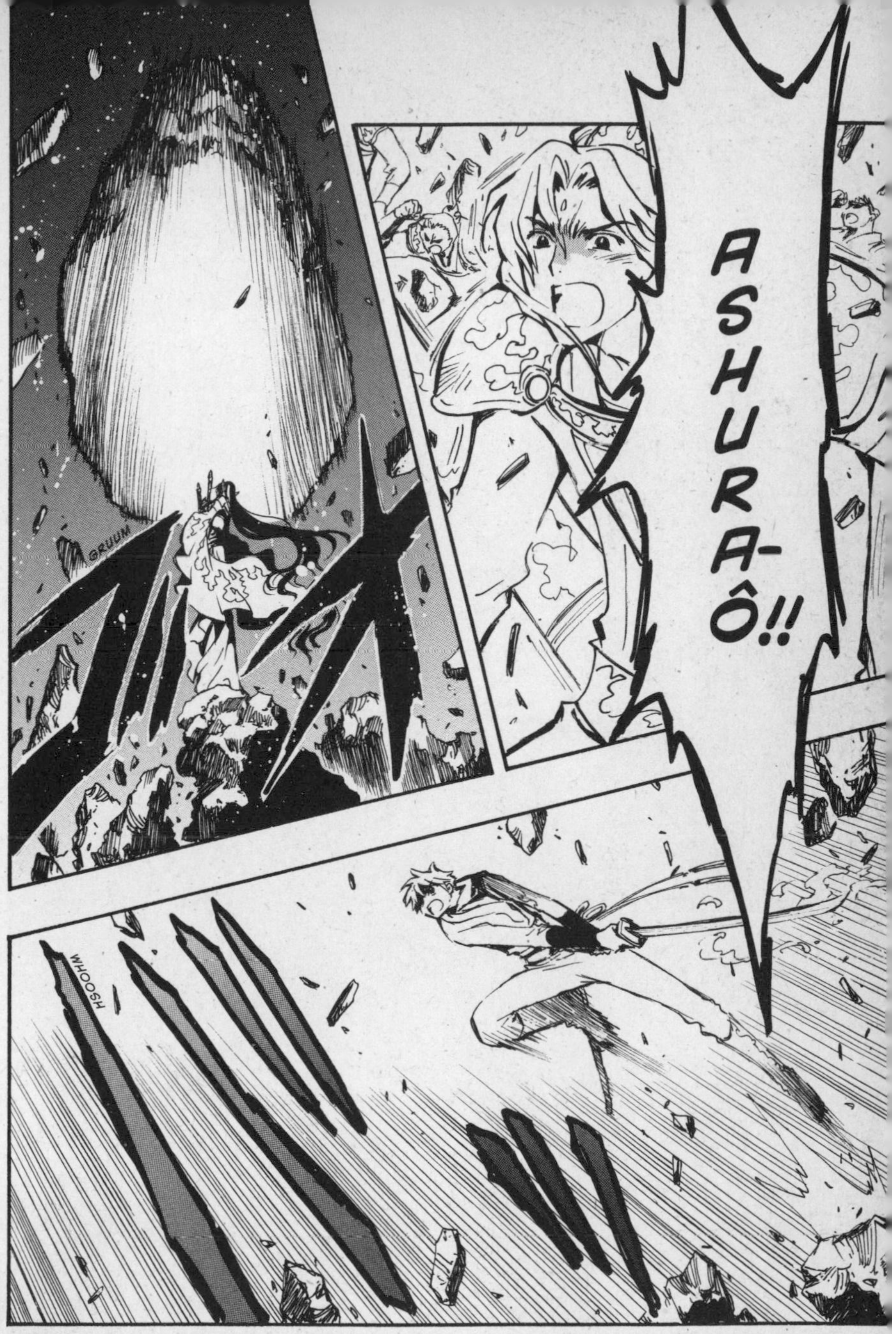
ASHURA-Ô!!
GRUUM
WHOOSH

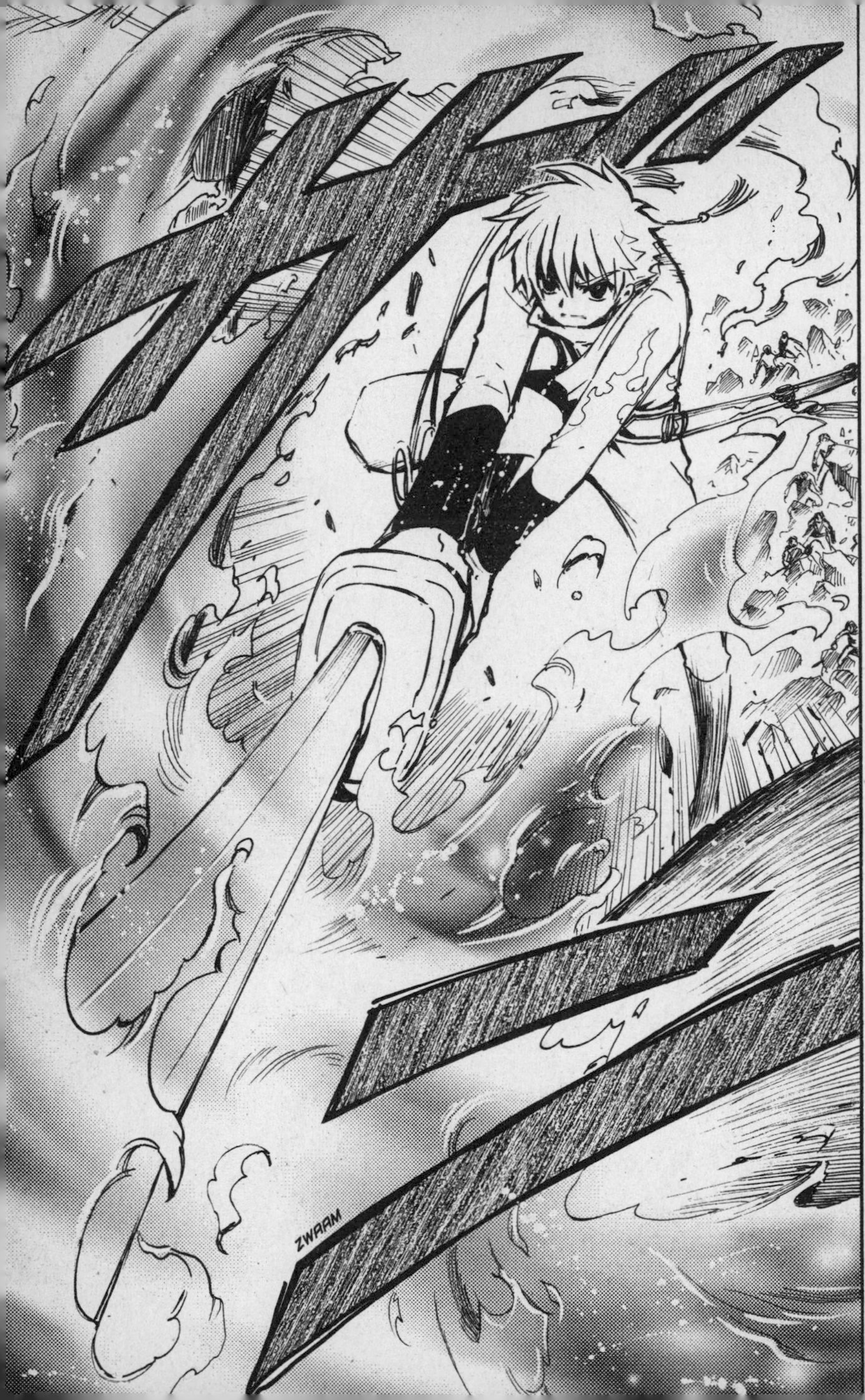
ZWAAM

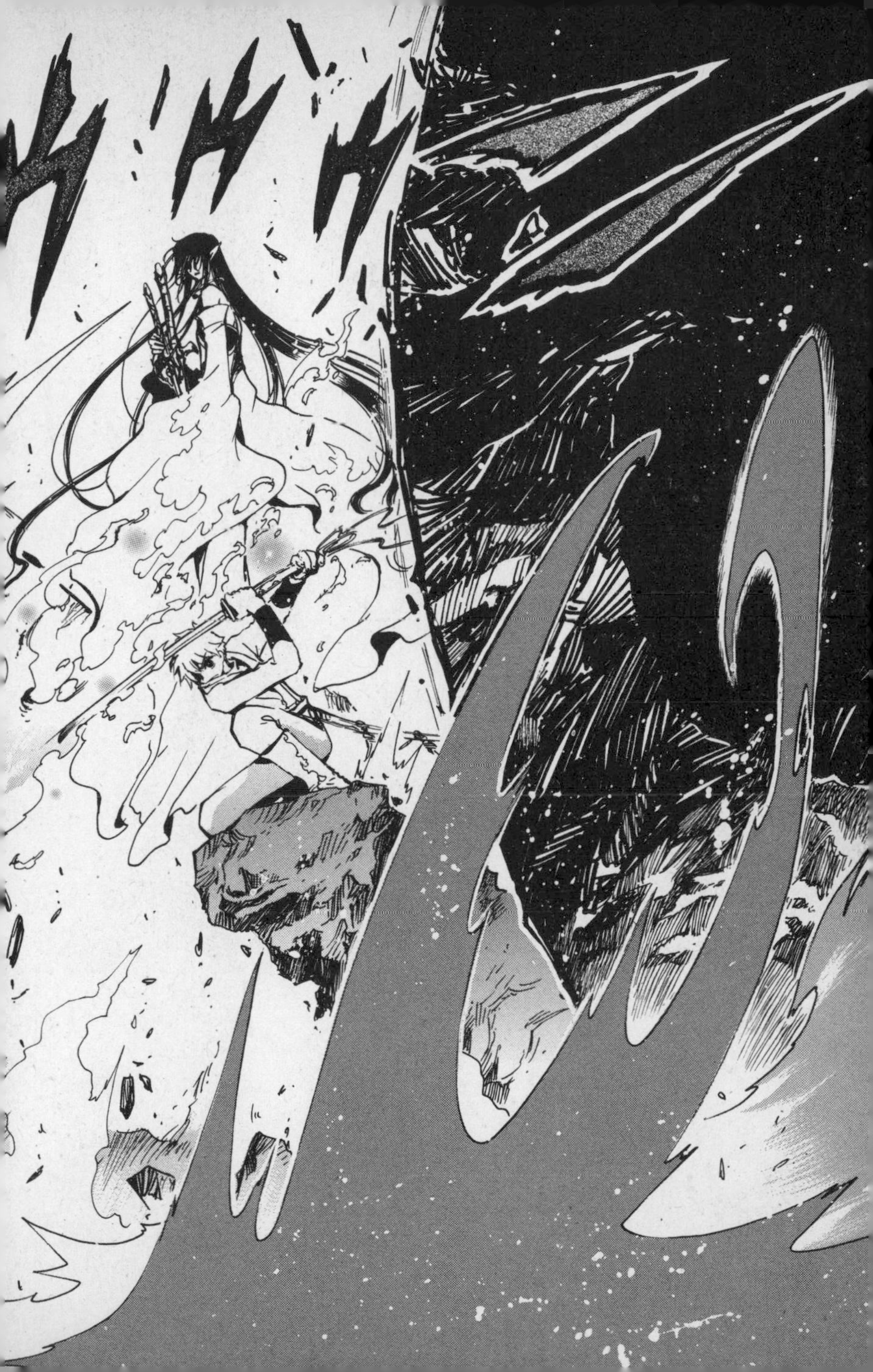

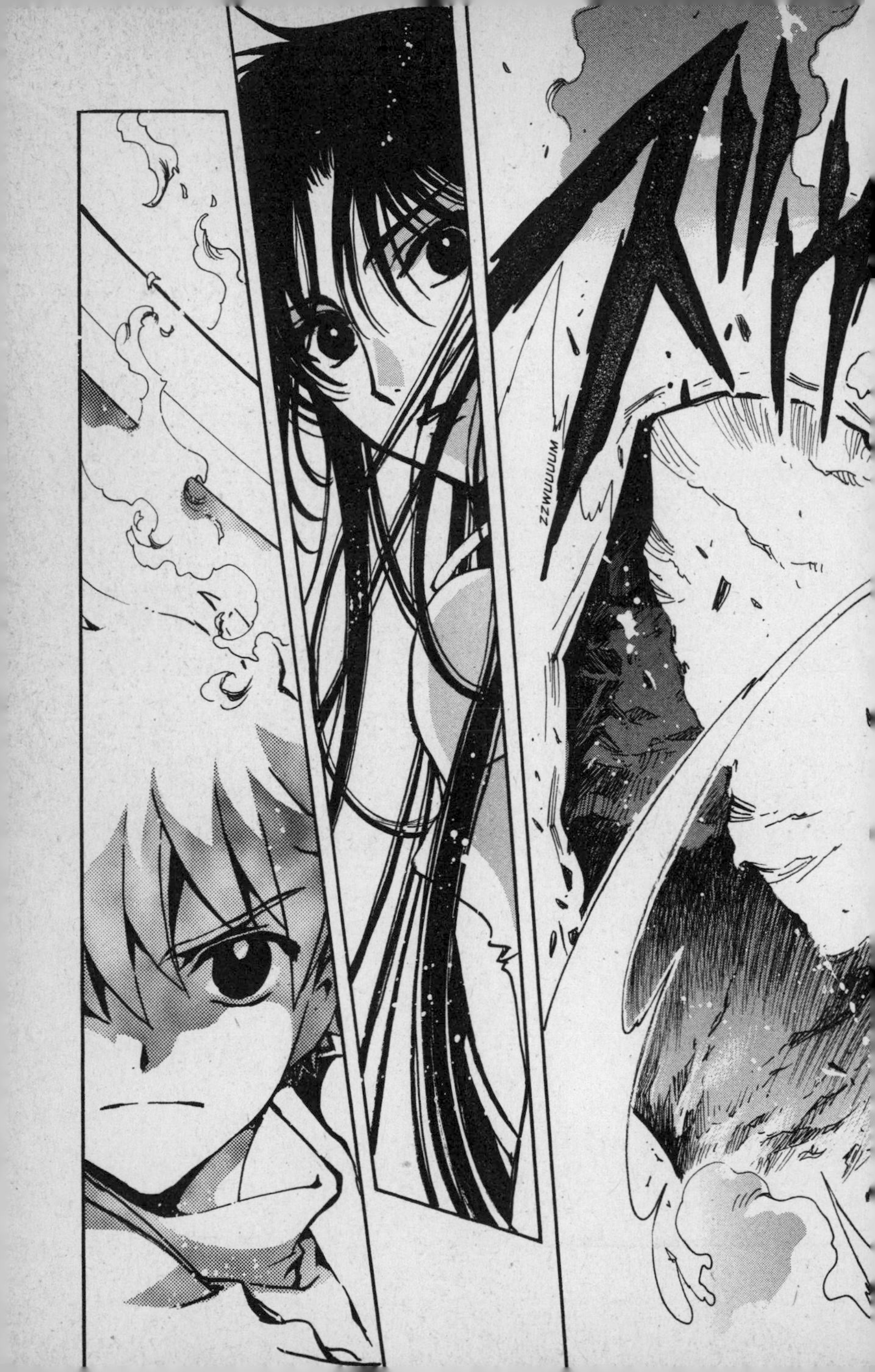
ZZWUUUUM

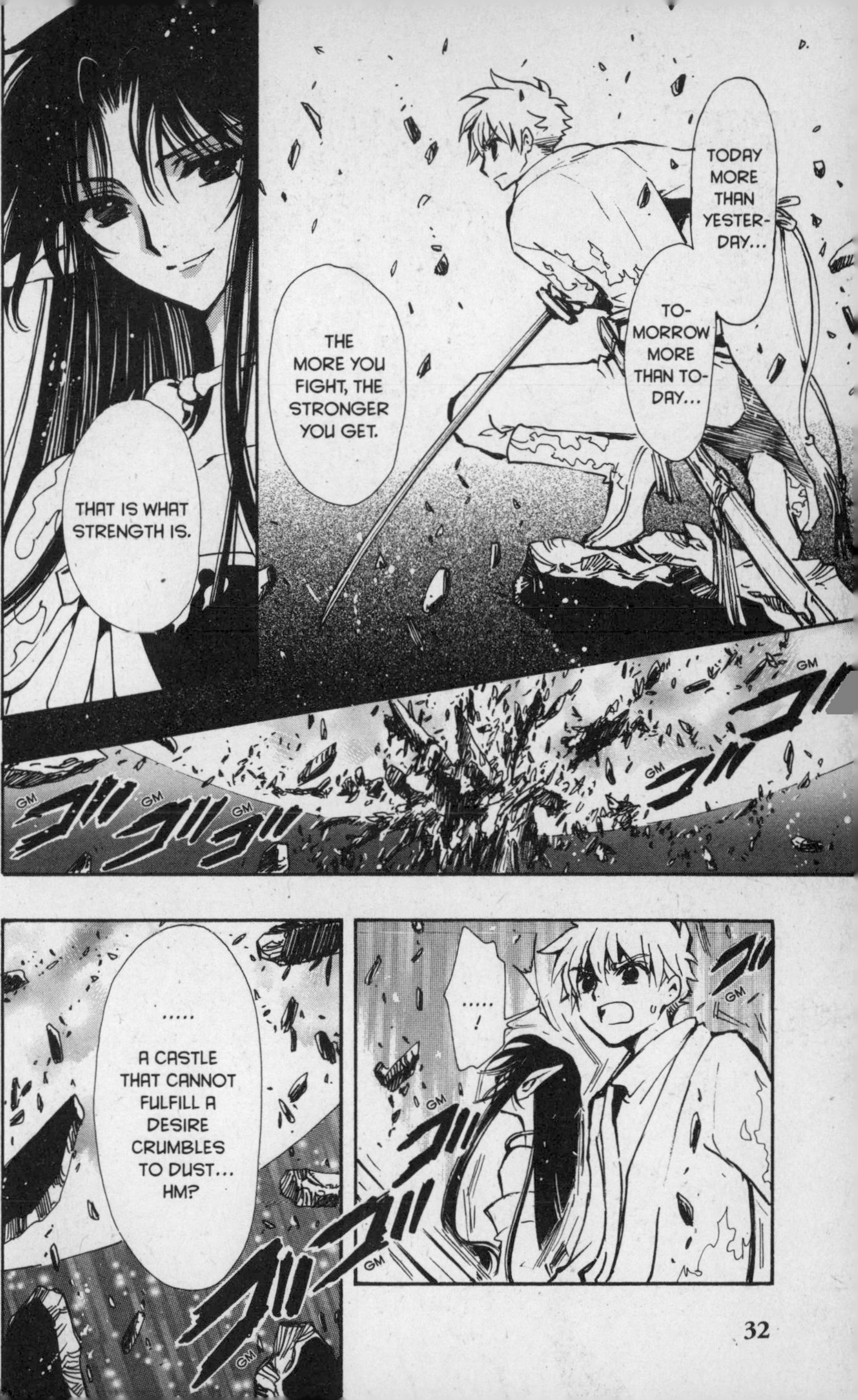
TODAY MORE THAN YESTER-DAY...
TO-MORROW MORE THAN TO-DAY...
THE MORE YOU FIGHT, THE STRONGER YOU GET.
THAT IS WHAT STRENGTH IS.
GM
GM
GM
GM
GM
GM
.....
!
GM
GM
.....
A CASTLE THAT CANNOT FULFILL A DESIRE CRUMBLES TO DUST... HM?
GM

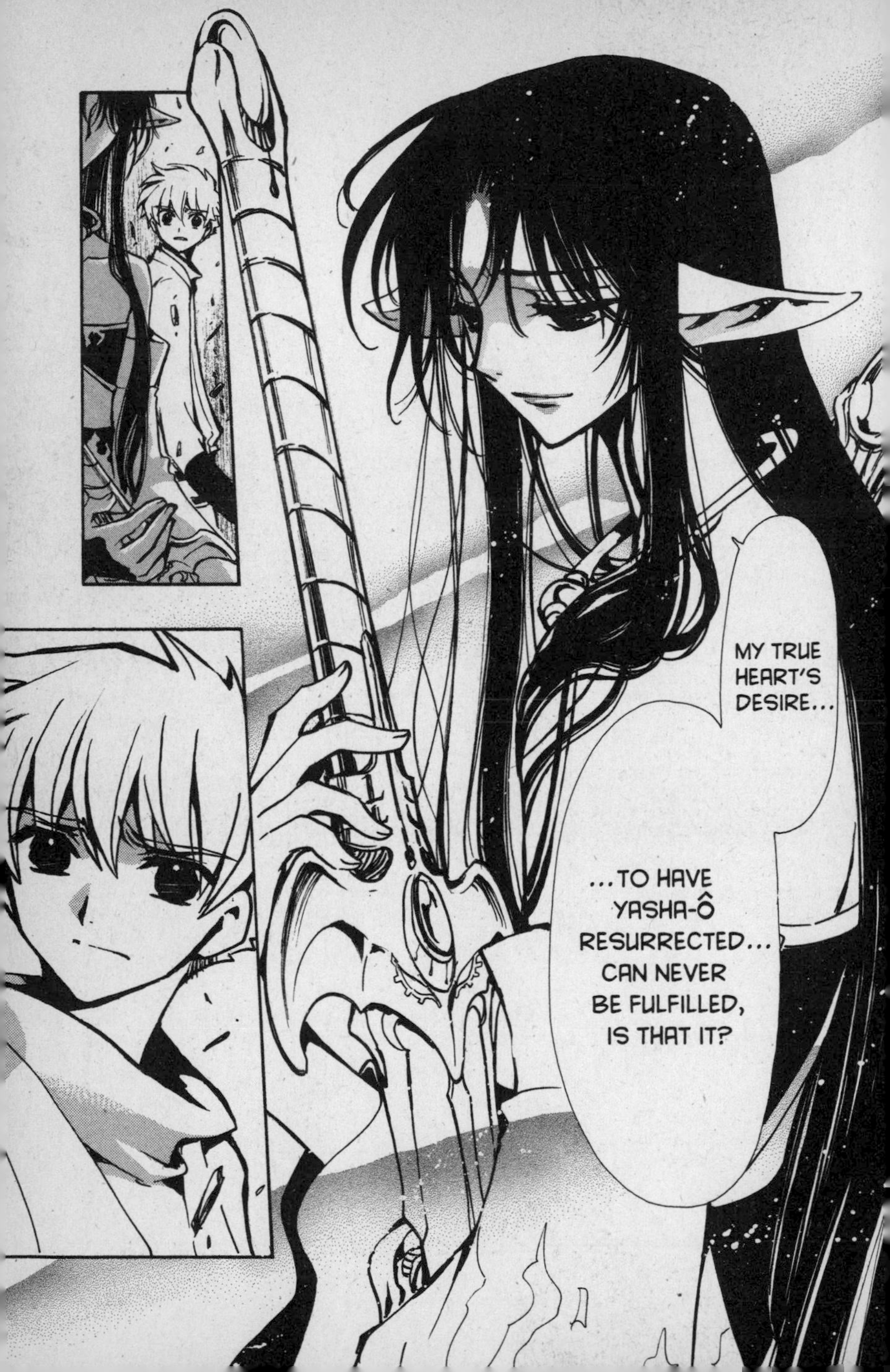
MY TRUE HEART'S DESIRE...
...TO HAVE YASHA-Ô RESURRECTED... CAN NEVER BE FULFILLED, IS THAT IT?

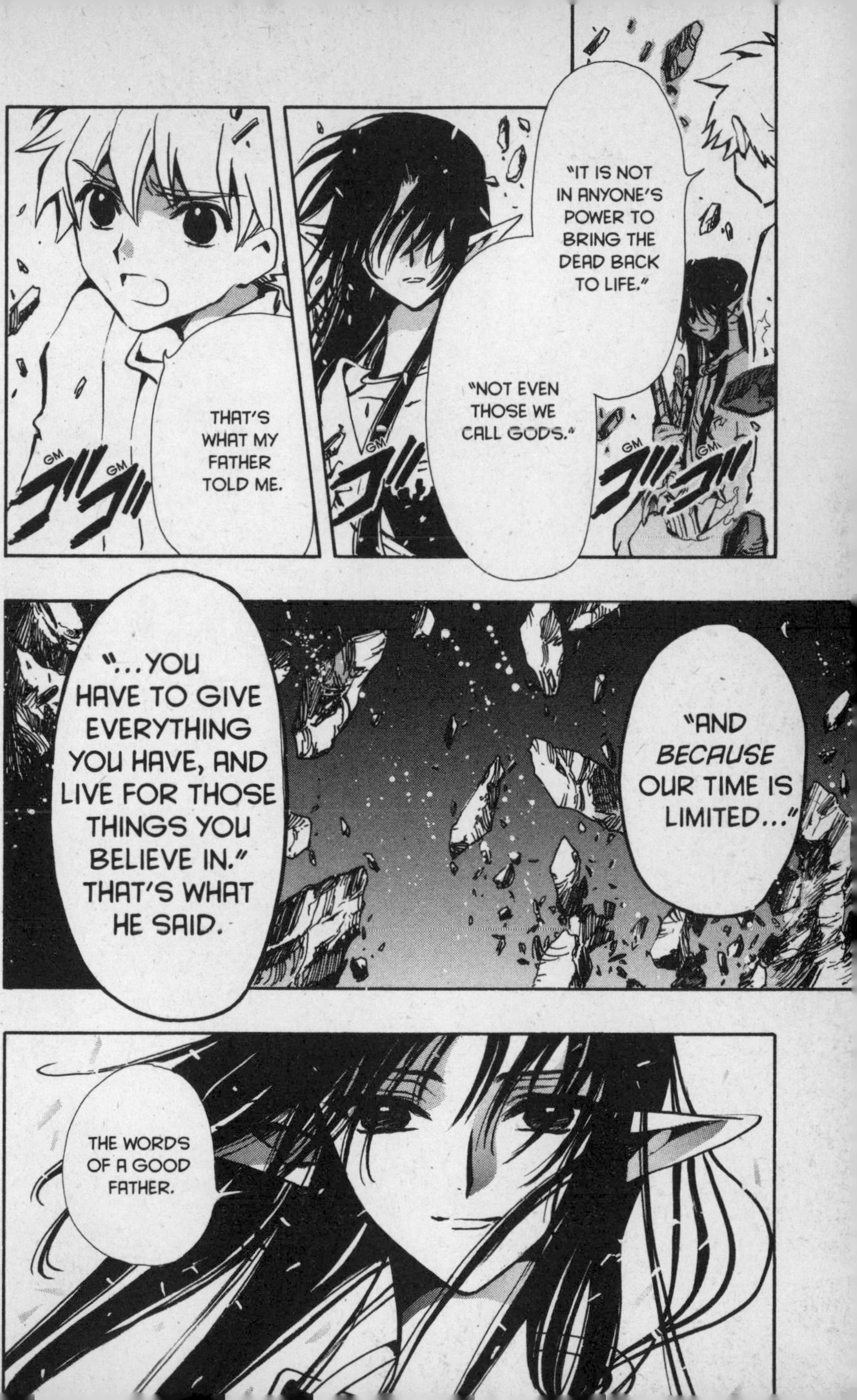
"IT IS NOT IN ANYONE'S POWER TO BRING THE DEAD BACK TO LIFE."
GM
GM
"NOT EVEN THOSE WE CALL GODS."
GM
THAT'S WHAT MY FATHER TOLD ME.
GM
GM
"AND *BECAUSE* OUR TIME IS LIMITED..."
"...YOU HAVE TO GIVE EVERYTHING YOU HAVE, AND LIVE FOR THOSE THINGS YOU BELIEVE IN." THAT'S WHAT HE SAID.
THE WORDS OF A GOOD FATHER.

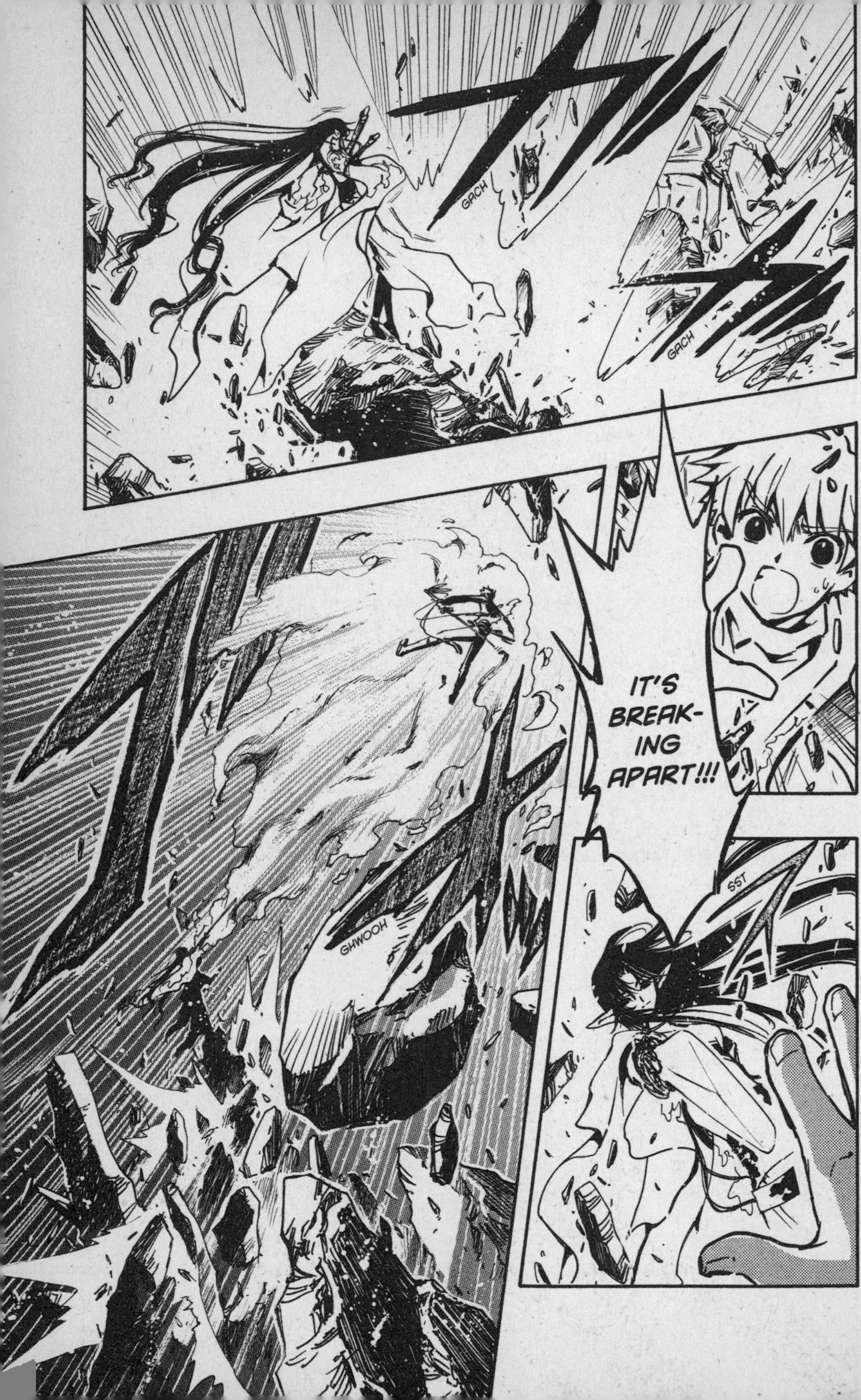
GACH
GACH
IT'S BREAKING-ING APART!!!
SST
GHWOOH

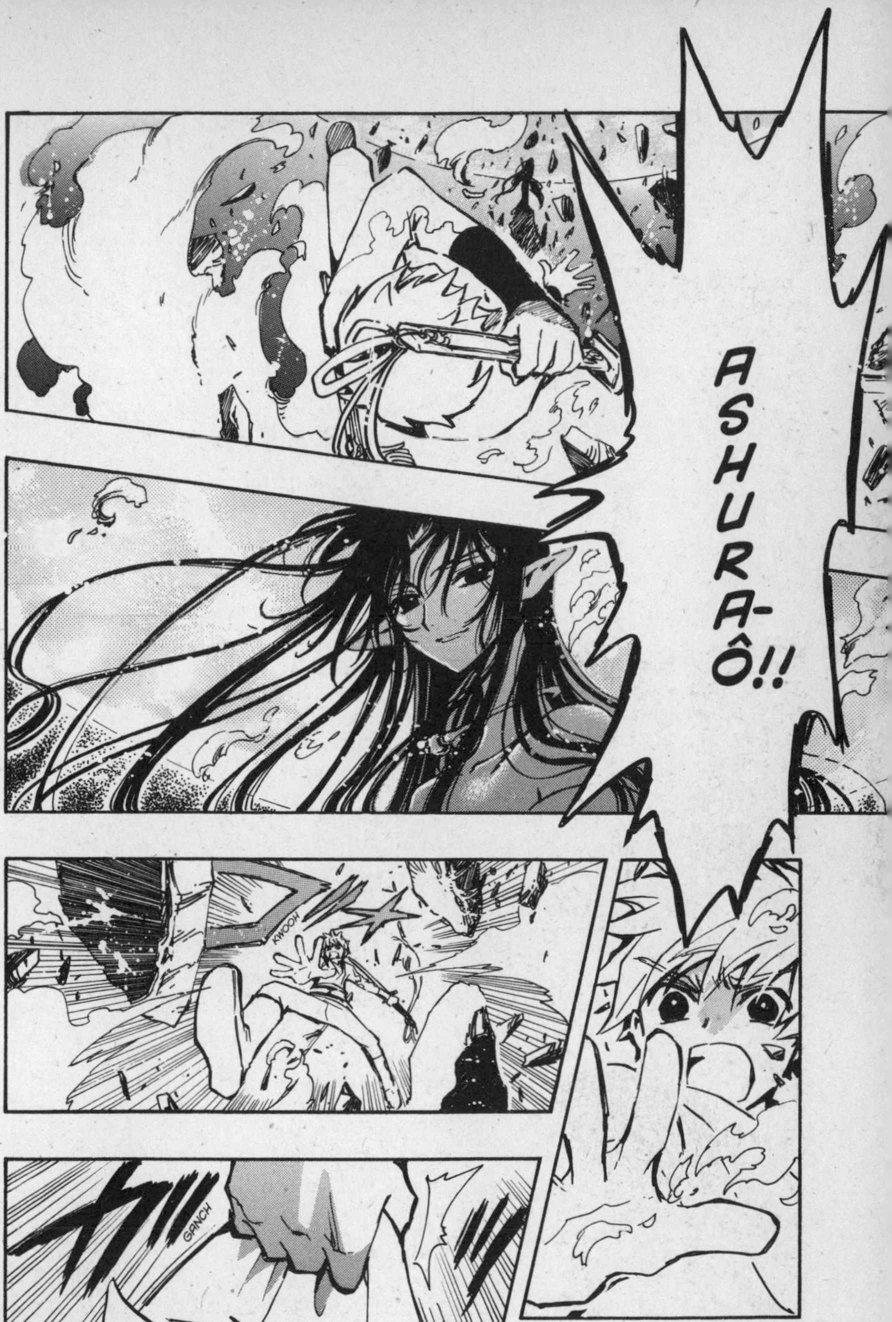
ASHURA-Ô!!
KWOOH
GANCH

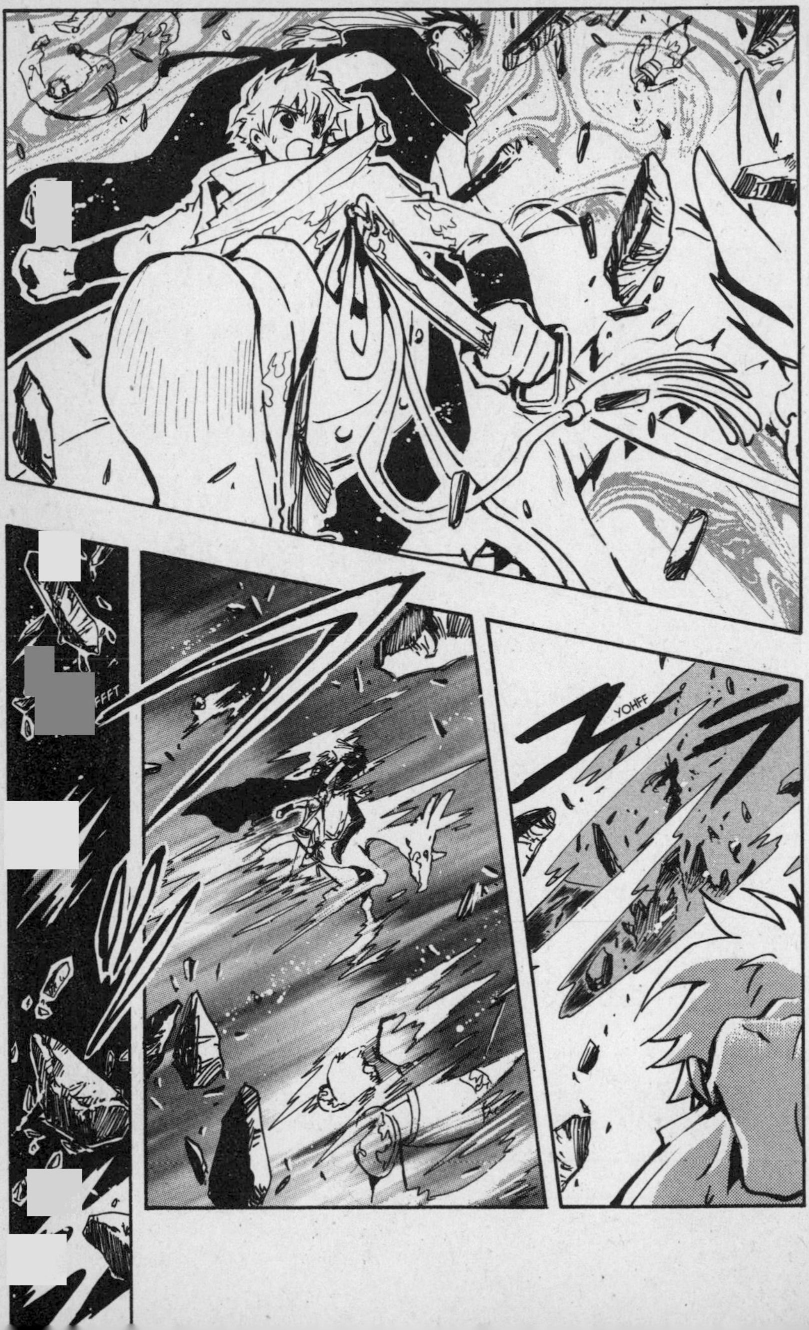
YOHFF

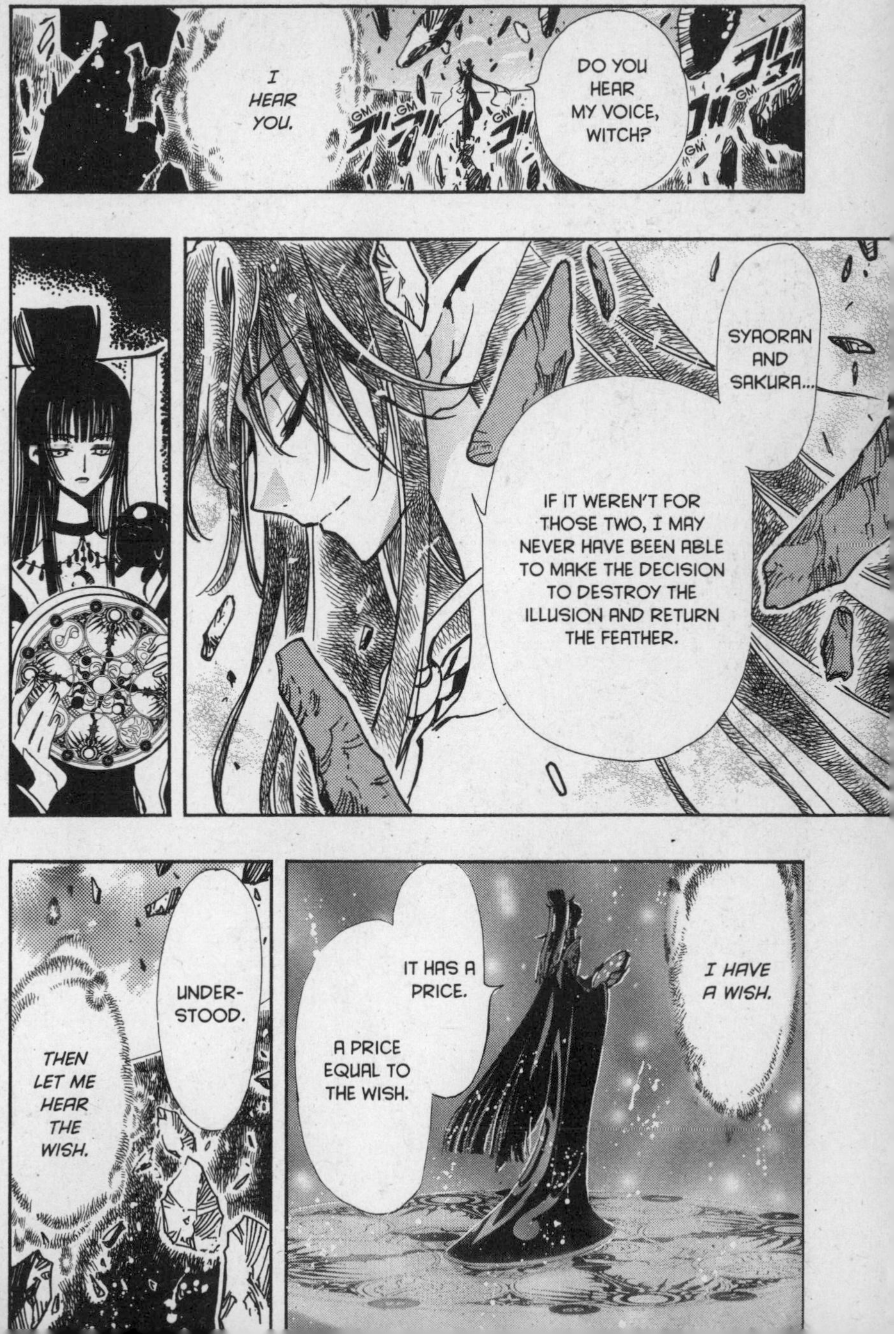
GM
GM
GM
GM
GM
DO YOU HEAR MY VOICE, WITCH?
I HEAR YOU.
SYAORAN AND SAKURA...
IF IT WEREN'T FOR THOSE TWO, I MAY NEVER HAVE BEEN ABLE TO MAKE THE DECISION TO DESTROY THE ILLUSION AND RETURN THE FEATHER.
I HAVE A WISH.
IT HAS A PRICE.
A PRICE EQUAL TO THE WISH.
UNDER-STOOD.
THEN LET ME HEAR THE WISH.

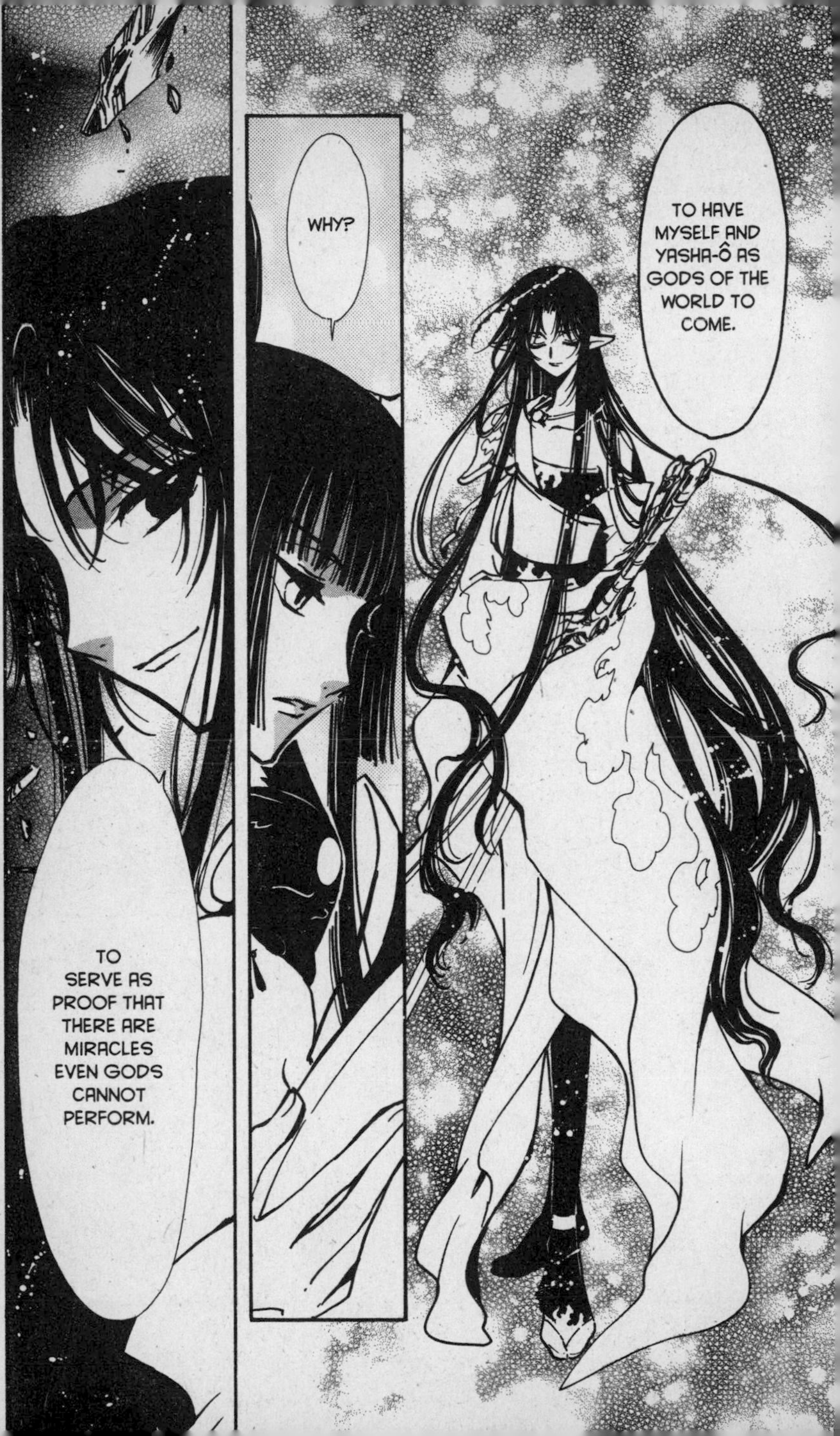
TO HAVE MYSELF AND YASHA-Ô AS GODS OF THE WORLD TO COME.
WHY?
TO SERVE AS PROOF THAT THERE ARE MIRACLES EVEN GODS CANNOT PERFORM.

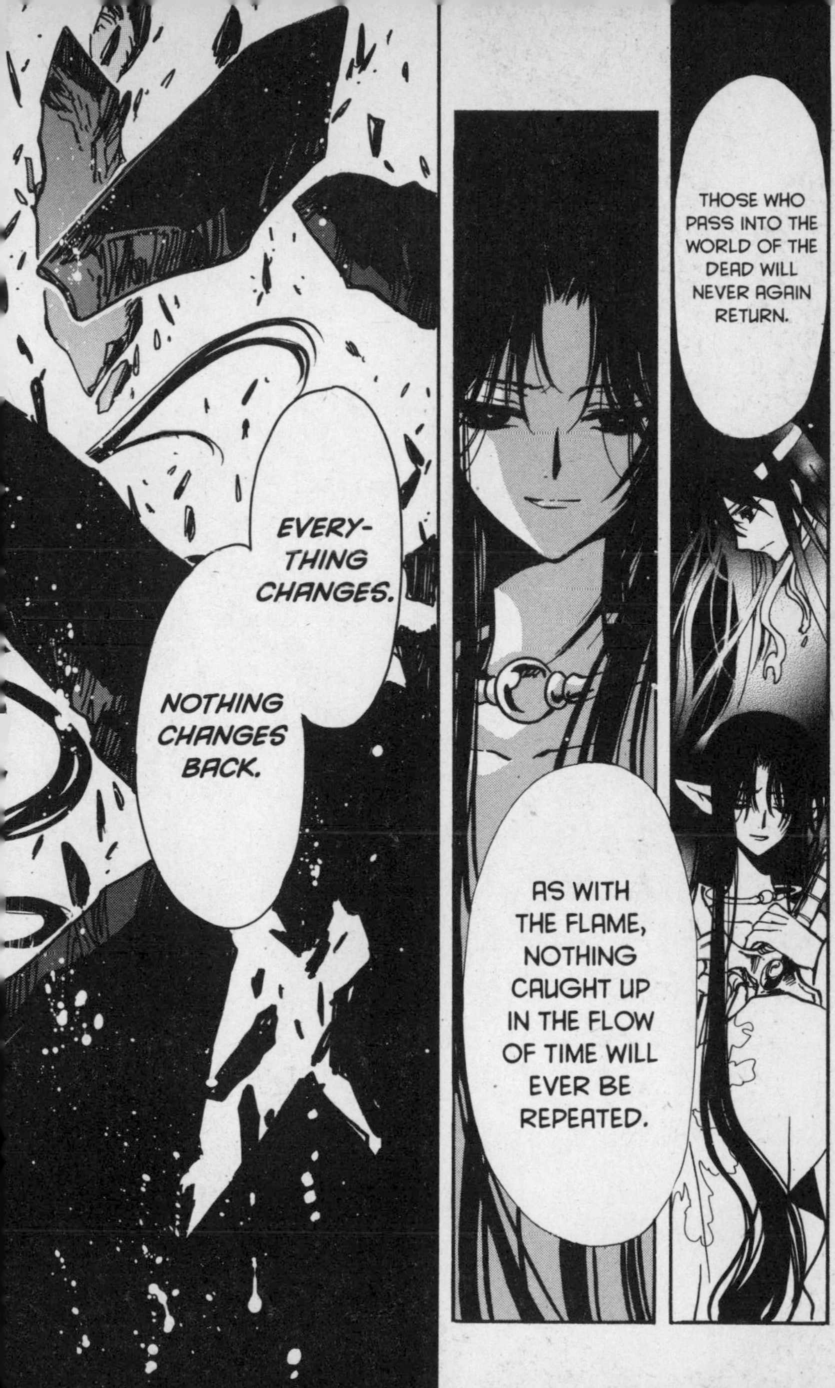
THOSE WHO PASS INTO THE WORLD OF THE DEAD WILL NEVER AGAIN RETURN.
AS WITH THE FLAME, NOTHING CAUGHT UP IN THE FLOW OF TIME WILL EVER BE REPEATED.
EVERY-THING CHANGES.
NOTHING CHANGES BACK.

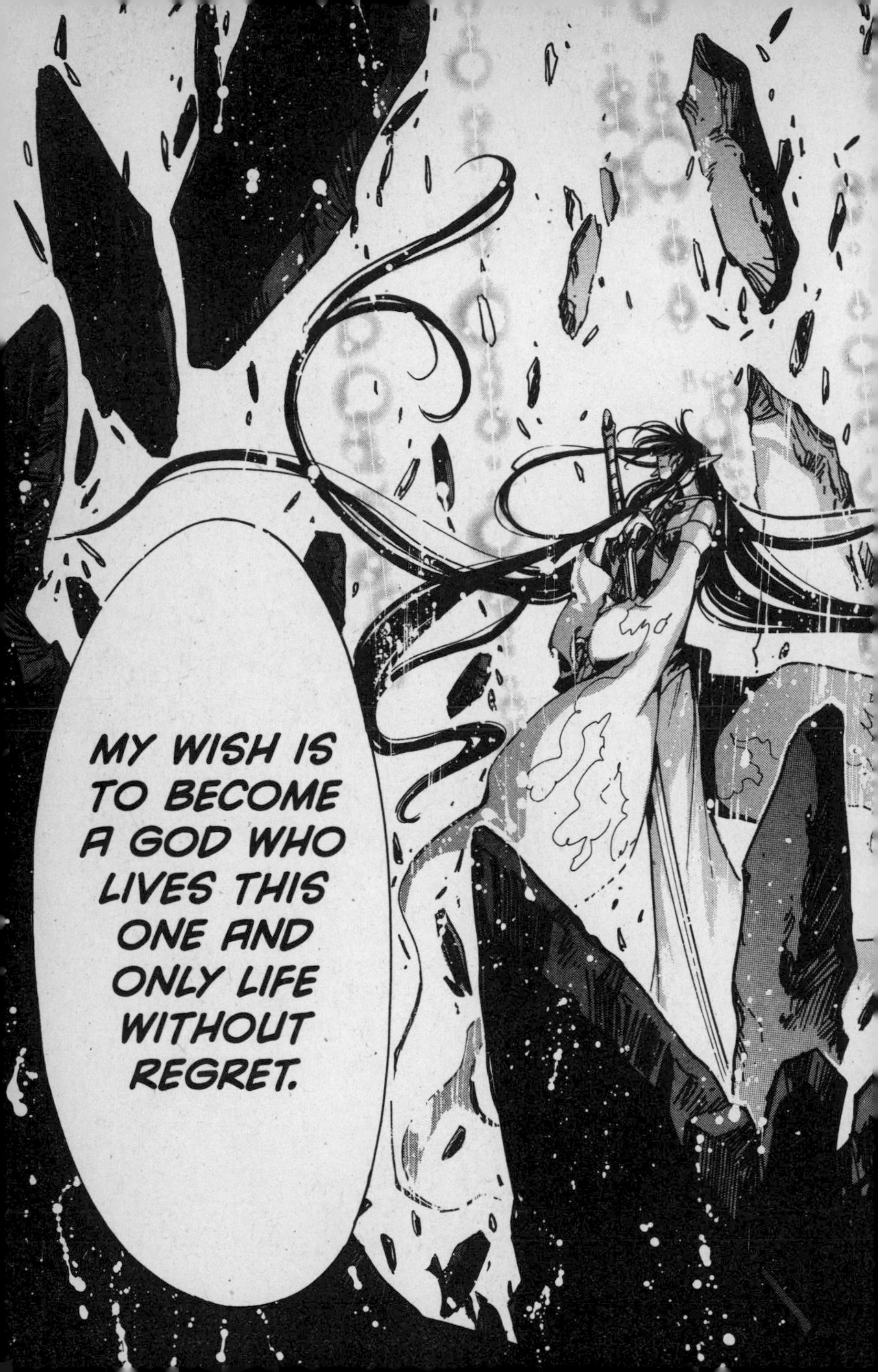
MY WISH IS TO BECOME A GOD WHO LIVES THIS ONE AND ONLY LIFE WITHOUT REGRET.

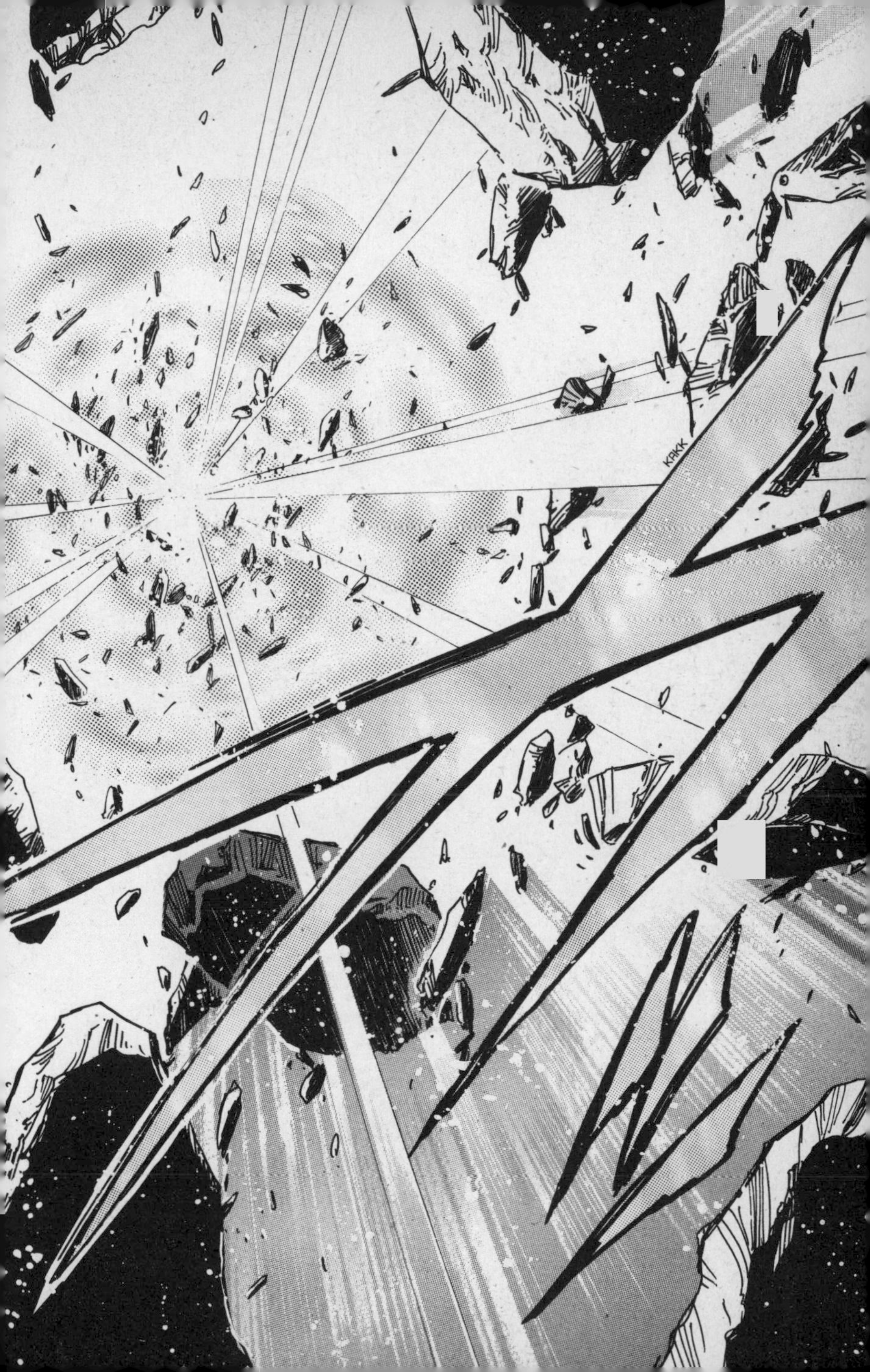
KAKK

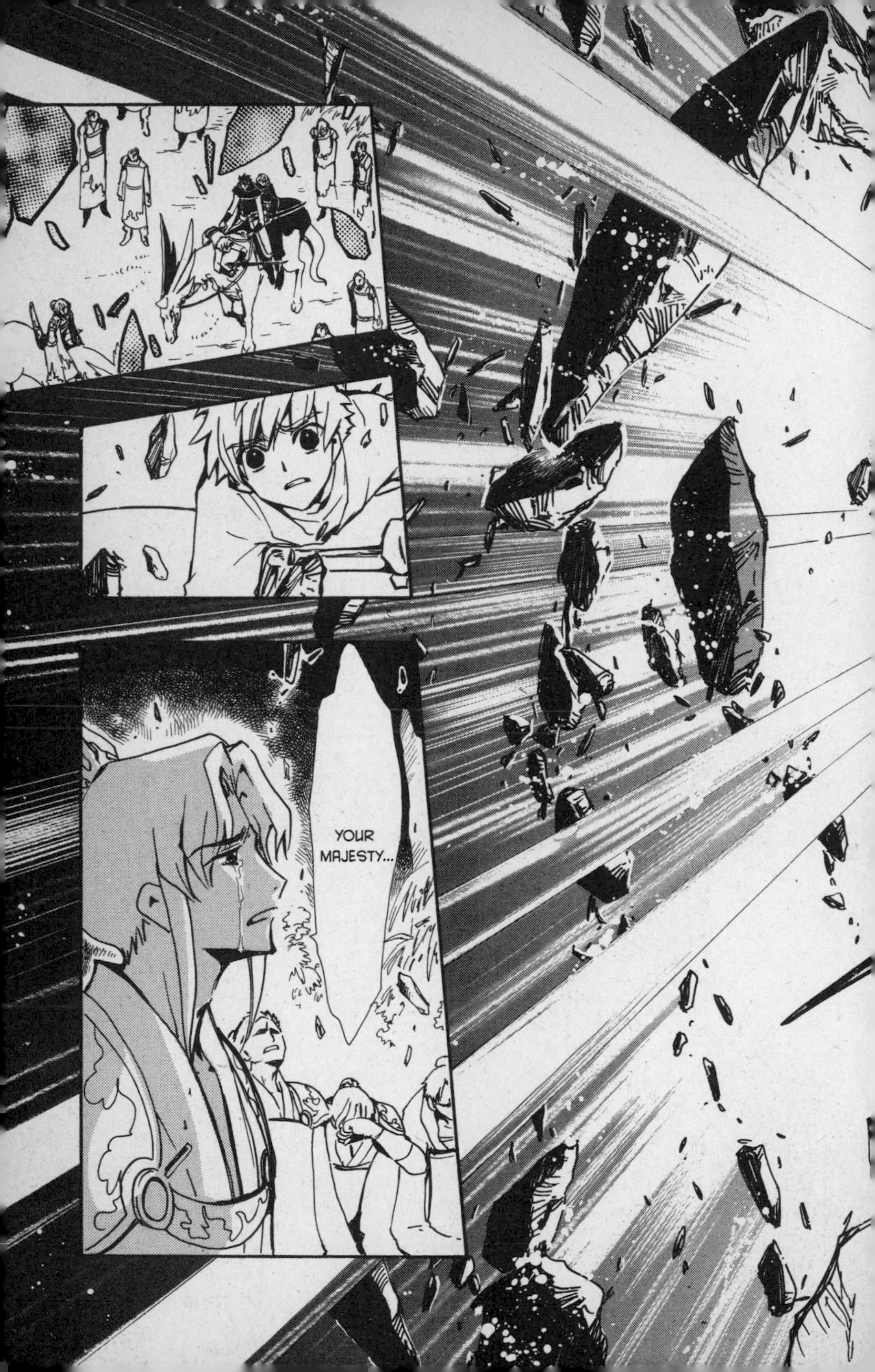
YOUR MAJESTY...

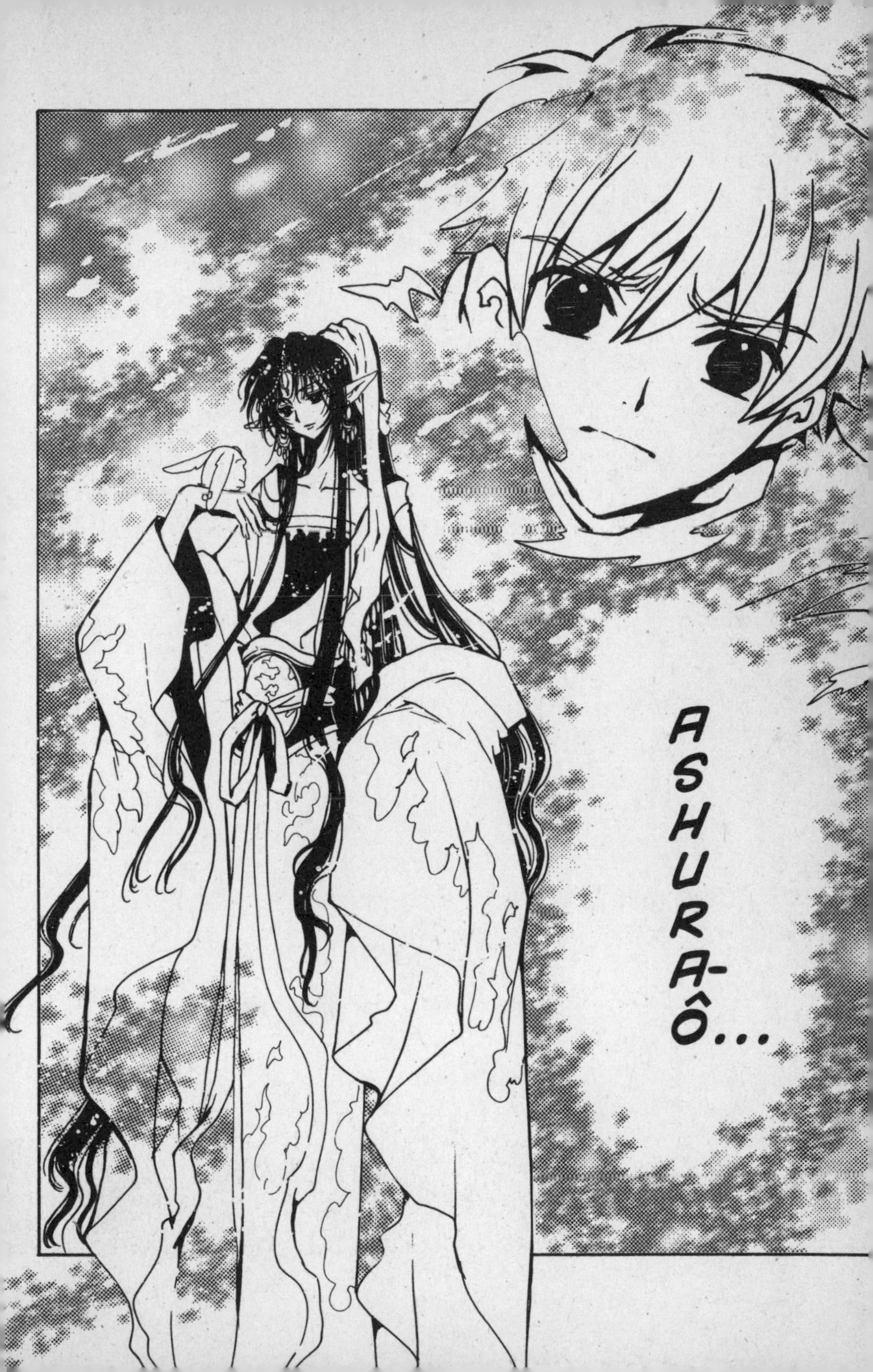
ASHURA-Ô...

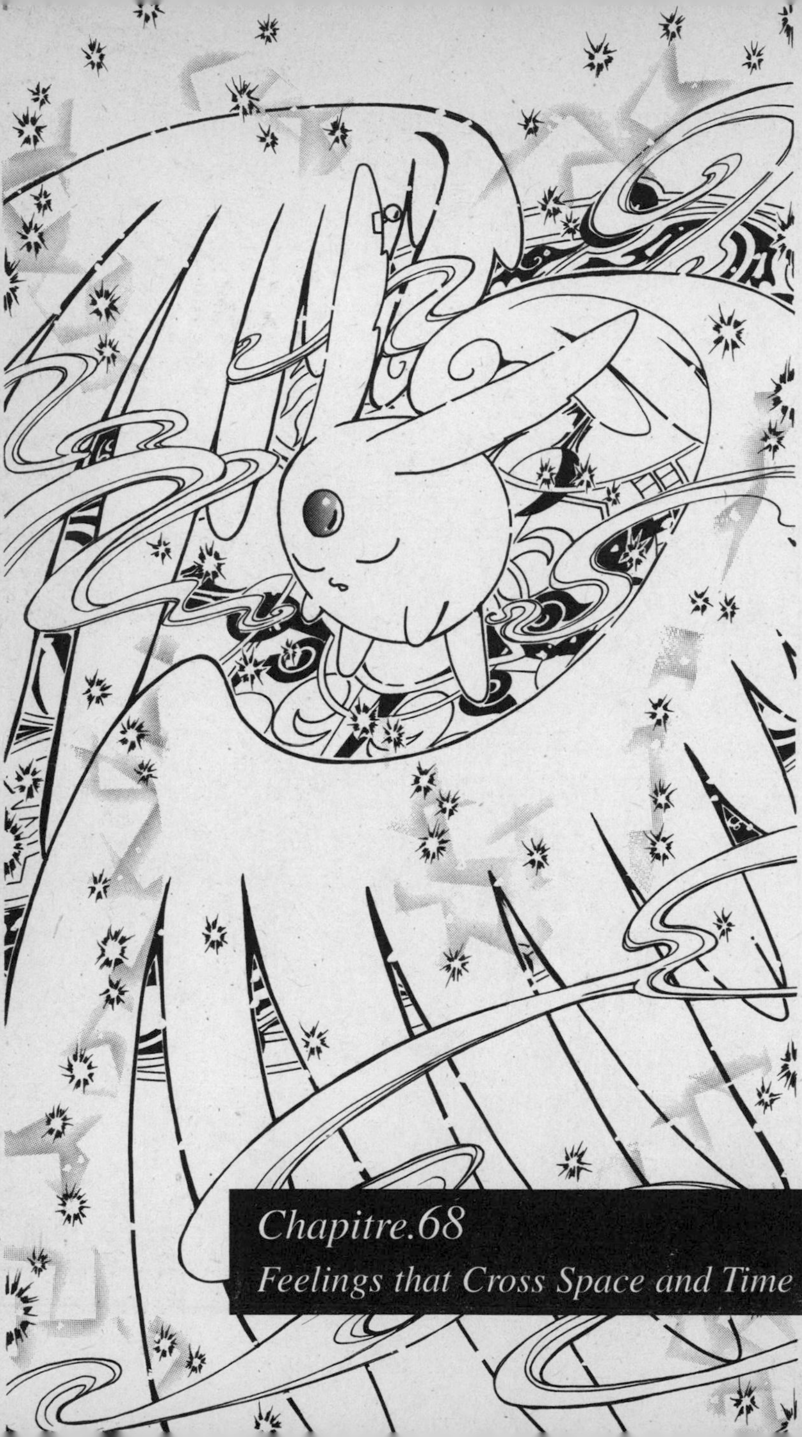
Chapitre.68
Feelings that Cross Space and Time

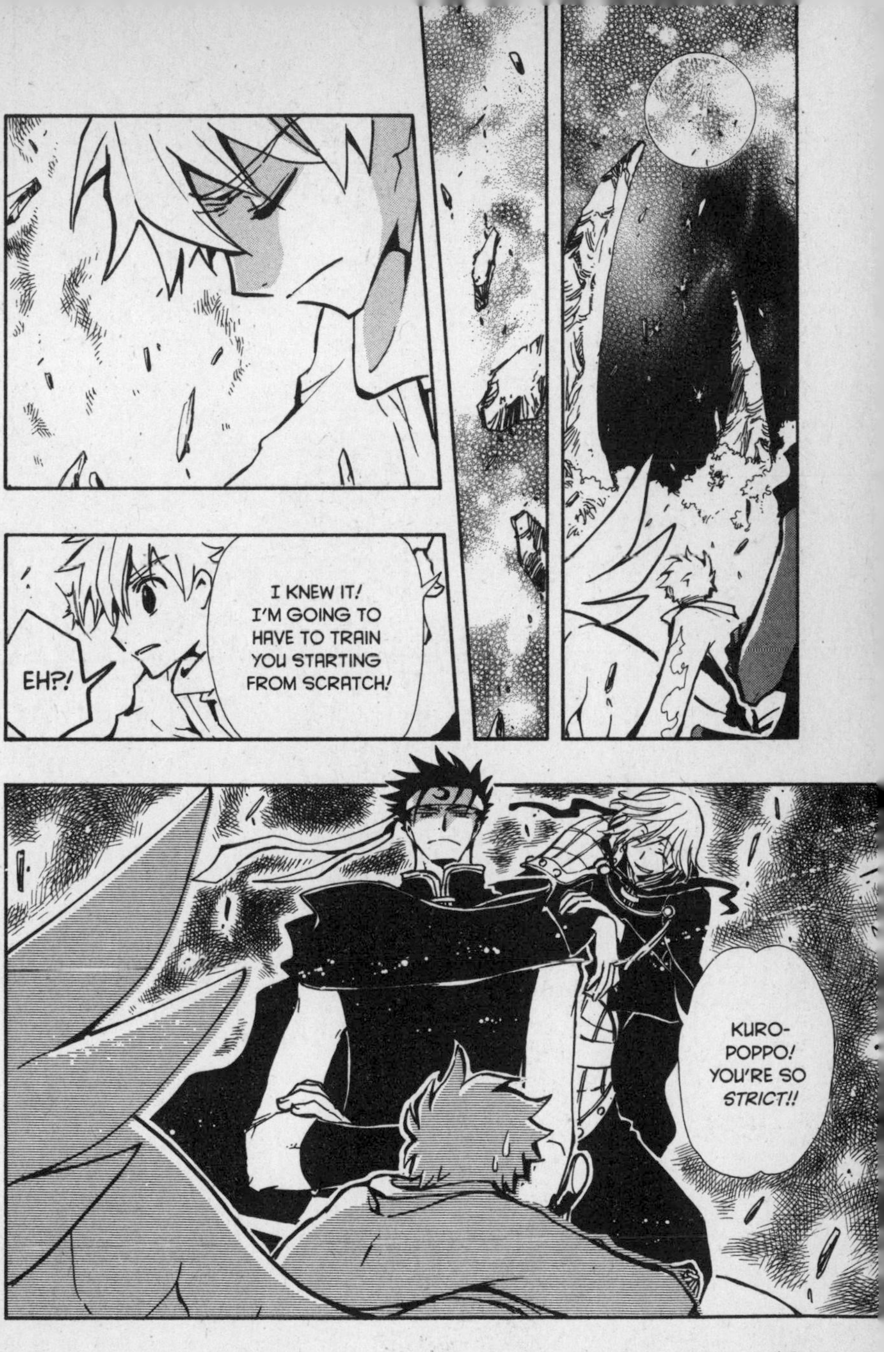
I KNEW IT! I'M GOING TO HAVE TO TRAIN YOU STARTING FROM SCRATCH!
EH?!
KURO-POPPO! YOU'RE SO STRICT!!

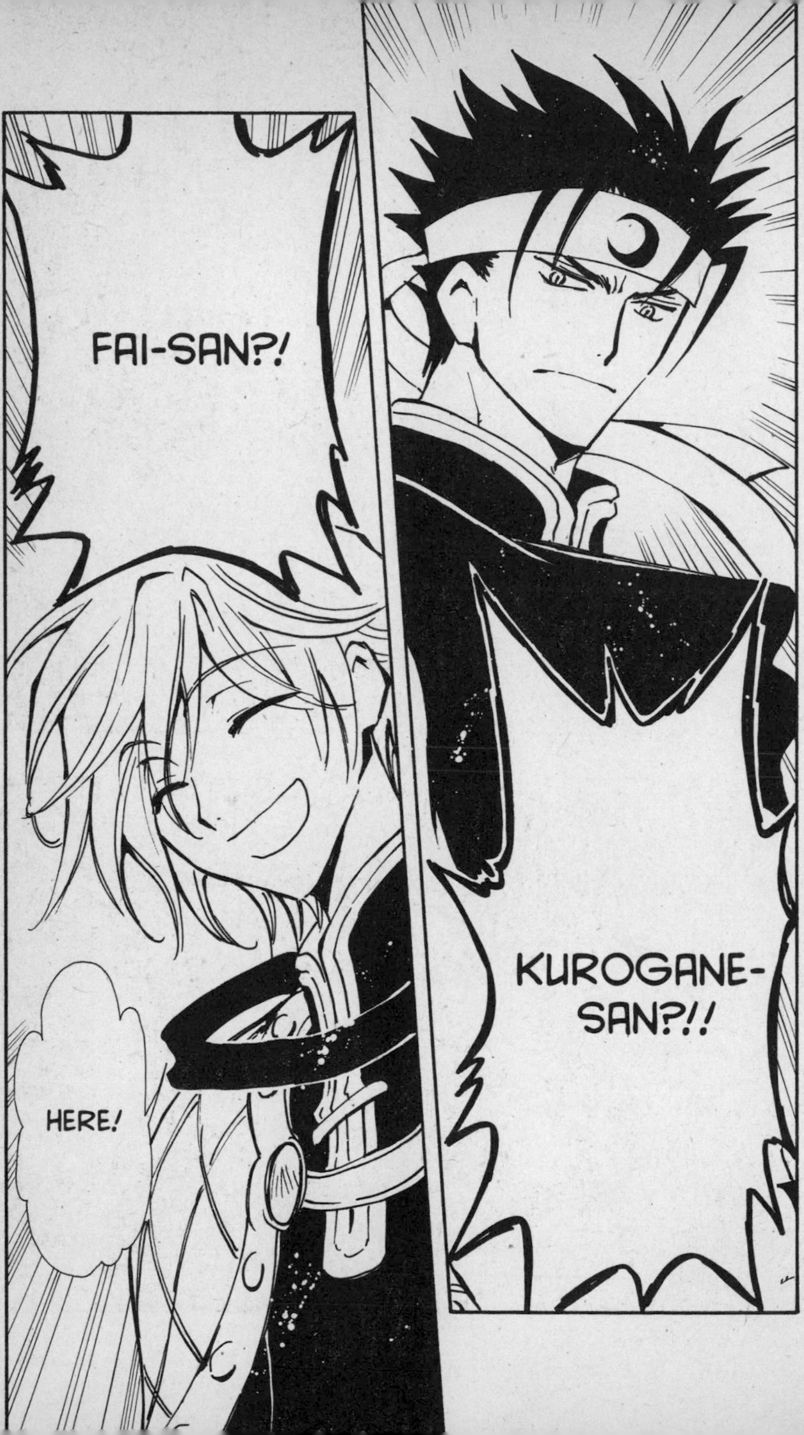
KUROGANE-SAN?!!
FAI-SAN?!
HERE!

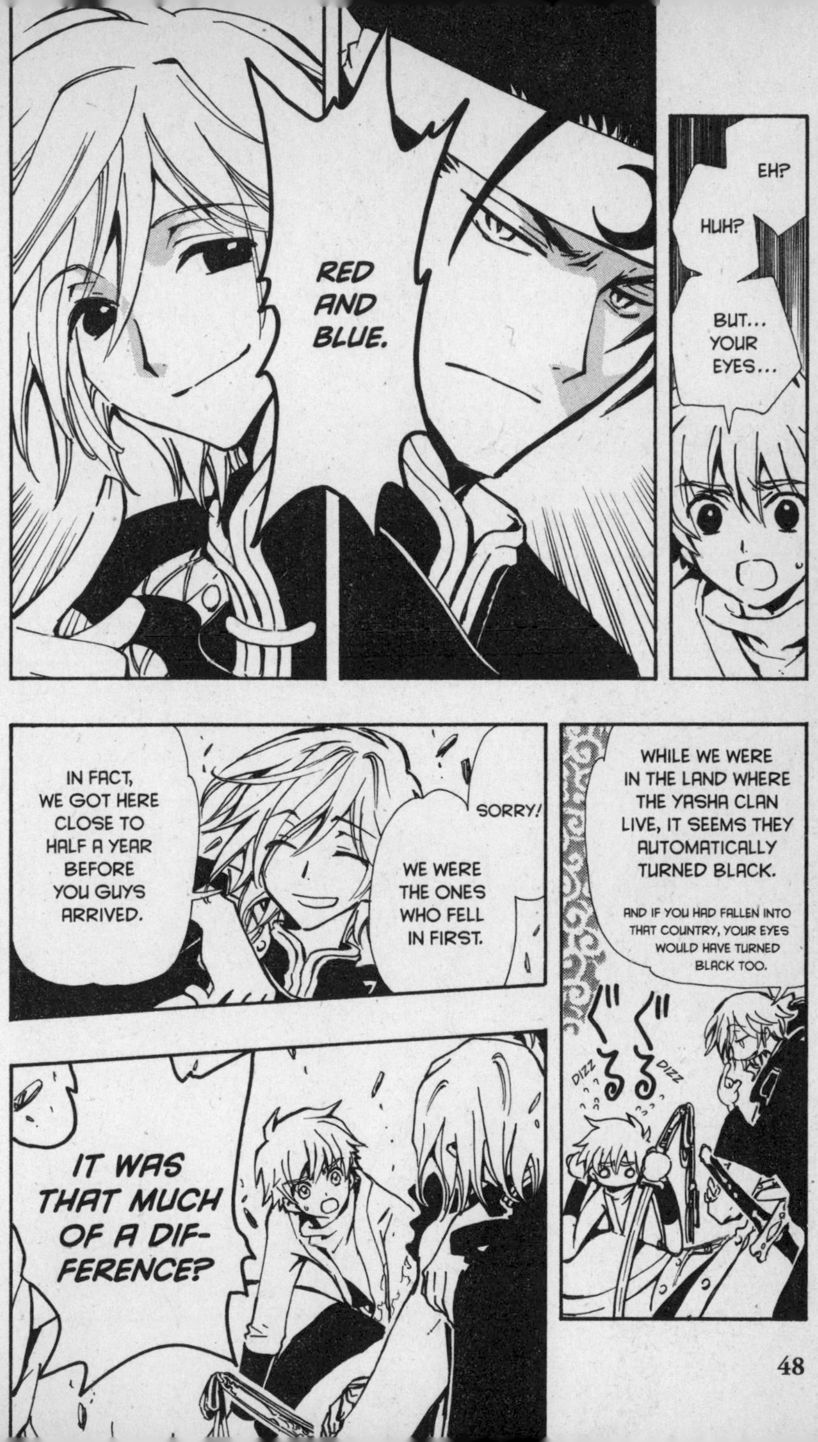
EH?
HUH?
BUT... YOUR EYES...
RED AND BLUE.
WHILE WE WERE IN THE LAND WHERE THE YASHA CLAN LIVE, IT SEEMS THEY AUTOMATICALLY TURNED BLACK.
AND IF YOU HAD FALLEN INTO THAT COUNTRY, YOUR EYES WOULD HAVE TURNED BLACK TOO.
ぐるぐる
DIZZ DIZZ
SORRY!
WE WERE THE ONES WHO FELL IN FIRST.
IN FACT, WE GOT HERE CLOSE TO HALF A YEAR BEFORE YOU GUYS ARRIVED.
IT WAS THAT MUCH OF A DIF-FERENCE?

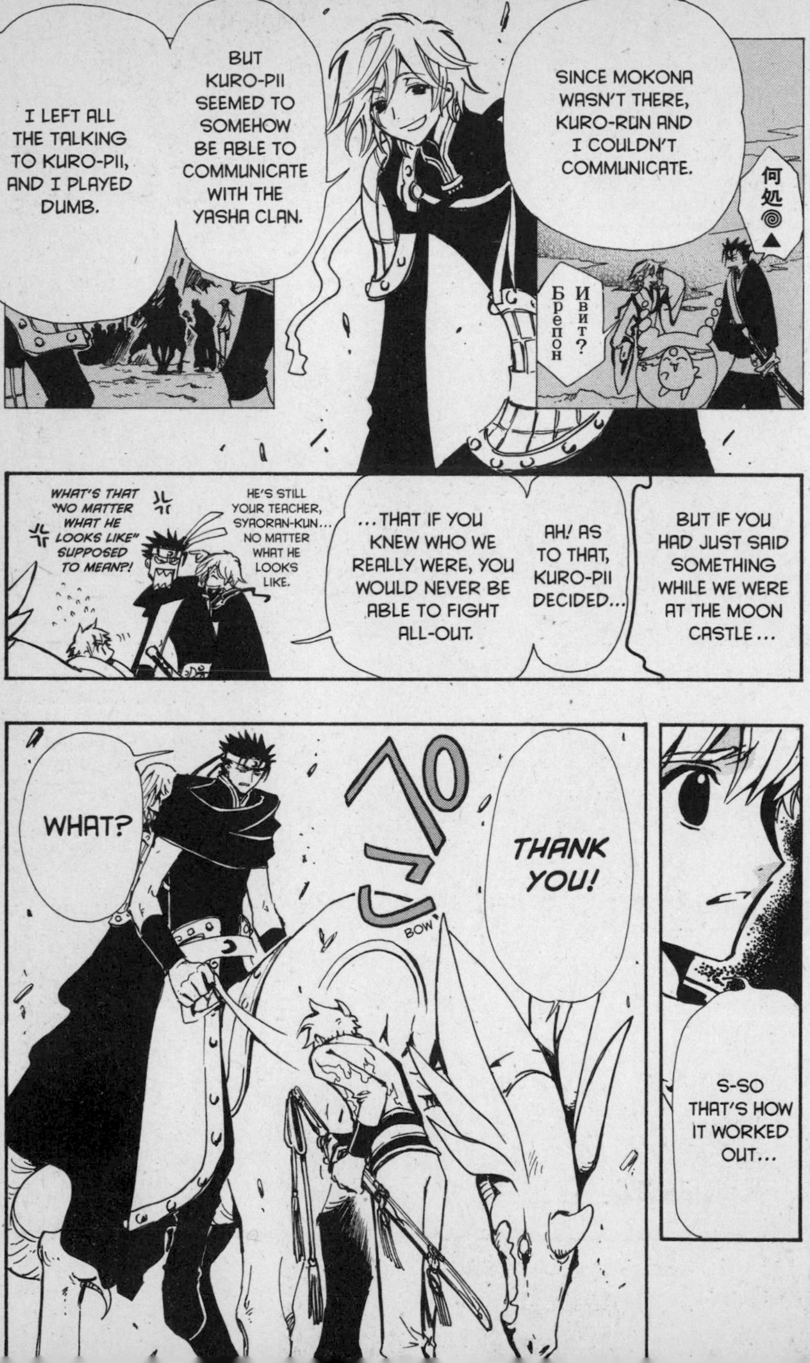
SINCE MOKONA WASN'T THERE, KURO-RUN AND I COULDN'T COMMUNICATE.
Ивит?
Брепон
何処◎▲
BUT KURO-PII SEEMED TO SOMEHOW BE ABLE TO COMMUNICATE WITH THE YASHA CLAN.
I LEFT ALL THE TALKING TO KURO-PII, AND I PLAYED DUMB.
BUT IF YOU HAD JUST SAID SOMETHING WHILE WE WERE AT THE MOON CASTLE...
AH! AS TO THAT, KURO-PII DECIDED...
...THAT IF YOU KNEW WHO WE REALLY WERE, YOU WOULD NEVER BE ABLE TO FIGHT ALL-OUT.
HE'S STILL YOUR TEACHER, SYAORAN-KUN... NO MATTER WHAT HE LOOKS LIKE.
WHAT'S THAT "NO MATTER WHAT HE LOOKS LIKE" SUPPOSED TO MEAN?!
S-SO THAT'S HOW IT WORKED OUT...
THANK YOU!
BOW
WHAT?

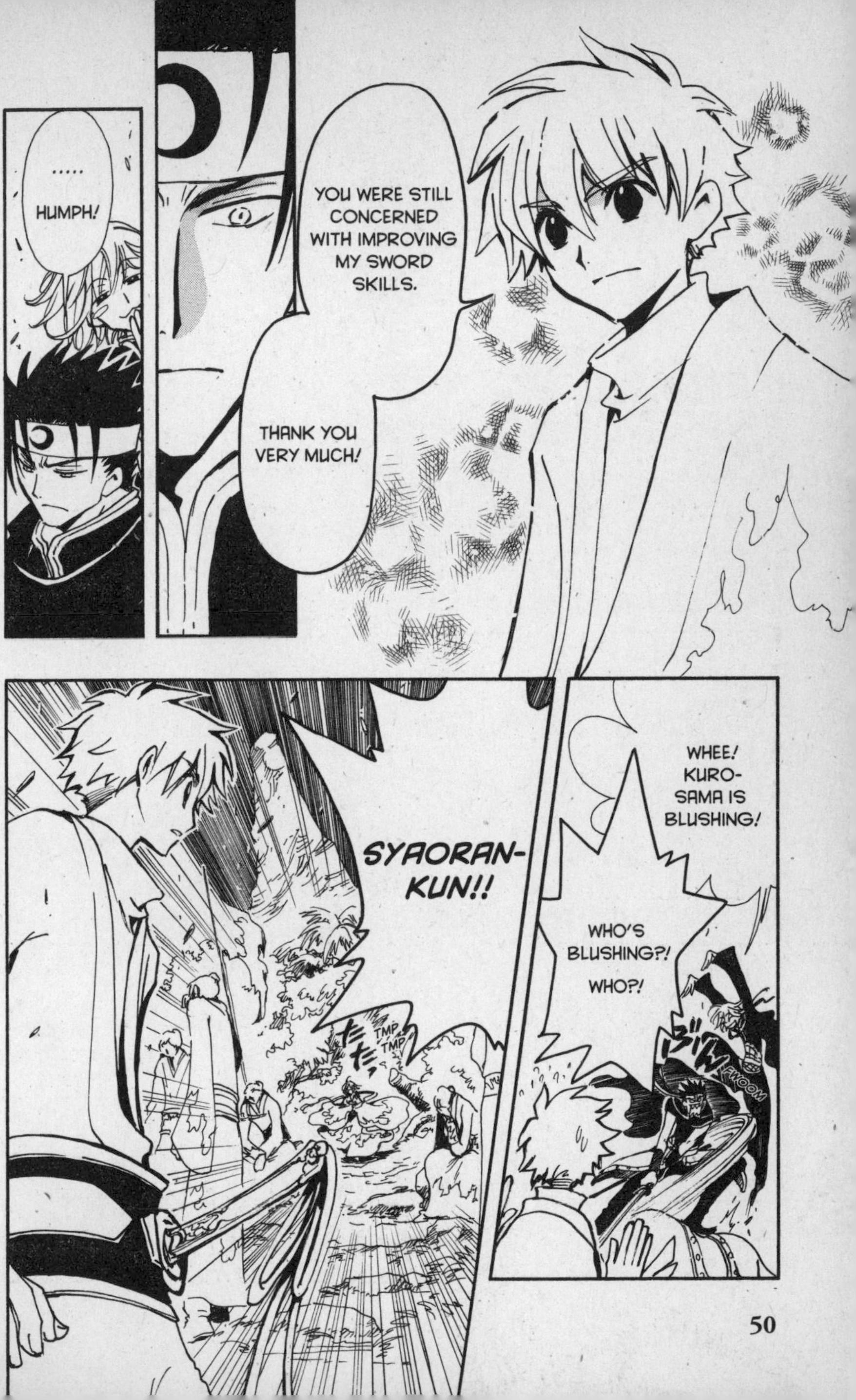
YOU WERE STILL CONCERNED WITH IMPROVING MY SWORD SKILLS.
THANK YOU VERY MUCH!
.....
HUMPH!
WHEE! KURO-SAMA IS BLUSHING!
WHO'S BLUSHING?!
WHO?!
FWOOM
SYAORAN-KUN!!
TMP TMP

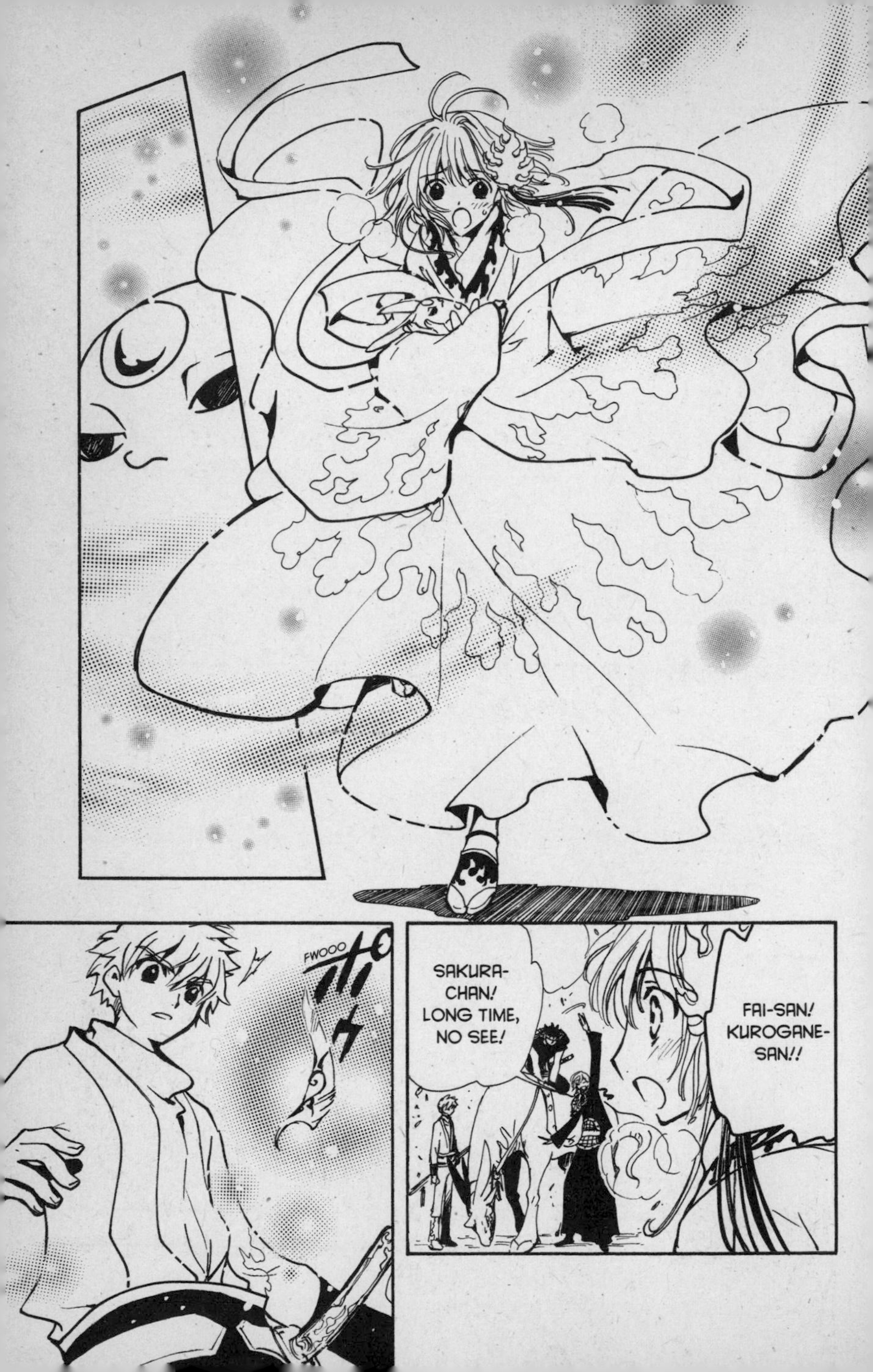
FAI-SAN! KUROGANE-SAN!!
SAKURA-CHAN! LONG TIME, NO SEE!
FWOOO

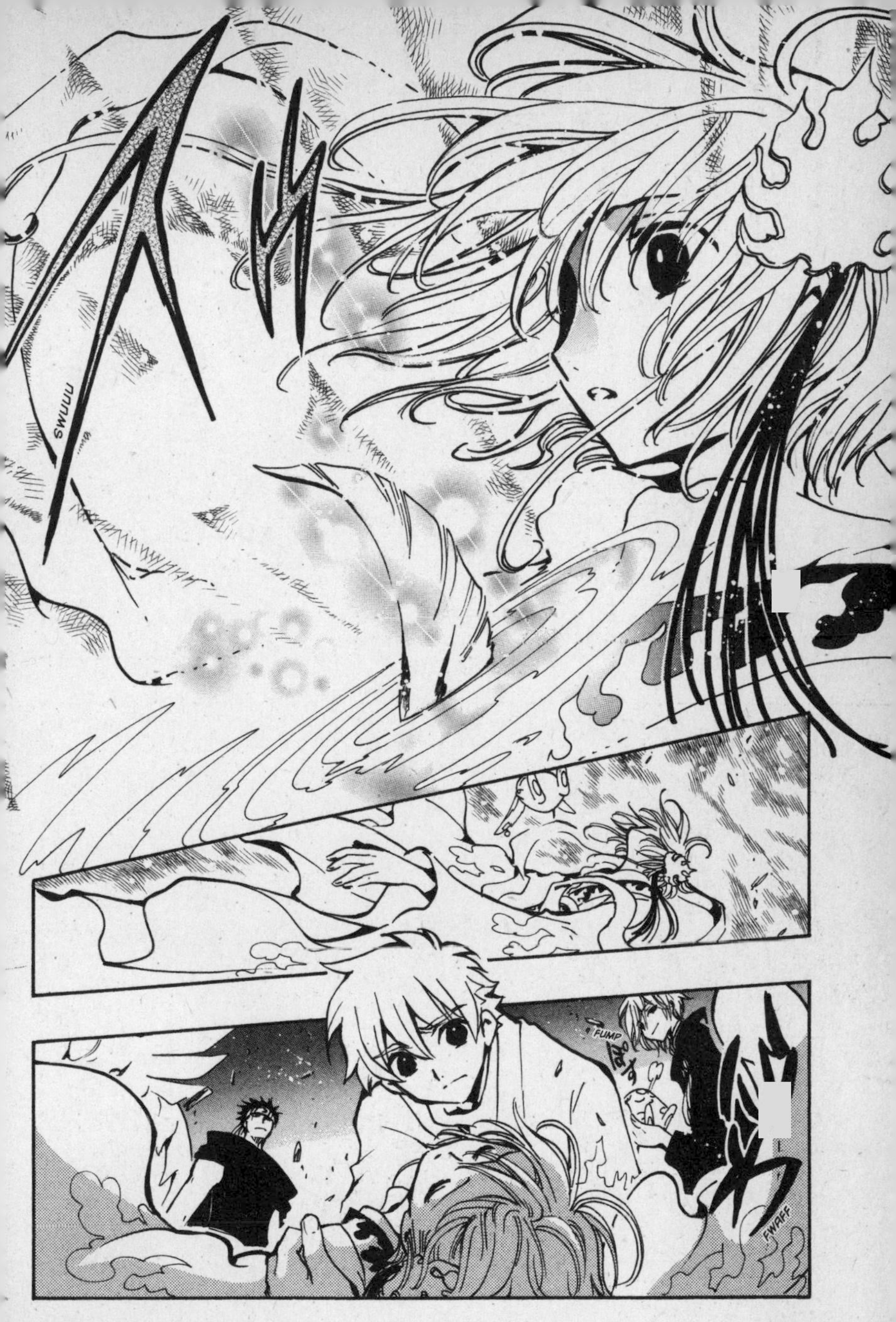
SWUUU
FUMP
FWAFF

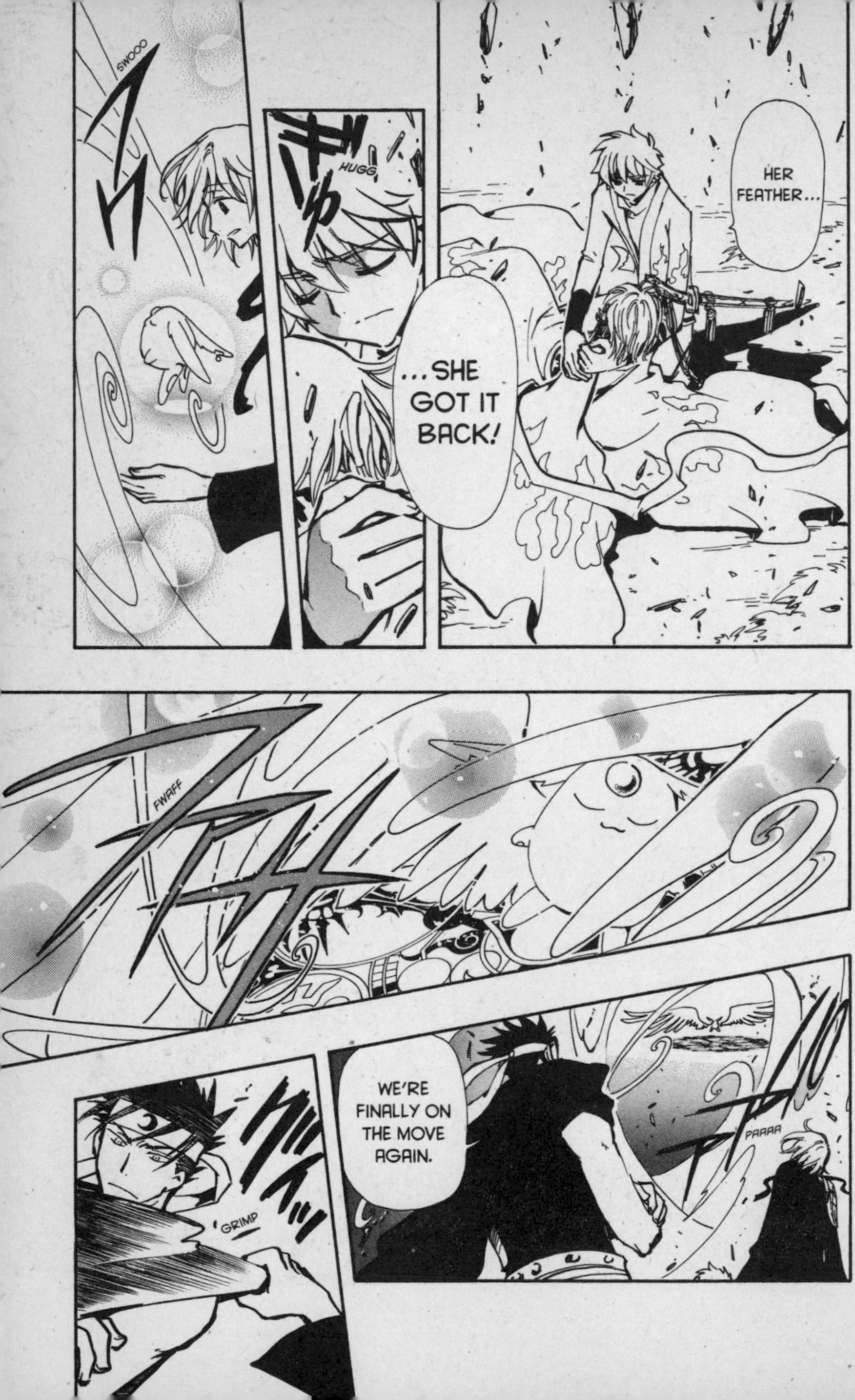
HER FEATHER...
HUGG
...SHE GOT IT BACK!
SWOOO
FWAFF
WE'RE FINALLY ON THE MOVE AGAIN.
PAAAA
GRIMP

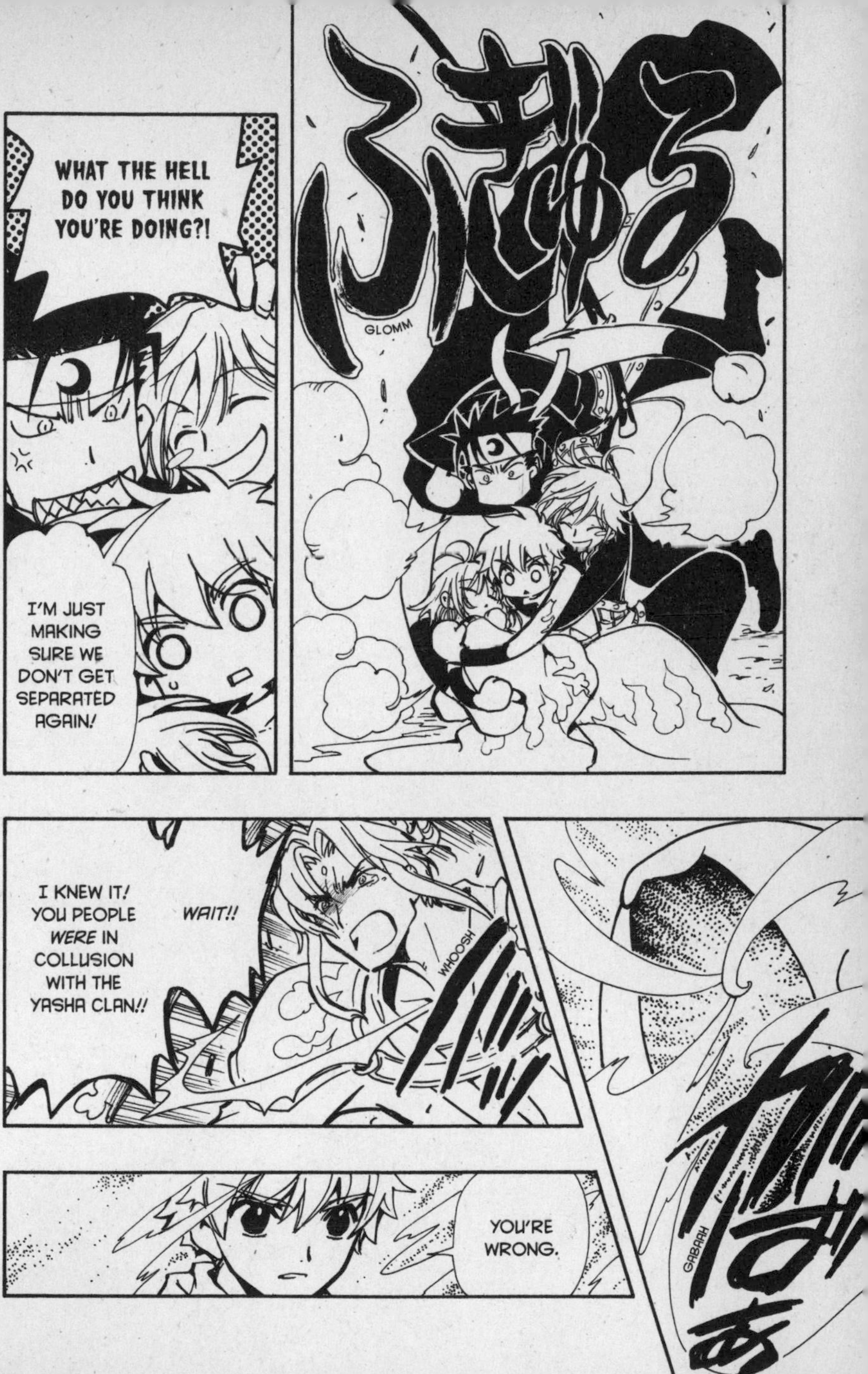
GLOMM
WHAT THE HELL DO YOU THINK YOU'RE DOING?!
I'M JUST MAKING SURE WE DON'T GET SEPARATED AGAIN!
GABAAH
WHOOSH
WAIT!!
I KNEW IT! YOU PEOPLE *WERE* IN COLLUSION WITH THE YASHA CLAN!!
YOU'RE WRONG.

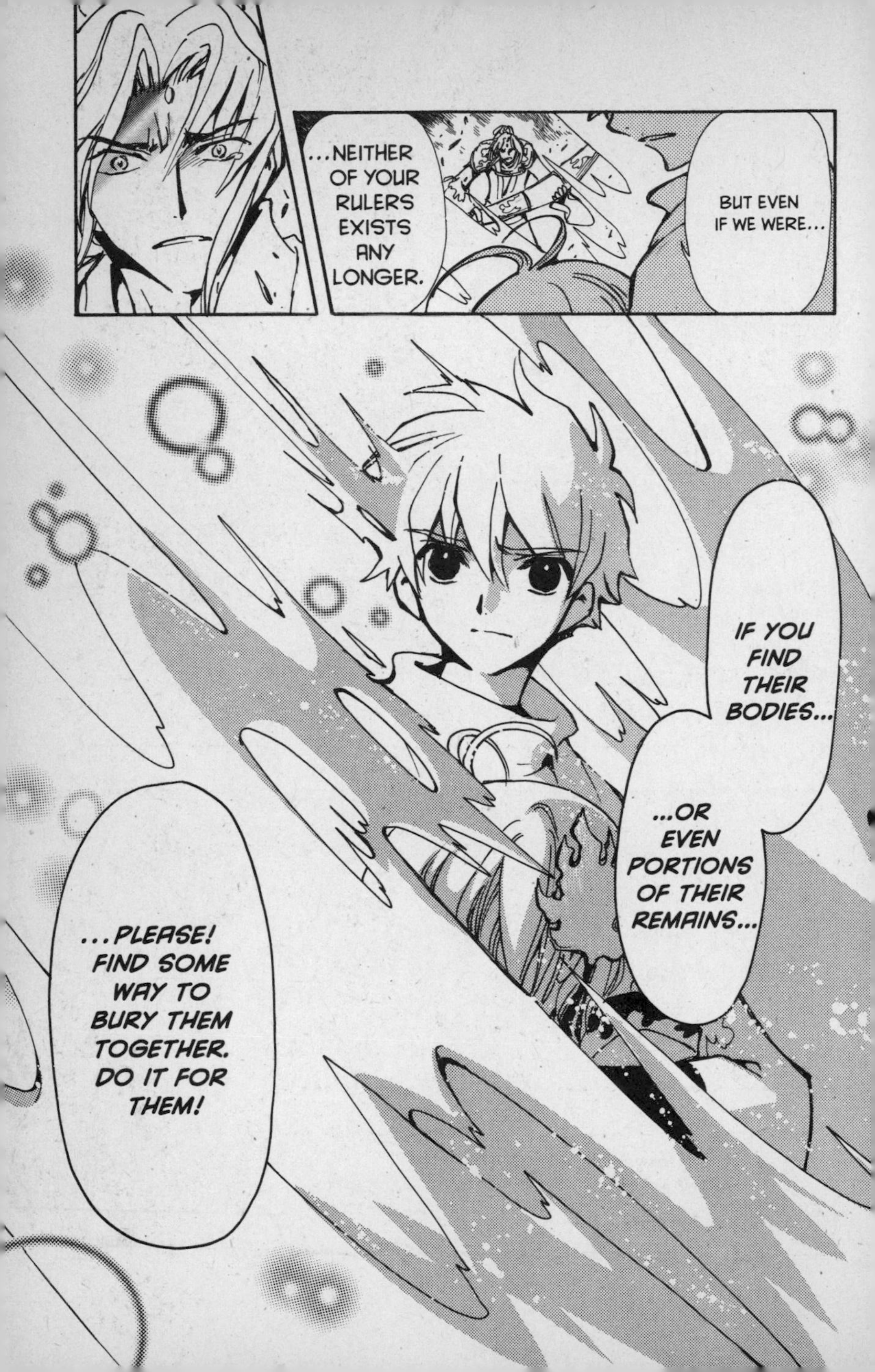
BUT EVEN IF WE WERE...
...NEITHER OF YOUR RULERS EXISTS ANY LONGER.
IF YOU FIND THEIR BODIES...
...OR EVEN PORTIONS OF THEIR REMAINS...
...PLEASE! FIND SOME WAY TO BURY THEM TOGETHER. DO IT FOR THEM!

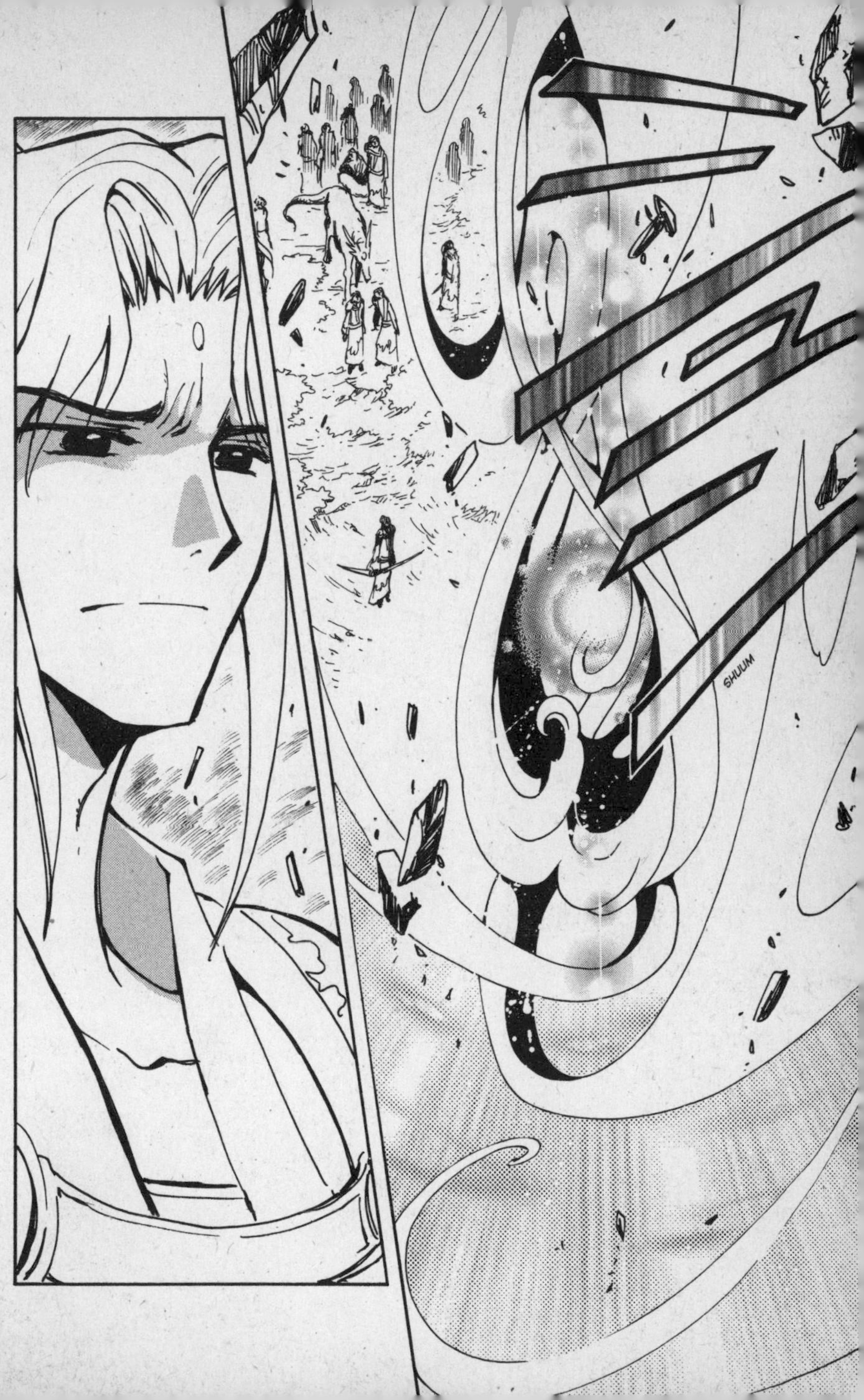
SHUUM

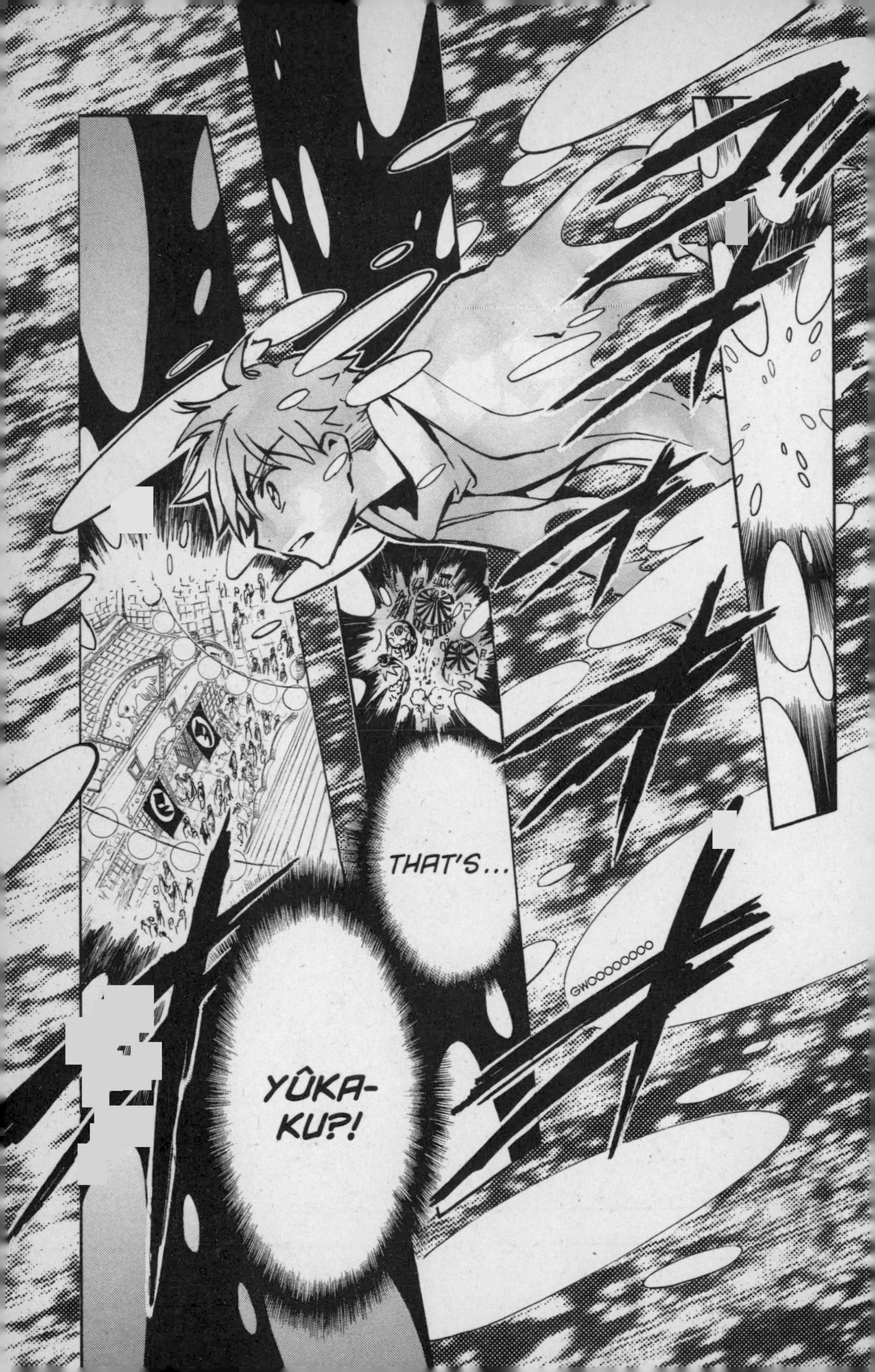
THAT'S...
GWOOOOOOOOO
YÛKA-KU?!

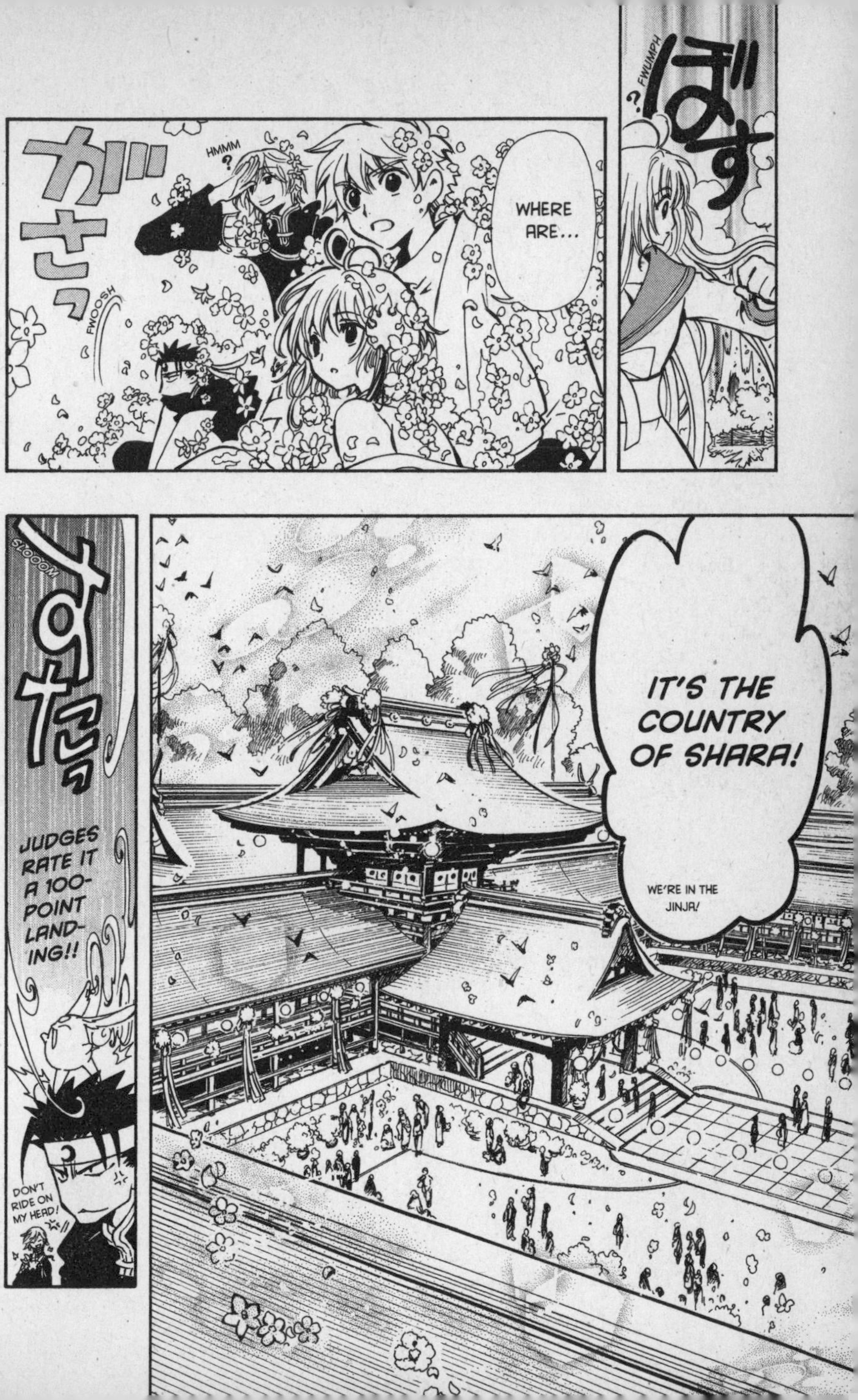
FWUMPH
ぼす
?
WHERE ARE...
HMMM
?
がさっ
FWOOSH
IT'S THE COUNTRY OF SHARA!
WE'RE IN THE JINJA!
すたっ
SLOOOM
JUDGES RATE IT A 100-POINT LAND-ING!!
DON'T RIDE ON MY HEAD!

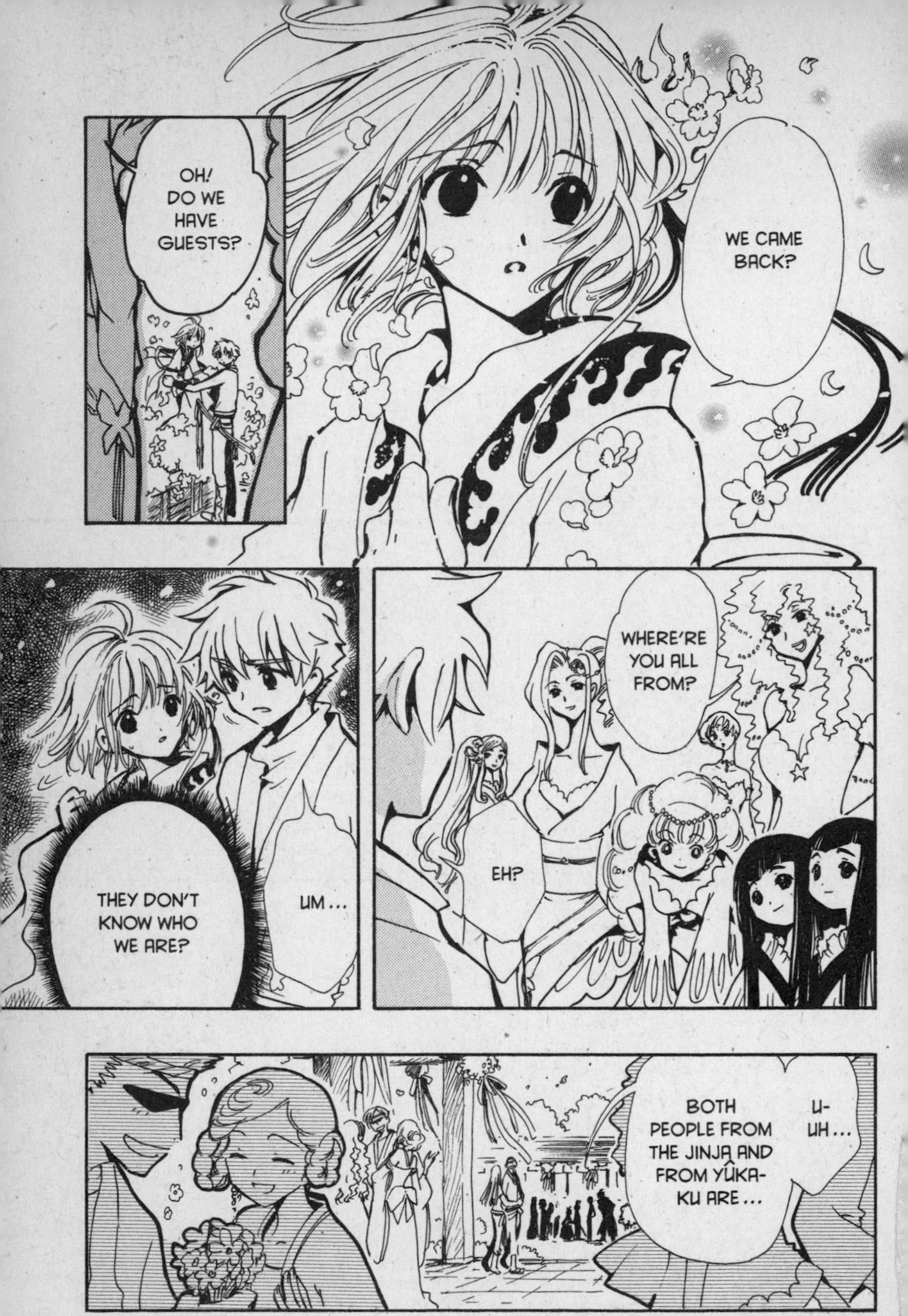
WE CAME BACK?
OH! DO WE HAVE GUESTS?
WHERE'RE YOU ALL FROM?
EH?
UM...
THEY DON'T KNOW WHO WE ARE?
U-UH...
BOTH PEOPLE FROM THE JINJA AND FROM YÛKA-KU ARE...

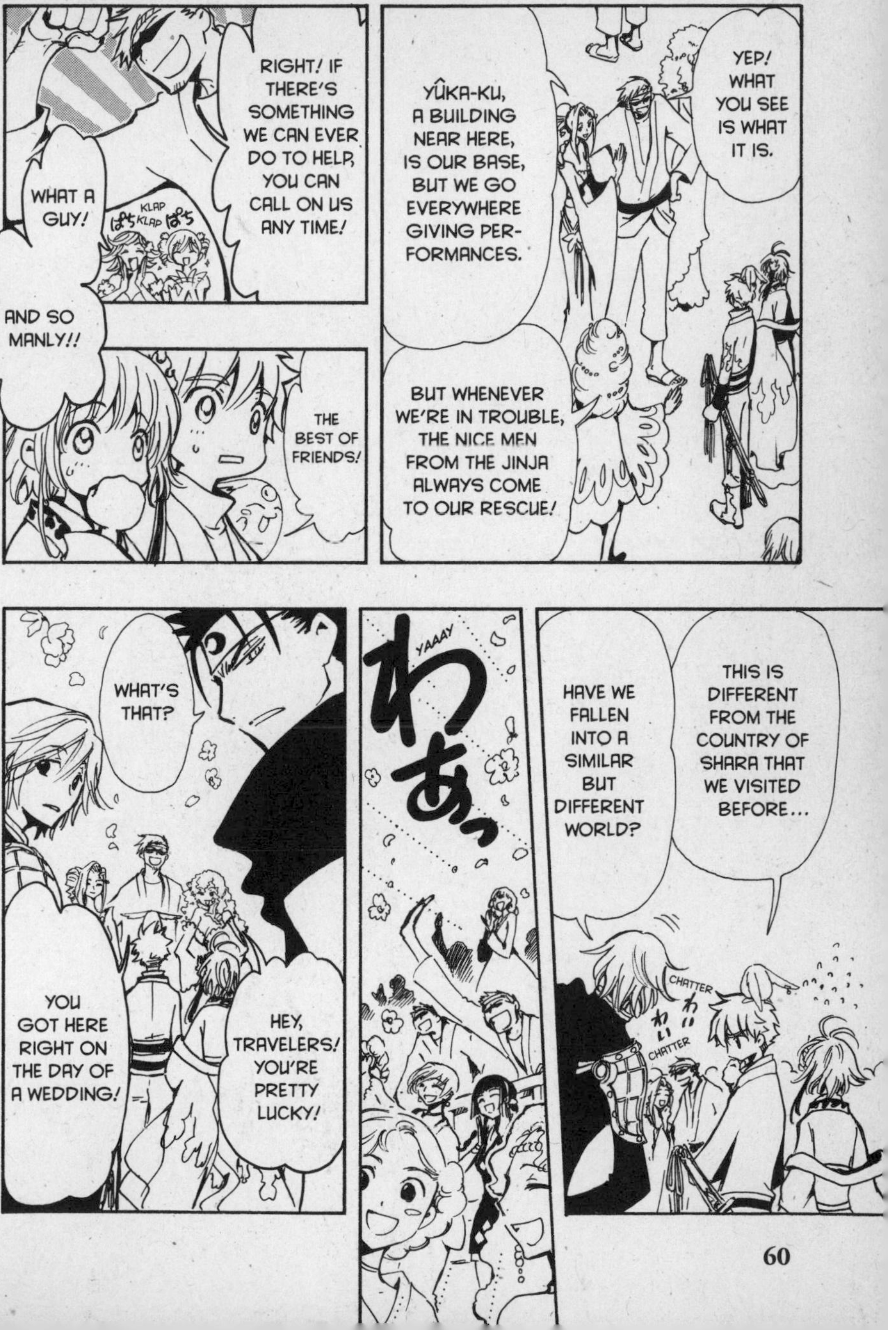
YEP! WHAT YOU SEE IS WHAT IT IS.
YÛKA-KU, A BUILDING NEAR HERE, IS OUR BASE, BUT WE GO EVERYWHERE GIVING PER-FORMANCES.
BUT WHENEVER WE'RE IN TROUBLE, THE NICE MEN FROM THE JINJA ALWAYS COME TO OUR RESCUE!
RIGHT! IF THERE'S SOMETHING WE CAN EVER DO TO HELP, YOU CAN CALL ON US ANY TIME!
ぱち KLAP ぱち KLAP
WHAT A GUY!
AND SO MANLY!!
THE BEST OF FRIENDS!
THIS IS DIFFERENT FROM THE COUNTRY OF SHARA THAT WE VISITED BEFORE...
HAVE WE FALLEN INTO A SIMILAR BUT DIFFERENT WORLD?
わい CHATTER わい CHATTER
わあっ YAAAY
WHAT'S THAT?
HEY, TRAVELERS! YOU'RE PRETTY LUCKY!
YOU GOT HERE RIGHT ON THE DAY OF A WEDDING!

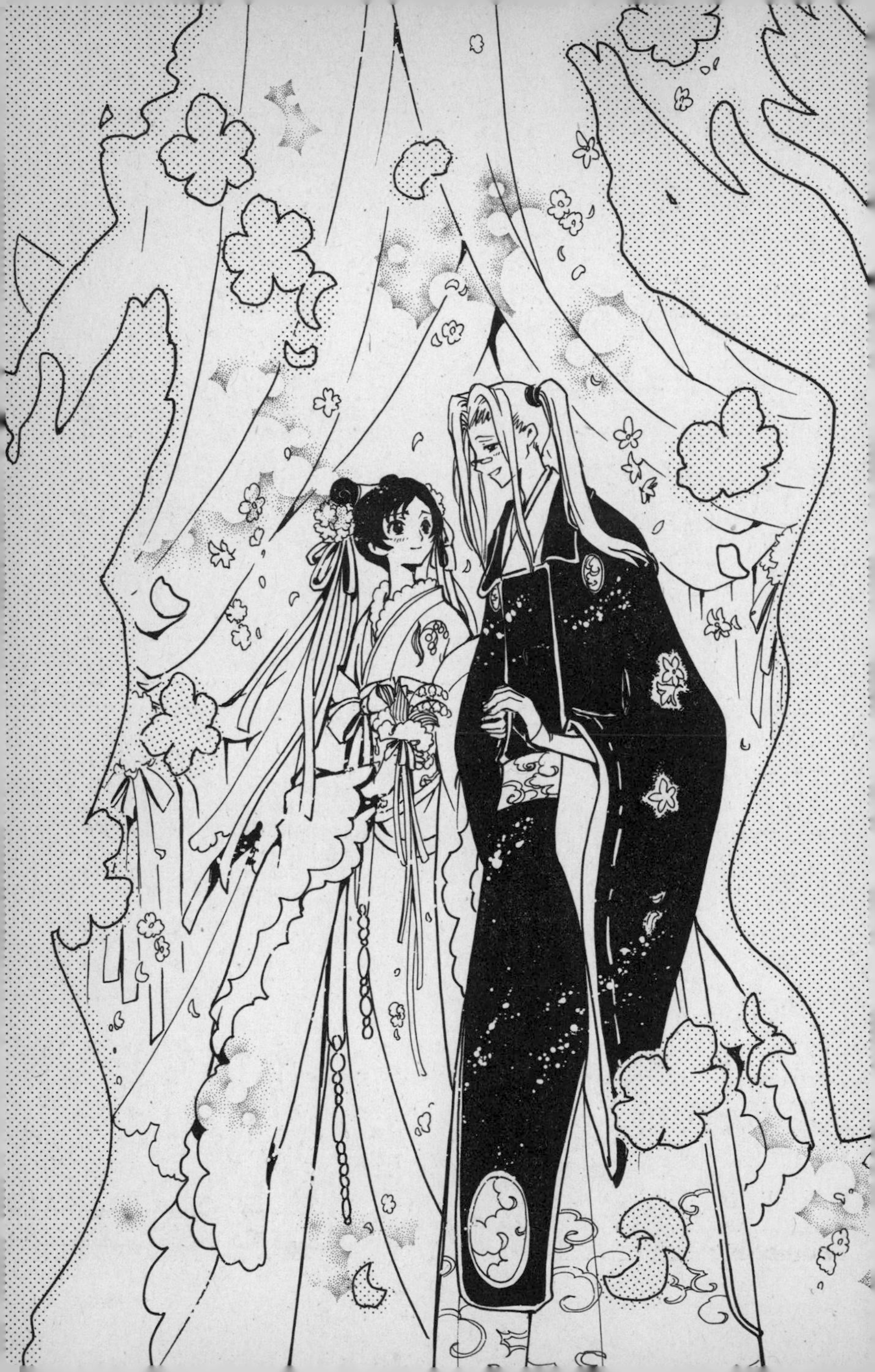

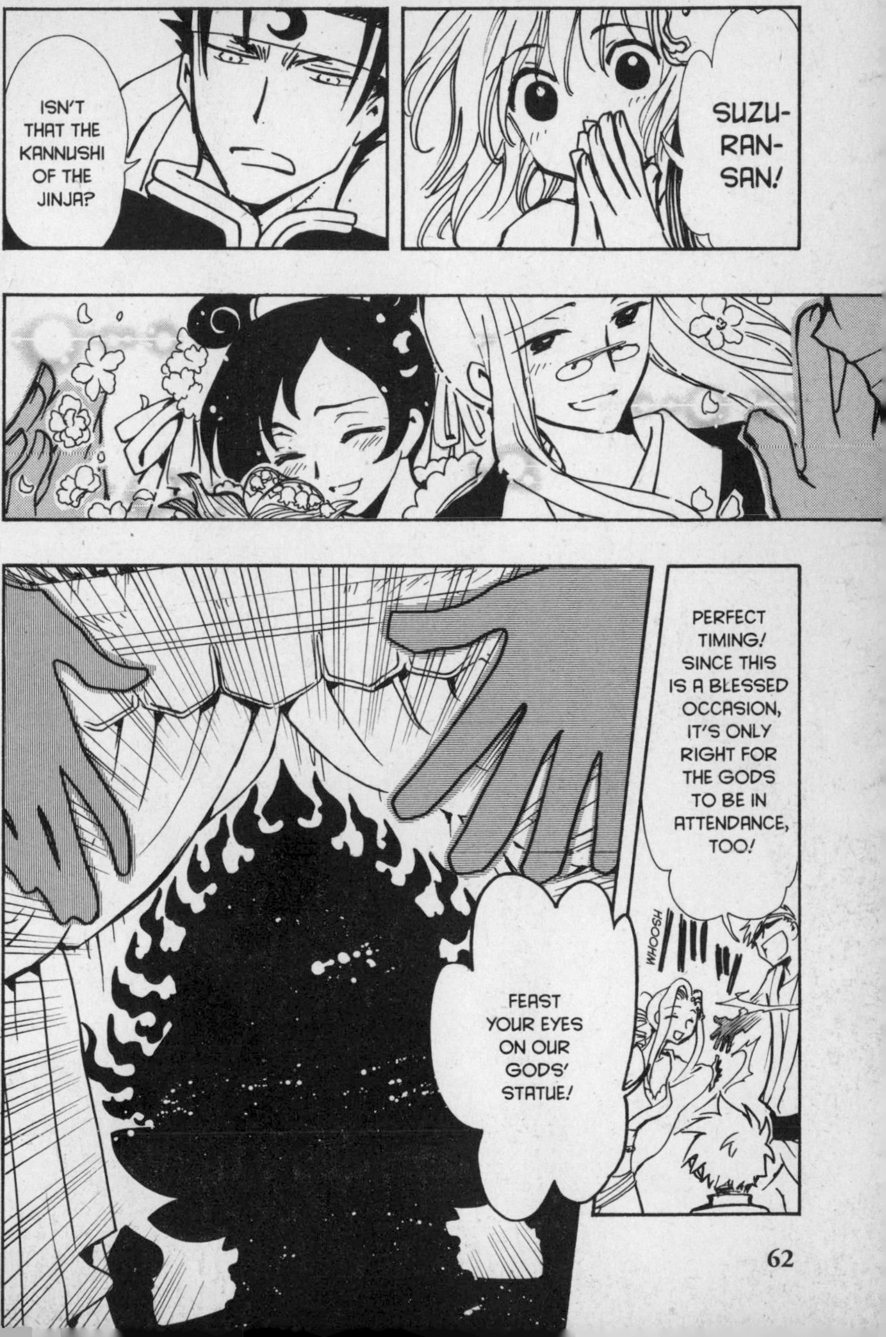
SUZU-RAN-SAN!
ISN'T THAT THE KANNUSHI OF THE JINJA?
PERFECT TIMING! SINCE THIS IS A BLESSED OCCASION, IT'S ONLY RIGHT FOR THE GODS TO BE IN ATTENDANCE, TOO!
WHOOSH
FEAST YOUR EYES ON OUR GODS' STATUE!

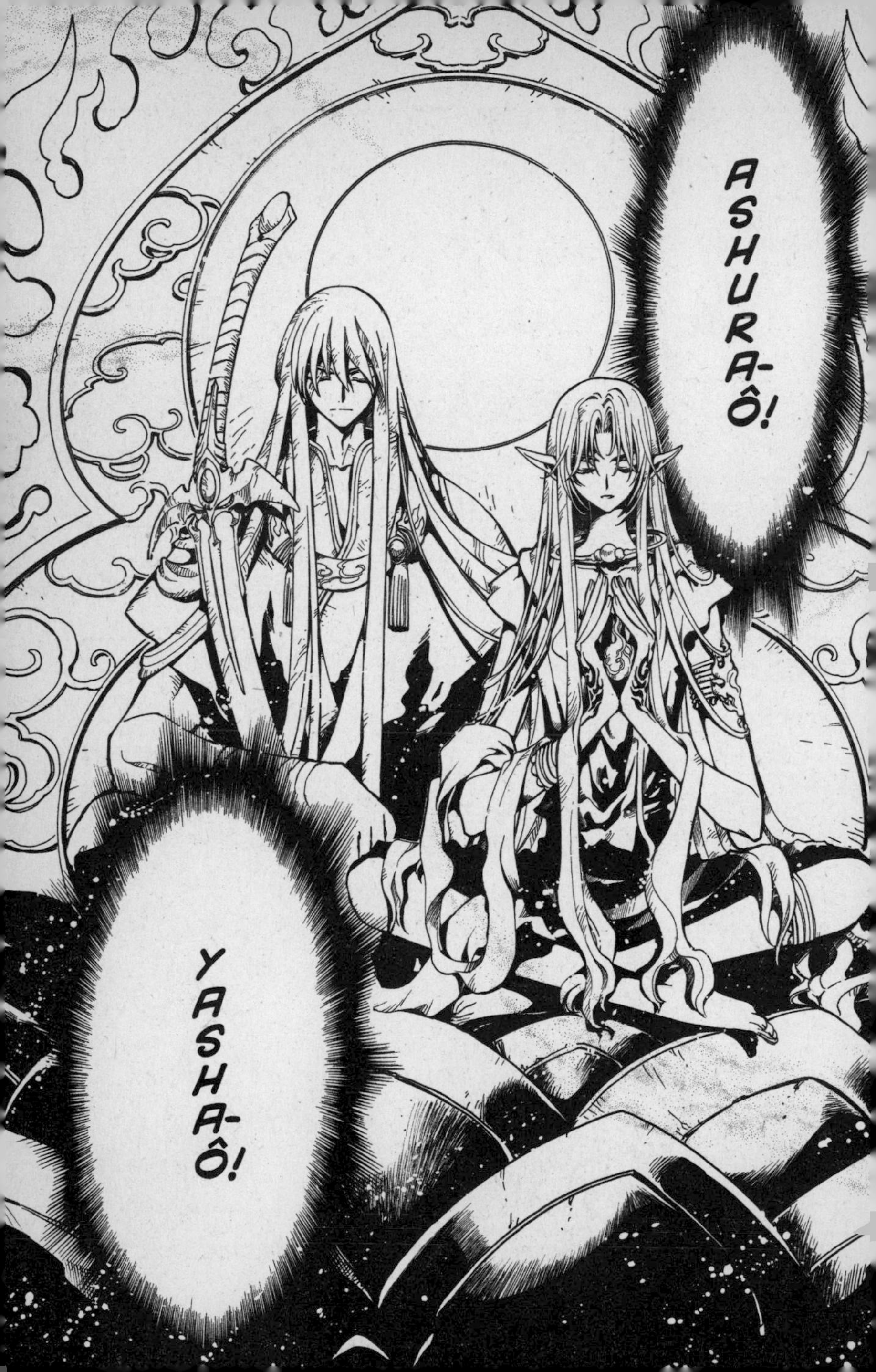
ASHURA-Ô!
YASHA-Ô!

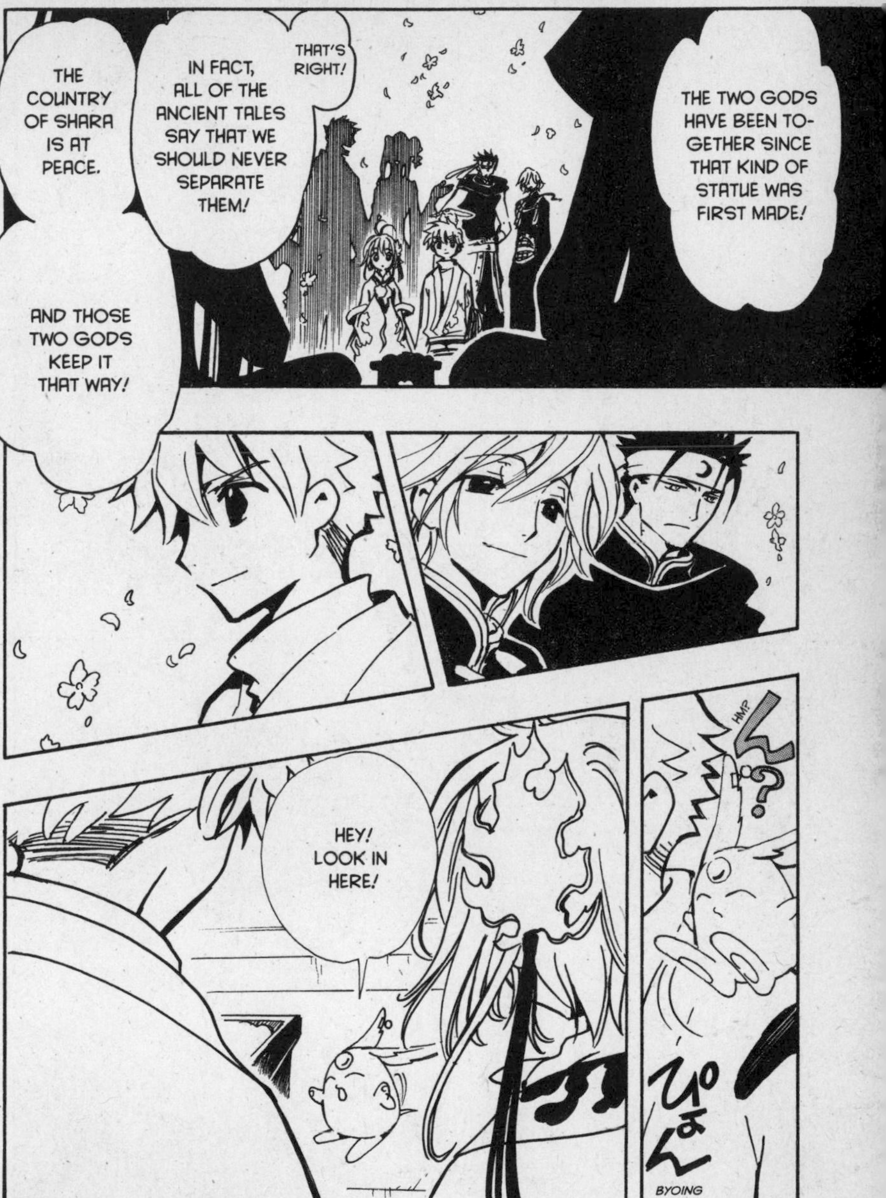
THE TWO GODS HAVE BEEN TO-GETHER SINCE THAT KIND OF STATUE WAS FIRST MADE!
THAT'S RIGHT!
IN FACT, ALL OF THE ANCIENT TALES SAY THAT WE SHOULD NEVER SEPARATE THEM!
THE COUNTRY OF SHARA IS AT PEACE.
AND THOSE TWO GODS KEEP IT THAT WAY!
HMP?
BYOING
HEY! LOOK IN HERE!

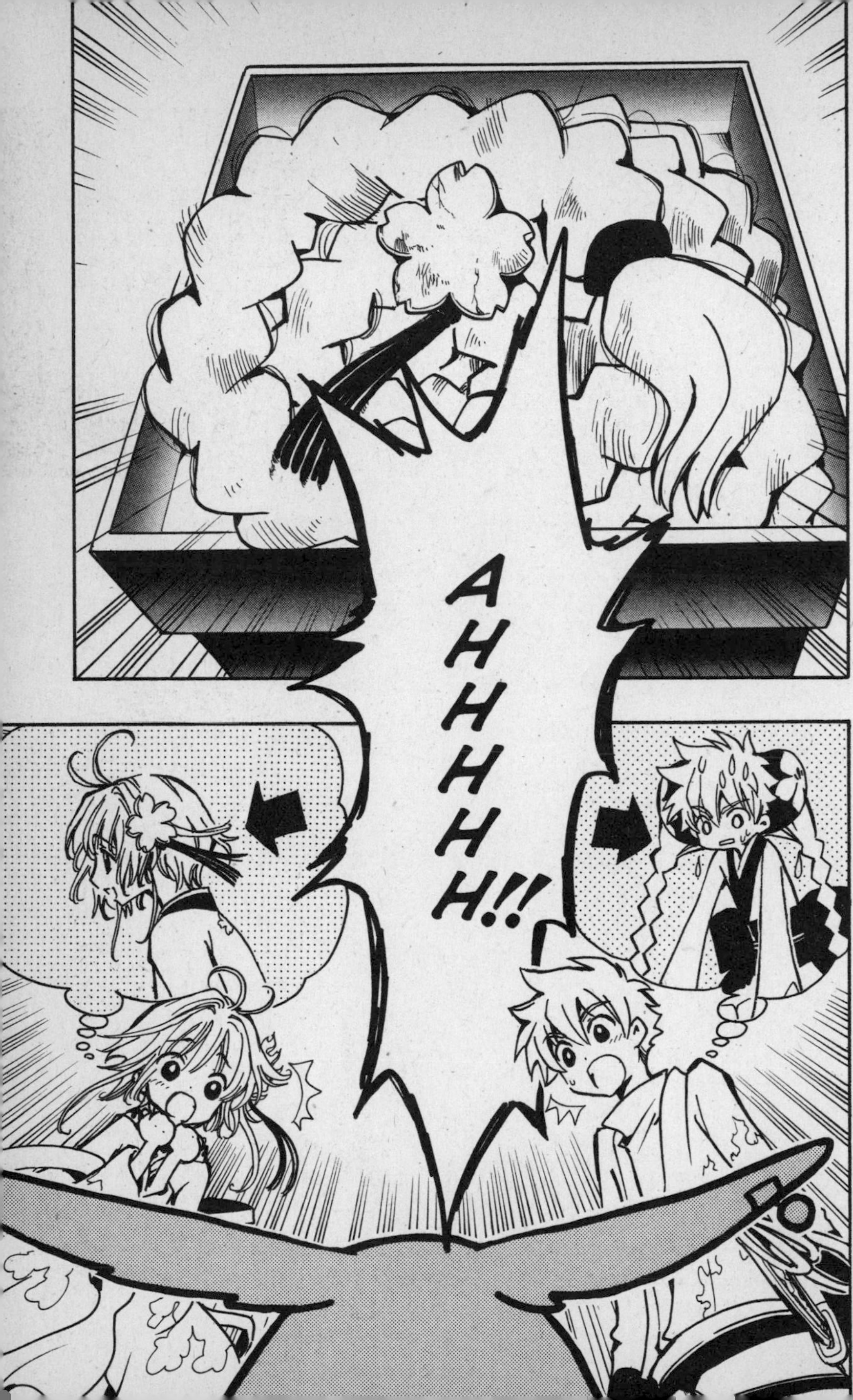
AHHHHH!!!

ツバサ

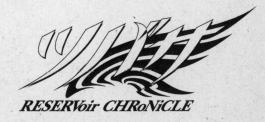

RESERVoir CHRoNiCLE

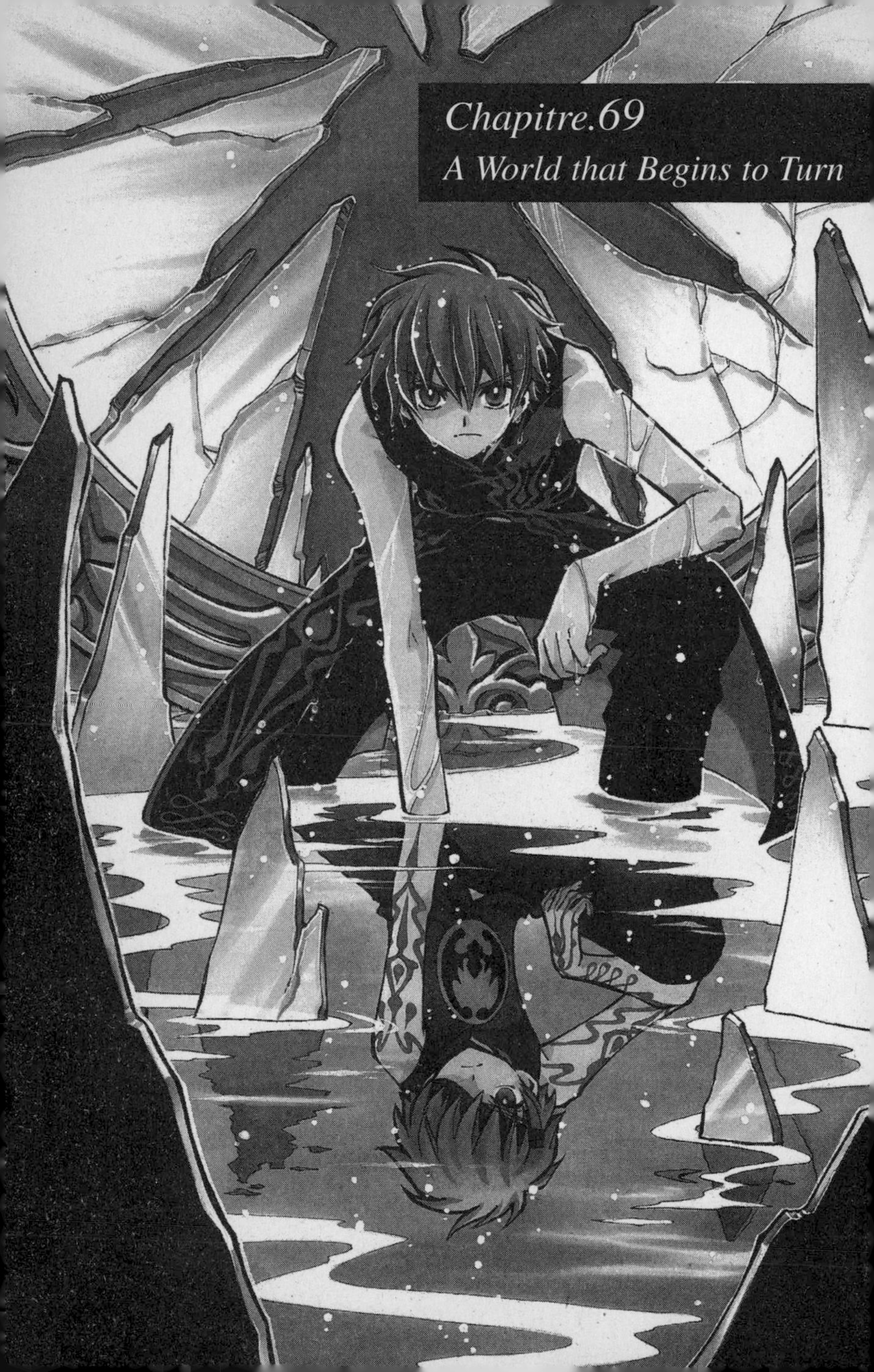
Chapitre.69
A World that Begins to Turn

ツバサ

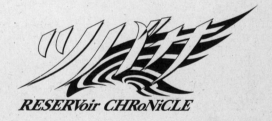

RESERVoir CHRoNiCLE

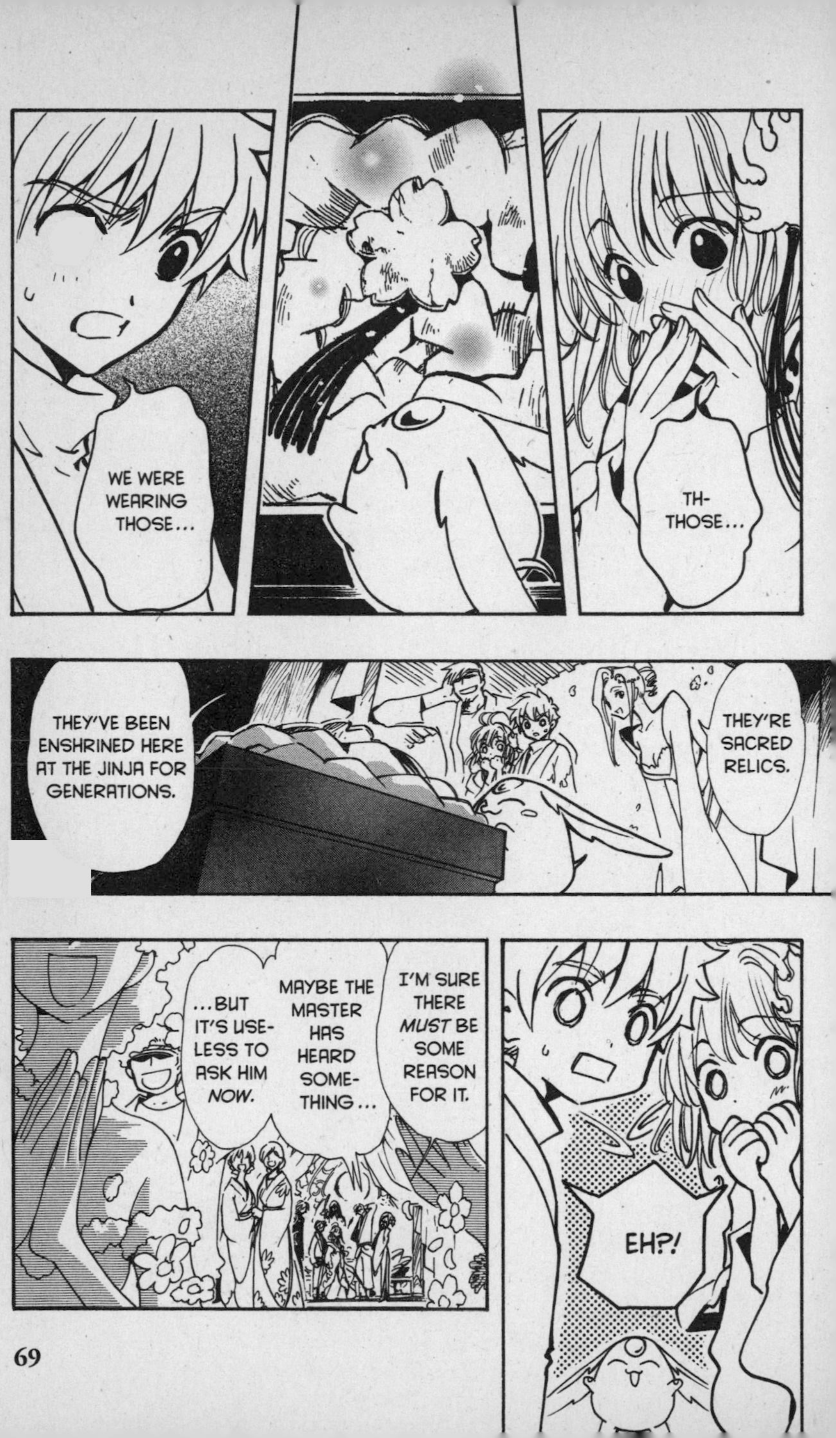
TH- THOSE...
WE WERE WEARING THOSE...
THEY'RE SACRED RELICS.
THEY'VE BEEN ENSHRINED HERE AT THE JINJA FOR GENERATIONS.
EH?!
I'M SURE THERE *MUST* BE SOME REASON FOR IT.
MAYBE THE MASTER HAS HEARD SOME-THING...
...BUT IT'S USE-LESS TO ASK HIM *NOW*.

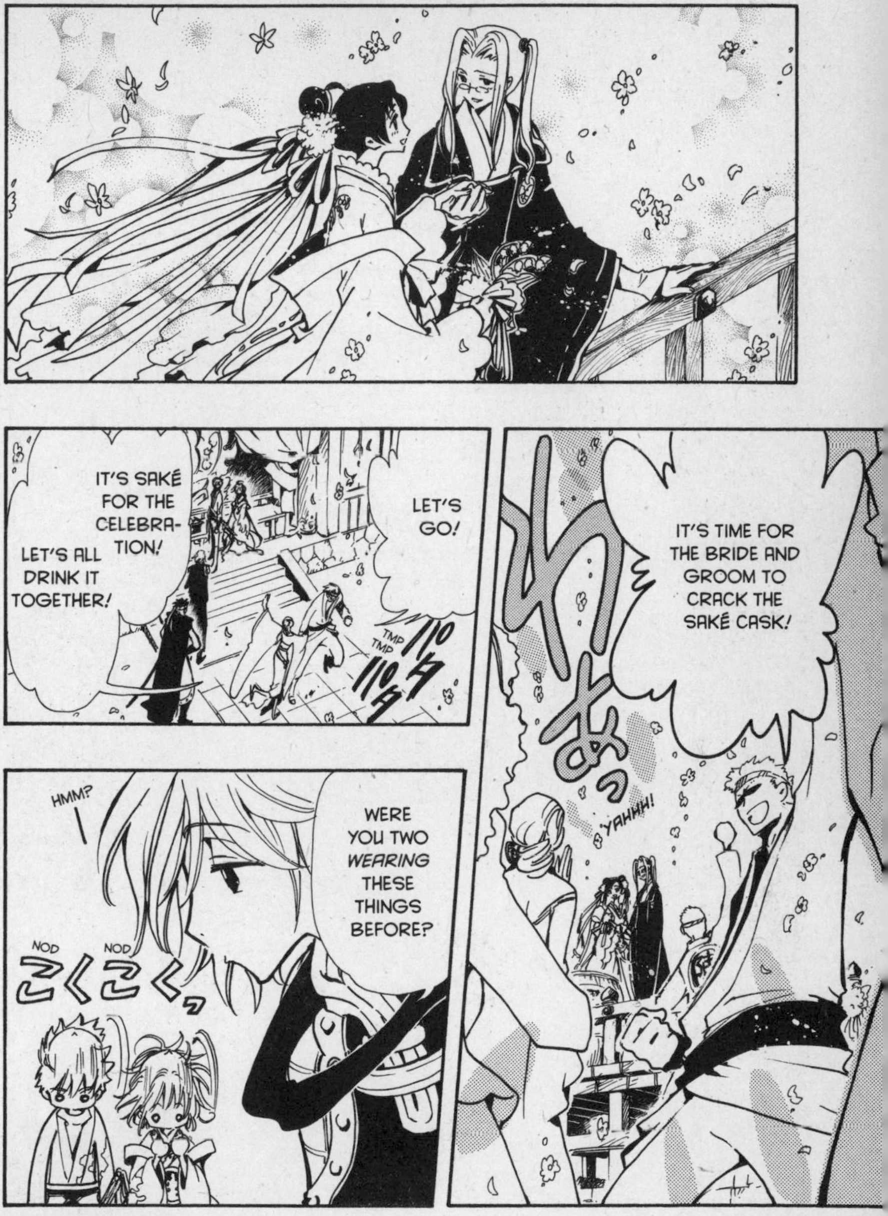
IT'S TIME FOR THE BRIDE AND GROOM TO CRACK THE SAKÉ CASK!
YAHHH!
LET'S GO!
IT'S SAKÉ FOR THE CELEBRATION!
LET'S ALL DRINK IT TOGETHER!
TMP TMP
WERE YOU TWO *WEARING* THESE THINGS BEFORE?
HMM?
NOD NOD

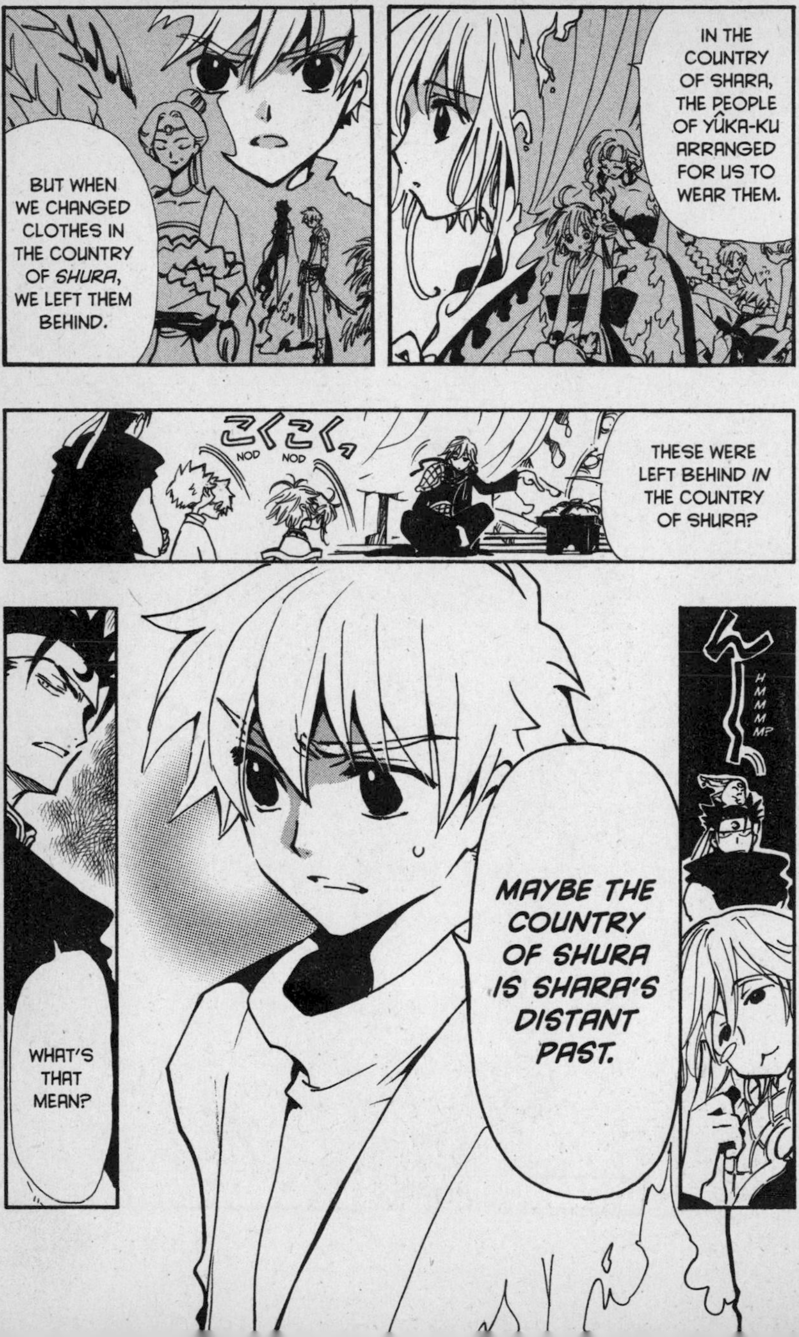
IN THE COUNTRY OF SHARA, THE PEOPLE OF YÛKA-KU ARRANGED FOR US TO WEAR THEM.
BUT WHEN WE CHANGED CLOTHES IN THE COUNTRY OF *SHURA*, WE LEFT THEM BEHIND.
THESE WERE LEFT BEHIND *IN* THE COUNTRY OF SHURA?
こくこく
NOD NOD
HMMMM?
MAYBE THE COUNTRY OF SHURA IS SHARA'S DISTANT PAST.
WHAT'S THAT MEAN?

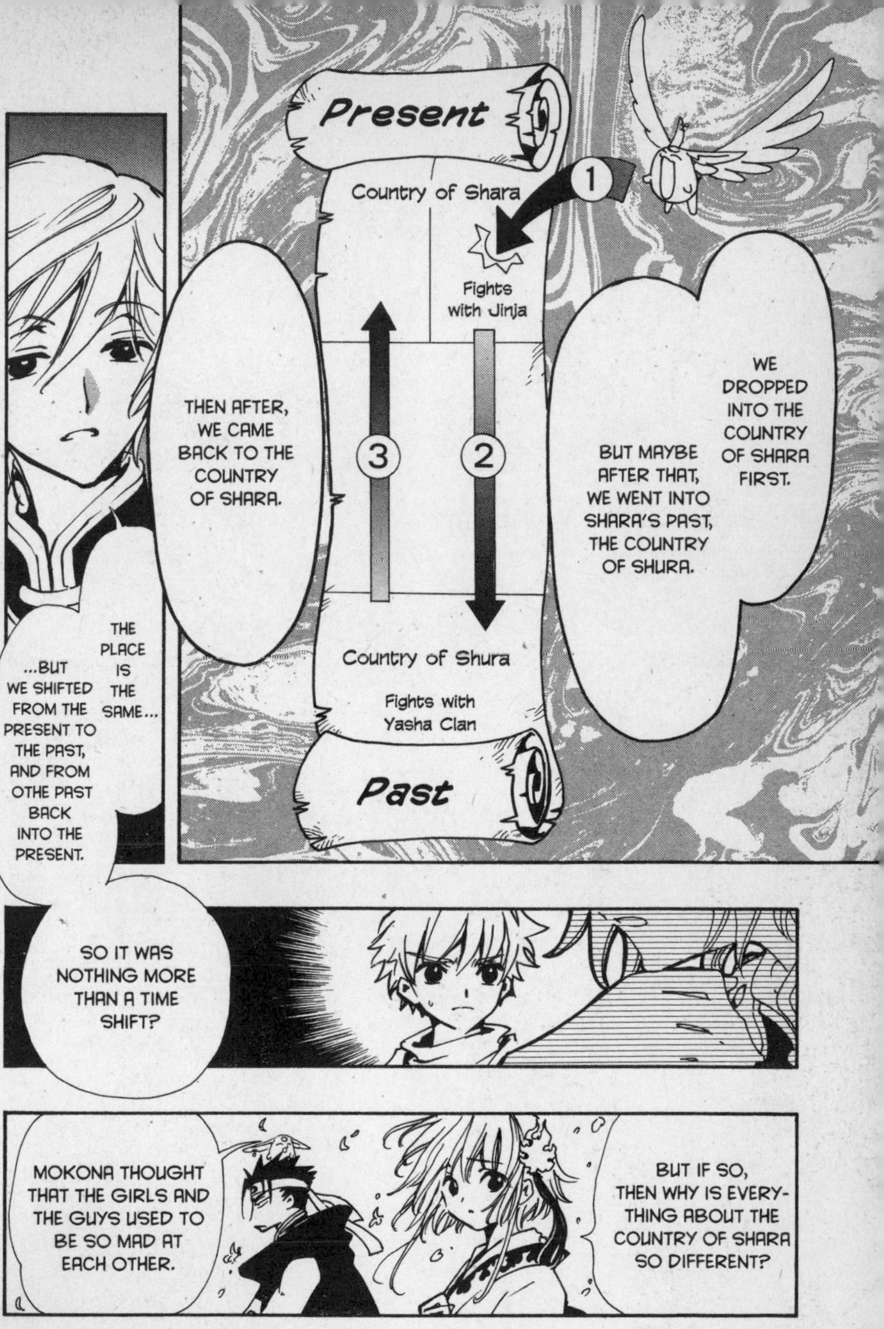
Present
Country of Shara
1
Fights with Jinja
2
3
Country of Shura
Fights with Yasha Clan
Past
WE DROPPED INTO THE COUNTRY OF SHARA FIRST.
BUT MAYBE AFTER THAT, WE WENT INTO SHARA'S PAST, THE COUNTRY OF SHURA.
THEN AFTER, WE CAME BACK TO THE COUNTRY OF SHARA.
THE PLACE IS THE SAME...
...BUT WE SHIFTED FROM THE PRESENT TO THE PAST, AND FROM OTHE PAST BACK INTO THE PRESENT.
SO IT WAS NOTHING MORE THAN A TIME SHIFT?
BUT IF SO, THEN WHY IS EVERY-THING ABOUT THE COUNTRY OF SHARA SO DIFFERENT?
MOKONA THOUGHT THAT THE GIRLS AND THE GUYS USED TO BE SO MAD AT EACH OTHER.

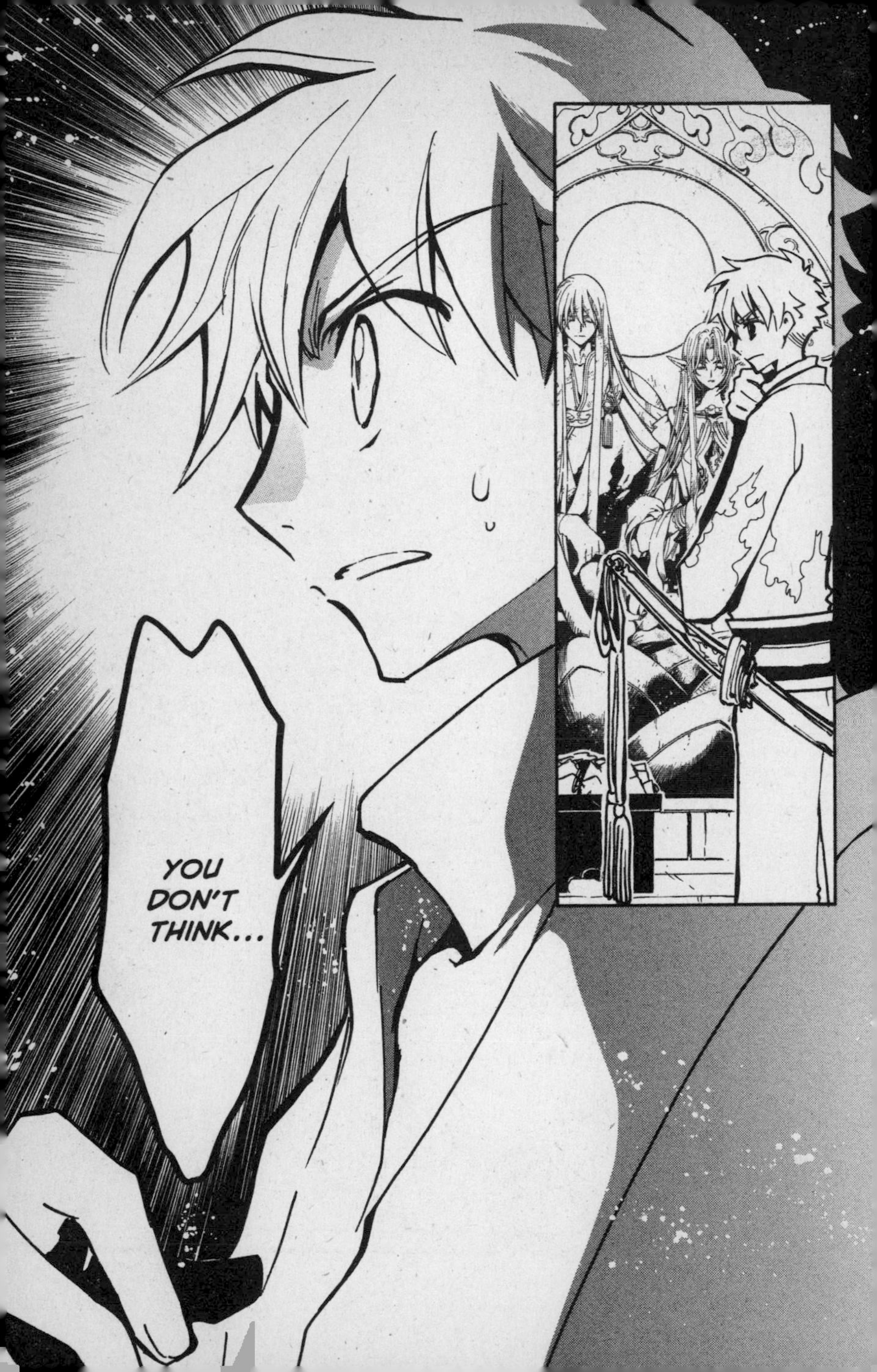
YOU DON'T THINK...

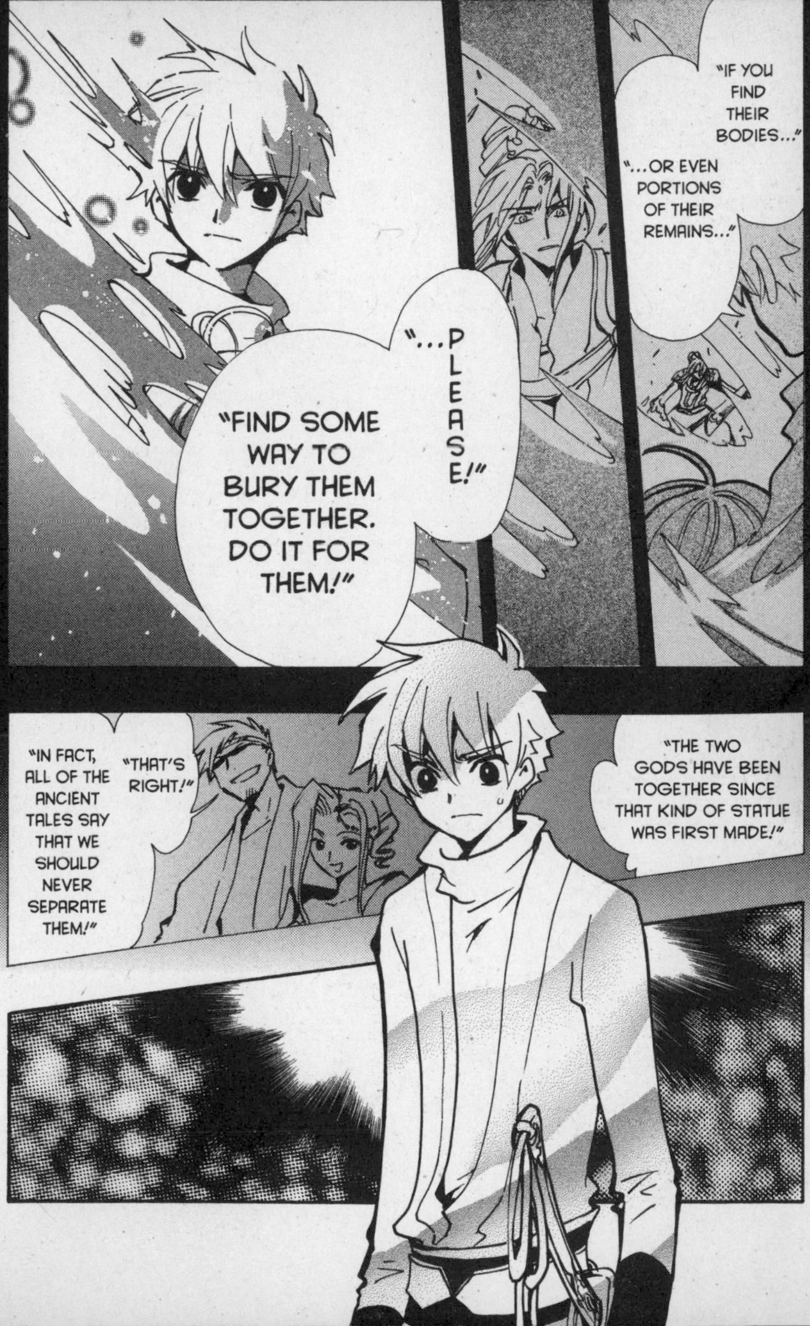
"IF YOU FIND THEIR BODIES..."
"...OR EVEN PORTIONS OF THEIR REMAINS..."
"FIND SOME WAY TO BURY THEM TOGETHER. DO IT FOR THEM!"
"...PLEASE!"
"THE TWO GODS HAVE BEEN TOGETHER SINCE THAT KIND OF STATUE WAS FIRST MADE!"
"THAT'S RIGHT!"
"IN FACT, ALL OF THE ANCIENT TALES SAY THAT WE SHOULD NEVER SEPARATE THEM!"

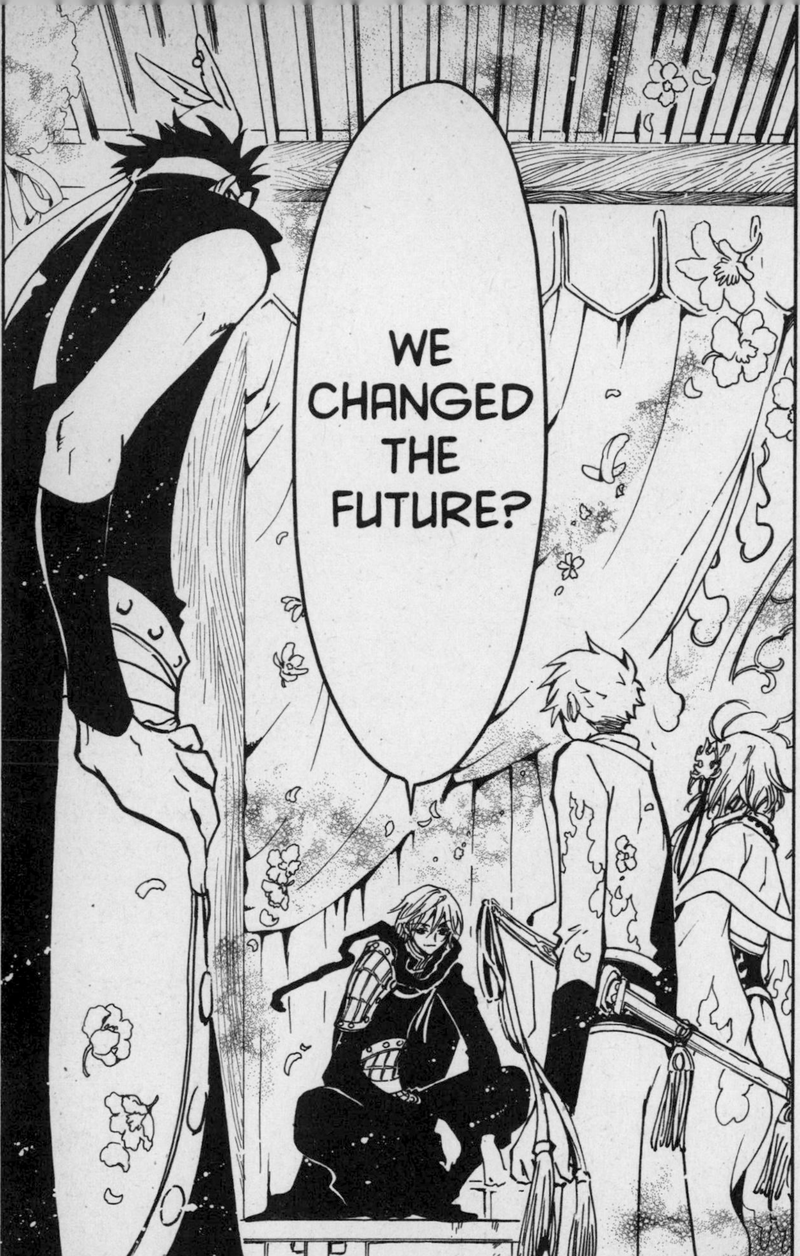
WE CHANGED THE FUTURE?

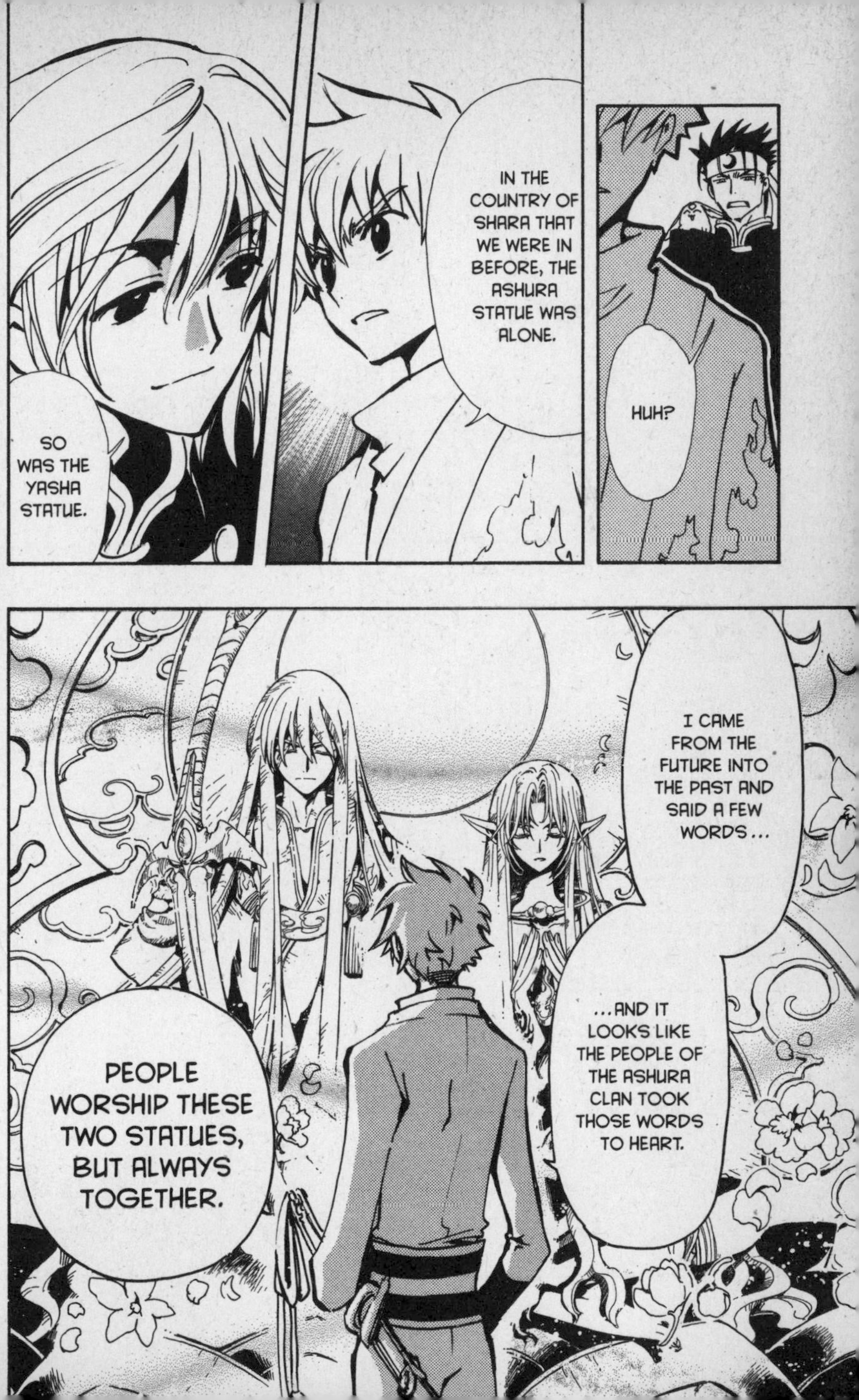
HUH?
IN THE COUNTRY OF SHARA THAT WE WERE IN BEFORE, THE ASHURA STATUE WAS ALONE.
SO WAS THE YASHA STATUE.
I CAME FROM THE FUTURE INTO THE PAST AND SAID A FEW WORDS...
...AND IT LOOKS LIKE THE PEOPLE OF THE ASHURA CLAN TOOK THOSE WORDS TO HEART.
PEOPLE WORSHIP THESE TWO STATUES, BUT ALWAYS TOGETHER.

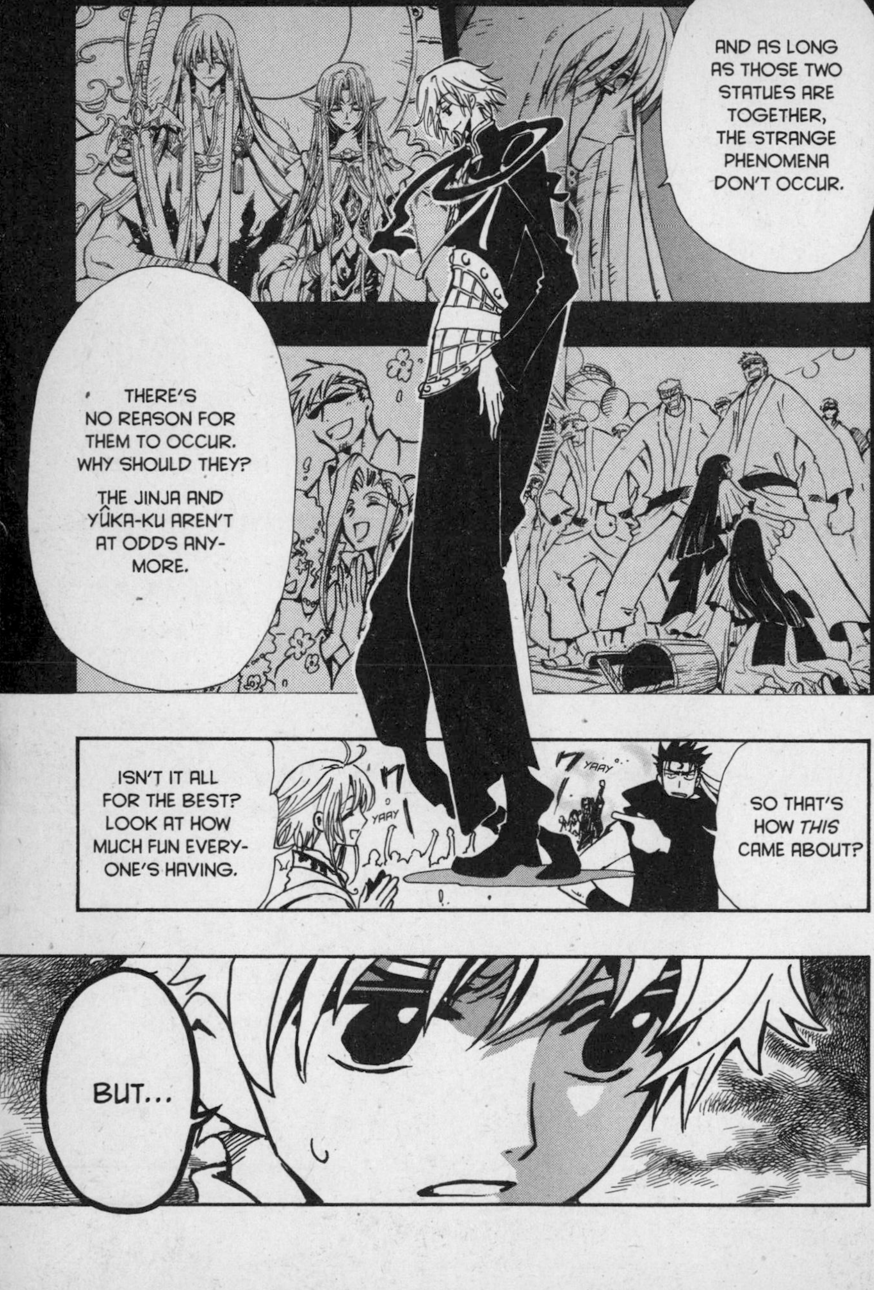
AND AS LONG AS THOSE TWO STATUES ARE TOGETHER, THE STRANGE PHENOMENA DON'T OCCUR.
THERE'S NO REASON FOR THEM TO OCCUR. WHY SHOULD THEY?
THE JINJA AND YÛKA-KU AREN'T AT ODDS ANY-MORE.
SO THAT'S HOW *THIS* CAME ABOUT?
YAAY
ISN'T IT ALL FOR THE BEST? LOOK AT HOW MUCH FUN EVERY-ONE'S HAVING.
YAAY
BUT...

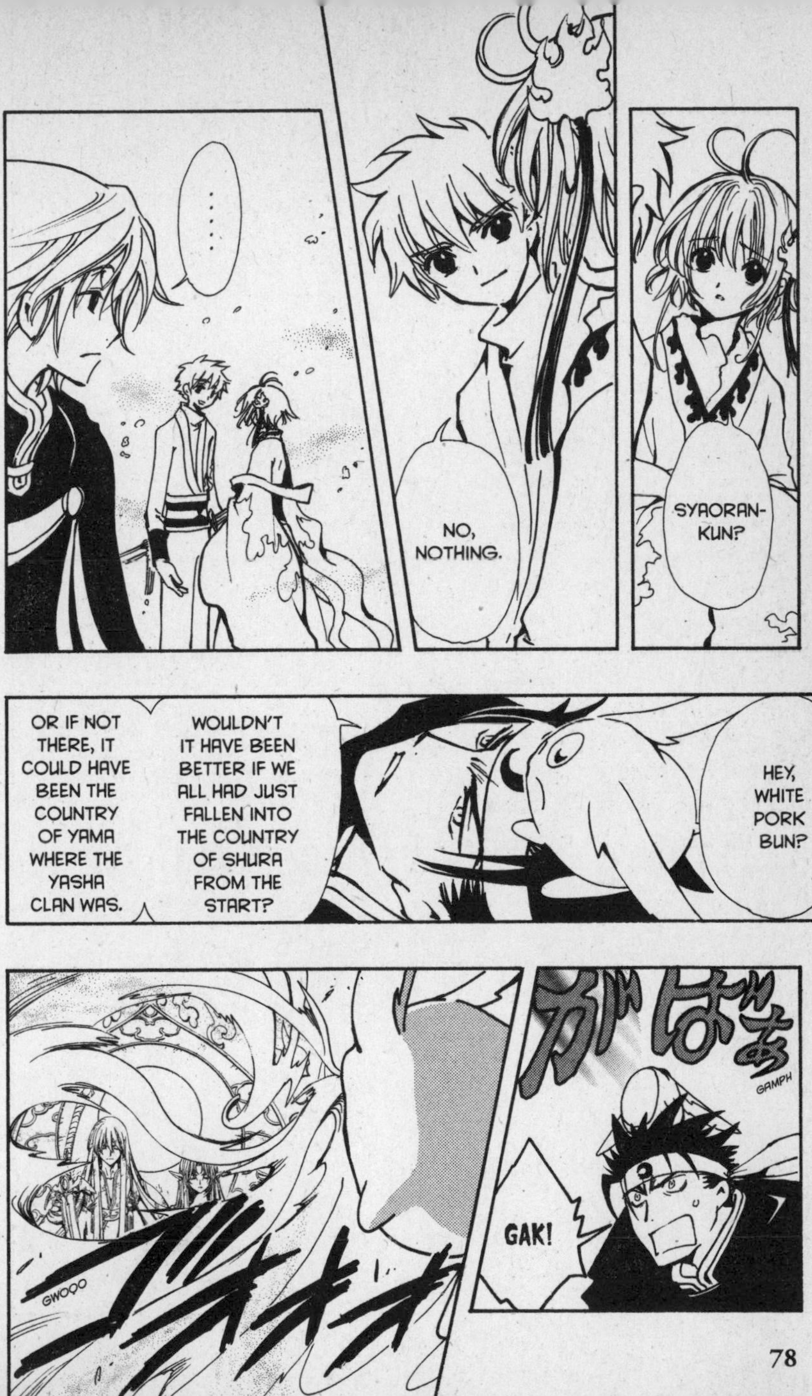
SYAORAN-KUN?
NO, NOTHING.
......
HEY, WHITE PORK BUN?
WOULDN'T IT HAVE BEEN BETTER IF WE ALL HAD JUST FALLEN INTO THE COUNTRY OF SHURA FROM THE START?
OR IF NOT THERE, IT COULD HAVE BEEN THE COUNTRY OF YAMA WHERE THE YASHA CLAN WAS.
GAMPH
GAK!
GWOOO

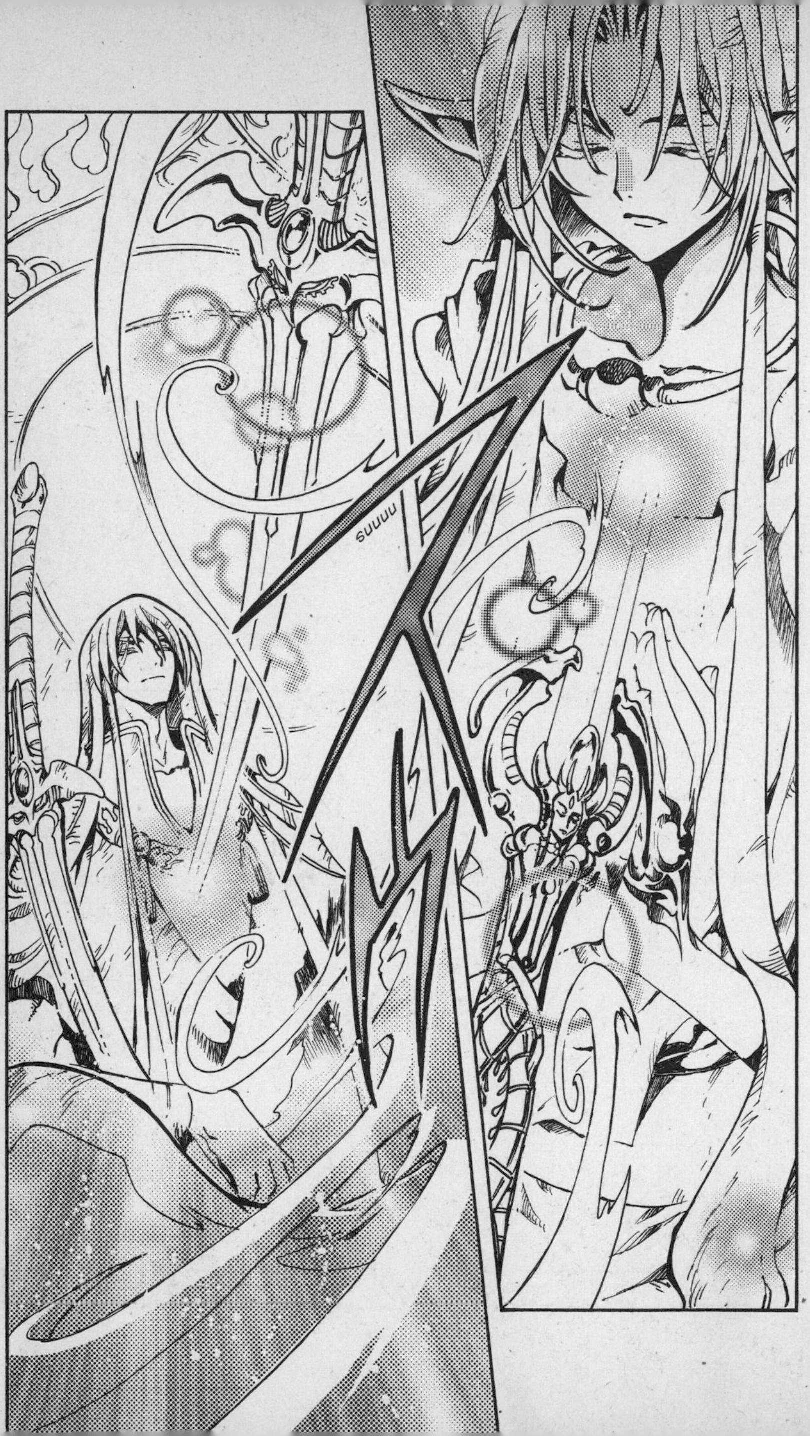
suuuu

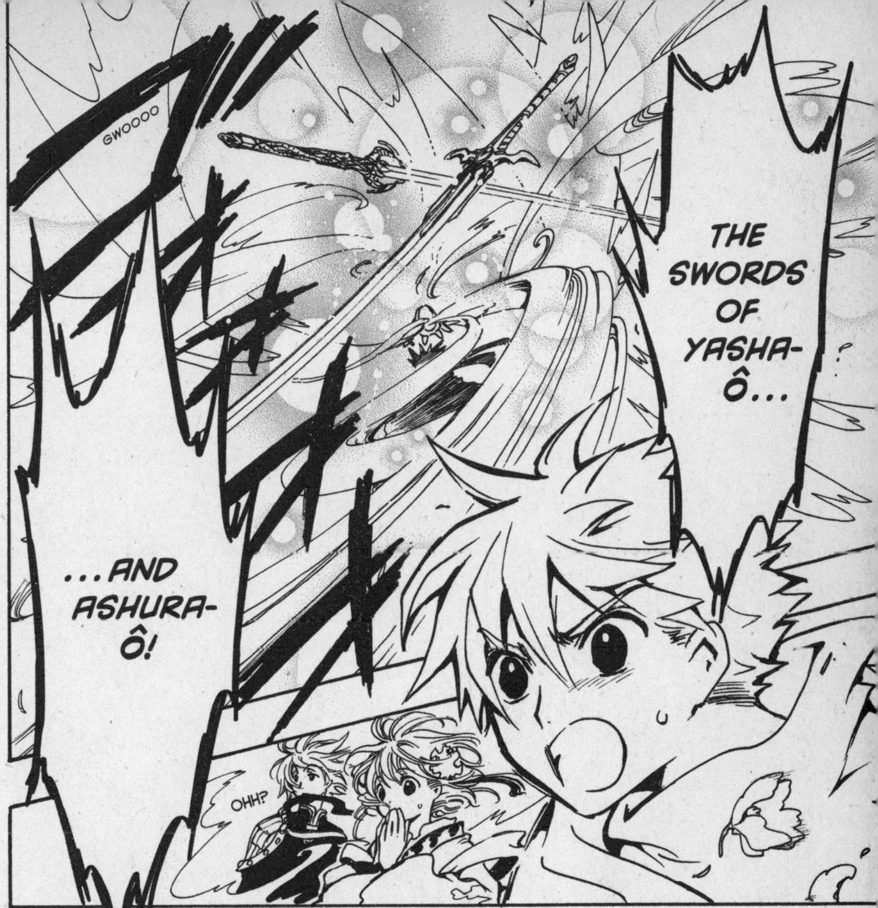
THE SWORDS OF YASHA-Ô...
GWOOOO
...AND ASHURA-Ô!
OHH?

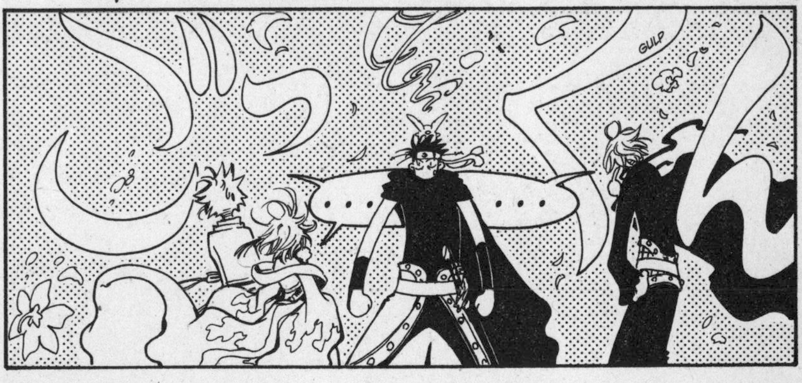
GULP
... ...

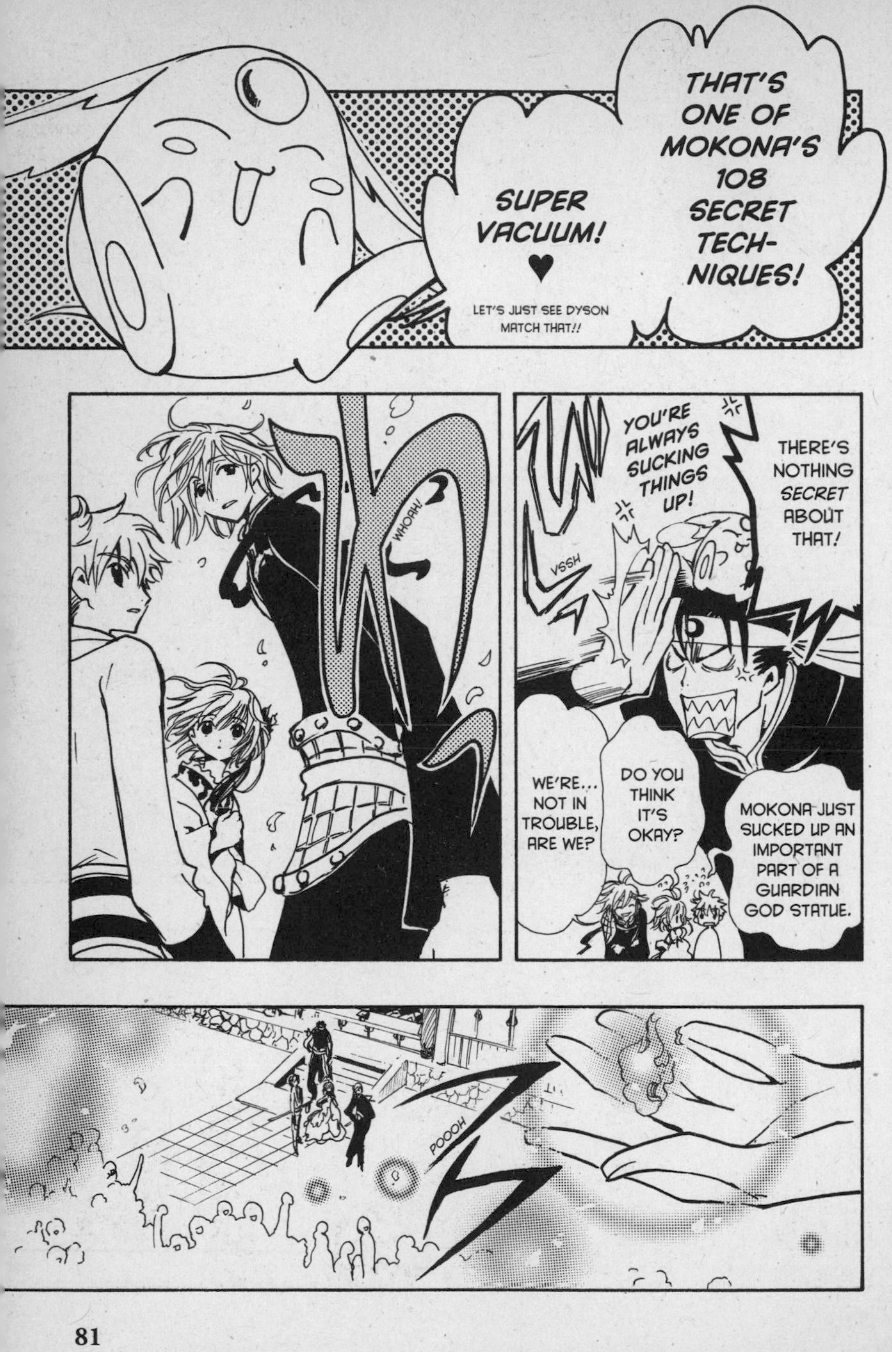
THAT'S ONE OF MOKONA'S 108 SECRET TECHNIQUES!
SUPER VACUUM! ♥
LET'S JUST SEE DYSON MATCH THAT!!
THERE'S NOTHING SECRET ABOUT THAT!
YOU'RE ALWAYS SUCKING THINGS UP!
VSSH
MOKONA JUST SUCKED UP AN IMPORTANT PART OF A GUARDIAN GOD STATUE.
DO YOU THINK IT'S OKAY?
WE'RE... NOT IN TROUBLE, ARE WE?
WHOAH!
POOOH

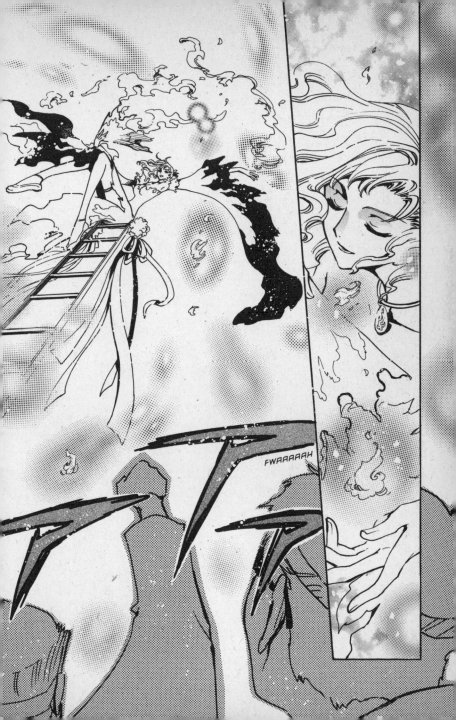

FWARRRRH

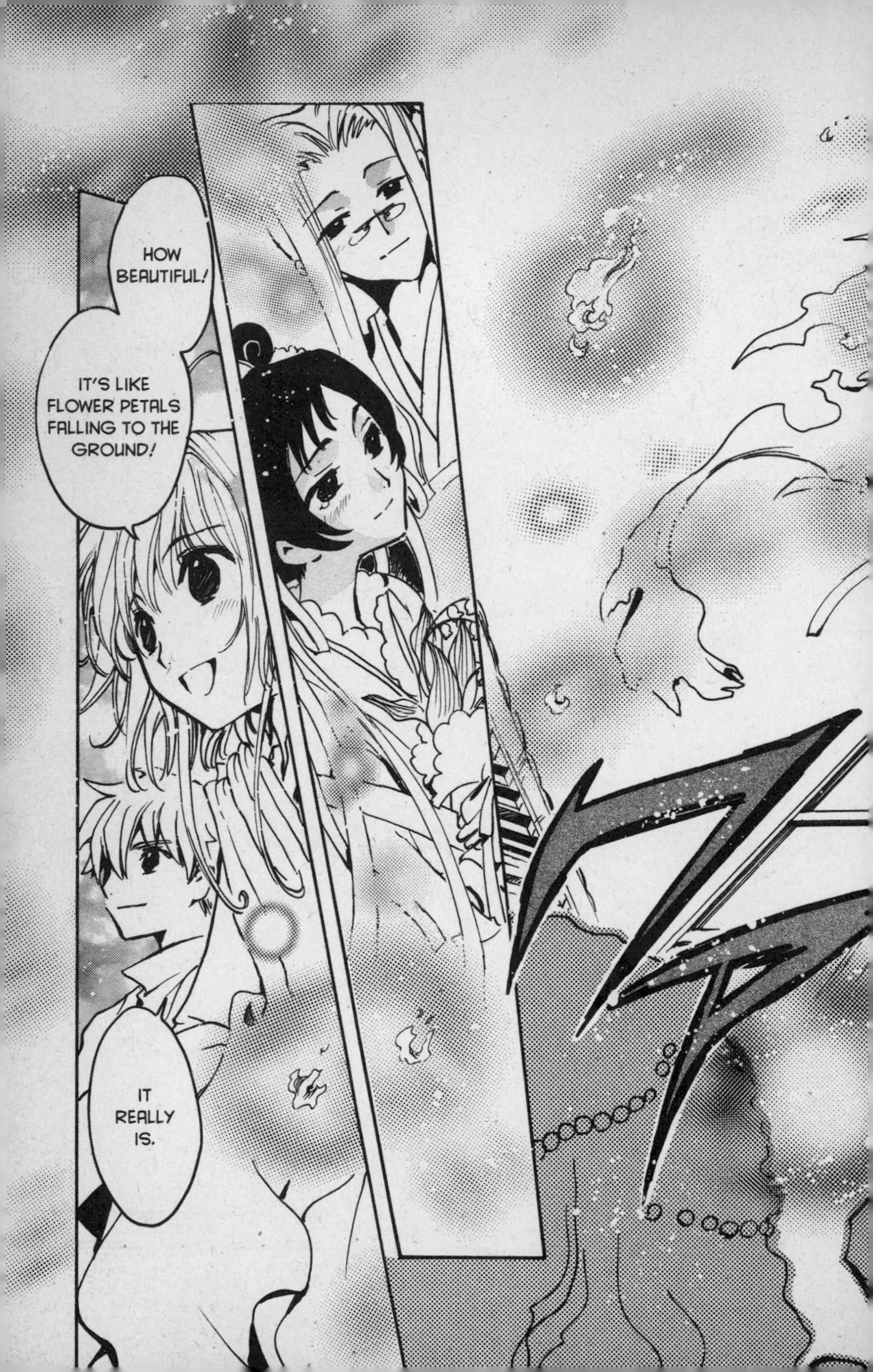
HOW BEAUTIFUL!
IT'S LIKE FLOWER PETALS FALLING TO THE GROUND!
IT REALLY IS.

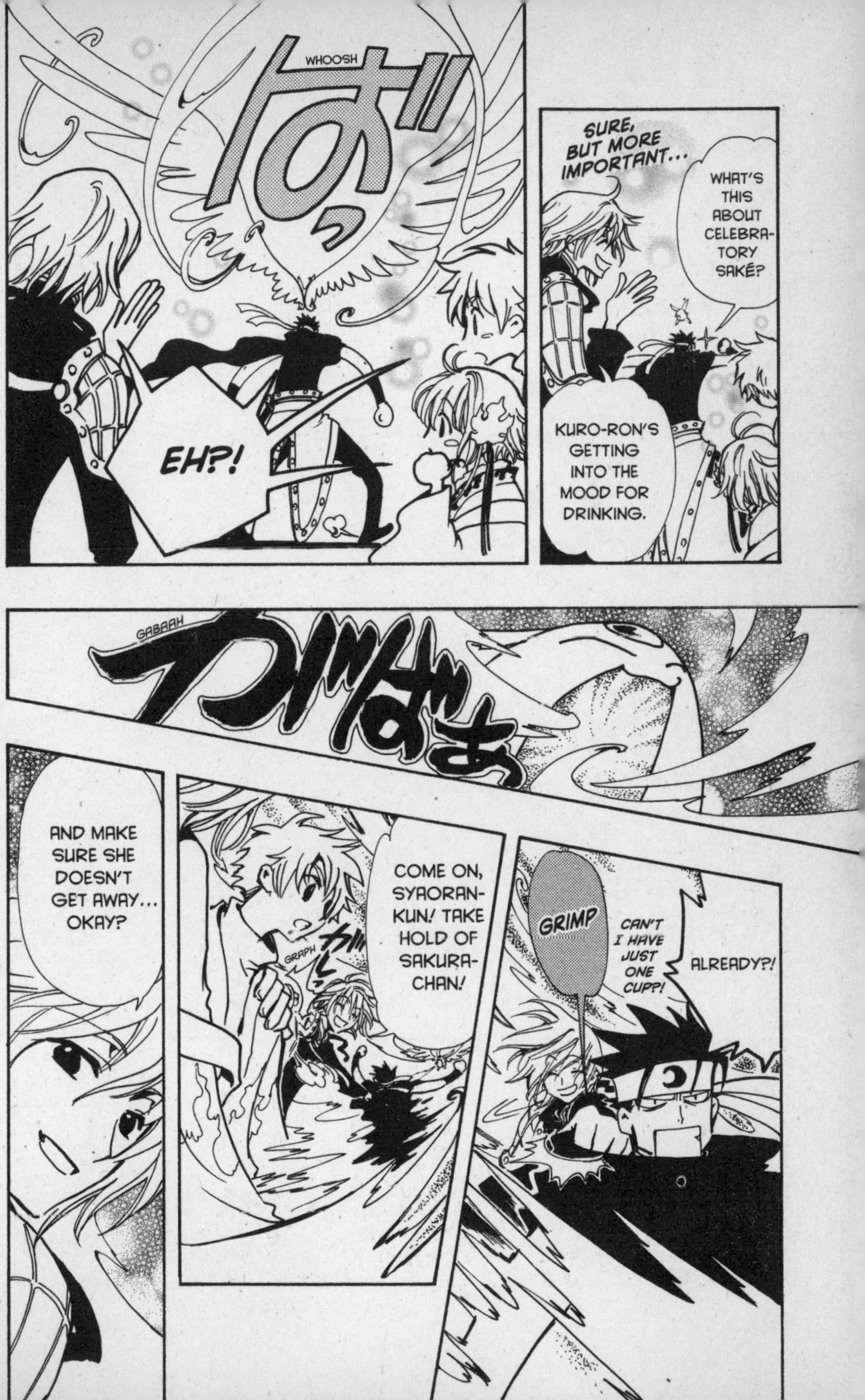
SURE, BUT MORE IMPORTANT...
WHAT'S THIS ABOUT CELEBRATORY SAKÉ?
KURO-RON'S GETTING INTO THE MOOD FOR DRINKING.
WHOOSH
EH?!
GABAAH
ALREADY?!
CAN'T I HAVE JUST ONE CUP?!
GRIMP
COME ON, SYAORAN-KUN! TAKE HOLD OF SAKURA-CHAN!
GRAPH
AND MAKE SURE SHE DOESN'T GET AWAY... OKAY?

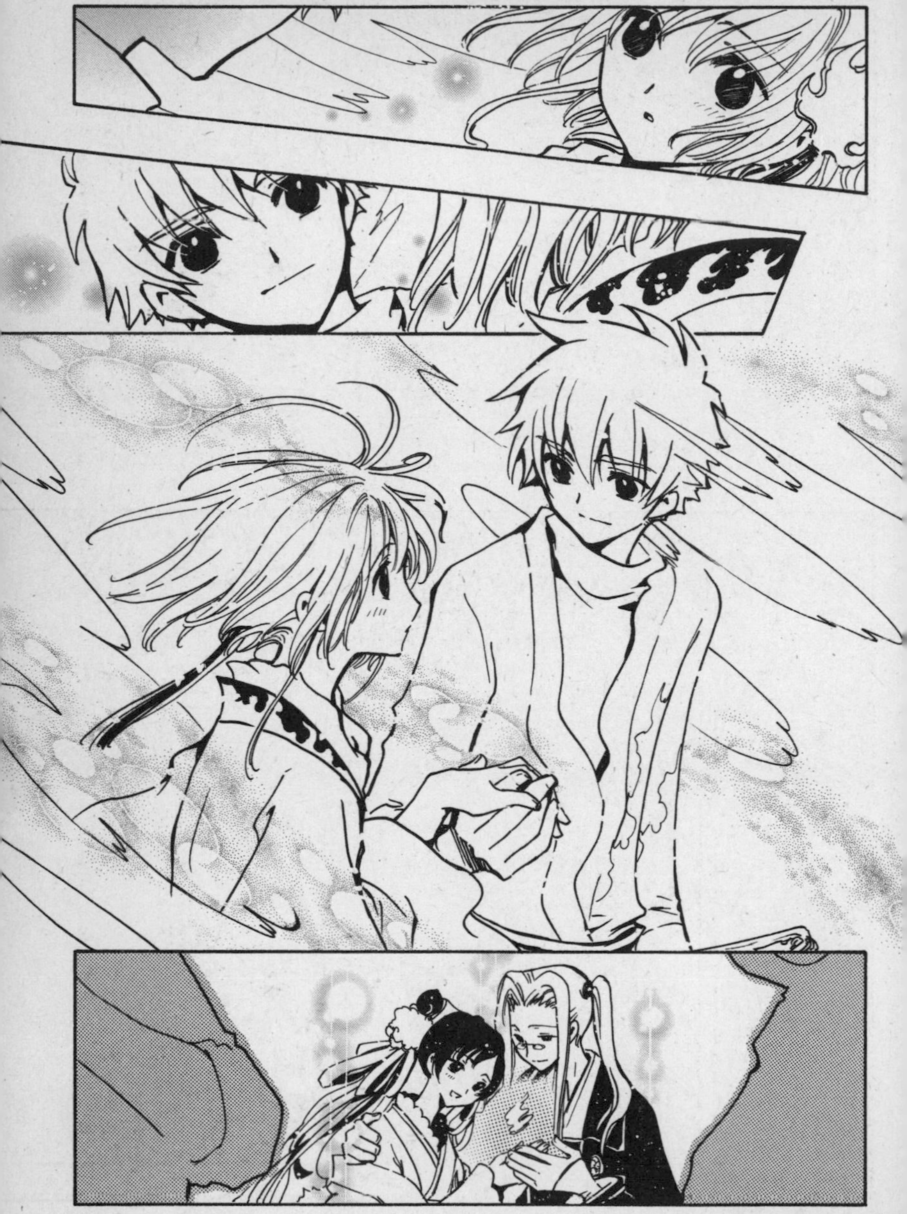

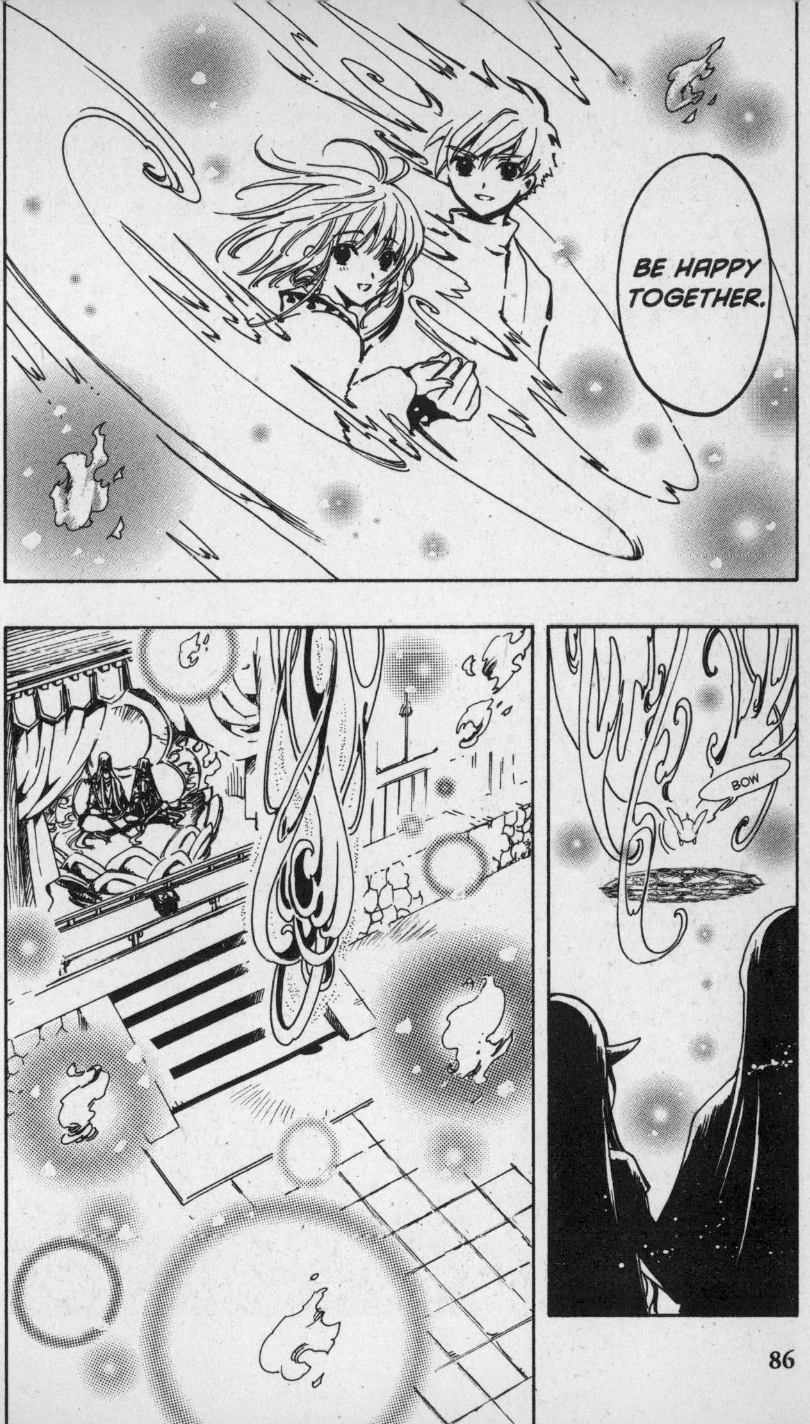
BE HAPPY TOGETHER.
BOW

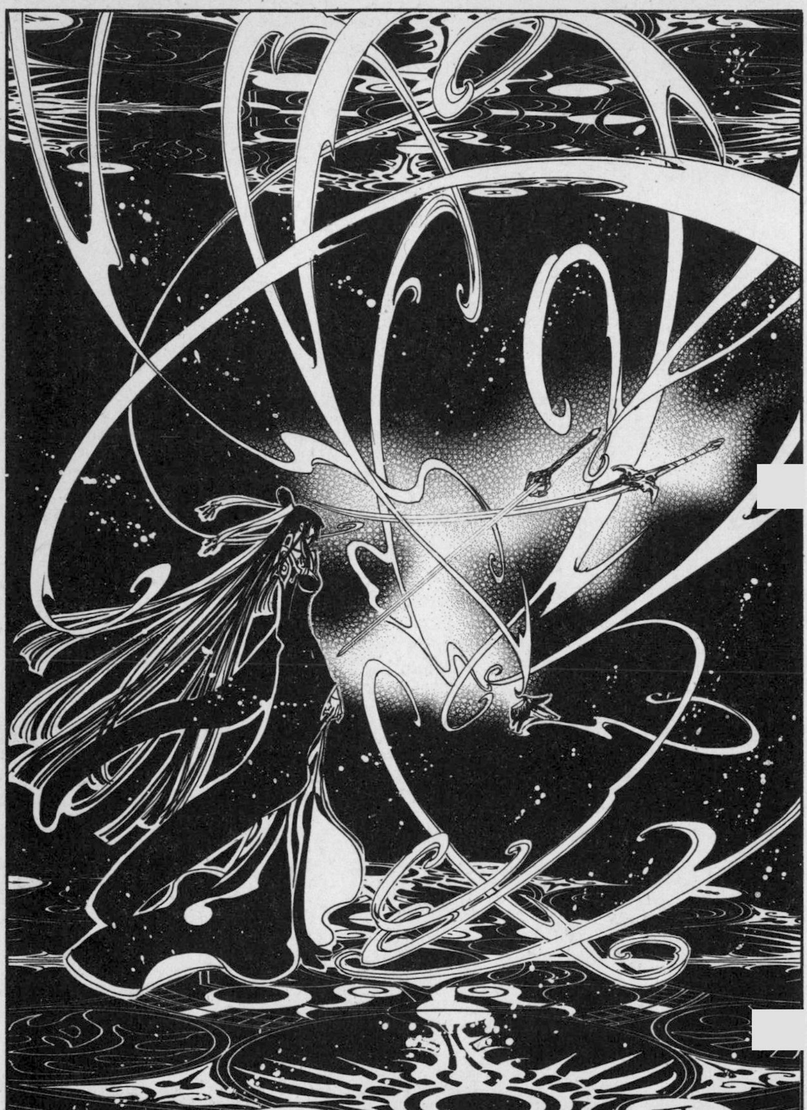

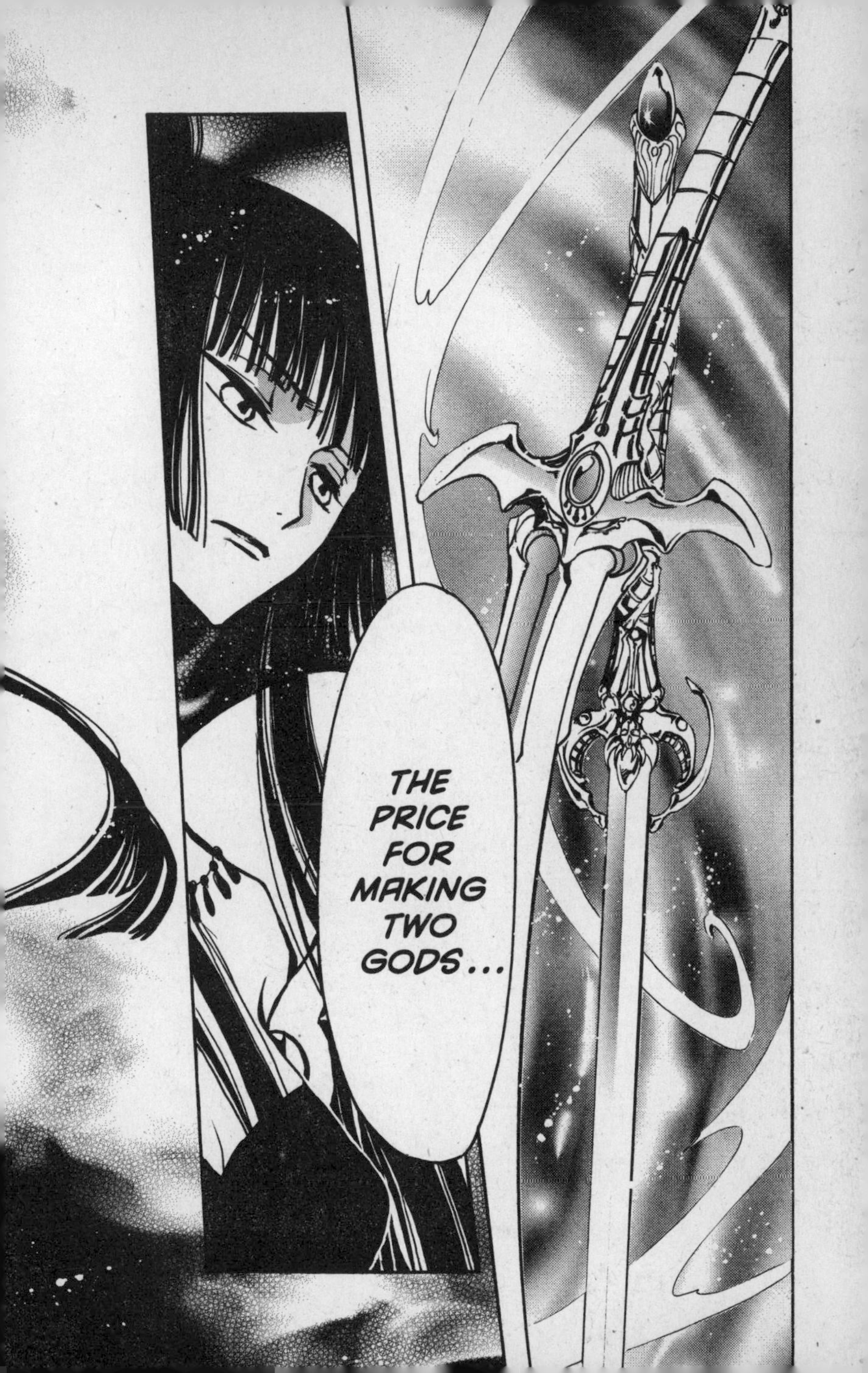
THE PRICE FOR MAKING TWO GODS...

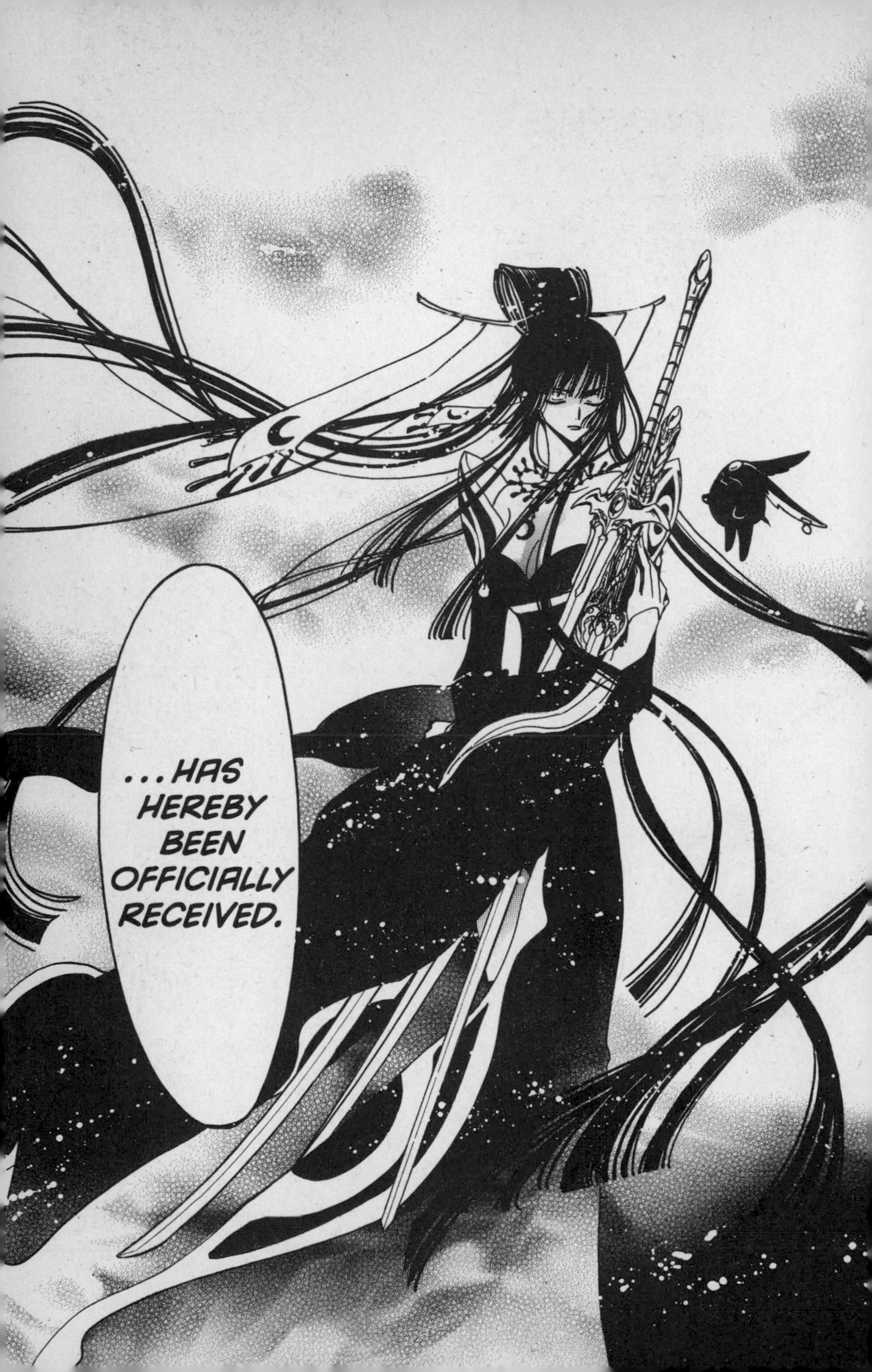
...HAS HEREBY BEEN OFFICIALLY RECEIVED.

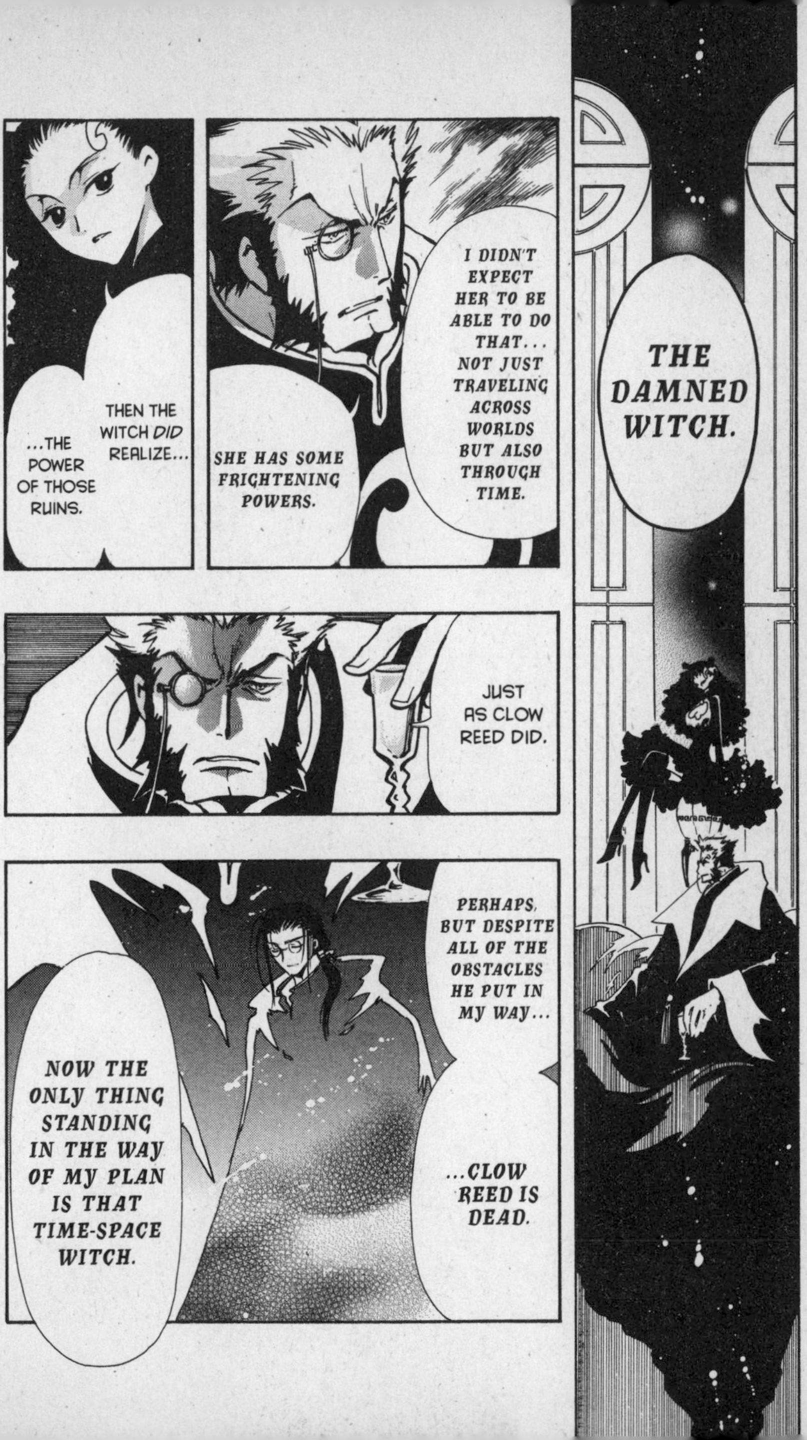
THE DAMNED WITCH.
I DIDN'T EXPECT HER TO BE ABLE TO DO THAT... NOT JUST TRAVELING ACROSS WORLDS BUT ALSO THROUGH TIME.
SHE HAS SOME FRIGHTENING POWERS.
THEN THE WITCH DID REALIZE...
...THE POWER OF THOSE RUINS.
JUST AS CLOW REED DID.
PERHAPS, BUT DESPITE ALL OF THE OBSTACLES HE PUT IN MY WAY...
...CLOW REED IS DEAD.
NOW THE ONLY THING STANDING IN THE WAY OF MY PLAN IS THAT TIME-SPACE WITCH.

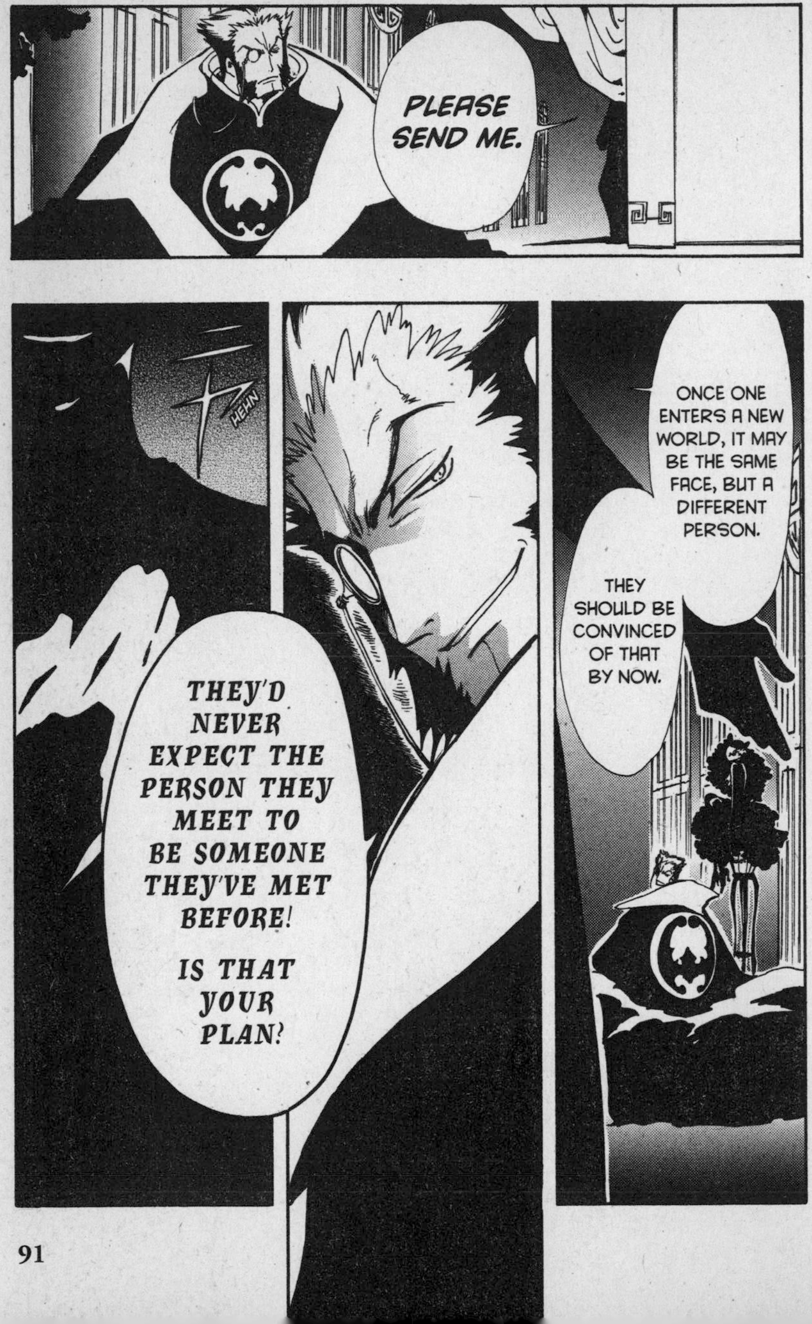
PLEASE SEND ME.
ONCE ONE ENTERS A NEW WORLD, IT MAY BE THE SAME FACE, BUT A DIFFERENT PERSON.
THEY SHOULD BE CONVINCED OF THAT BY NOW.
HEHN
THEY'D NEVER EXPECT THE PERSON THEY MEET TO BE SOMEONE THEY'VE MET BEFORE!
IS THAT YOUR PLAN?

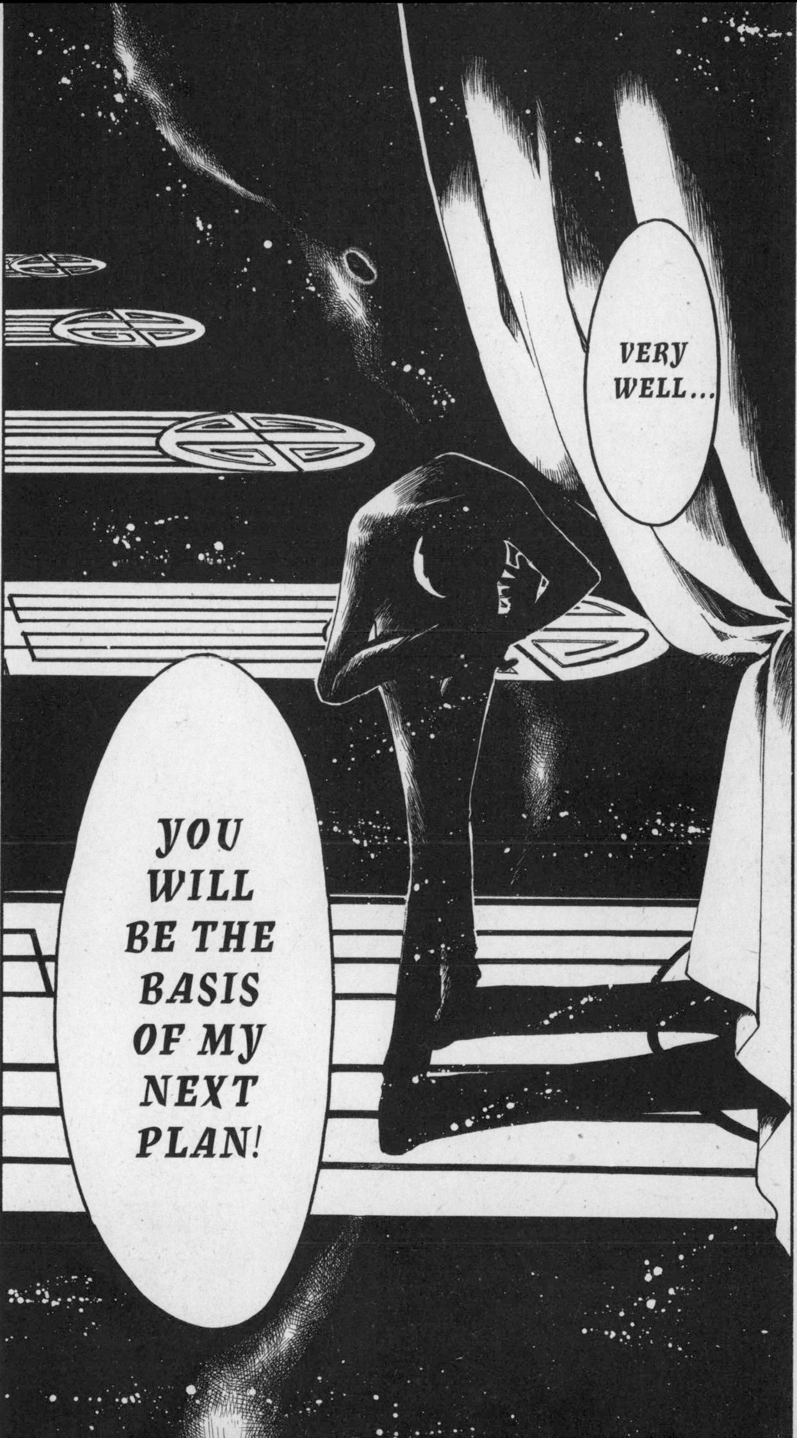
VERY WELL...
YOU WILL BE THE BASIS OF MY NEXT PLAN!

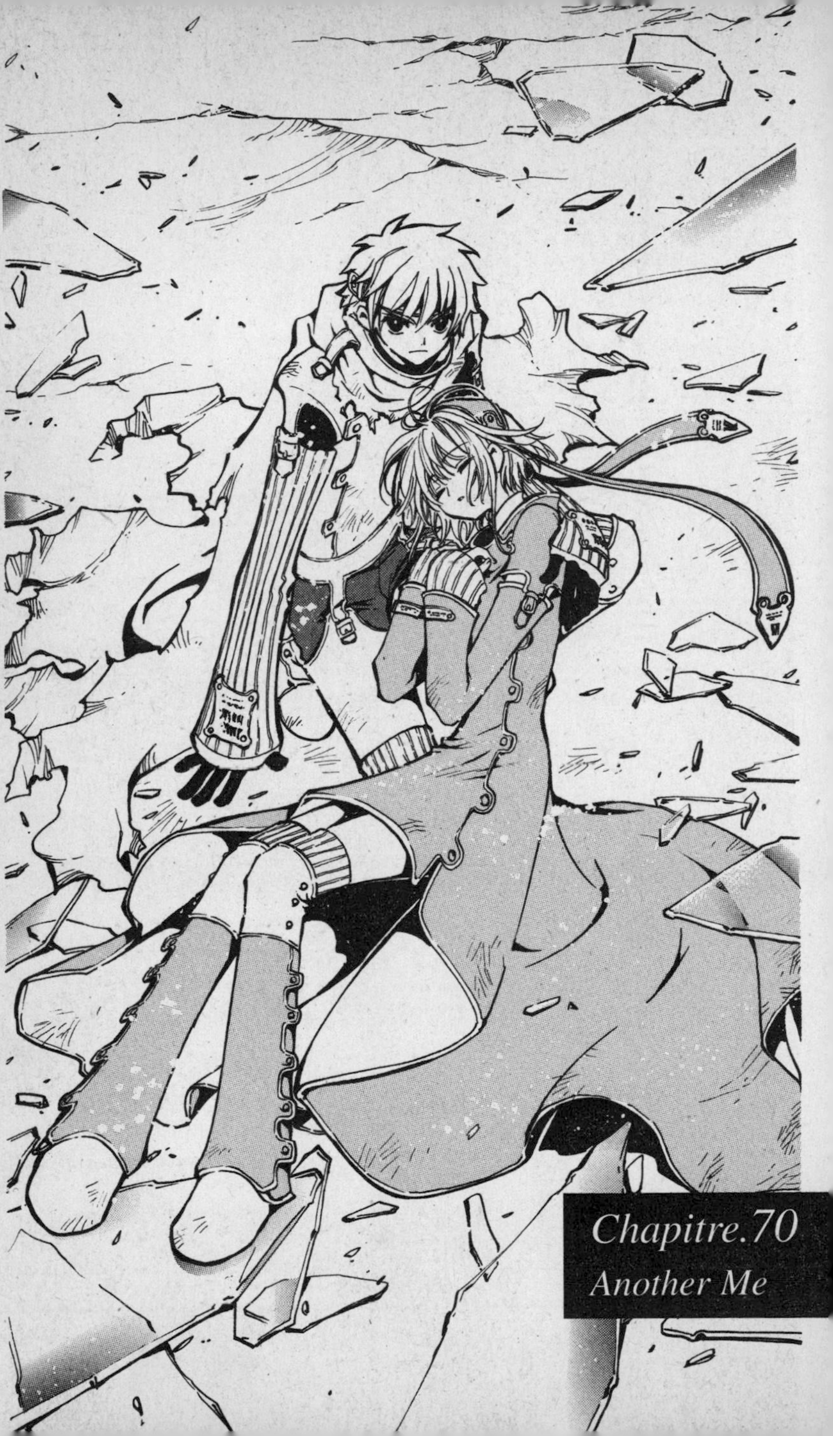
Chapitre.70
Another Me

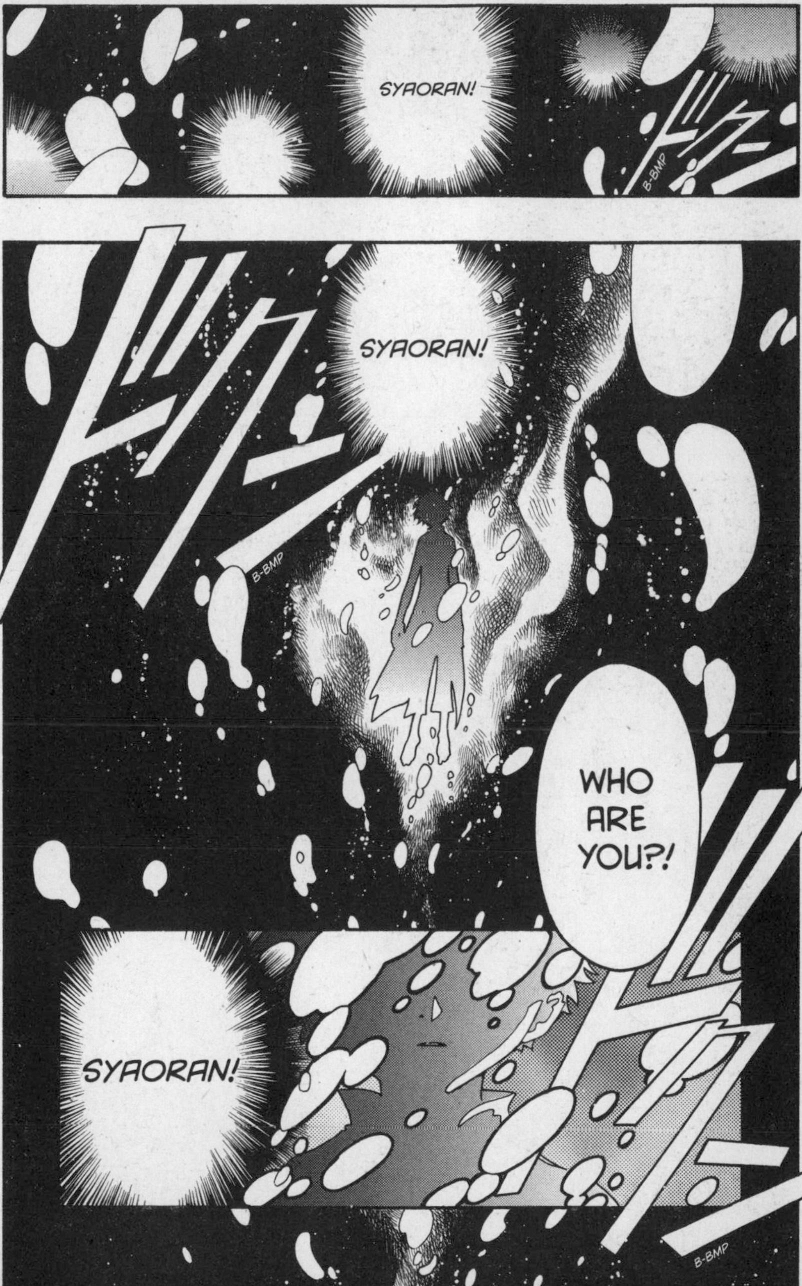
B-BMP
SYAORAN!
SYAORAN!
B-BMP
WHO ARE YOU?!
B-BMP
SYAORAN!

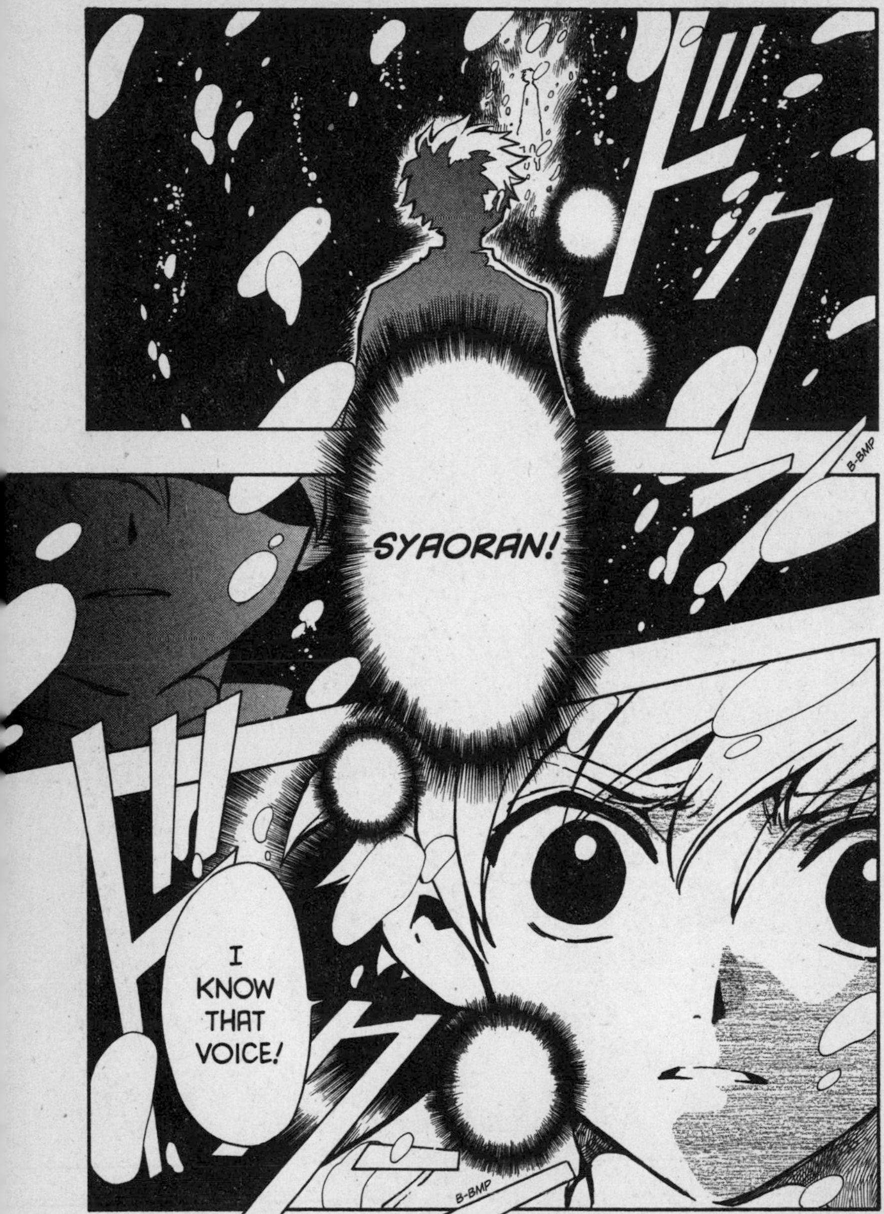
B-BMP
SYAORAN!
I KNOW THAT VOICE!
B-BMP

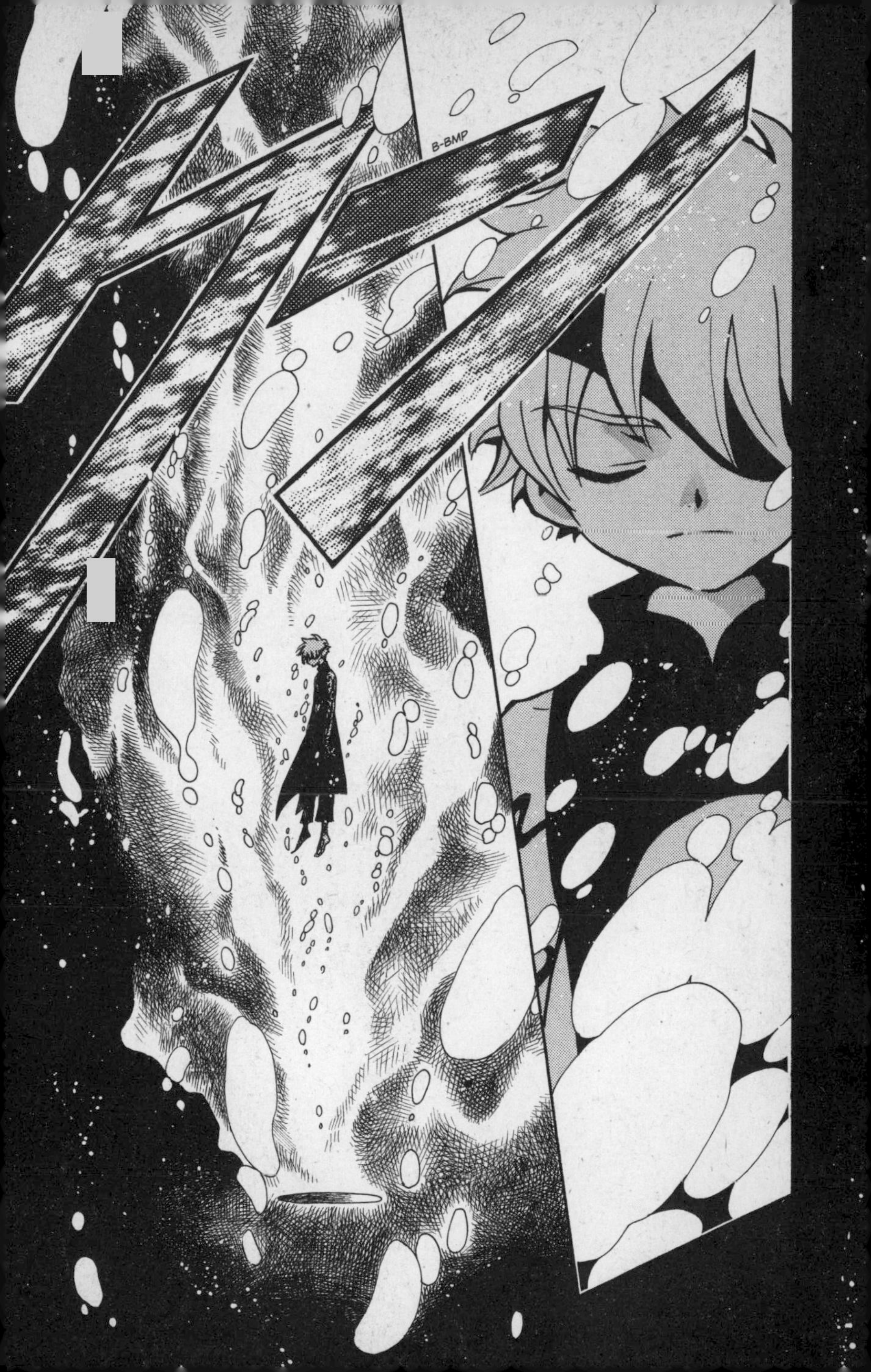
B-BMP

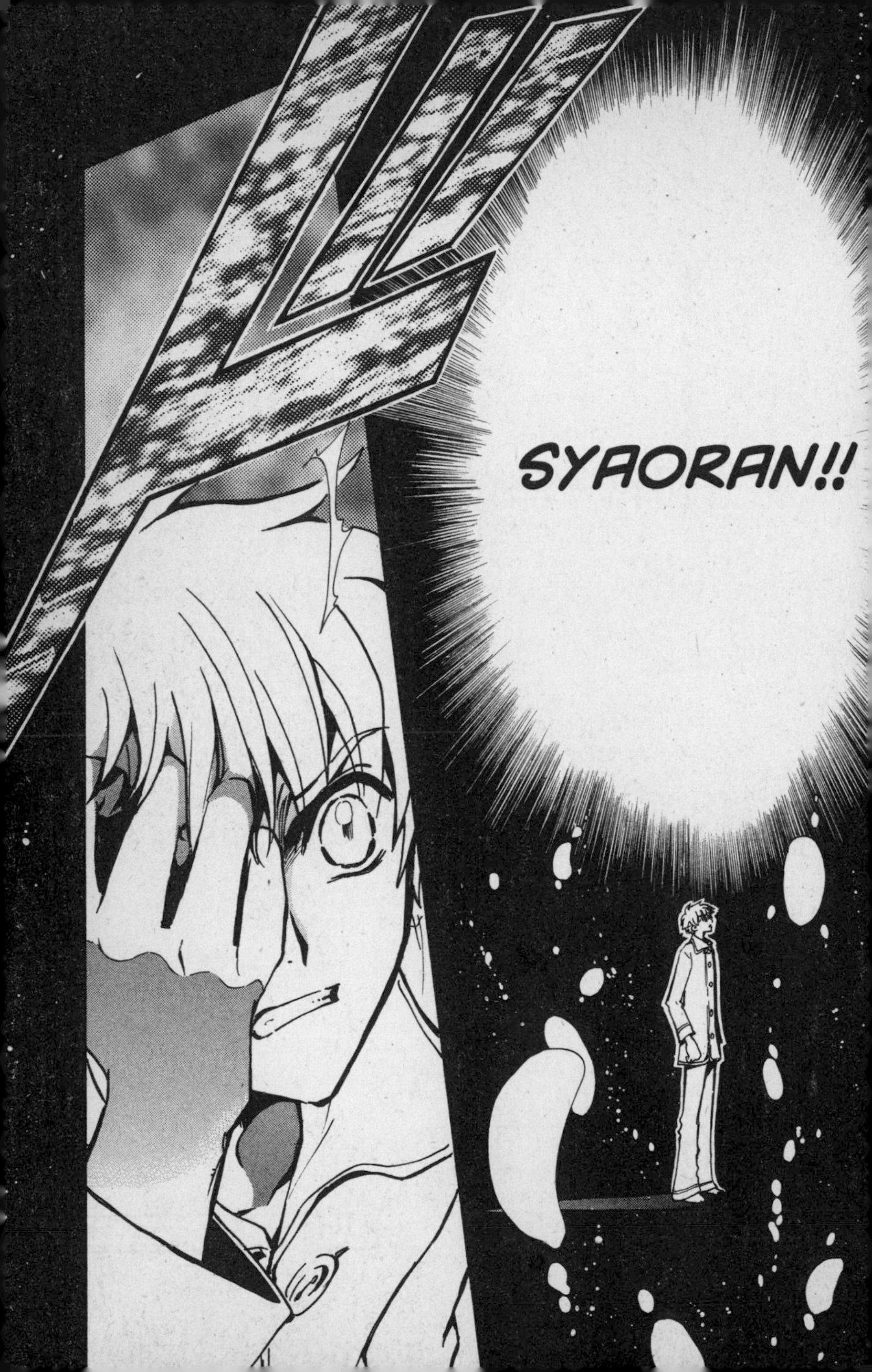
SYAORAN!!

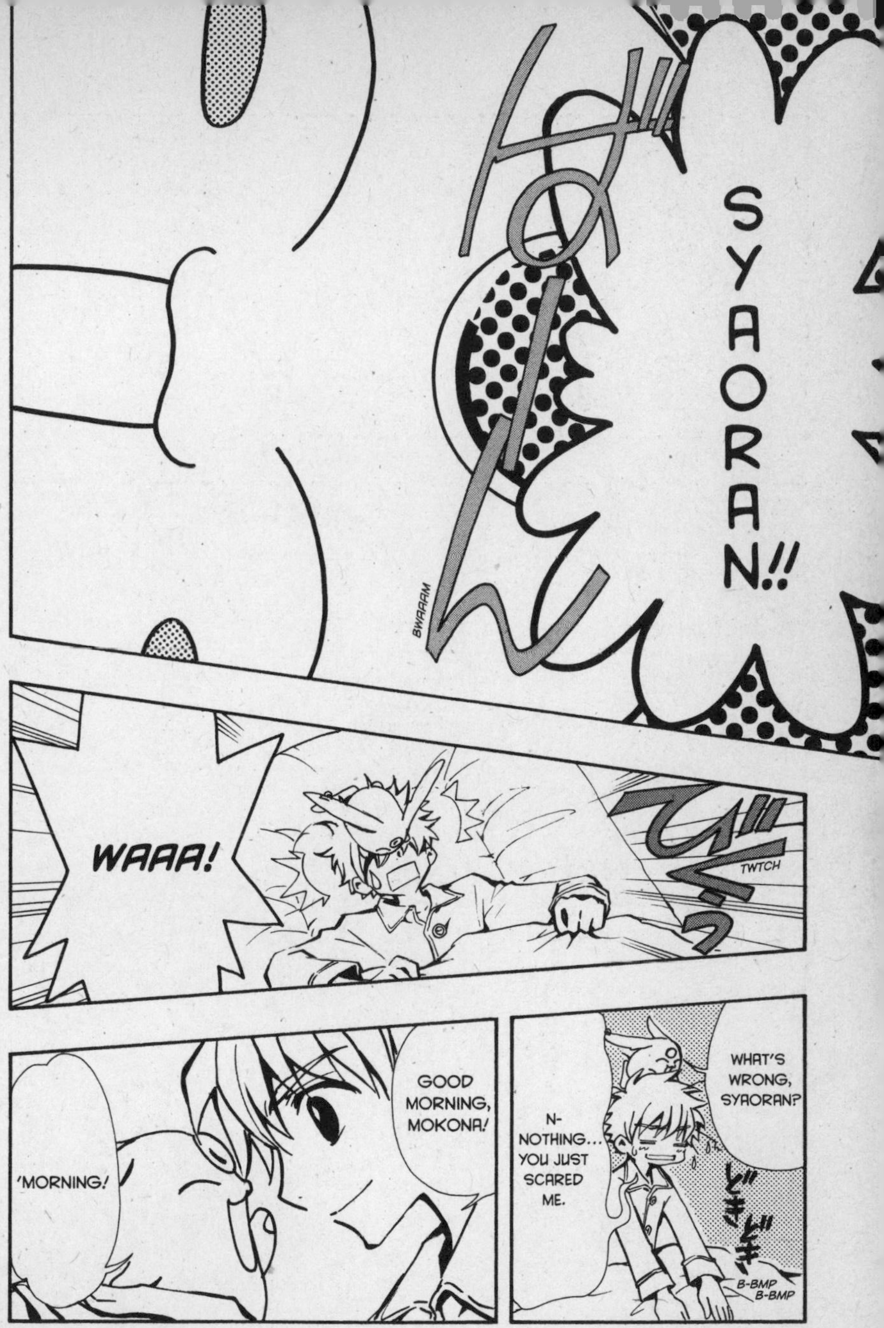
SYAORAN!!
BWAAAM
TWTCH
WAAA!
WHAT'S WRONG, SYAORAN?
N-NOTHING... YOU JUST SCARED ME.
B-BMP B-BMP
GOOD MORNING, MOKONA!
'MORNING!

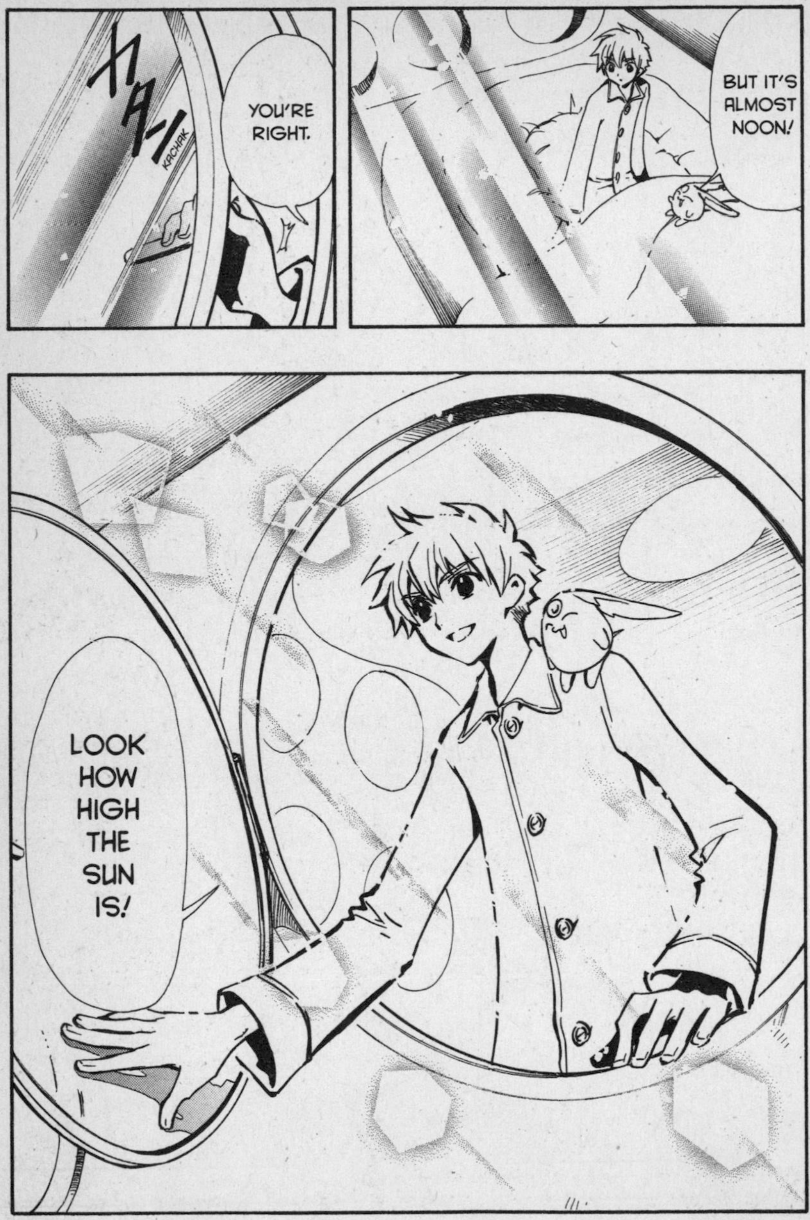
BUT IT'S ALMOST NOON!
YOU'RE RIGHT.
KACHAK
LOOK HOW HIGH THE SUN IS!

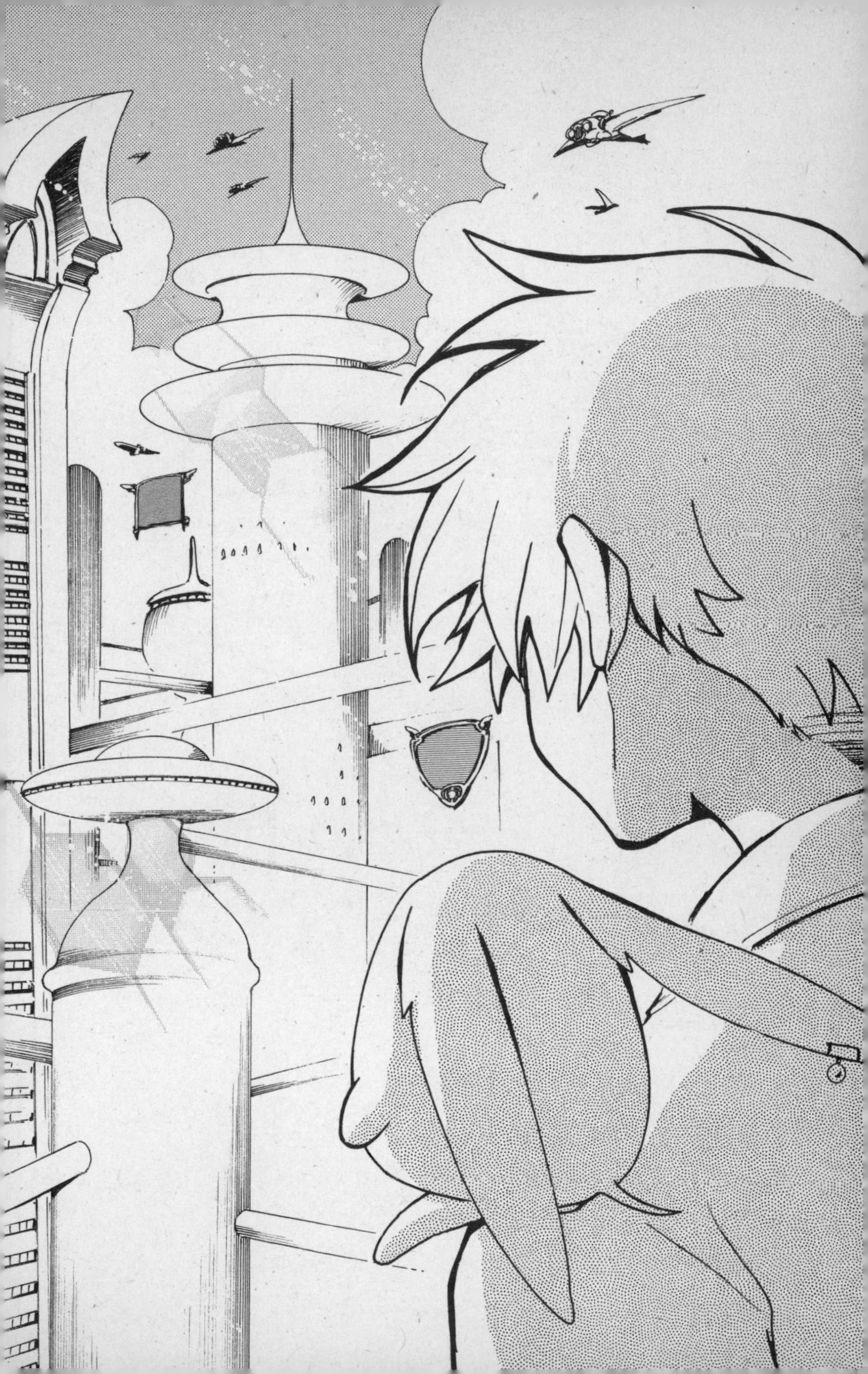

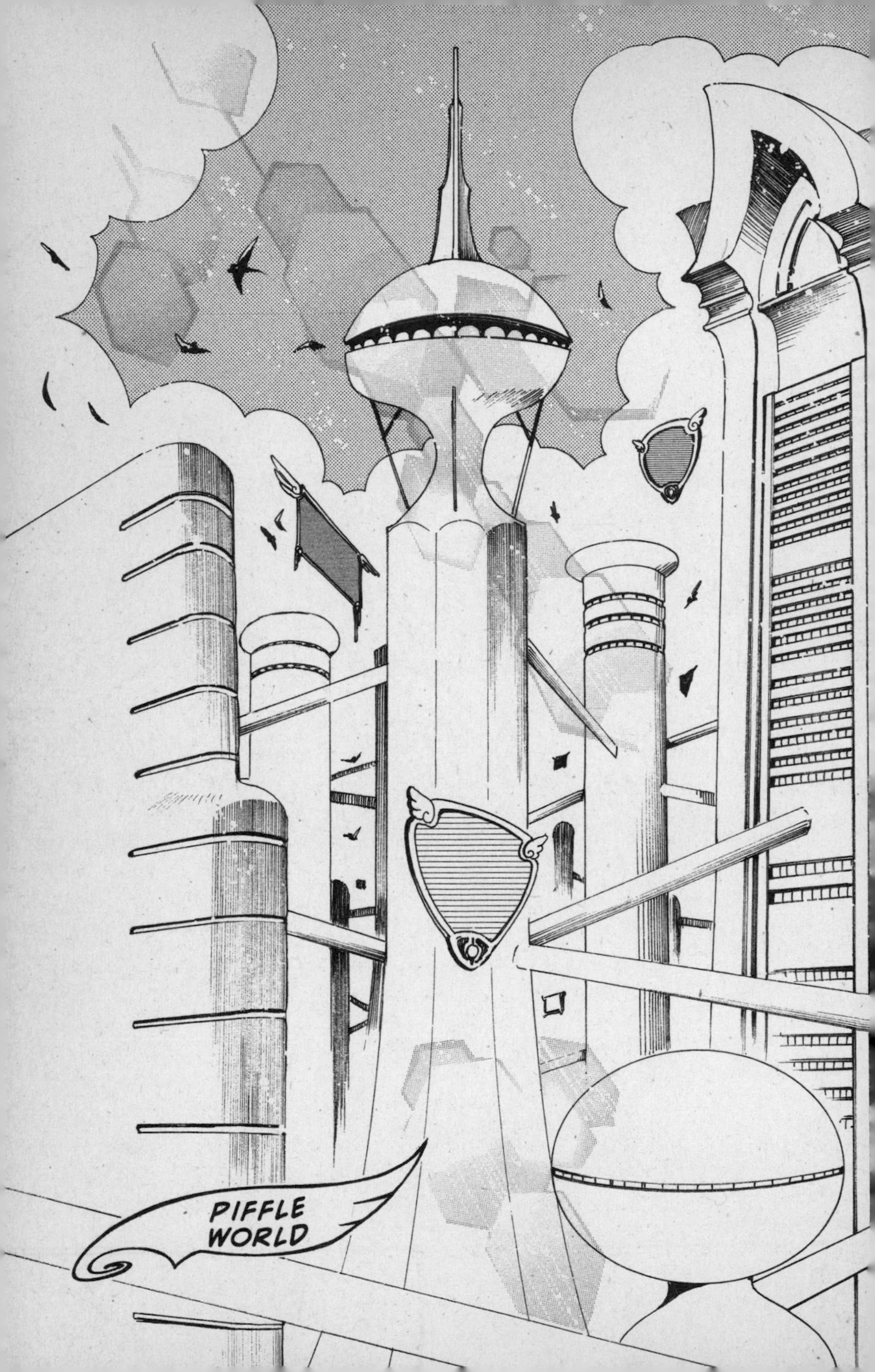
PIFFLE WORLD

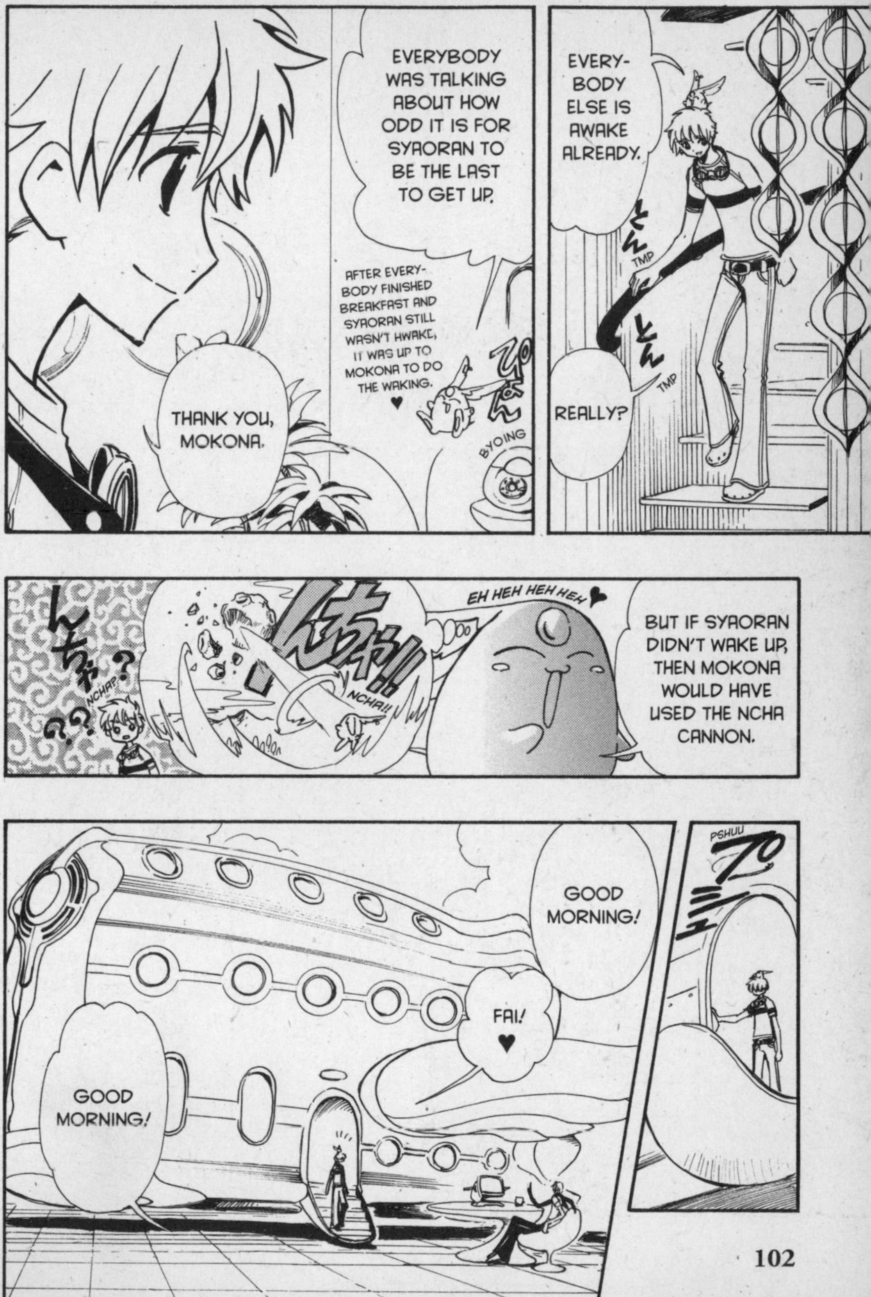
EVERY-BODY ELSE IS AWAKE ALREADY.
TMP
TMP
REALLY?
EVERYBODY WAS TALKING ABOUT HOW ODD IT IS FOR SYAORAN TO BE THE LAST TO GET UP.
AFTER EVERY-BODY FINISHED BREAKFAST AND SYAORAN STILL WASN'T AWAKE, IT WAS UP TO MOKONA TO DO THE WAKING. ♥
BYOING
THANK YOU, MOKONA.
BUT IF SYAORAN DIDN'T WAKE UP, THEN MOKONA WOULD HAVE USED THE NCHA CANNON.
EH HEH HEH HEH ♥
NCHA!!
NCHA?
PSHUU
GOOD MORNING!
FAI! ♥
GOOD MORNING!

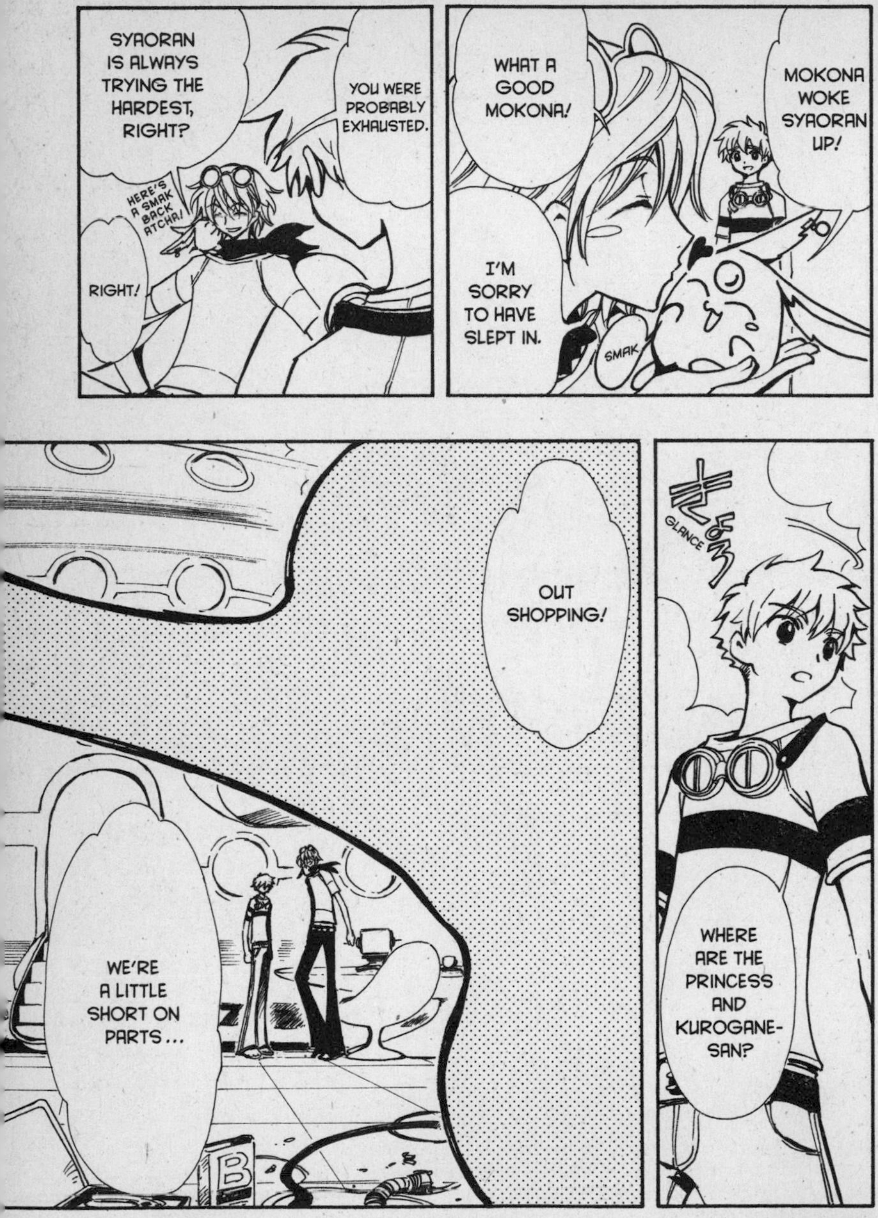
MOKONA WOKE SYAORAN UP!
WHAT A GOOD MOKONA!
I'M SORRY TO HAVE SLEPT IN.
SMAK
YOU WERE PROBABLY EXHAUSTED.
SYAORAN IS ALWAYS TRYING THE HARDEST, RIGHT?
HERE'S A SMAK BACK ATCHA!
RIGHT!
GLANCE
WHERE ARE THE PRINCESS AND KUROGANE-SAN?
OUT SHOPPING!
WE'RE A LITTLE SHORT ON PARTS...

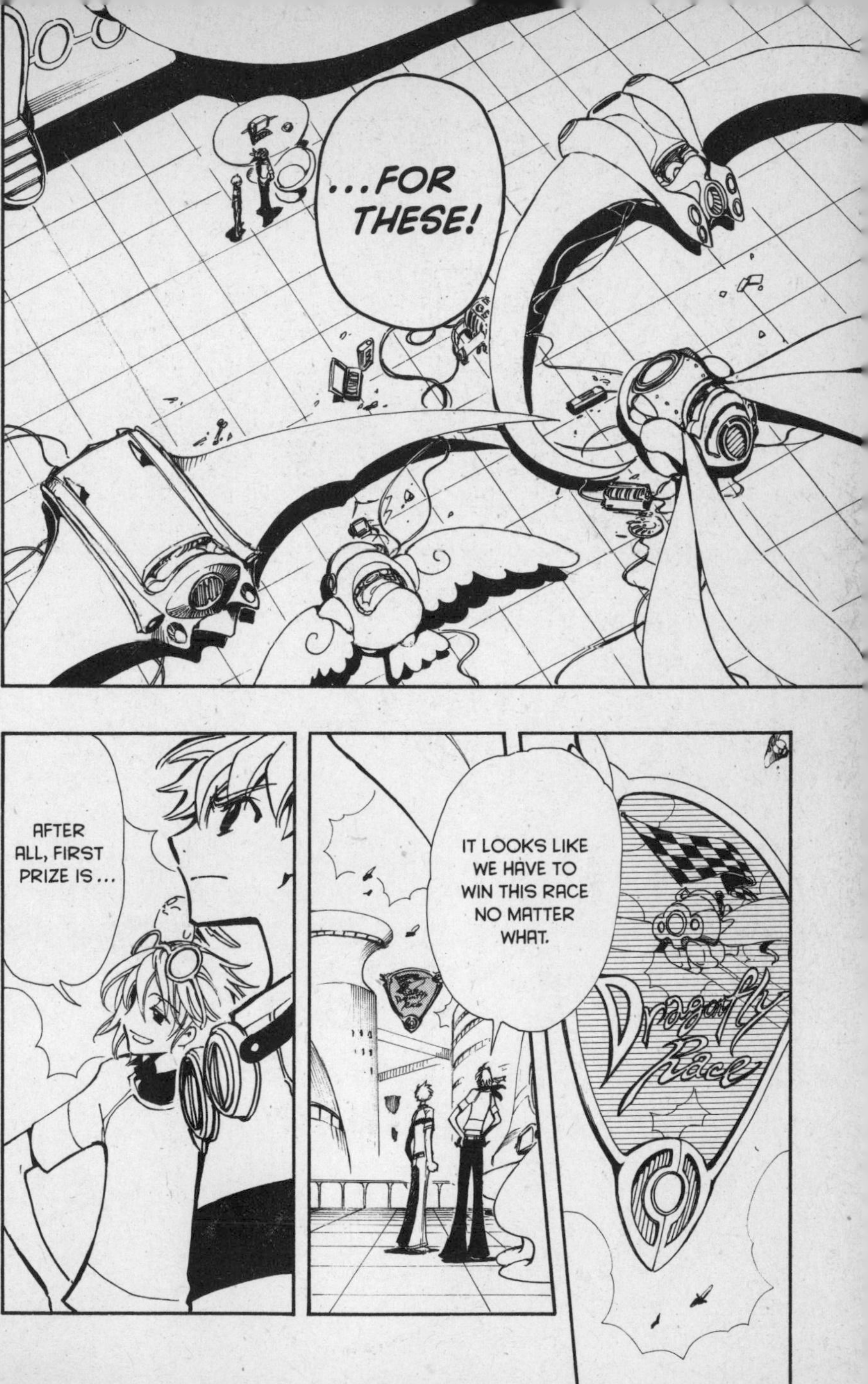
...FOR THESE!
Dragonfly Race
IT LOOKS LIKE WE HAVE TO WIN THIS RACE NO MATTER WHAT.
AFTER ALL, FIRST PRIZE IS...

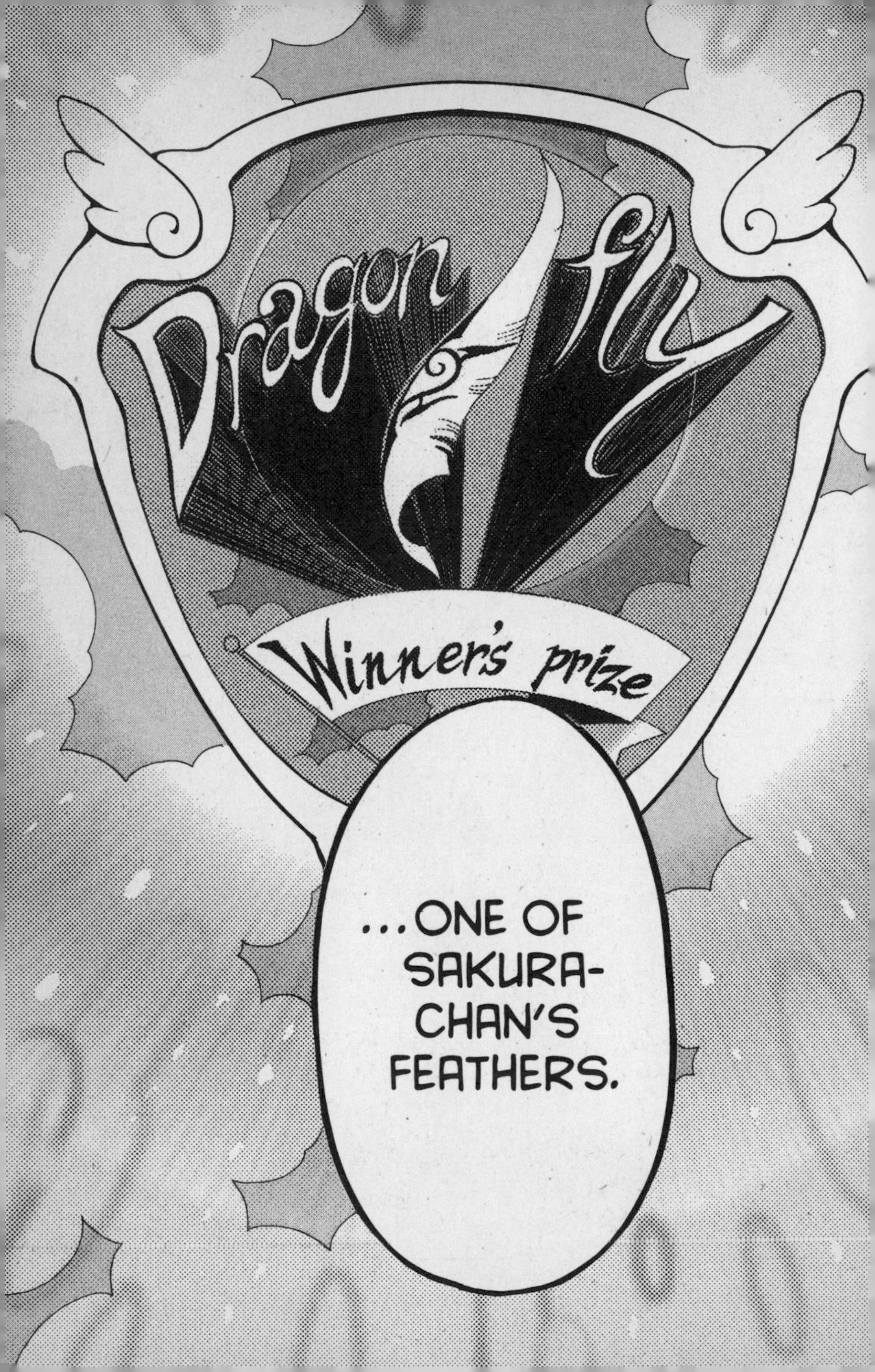
Dragon fly
Winner's prize
...ONE OF SAKURA-CHAN'S FEATHERS.

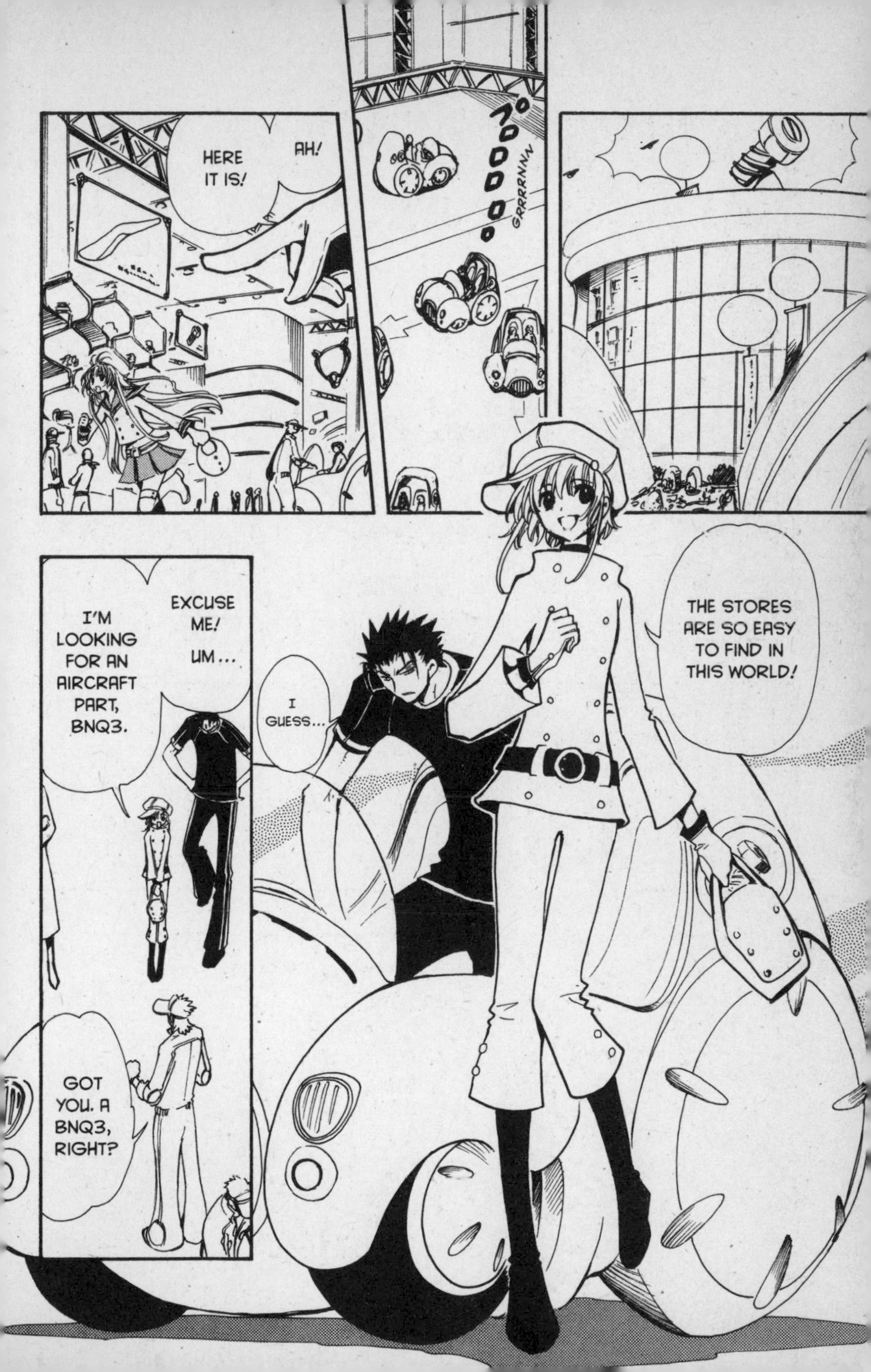
GRRRNNN
AH!
HERE IT IS!
THE STORES ARE SO EASY TO FIND IN THIS WORLD!
I GUESS...
EXCUSE ME! UM...
I'M LOOKING FOR AN AIRCRAFT PART, BNQ3.
GOT YOU. A BNQ3, RIGHT?

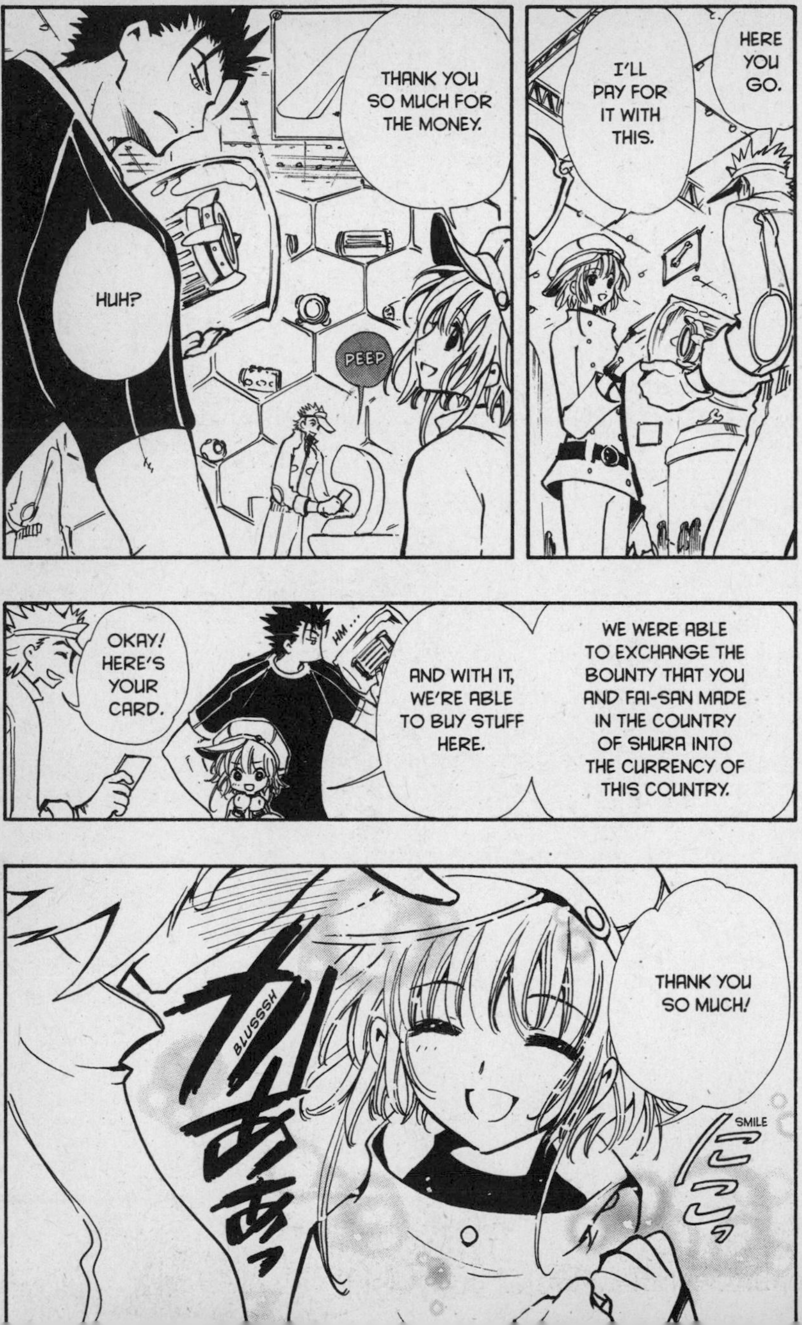
HERE YOU GO.
I'LL PAY FOR IT WITH THIS.
THANK YOU SO MUCH FOR THE MONEY.
PEEP
HUH?
WE WERE ABLE TO EXCHANGE THE BOUNTY THAT YOU AND FAI-SAN MADE IN THE COUNTRY OF SHURA INTO THE CURRENCY OF THIS COUNTRY.
AND WITH IT, WE'RE ABLE TO BUY STUFF HERE.
HM...
OKAY! HERE'S YOUR CARD.
THANK YOU SO MUCH!
SMILE
BLUSSSH

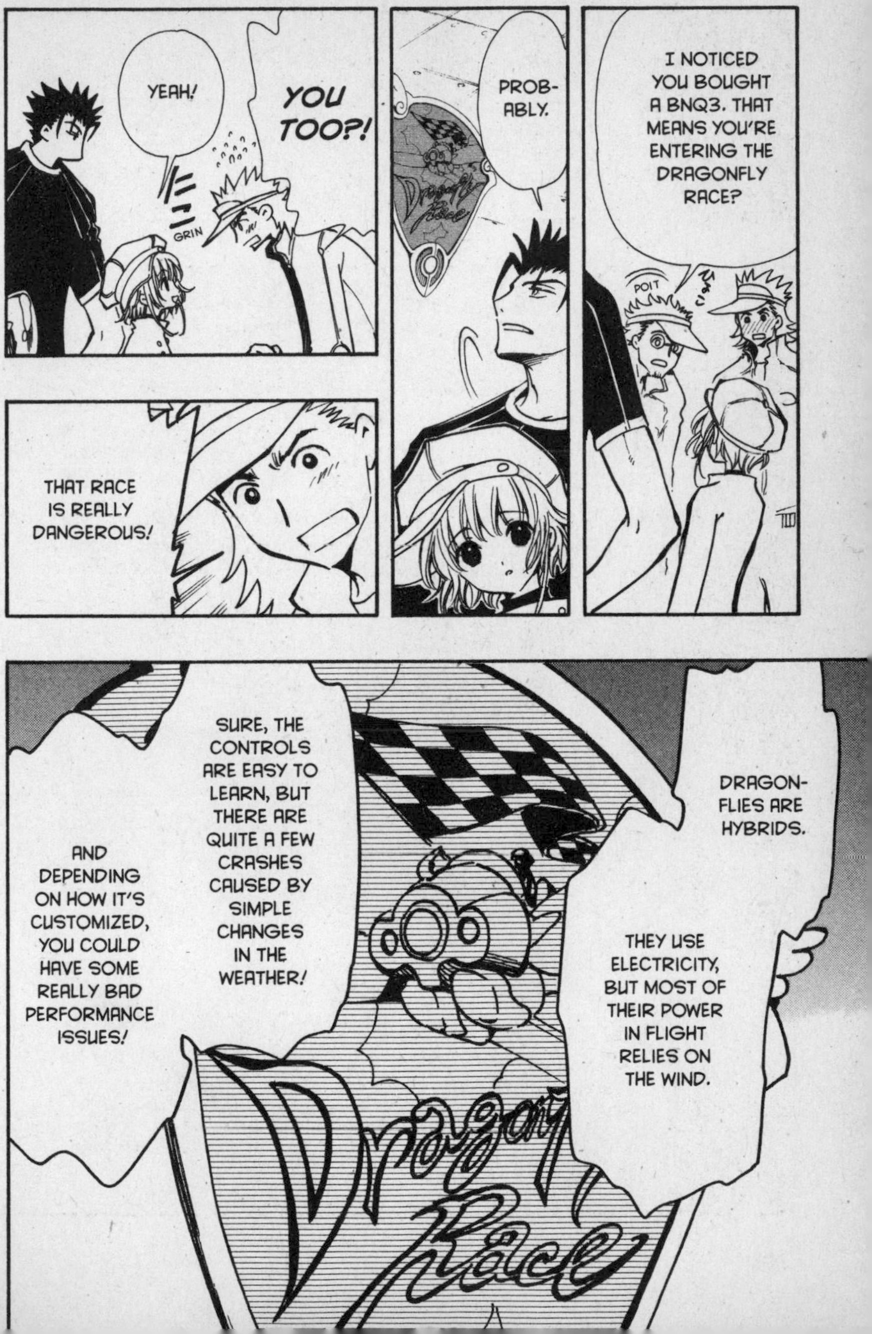
I NOTICED YOU BOUGHT A BNQ3. THAT MEANS YOU'RE ENTERING THE DRAGONFLY RACE?
POIT
PROB-ABLY.
YOU TOO?!
YEAH!
GRIN
THAT RACE IS REALLY DANGEROUS!
DRAGON-FLIES ARE HYBRIDS.
THEY USE ELECTRICITY, BUT MOST OF THEIR POWER IN FLIGHT RELIES ON THE WIND.
SURE, THE CONTROLS ARE EASY TO LEARN, BUT THERE ARE QUITE A FEW CRASHES CAUSED BY SIMPLE CHANGES IN THE WEATHER!
AND DEPENDING ON HOW IT'S CUSTOMIZED, YOU COULD HAVE SOME REALLY BAD PERFORMANCE ISSUES!

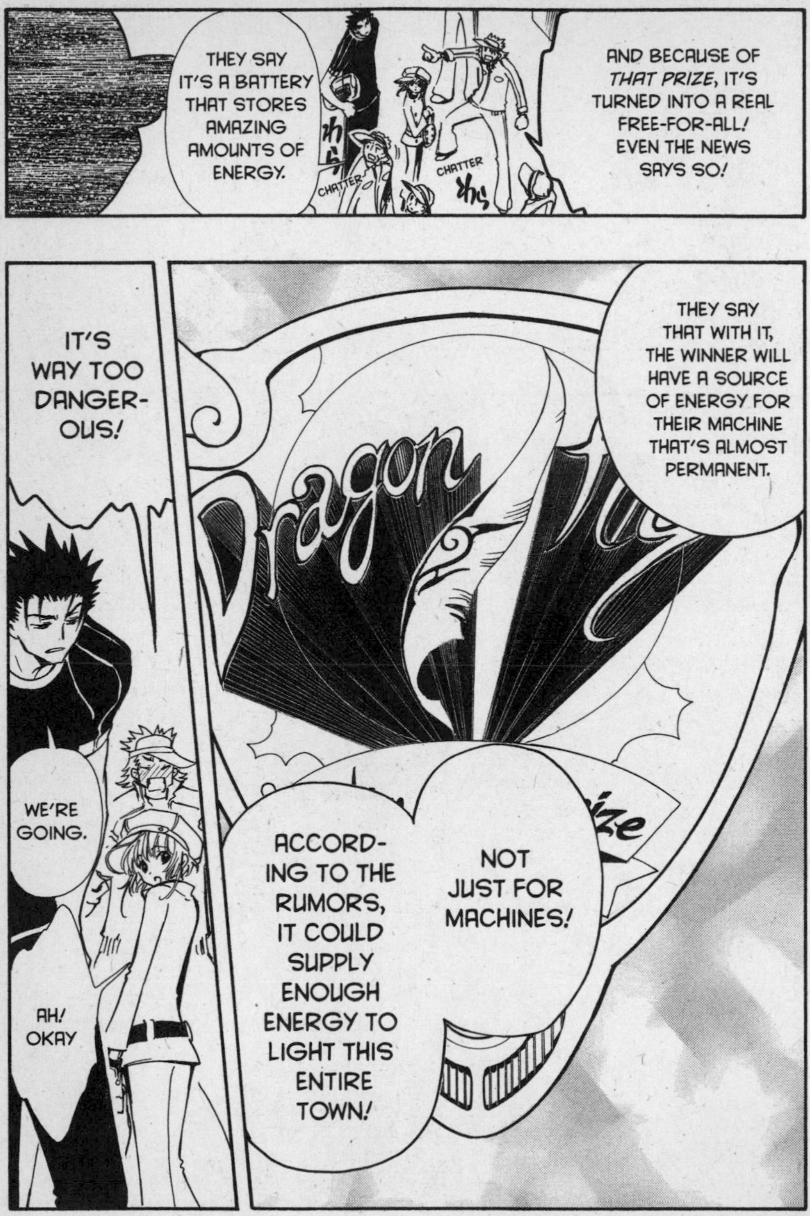
AND BECAUSE OF *THAT PRIZE*, IT'S TURNED INTO A REAL FREE-FOR-ALL! EVEN THE NEWS SAYS SO!
THEY SAY IT'S A BATTERY THAT STORES AMAZING AMOUNTS OF ENERGY.
CHATTER
CHATTER
THEY SAY THAT WITH IT, THE WINNER WILL HAVE A SOURCE OF ENERGY FOR THEIR MACHINE THAT'S ALMOST PERMANENT.
Dragon
NOT JUST FOR MACHINES!
ACCORDING TO THE RUMORS, IT COULD SUPPLY ENOUGH ENERGY TO LIGHT THIS ENTIRE TOWN!
IT'S WAY TOO DANGEROUS!
WE'RE GOING.
AH! OKAY

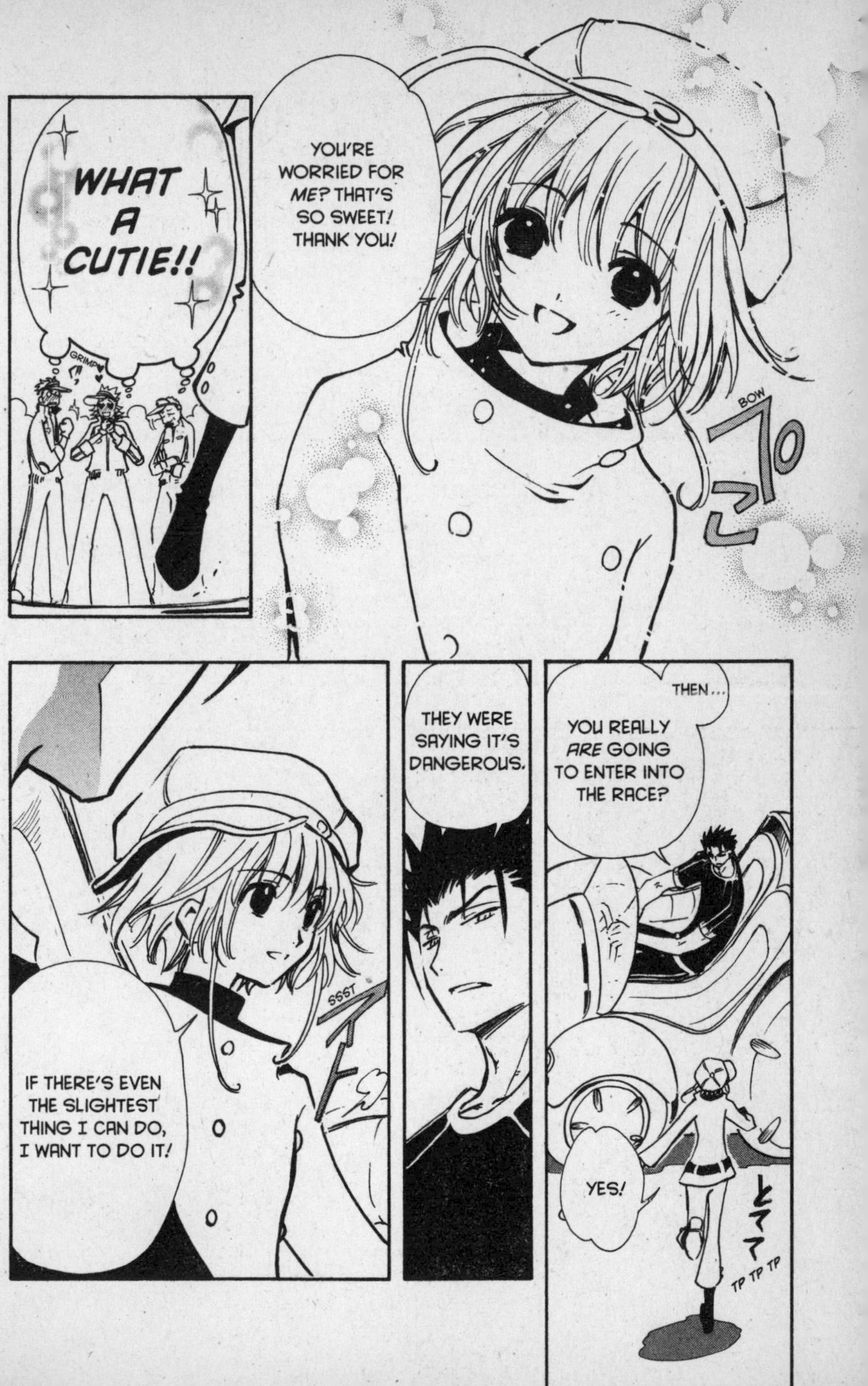
YOU'RE WORRIED FOR *ME*? THAT'S SO SWEET! THANK YOU!
BOW
WHAT A CUTIE!!
GRIMP
THEN...
YOU REALLY *ARE* GOING TO ENTER INTO THE RACE?
YES!
TP TP TP
THEY WERE SAYING IT'S DANGEROUS.
SSST
IF THERE'S EVEN THE SLIGHTEST THING I CAN DO, I WANT TO DO IT!

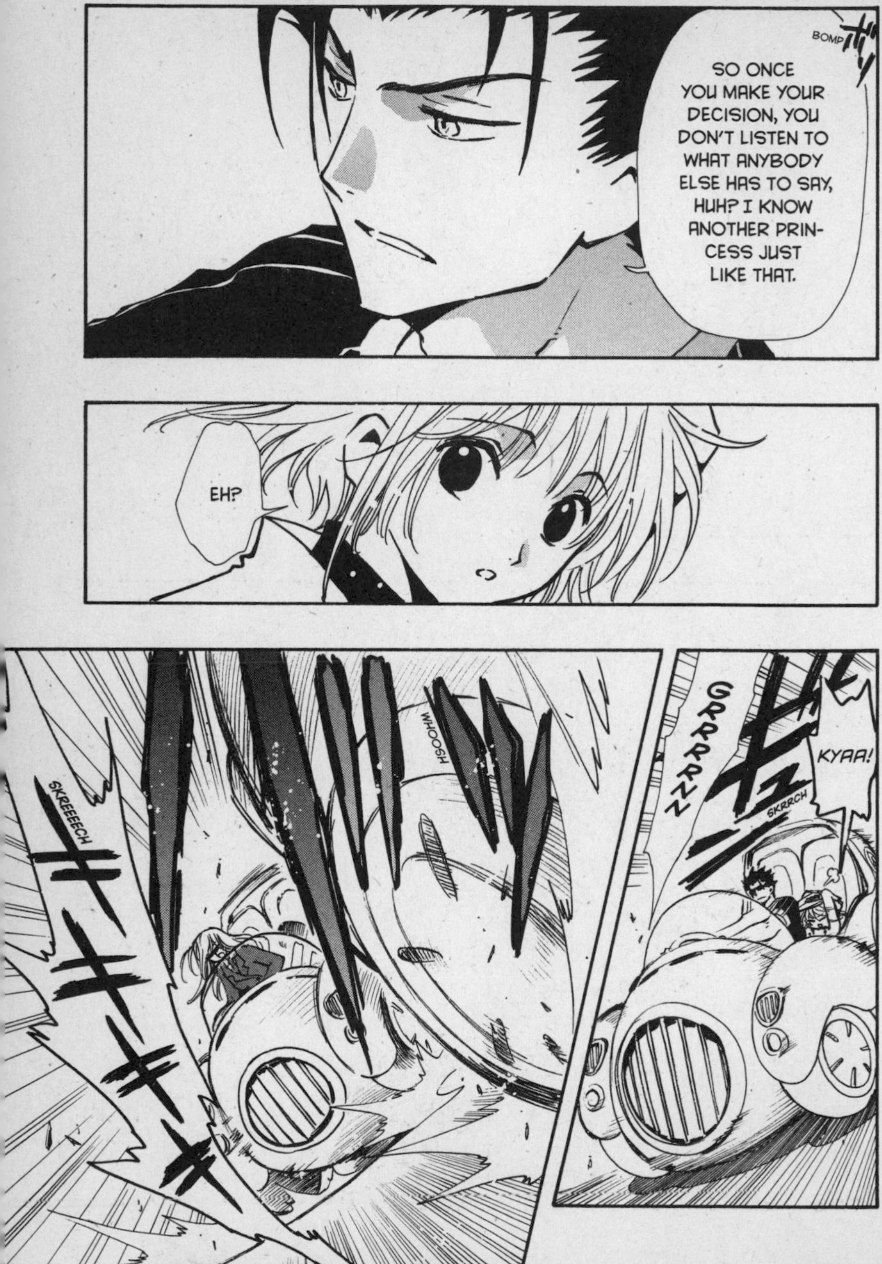
BOMP
SO ONCE YOU MAKE YOUR DECISION, YOU DON'T LISTEN TO WHAT ANYBODY ELSE HAS TO SAY, HUH? I KNOW ANOTHER PRINCESS JUST LIKE THAT.
EH?
GRRRRNN
KYAA!
SKRRCH
WHOOSH
SKREEEECH

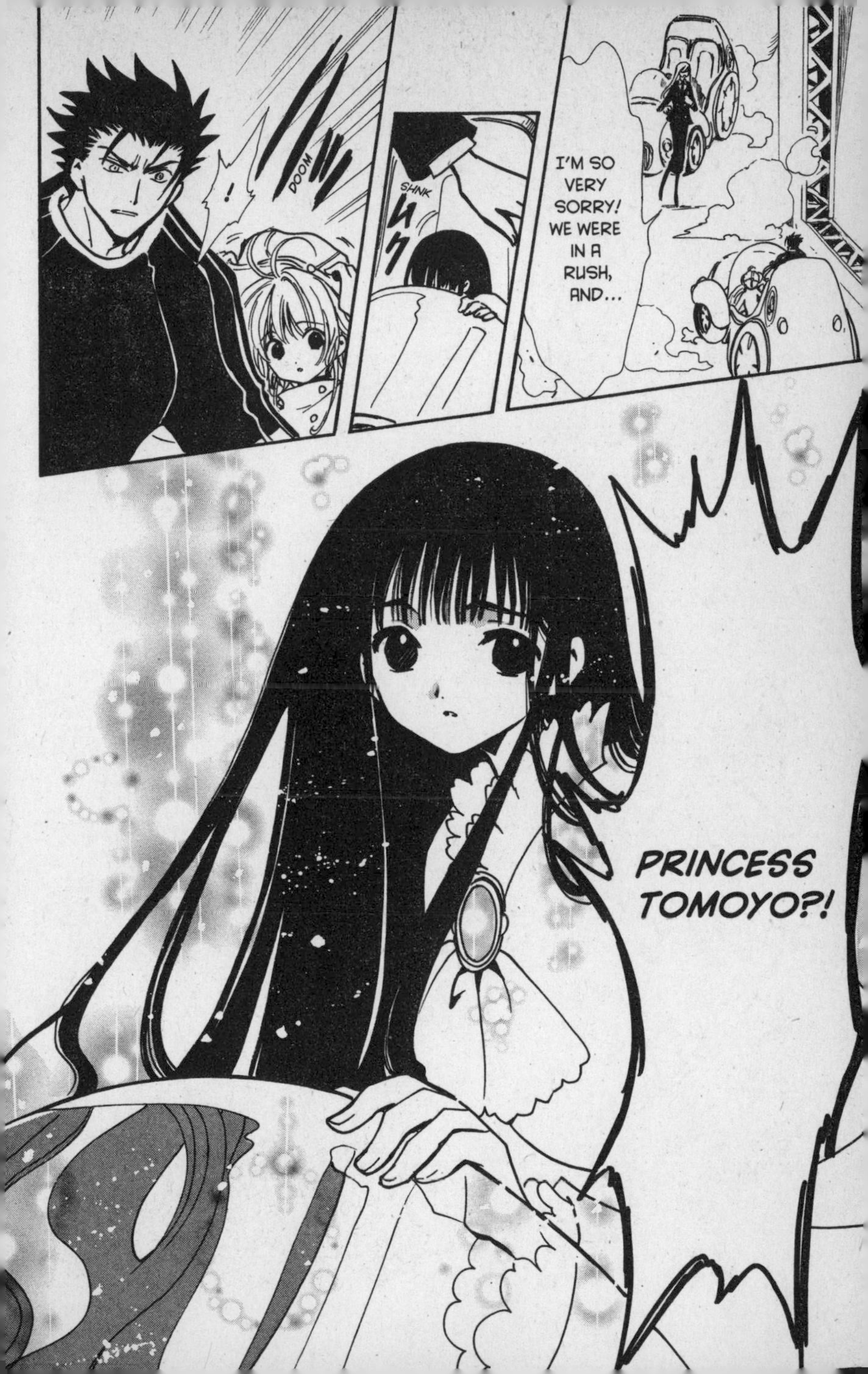
I'M SO VERY SORRY! WE WERE IN A RUSH, AND...
SHNK
DOOM
!
PRINCESS TOMOYO?!

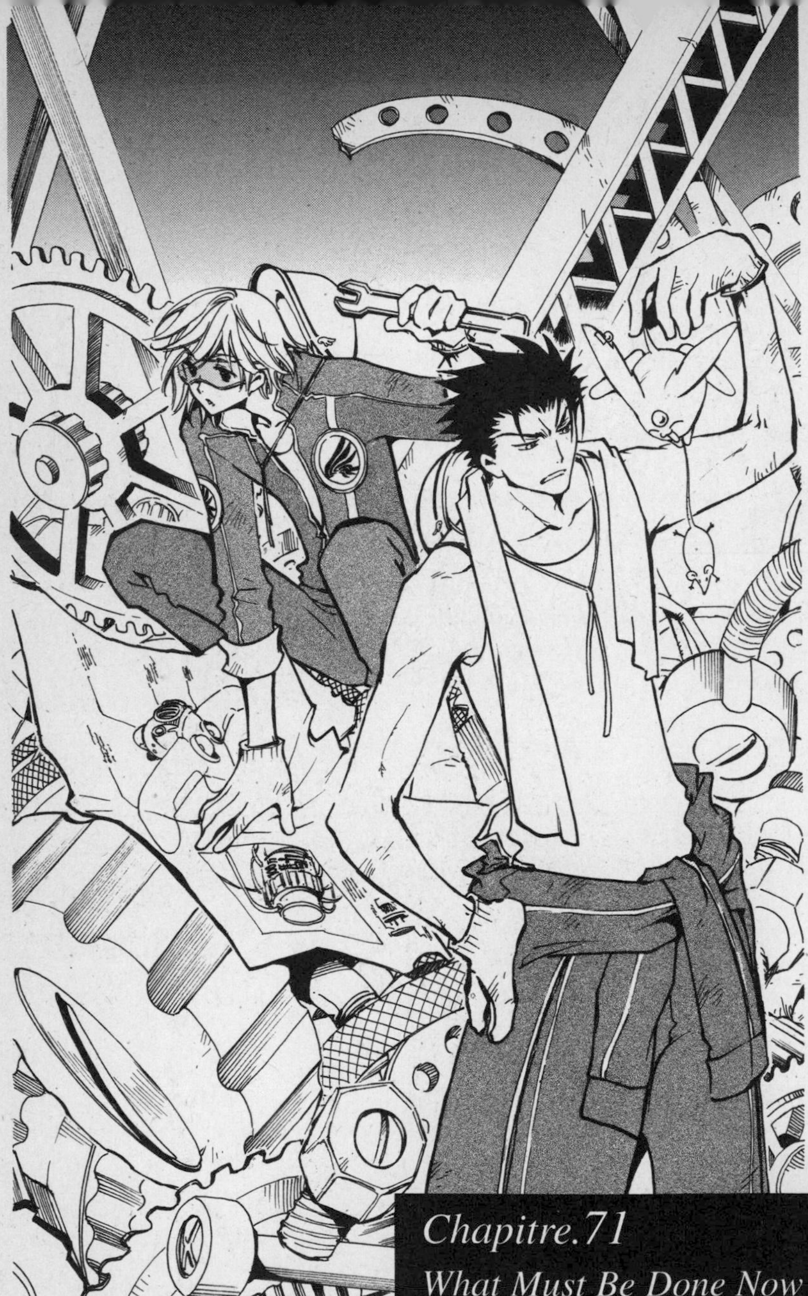
Chapitre.71
What Must Be Done Now

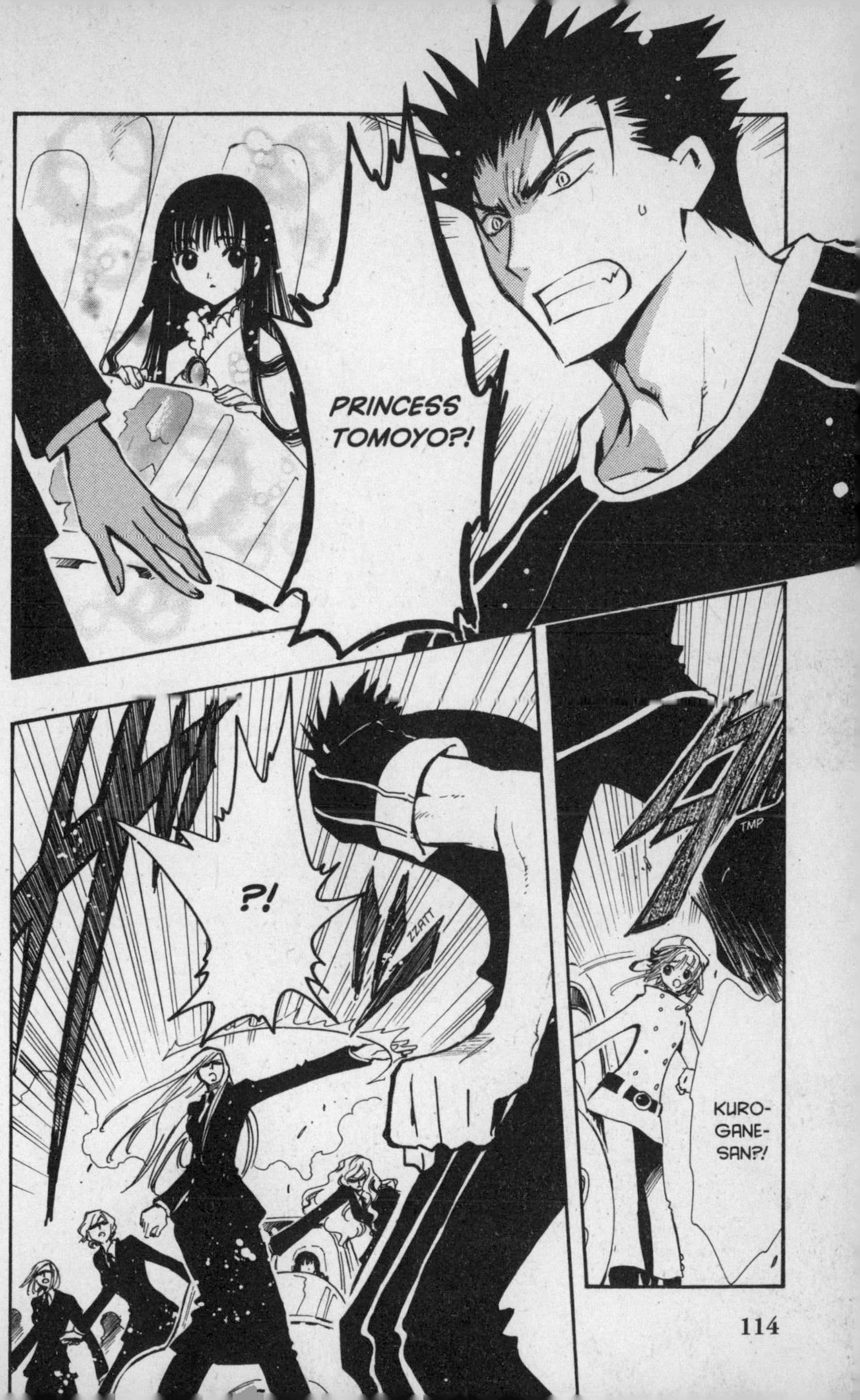
PRINCESS TOMOYO?!
TMP
KURO-GANE-SAN?!
?!
ZZATT

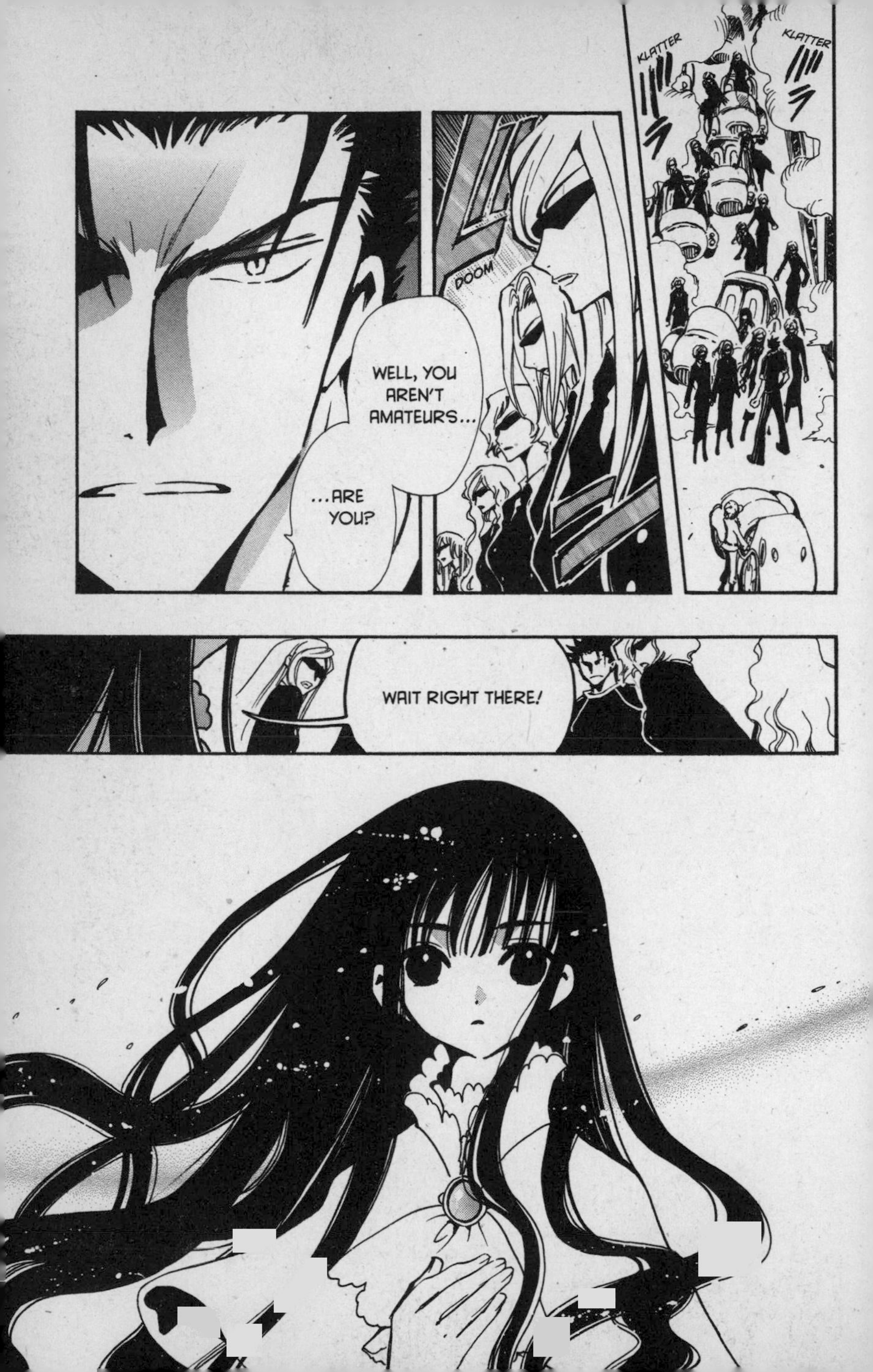
KLATTER
KLATTER
DOOM
WELL, YOU AREN'T AMATEURS...
...ARE YOU?
WAIT RIGHT THERE!

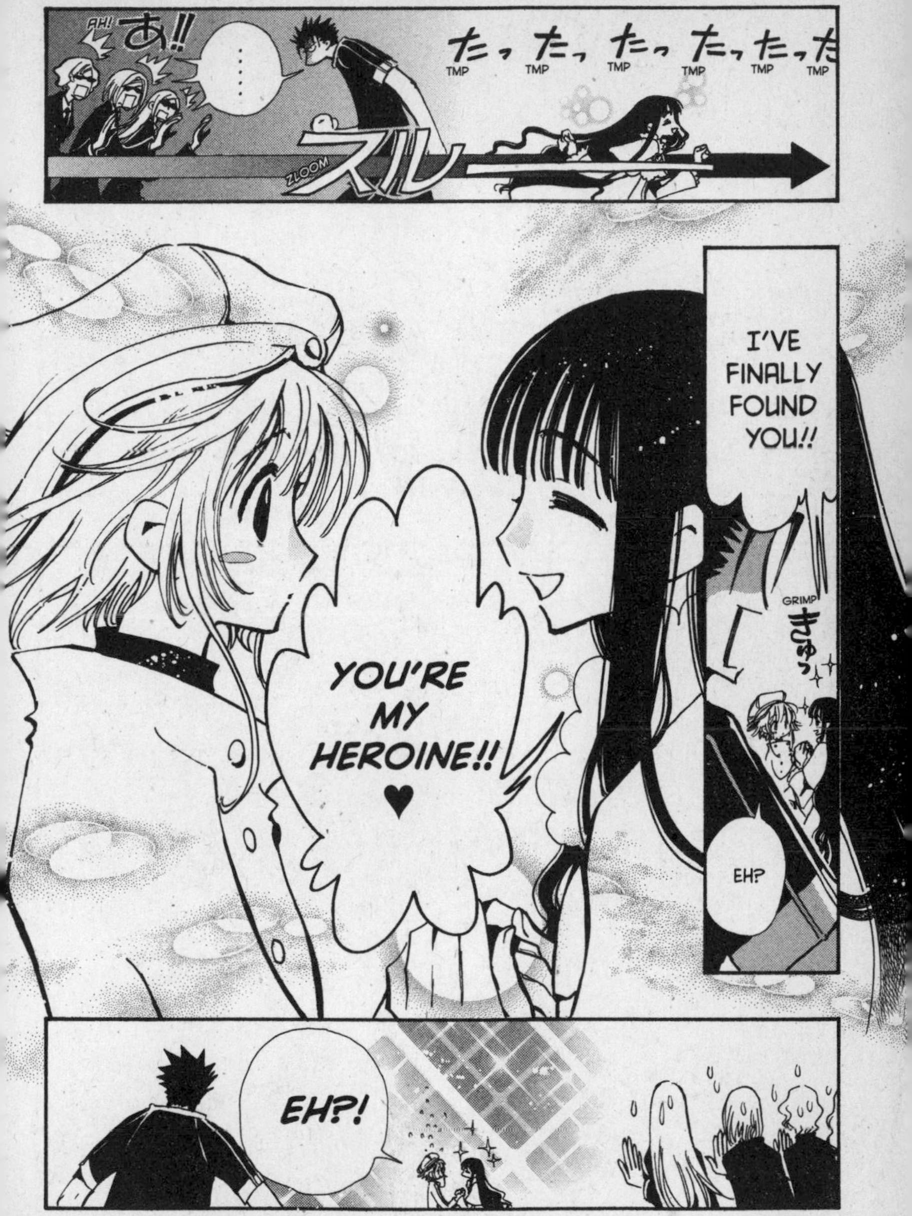
たっ たっ たっ たっ たっ た
TMP TMP TMP TMP TMP TMP
スル
ZLOOM
.....
あ!!
AH!
I'VE FINALLY FOUND YOU!!
きゅっ
GRIMP
EH?
YOU'RE MY HEROINE!! ♥
EH?!

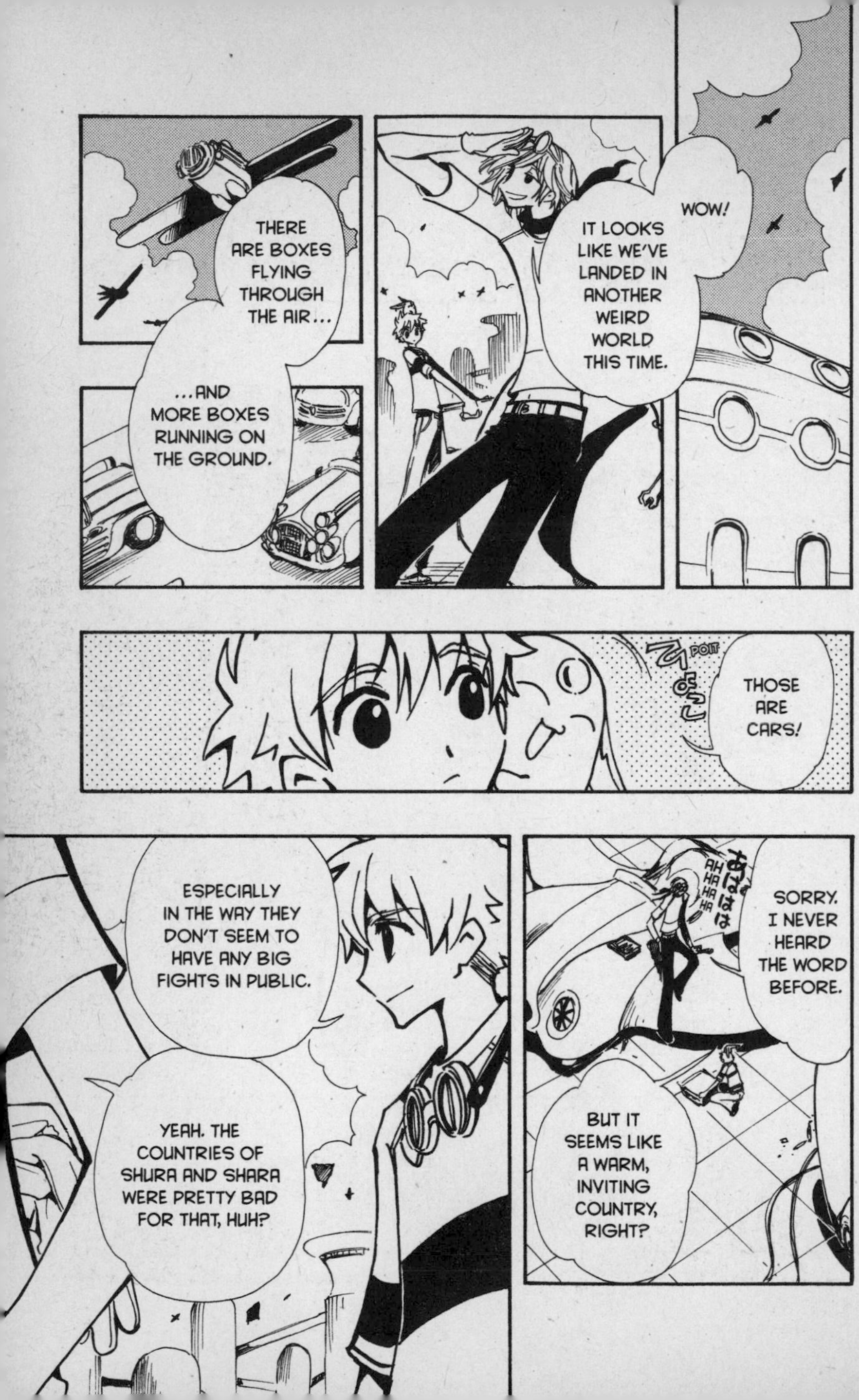
WOW!
IT LOOKS LIKE WE'VE LANDED IN ANOTHER WEIRD WORLD THIS TIME.
THERE ARE BOXES FLYING THROUGH THE AIR...
...AND MORE BOXES RUNNING ON THE GROUND.
POIT
THOSE ARE CARS!
あははは
AH HA HA HA HA
SORRY. I NEVER HEARD THE WORD BEFORE.
BUT IT SEEMS LIKE A WARM, INVITING COUNTRY, RIGHT?
ESPECIALLY IN THE WAY THEY DON'T SEEM TO HAVE ANY BIG FIGHTS IN PUBLIC.
YEAH. THE COUNTRIES OF SHURA AND SHARA WERE PRETTY BAD FOR THAT, HUH?

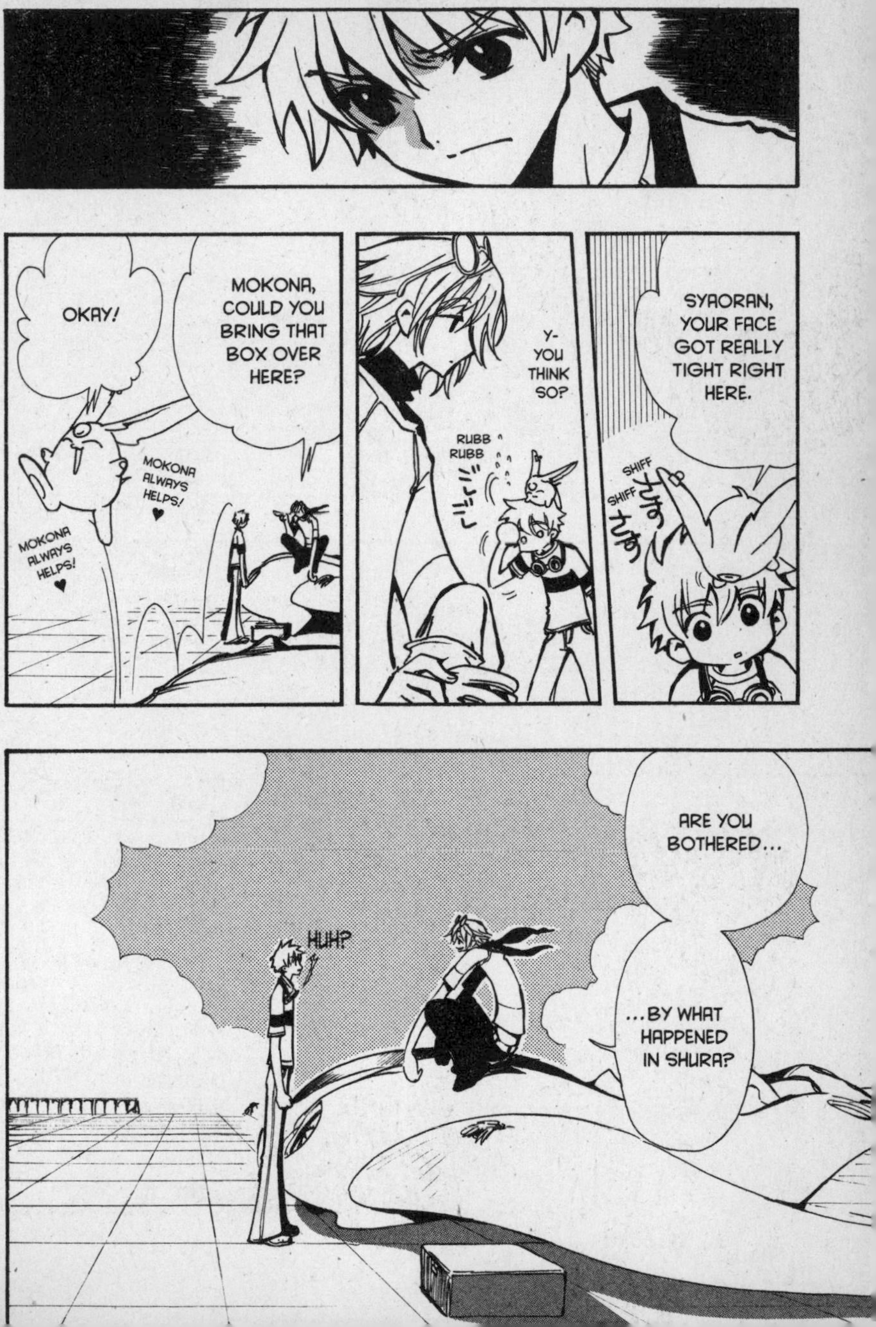
SYAORAN, YOUR FACE GOT REALLY TIGHT RIGHT HERE.
SHIFF SHIFF
Y-YOU THINK SO?
RUBB RUBB
MOKONA, COULD YOU BRING THAT BOX OVER HERE?
OKAY!
MOKONA ALWAYS HELPS! ♥
MOKONA ALWAYS HELPS! ♥
ARE YOU BOTHERED...
HUH?
...BY WHAT HAPPENED IN SHURA?

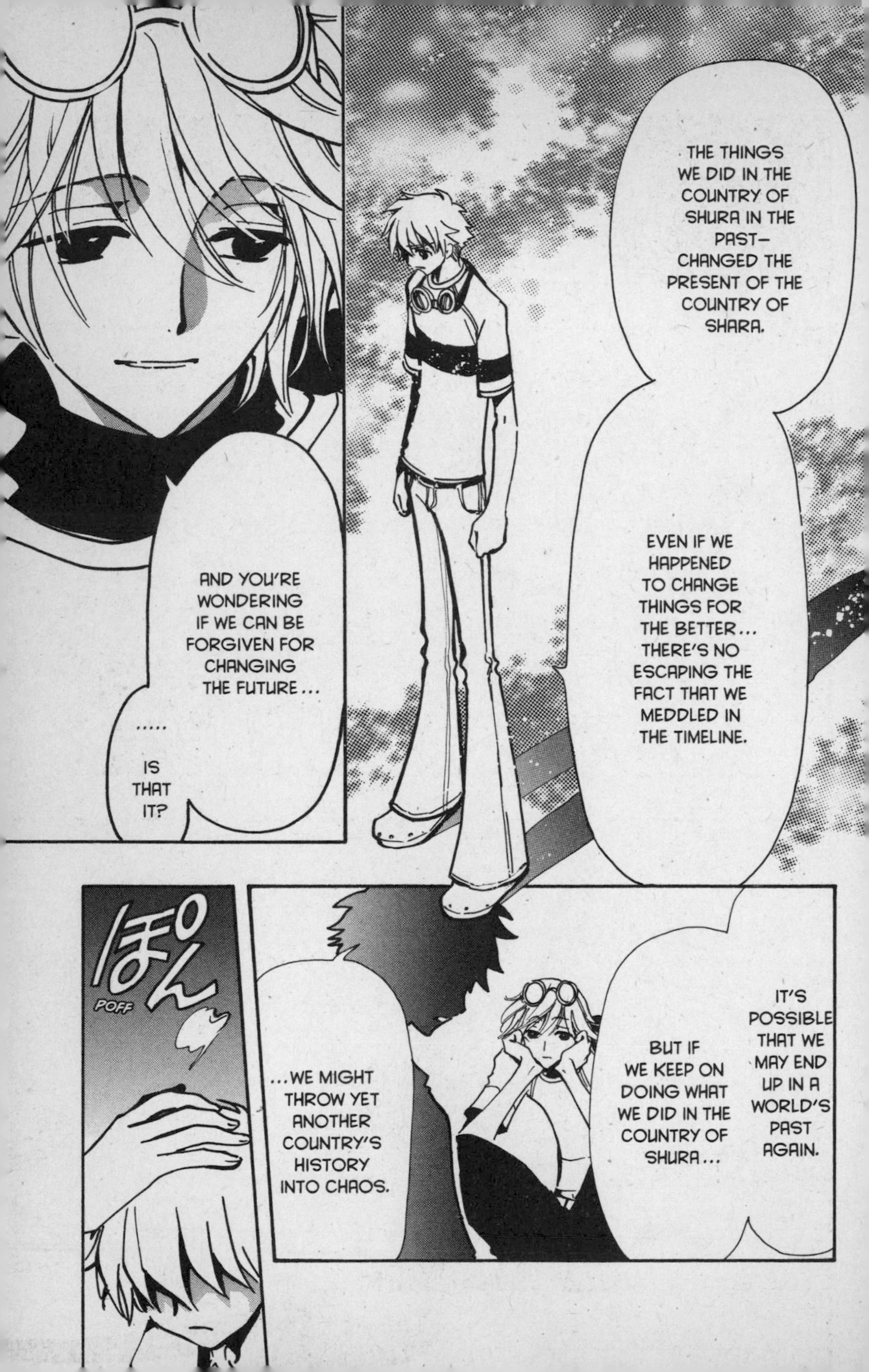
THE THINGS WE DID IN THE COUNTRY OF SHURA IN THE PAST—CHANGED THE PRESENT OF THE COUNTRY OF SHARA.
EVEN IF WE HAPPENED TO CHANGE THINGS FOR THE BETTER... THERE'S NO ESCAPING THE FACT THAT WE MEDDLED IN THE TIMELINE.
AND YOU'RE WONDERING IF WE CAN BE FORGIVEN FOR CHANGING THE FUTURE...
.....
IS THAT IT?
IT'S POSSIBLE THAT WE MAY END UP IN A WORLD'S PAST AGAIN.
BUT IF WE KEEP ON DOING WHAT WE DID IN THE COUNTRY OF SHURA...
...WE MIGHT THROW YET ANOTHER COUNTRY'S HISTORY INTO CHAOS.
ぽん
POFF

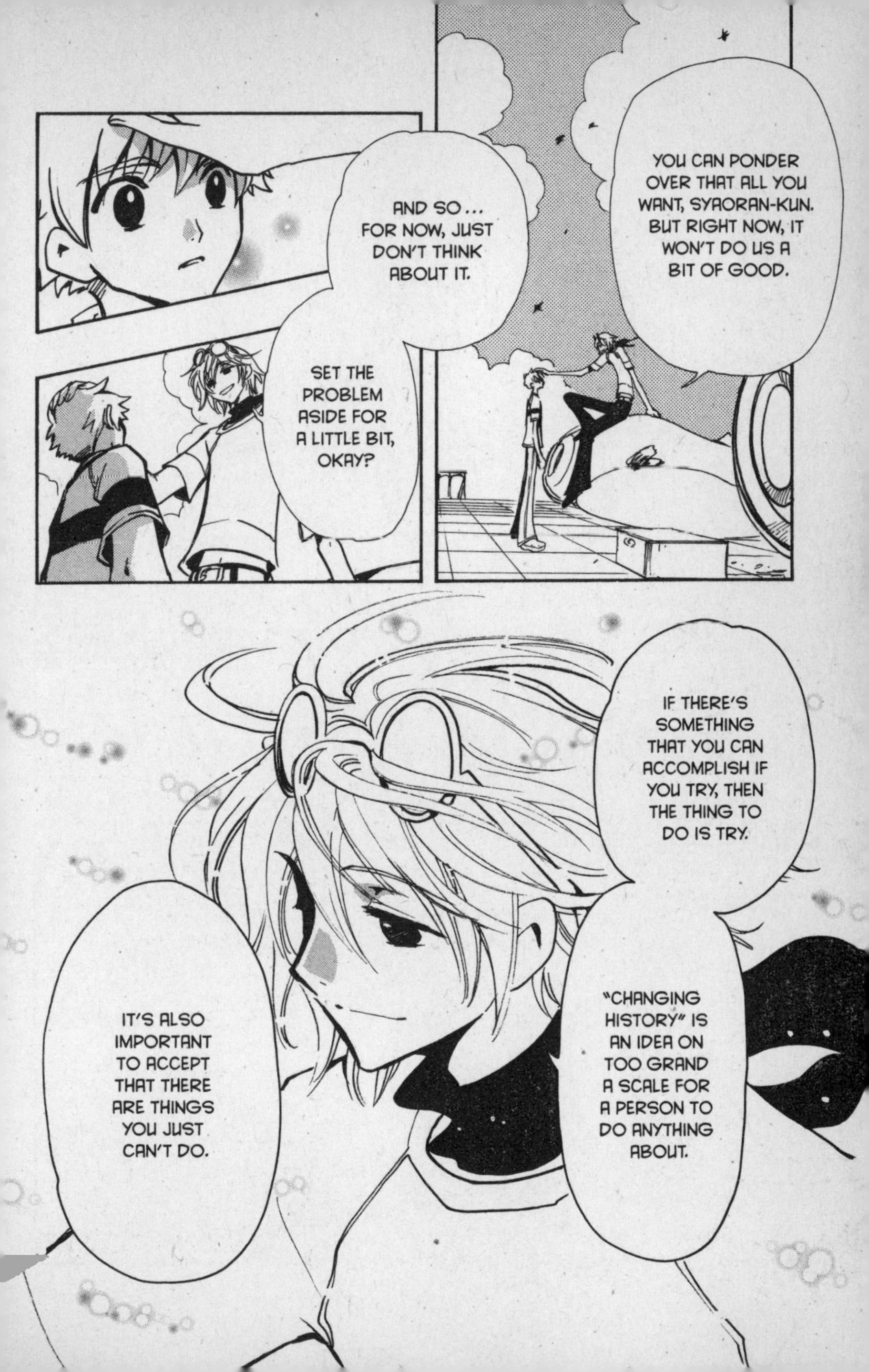
YOU CAN PONDER OVER THAT ALL YOU WANT, SYAORAN-KUN. BUT RIGHT NOW, IT WON'T DO US A BIT OF GOOD.
AND SO... FOR NOW, JUST DON'T THINK ABOUT IT.
SET THE PROBLEM ASIDE FOR A LITTLE BIT, OKAY?
IF THERE'S SOMETHING THAT YOU CAN ACCOMPLISH IF YOU TRY, THEN THE THING TO DO IS TRY.
"CHANGING HISTORY" IS AN IDEA ON TOO GRAND A SCALE FOR A PERSON TO DO ANYTHING ABOUT.
IT'S ALSO IMPORTANT TO ACCEPT THAT THERE ARE THINGS YOU JUST CAN'T DO.

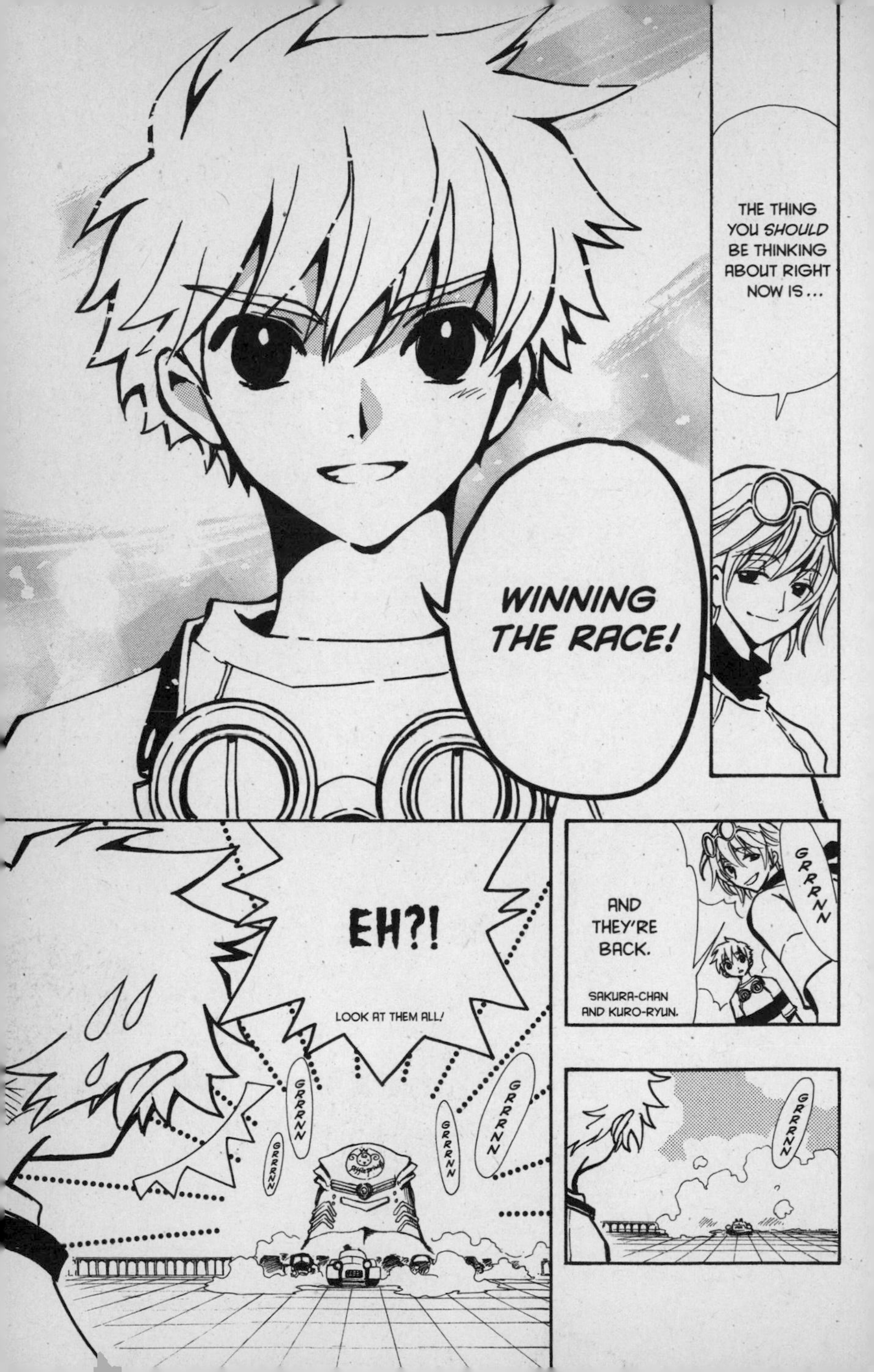
THE THING YOU SHOULD BE THINKING ABOUT RIGHT NOW IS...
WINNING THE RACE!
AND THEY'RE BACK.
SAKURA-CHAN AND KURO-RYUN.
GRRRNN
GRRRNN
EH?!
LOOK AT THEM ALL!
GRRRNN
GRRRNN
GRRRNN
GRRRNN

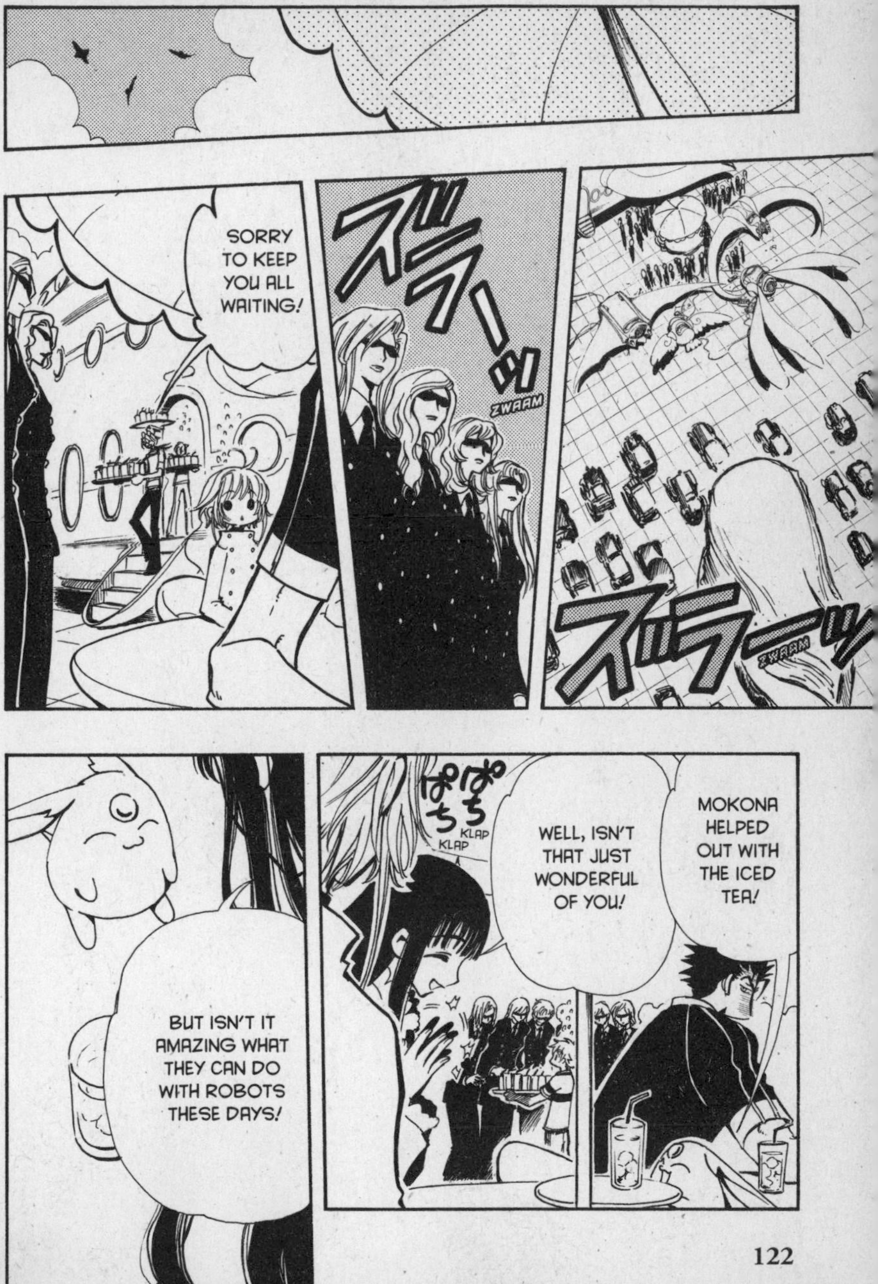
スッラーッ
ZWAAM
ズラーッ
ZWAAM
SORRY TO KEEP YOU ALL WAITING!
MOKONA HELPED OUT WITH THE ICED TEA!
WELL, ISN'T THAT JUST WONDERFUL OF YOU!
ぱちぱち
KLAP KLAP
BUT ISN'T IT AMAZING WHAT THEY CAN DO WITH ROBOTS THESE DAYS!

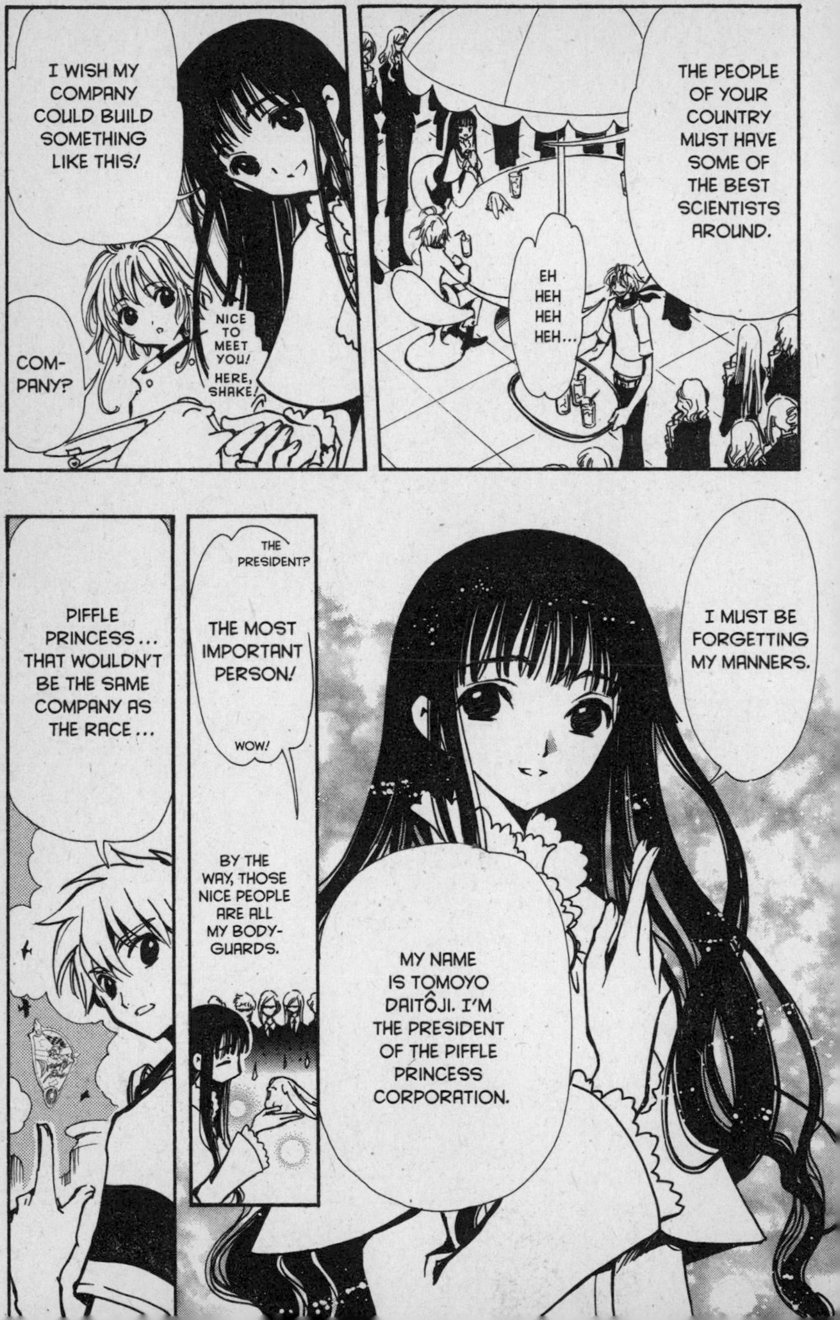
THE PEOPLE OF YOUR COUNTRY MUST HAVE SOME OF THE BEST SCIENTISTS AROUND.
EH HEH HEH HEH...
I WISH MY COMPANY COULD BUILD SOMETHING LIKE THIS!
NICE TO MEET YOU! HERE, SHAKE!
COM-PANY?
I MUST BE FORGETTING MY MANNERS.
MY NAME IS TOMOYO DAITÔJI. I'M THE PRESIDENT OF THE PIFFLE PRINCESS CORPORATION.
THE PRESIDENT?
THE MOST IMPORTANT PERSON!
WOW!
BY THE WAY, THOSE NICE PEOPLE ARE ALL MY BODY-GUARDS.
PIFFLE PRINCESS... THAT WOULDN'T BE THE SAME COMPANY AS THE RACE...

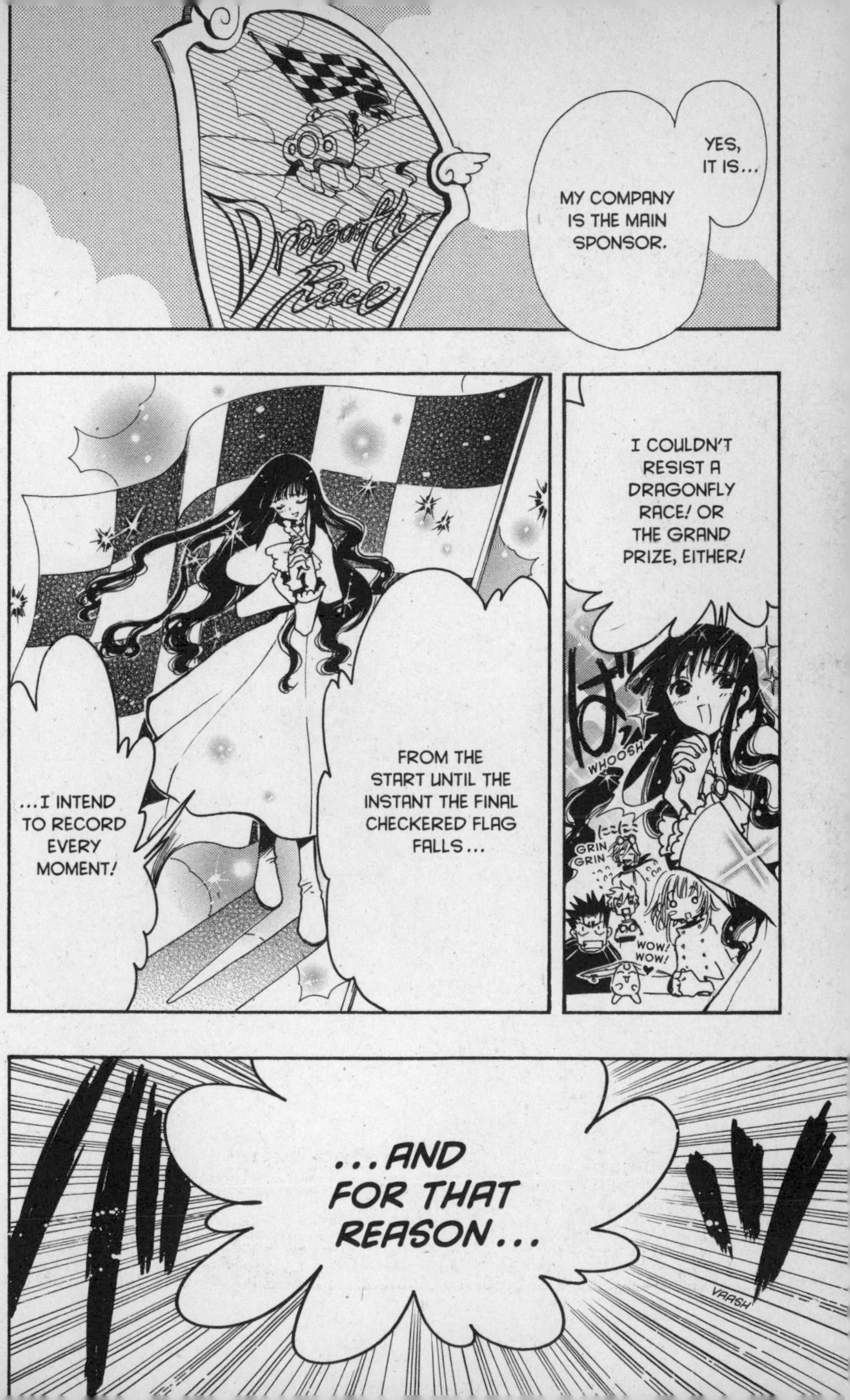
YES, IT IS...
MY COMPANY IS THE MAIN SPONSOR.
I COULDN'T RESIST A DRAGONFLY RACE! OR THE GRAND PRIZE, EITHER!
WHOOSH
GRIN GRIN
WOW! WOW!
FROM THE START UNTIL THE INSTANT THE FINAL CHECKERED FLAG FALLS...
...I INTEND TO RECORD EVERY MOMENT!
...AND FOR THAT REASON...
VRASH

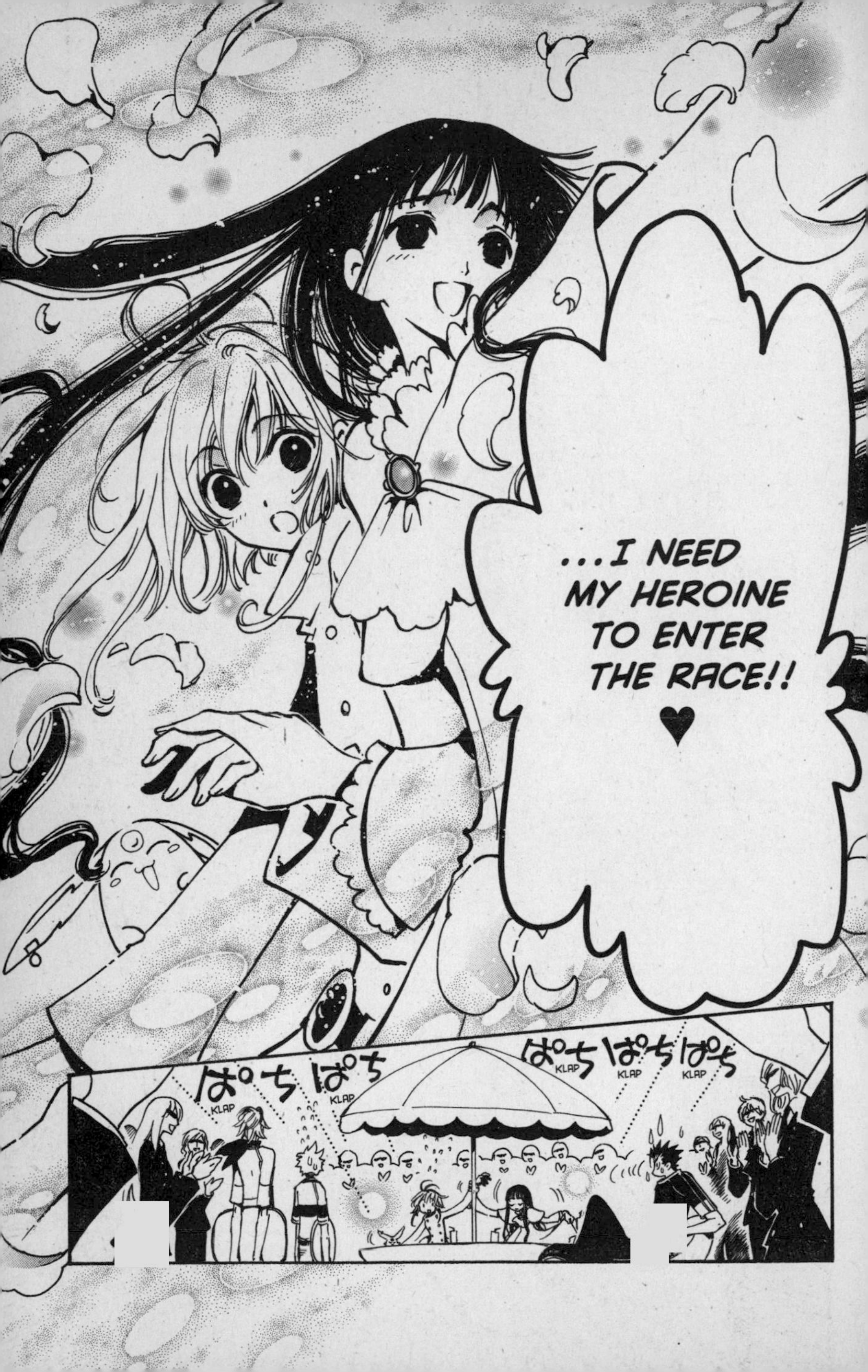
...I NEED MY HEROINE TO ENTER THE RACE!! ♥
ぱちぱちぱち
KLAP KLAP KLAP
ぱちぱち
KLAP KLAP

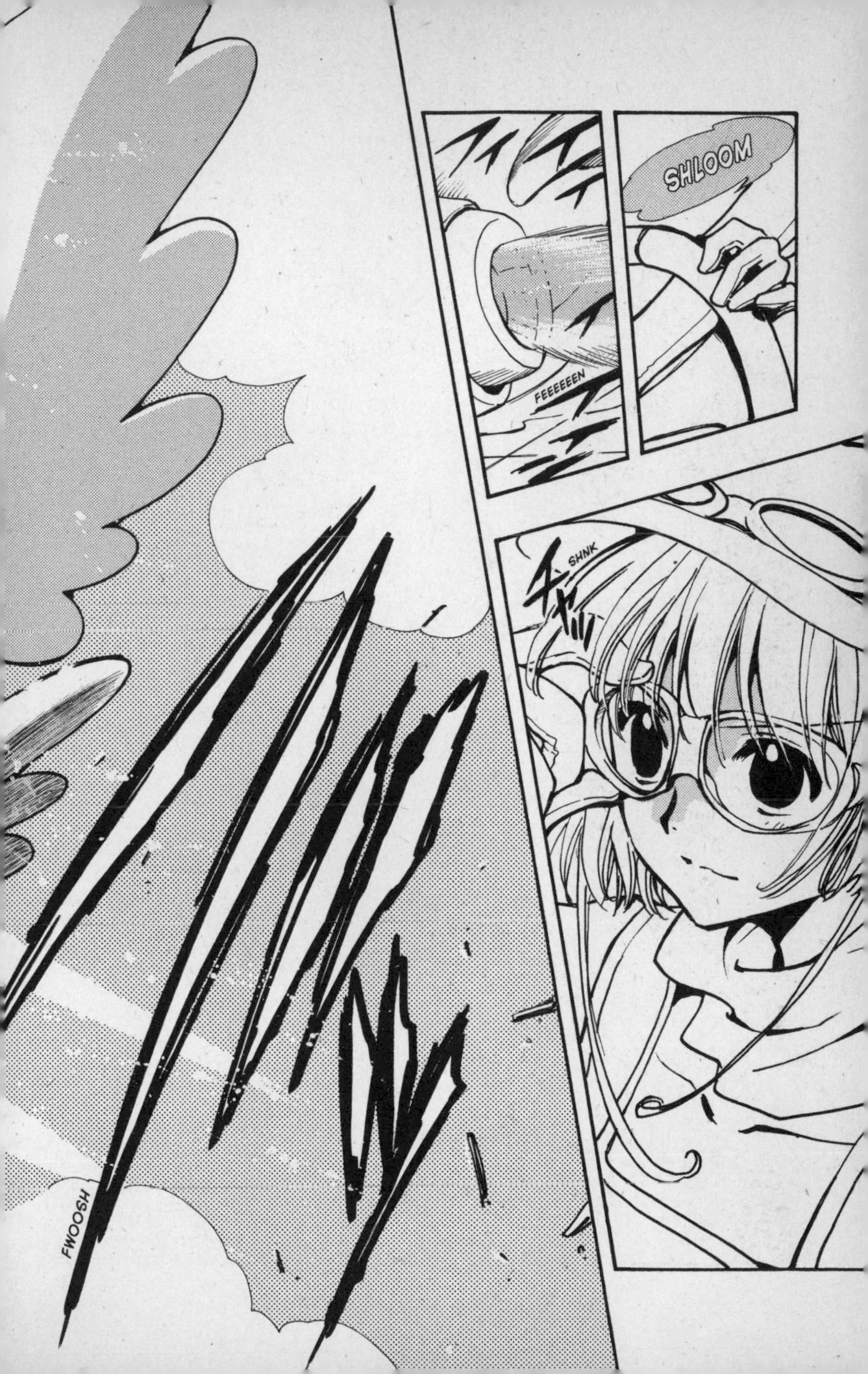
SHLOOM
FEEEEEEN
SHNK
FWOOSH

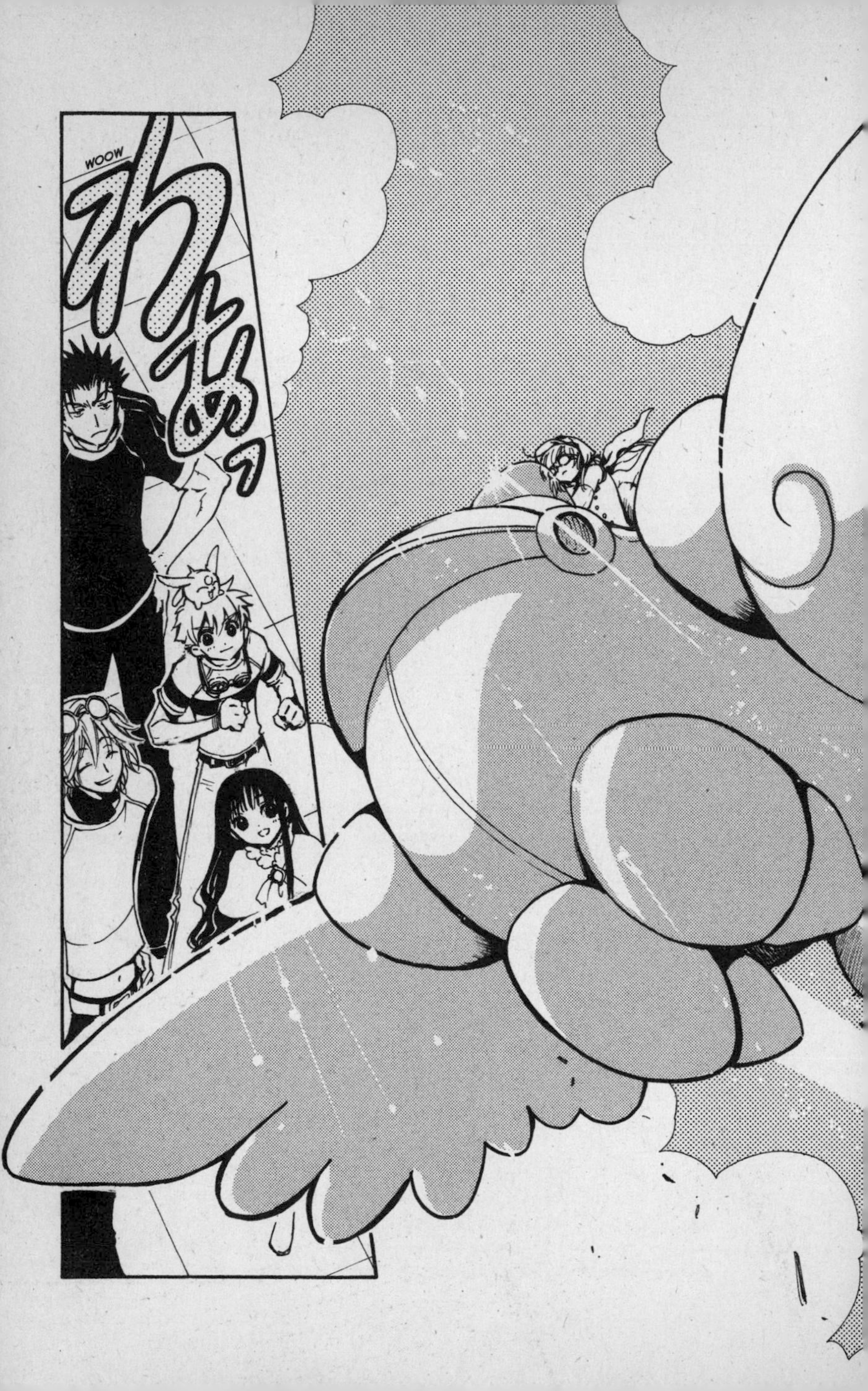
WOOW
わぁっ

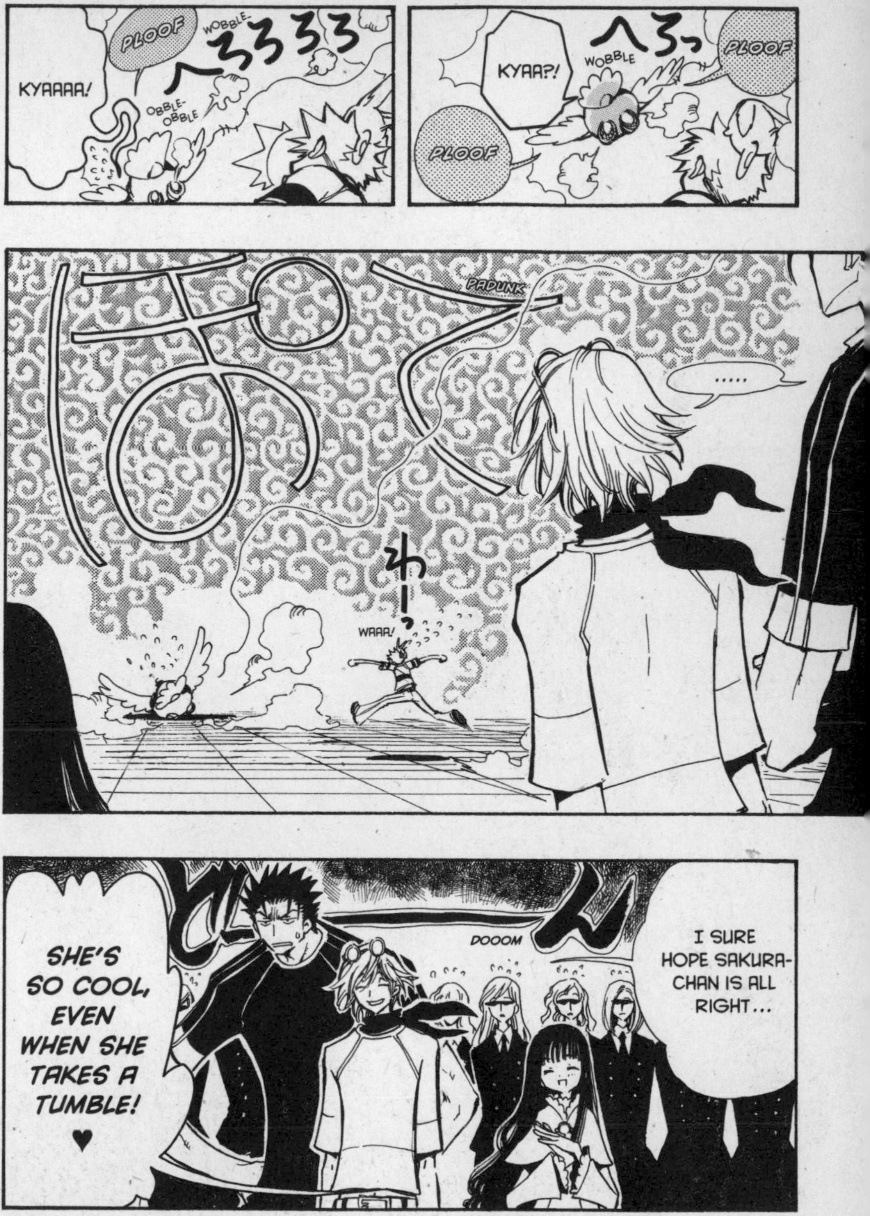
KYAA?!
WOBBLE
PLOOF
PLOOF
KYAAAA!
PLOOF
WOBBLE-
OBBLE-OBBLE
PADUNK
.....
WAAA!
I SURE HOPE SAKURA-CHAN IS ALL RIGHT...
DOOOM
SHE'S SO COOL, EVEN WHEN SHE TAKES A TUMBLE! ♥

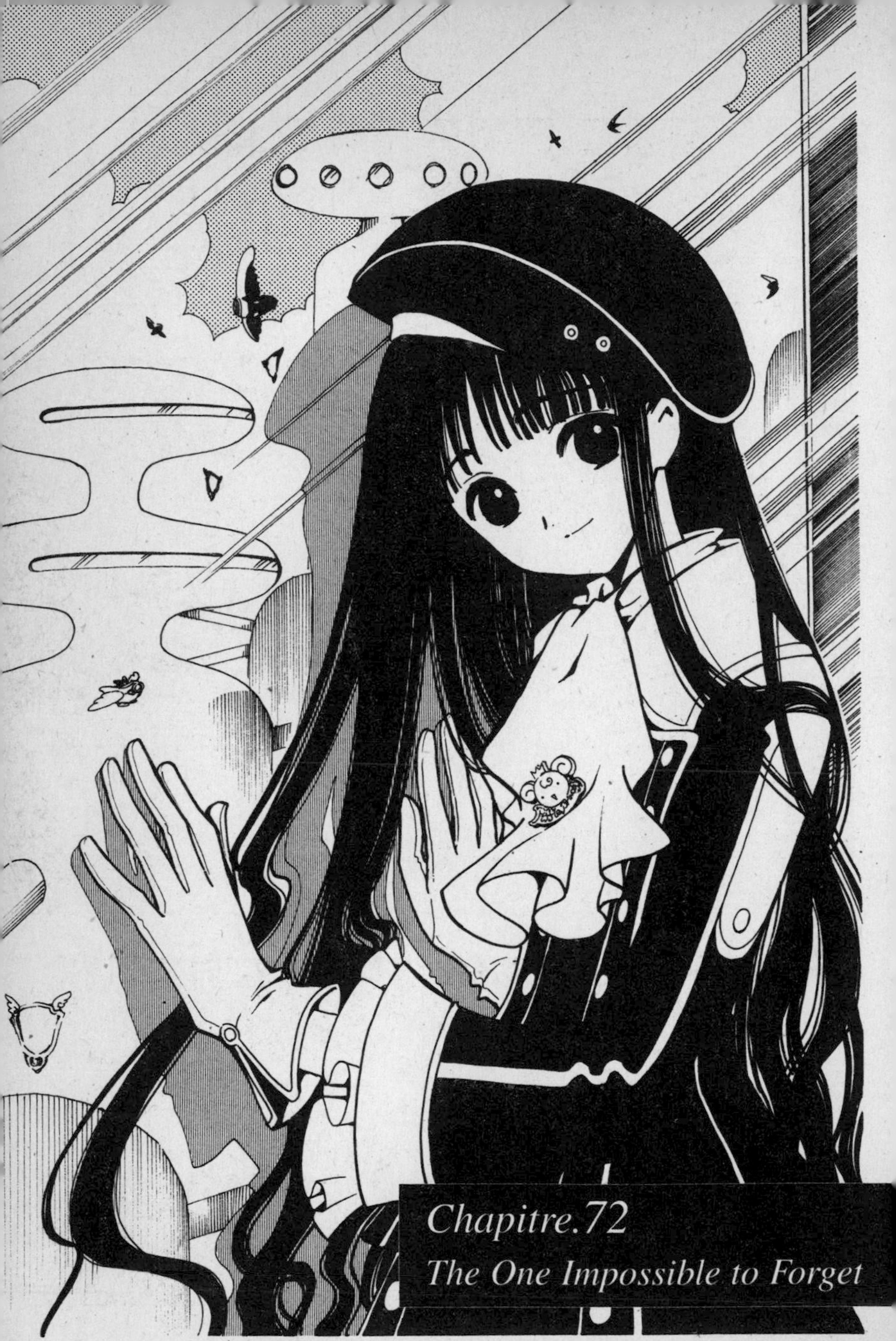
Chapitre.72
The One Impossible to Forget

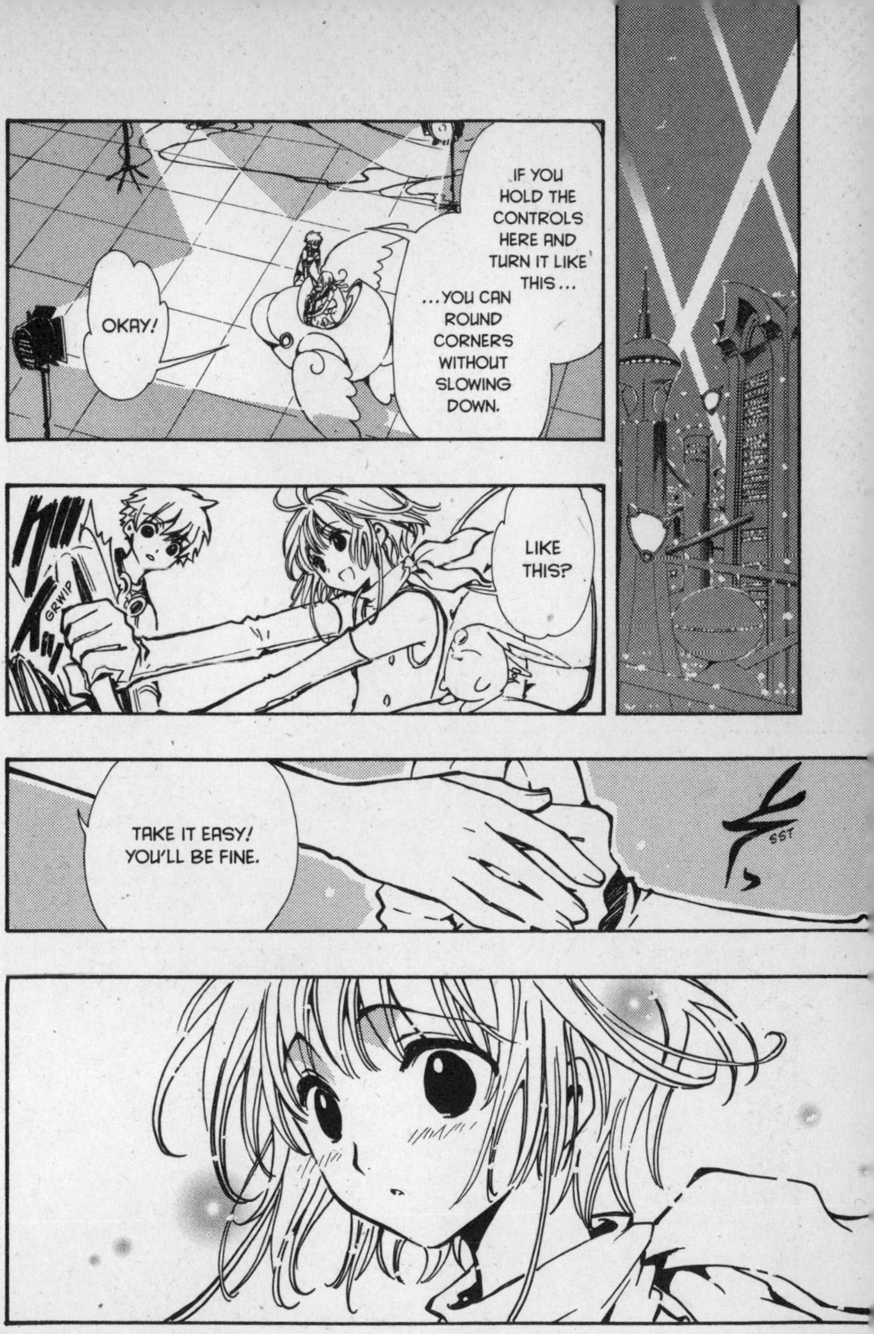
IF YOU HOLD THE CONTROLS HERE AND TURN IT LIKE THIS...
...YOU CAN ROUND CORNERS WITHOUT SLOWING DOWN.
OKAY!
LIKE THIS?
GRWIP
SST
TAKE IT EASY! YOU'LL BE FINE.

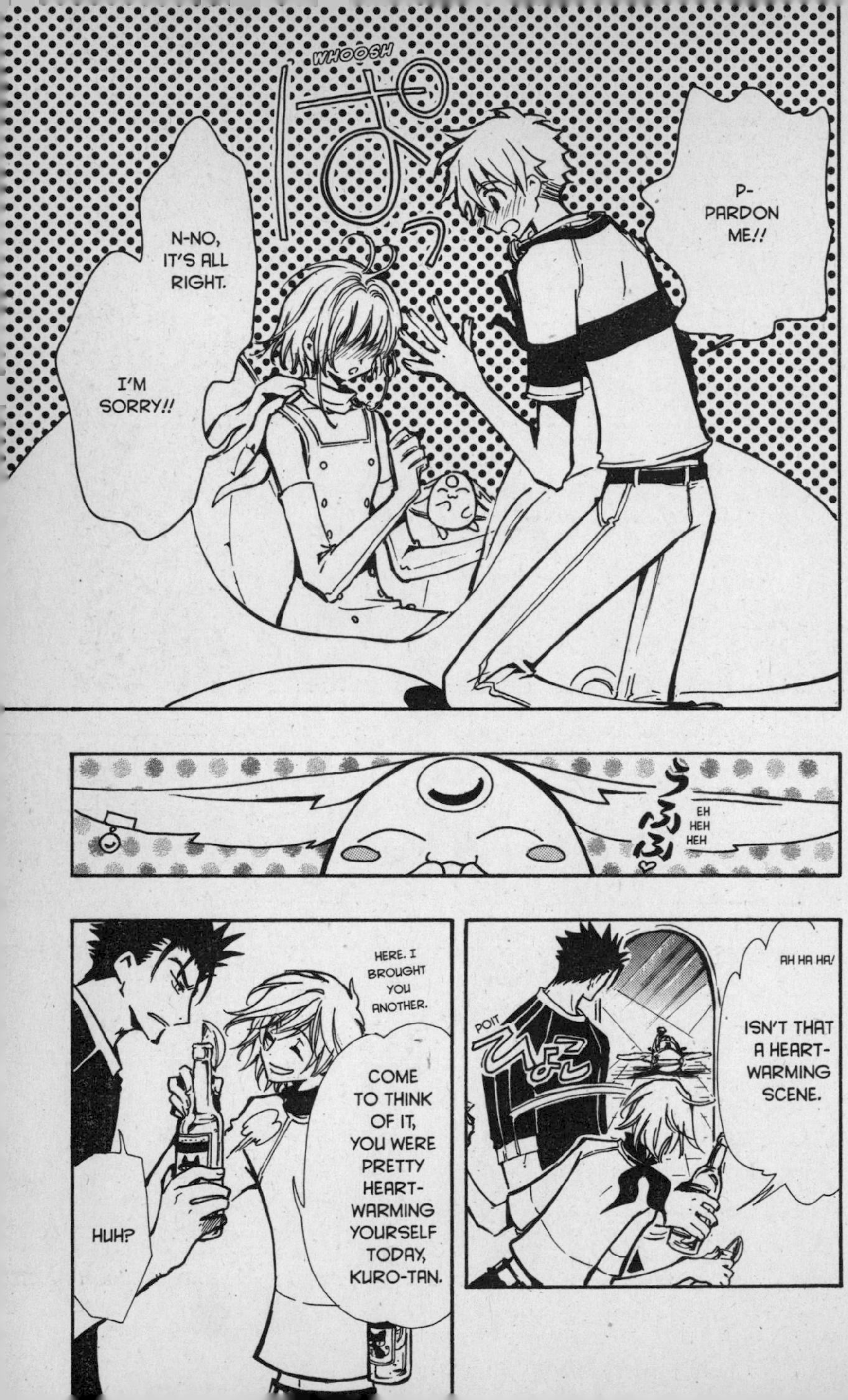
WHOOSH
P-PARDON ME!!
N-NO, IT'S ALL RIGHT.
I'M SORRY!!
EH HEH HEH
AH HA HA!
ISN'T THAT A HEART-WARMING SCENE.
POIT
HERE. I BROUGHT YOU ANOTHER.
COME TO THINK OF IT, YOU WERE PRETTY HEART-WARMING YOURSELF TODAY, KURO-TAN.
HUH?

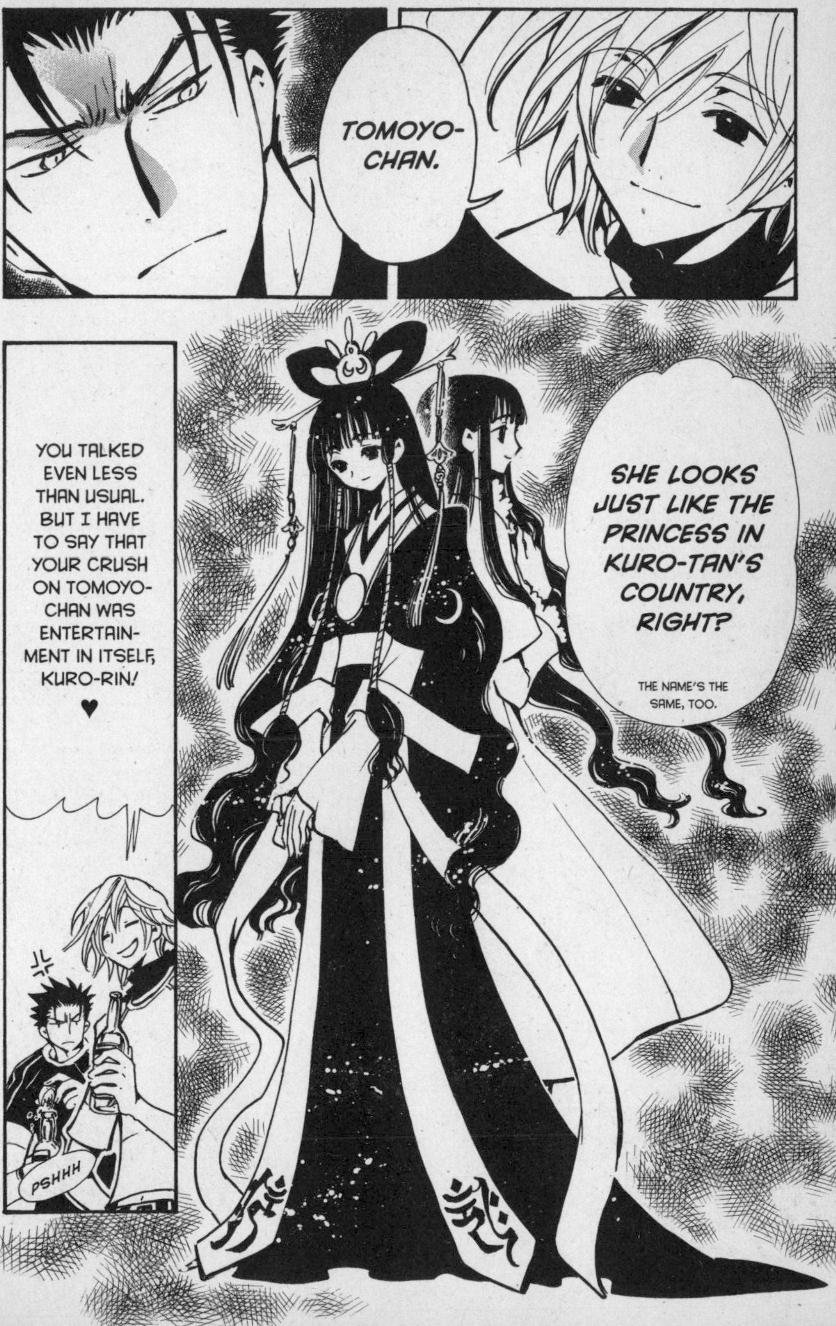
TOMOYO-CHAN.
SHE LOOKS JUST LIKE THE PRINCESS IN KURO-TAN'S COUNTRY, RIGHT?
THE NAME'S THE SAME, TOO.
YOU TALKED EVEN LESS THAN USUAL. BUT I HAVE TO SAY THAT YOUR CRUSH ON TOMOYO-CHAN WAS ENTERTAINMENT IN ITSELF, KURO-RIN! ♥
PSHHH

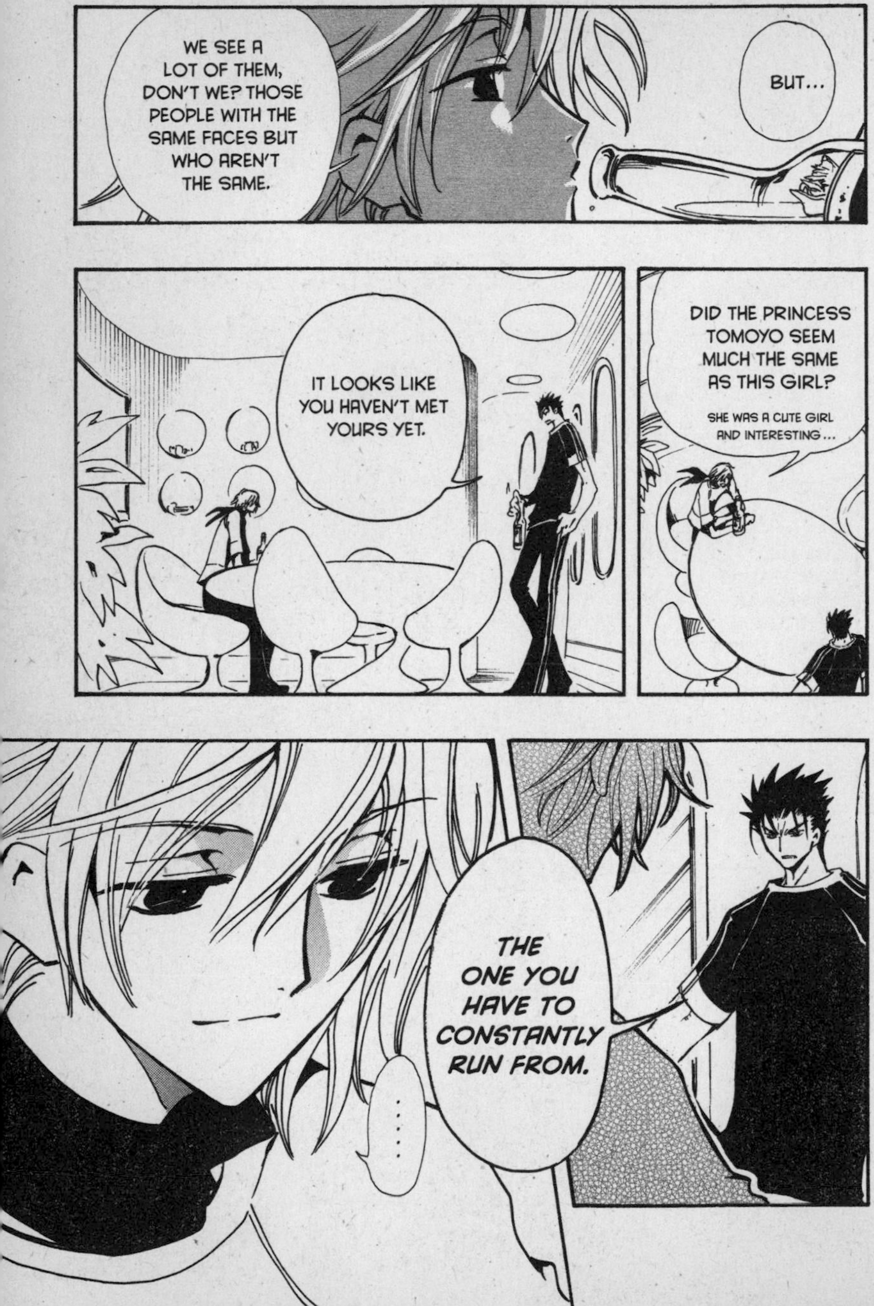
BUT...
WE SEE A LOT OF THEM, DON'T WE? THOSE PEOPLE WITH THE SAME FACES BUT WHO AREN'T THE SAME.
DID THE PRINCESS TOMOYO SEEM MUCH THE SAME AS THIS GIRL?
SHE WAS A CUTE GIRL AND INTERESTING...
IT LOOKS LIKE YOU HAVEN'T MET YOURS YET.
THE ONE YOU HAVE TO CONSTANTLY RUN FROM.
.....

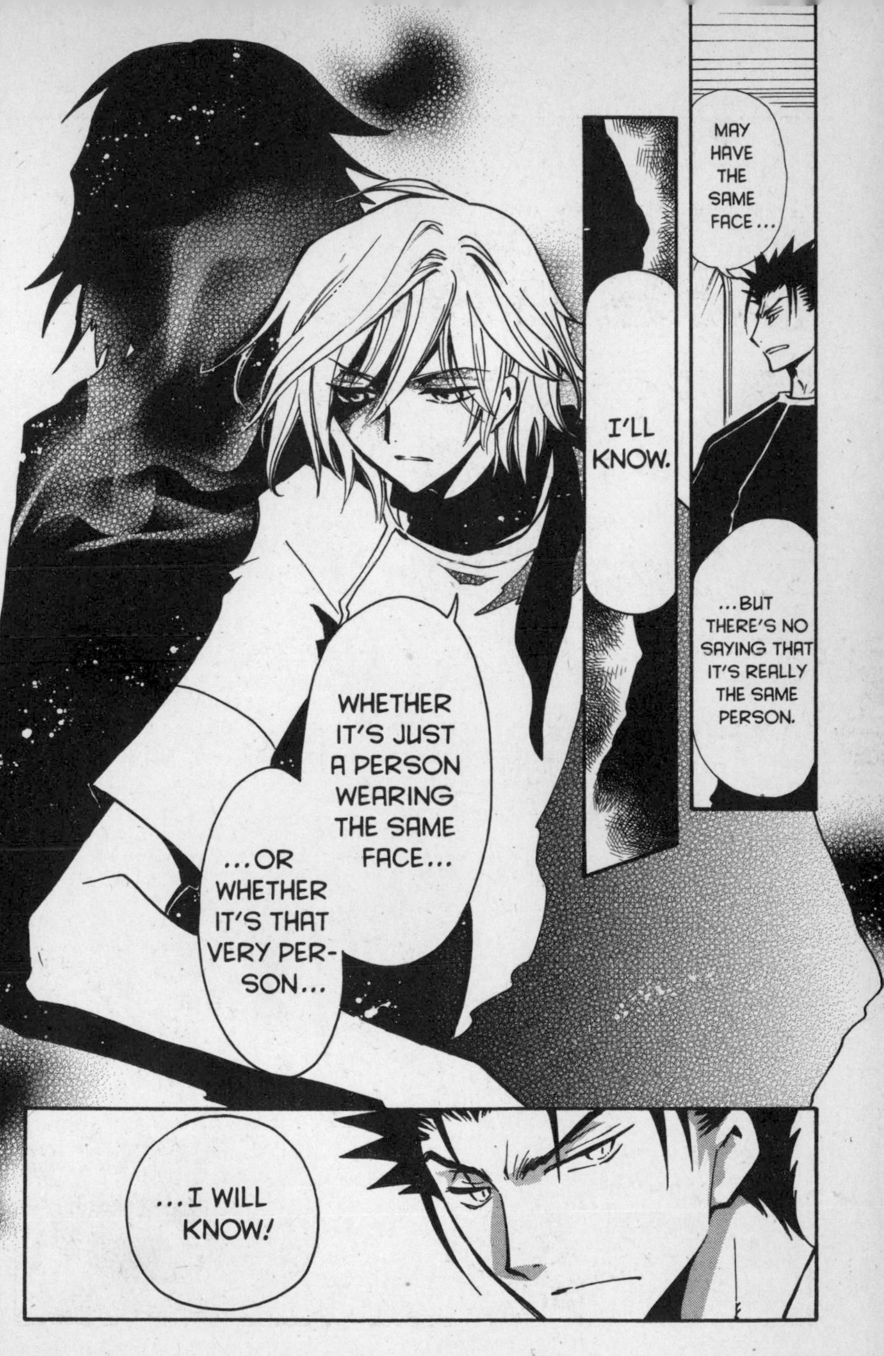

MAY HAVE THE SAME FACE...
...BUT THERE'S NO SAYING THAT IT'S REALLY THE SAME PERSON.
I'LL KNOW.
WHETHER IT'S JUST A PERSON WEARING THE SAME FACE...
...OR WHETHER IT'S THAT VERY PER-SON...
...I WILL KNOW!

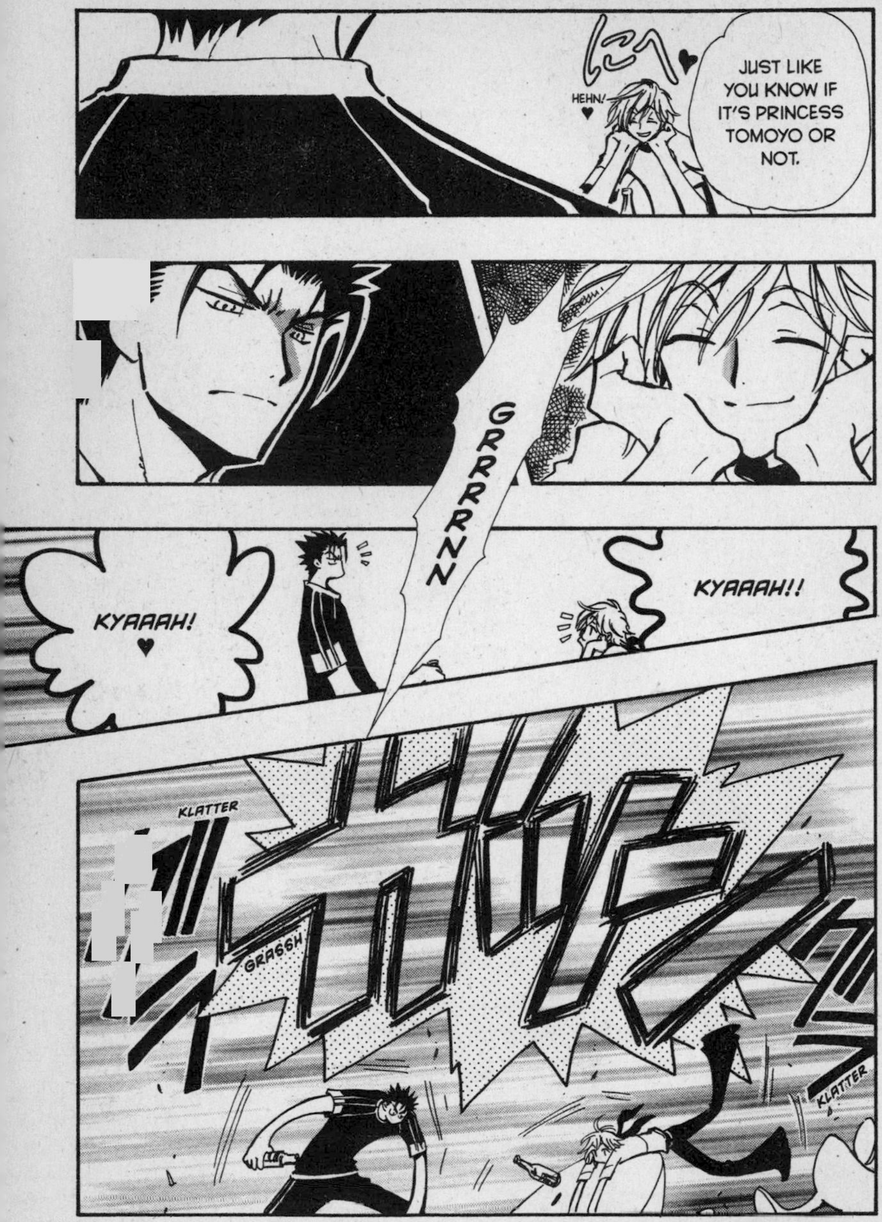
JUST LIKE YOU KNOW IF IT'S PRINCESS TOMOYO OR NOT.
にへ
HEHN!
GRRRRNN
KYAAAH!!
KYAAAH!
KLATTER
GRASSH
KLATTER

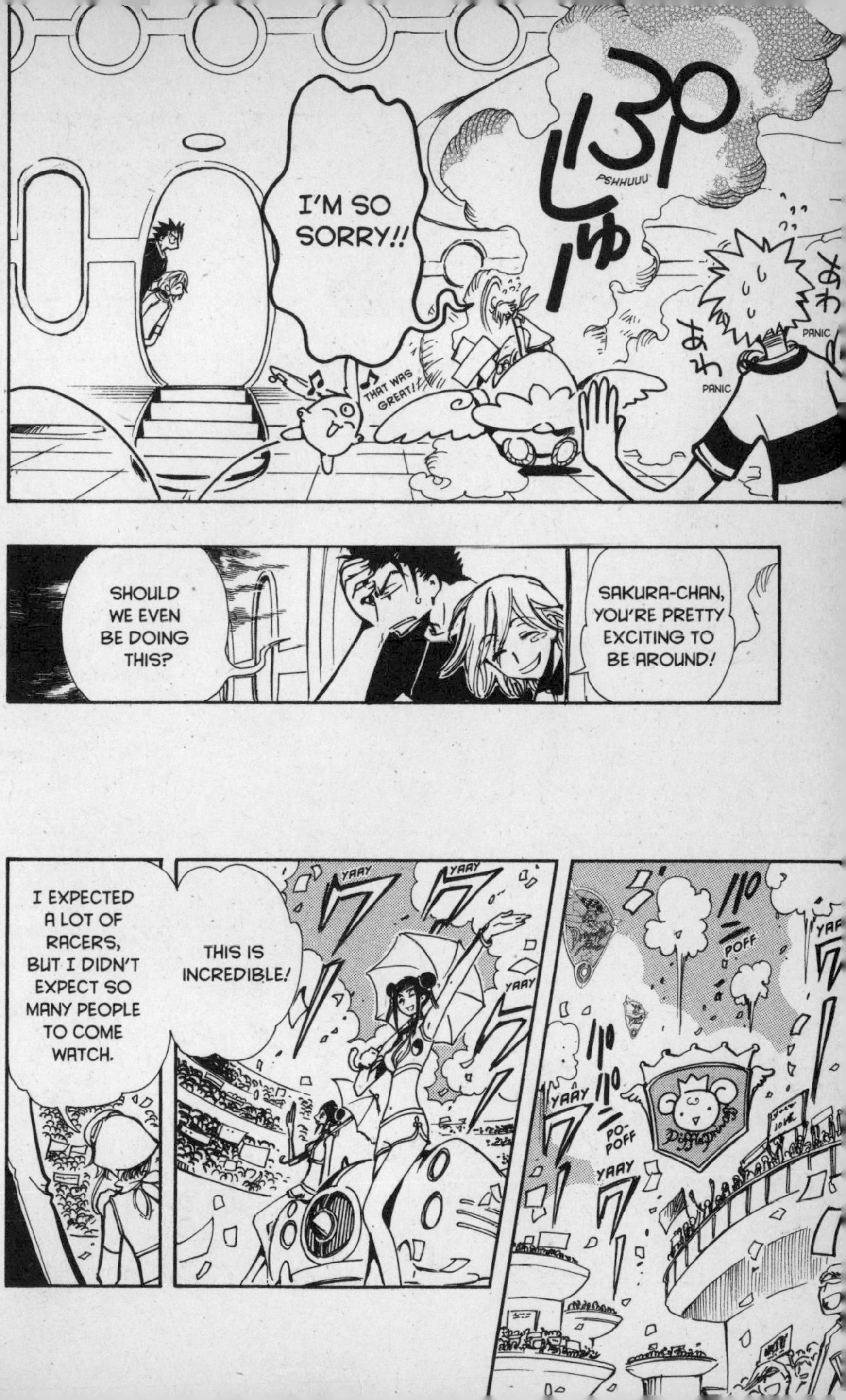
しゅー
PSHHUUU
あわ
PANIC
あわ
PANIC
I'M SO SORRY!!
THAT WAS GREAT!
SAKURA-CHAN, YOU'RE PRETTY EXCITING TO BE AROUND!
SHOULD WE EVEN BE DOING THIS?
YAAY
POFF
PO-POFF
YAAY
YAAY
YAAY
YAAY
YAAY
THIS IS INCREDIBLE!
I EXPECTED A LOT OF RACERS, BUT I DIDN'T EXPECT SO MANY PEOPLE TO COME WATCH.

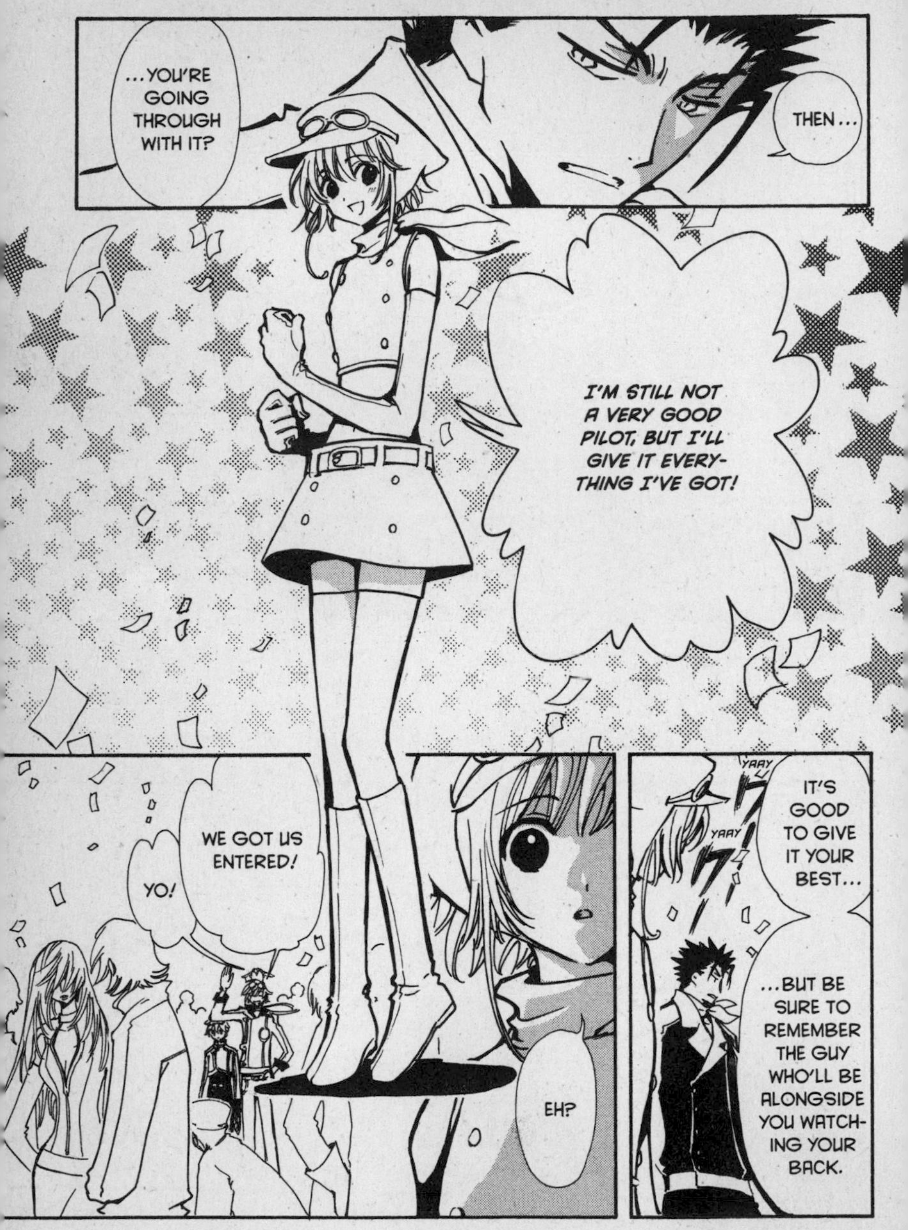
THEN...
...YOU'RE GOING THROUGH WITH IT?
I'M STILL NOT A VERY GOOD PILOT, BUT I'LL GIVE IT EVERY-THING I'VE GOT!
YAAY
YAAY
IT'S GOOD TO GIVE IT YOUR BEST...
...BUT BE SURE TO REMEMBER THE GUY WHO'LL BE ALONGSIDE YOU WATCH-ING YOUR BACK.
EH?
WE GOT US ENTERED!
YO!

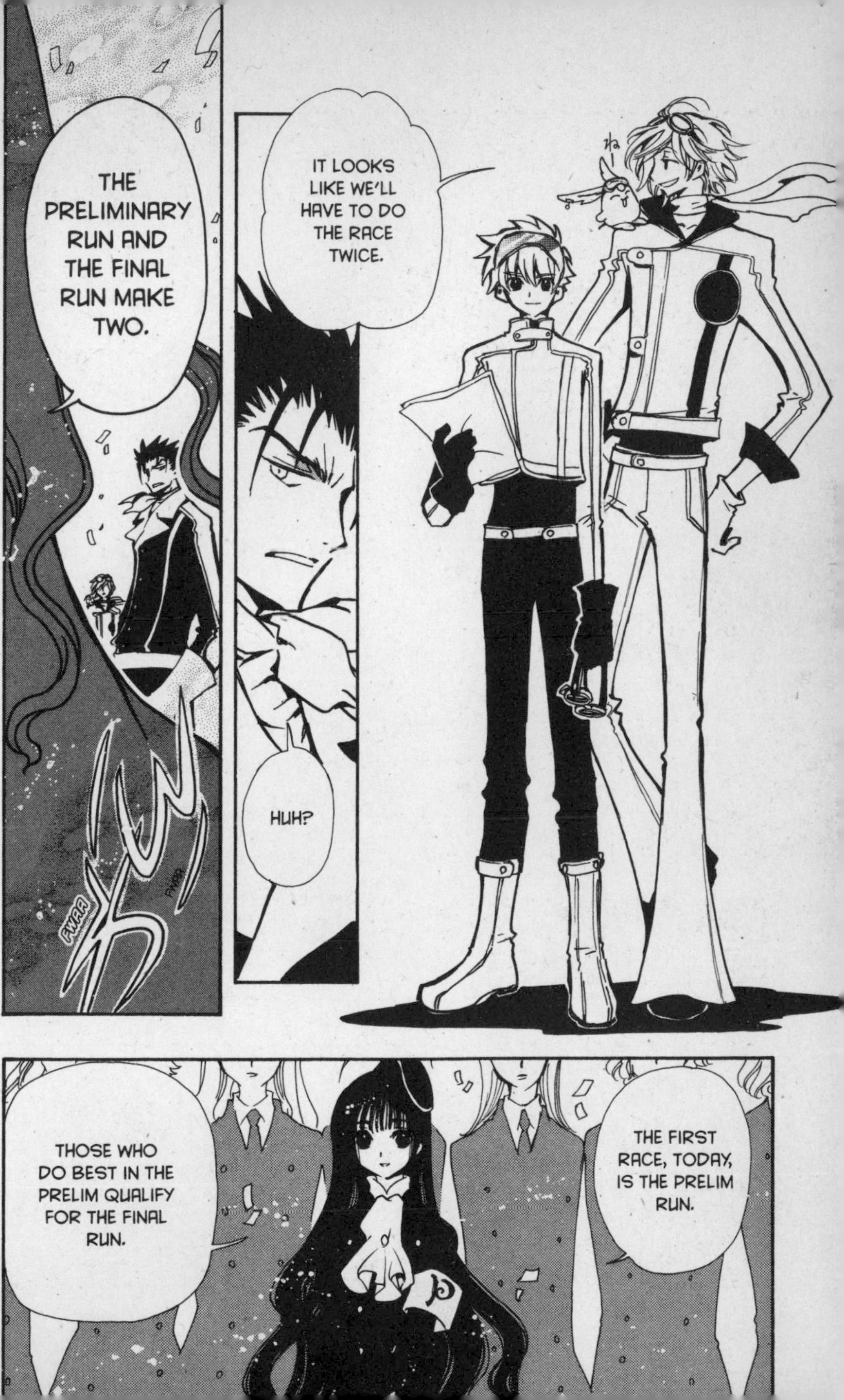
IT LOOKS LIKE WE'LL HAVE TO DO THE RACE TWICE.
HUH?
THE PRELIMINARY RUN AND THE FINAL RUN MAKE TWO.
FWAA
THE FIRST RACE, TODAY, IS THE PRELIM RUN.
THOSE WHO DO BEST IN THE PRELIM QUALIFY FOR THE FINAL RUN.

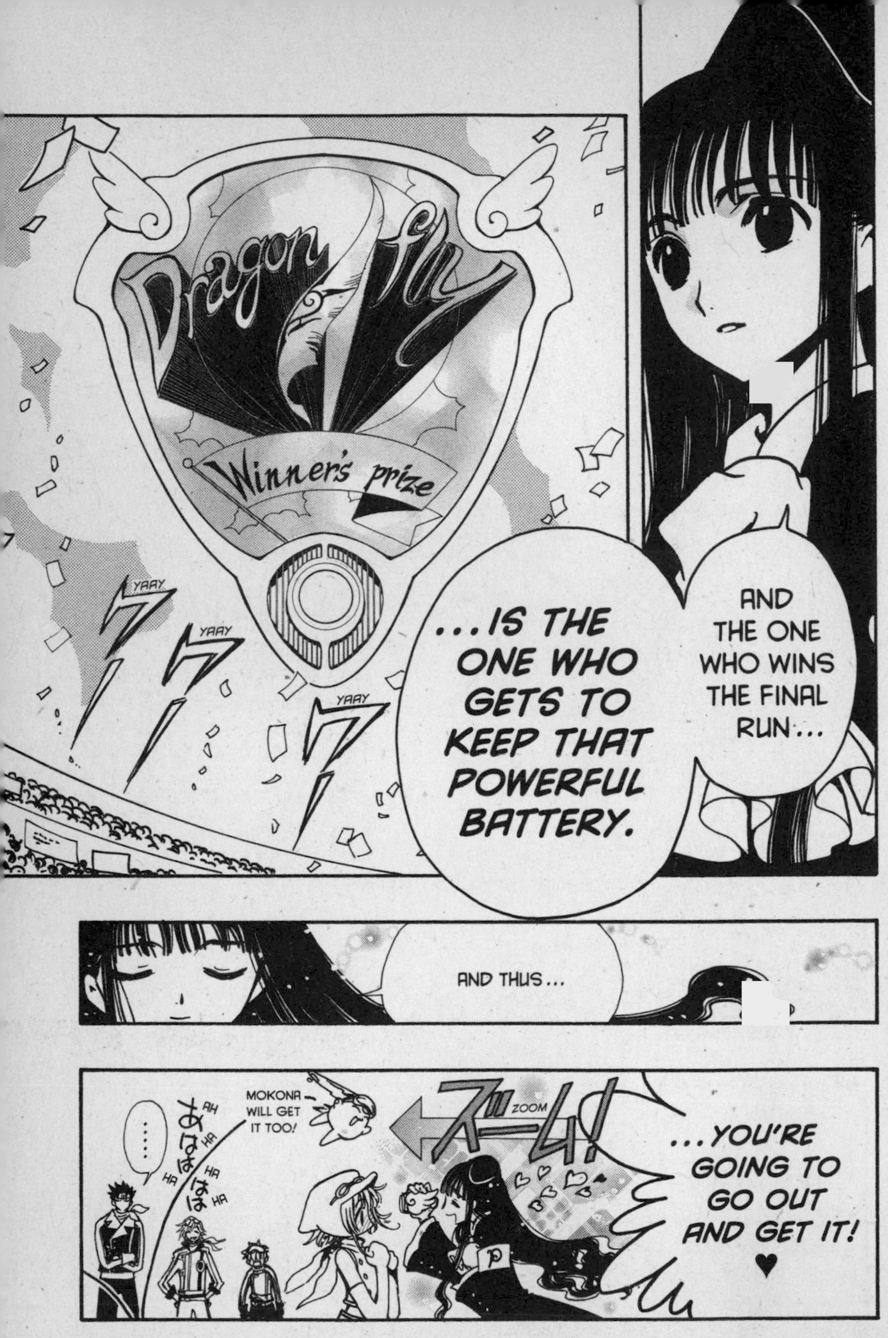
AND THE ONE WHO WINS THE FINAL RUN...
...IS THE ONE WHO GETS TO KEEP THAT POWERFUL BATTERY.
Dragon fly
Winner's prize
YAAY
YAAY
YAAY
AND THUS...
...YOU'RE GOING TO GO OUT AND GET IT! ♥
ZOOM
MOKONA WILL GET IT TOO!
AH HA HA HA HA HA
......

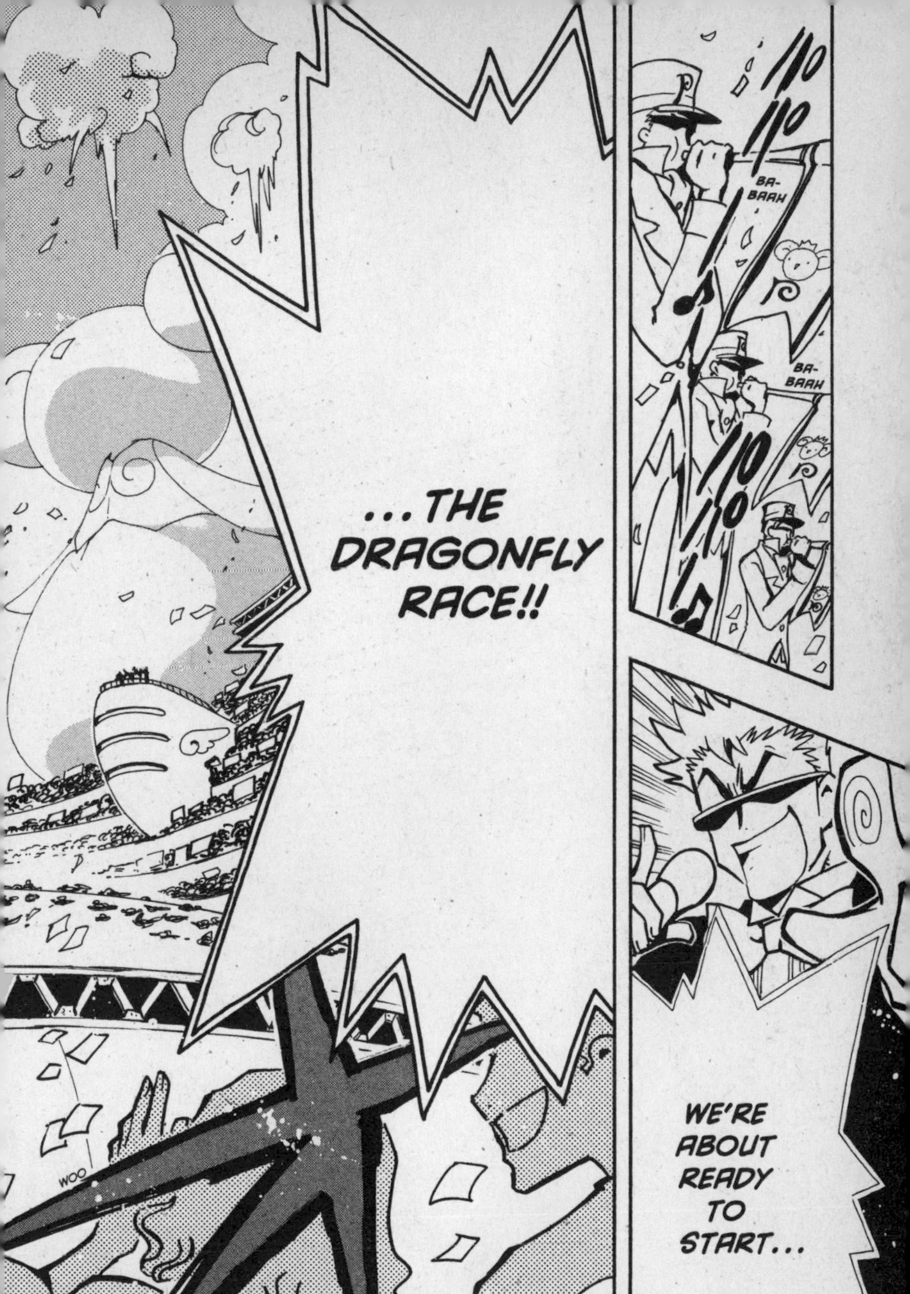
BA-BAAH
BA-BAAH
WE'RE ABOUT READY TO START...
...THE DRAGONFLY RACE!!
WOO

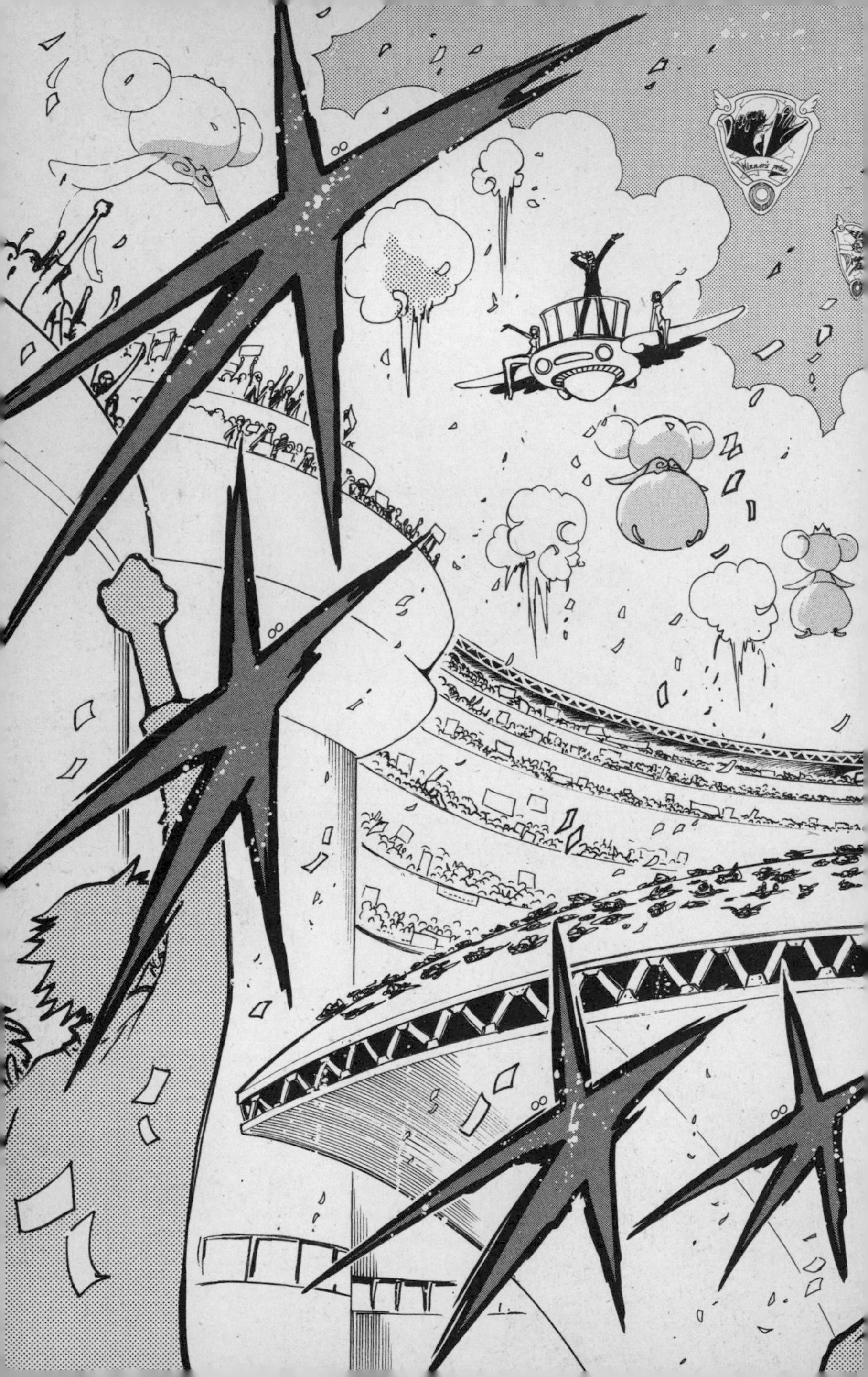
Dragon Fly
Winner's prize

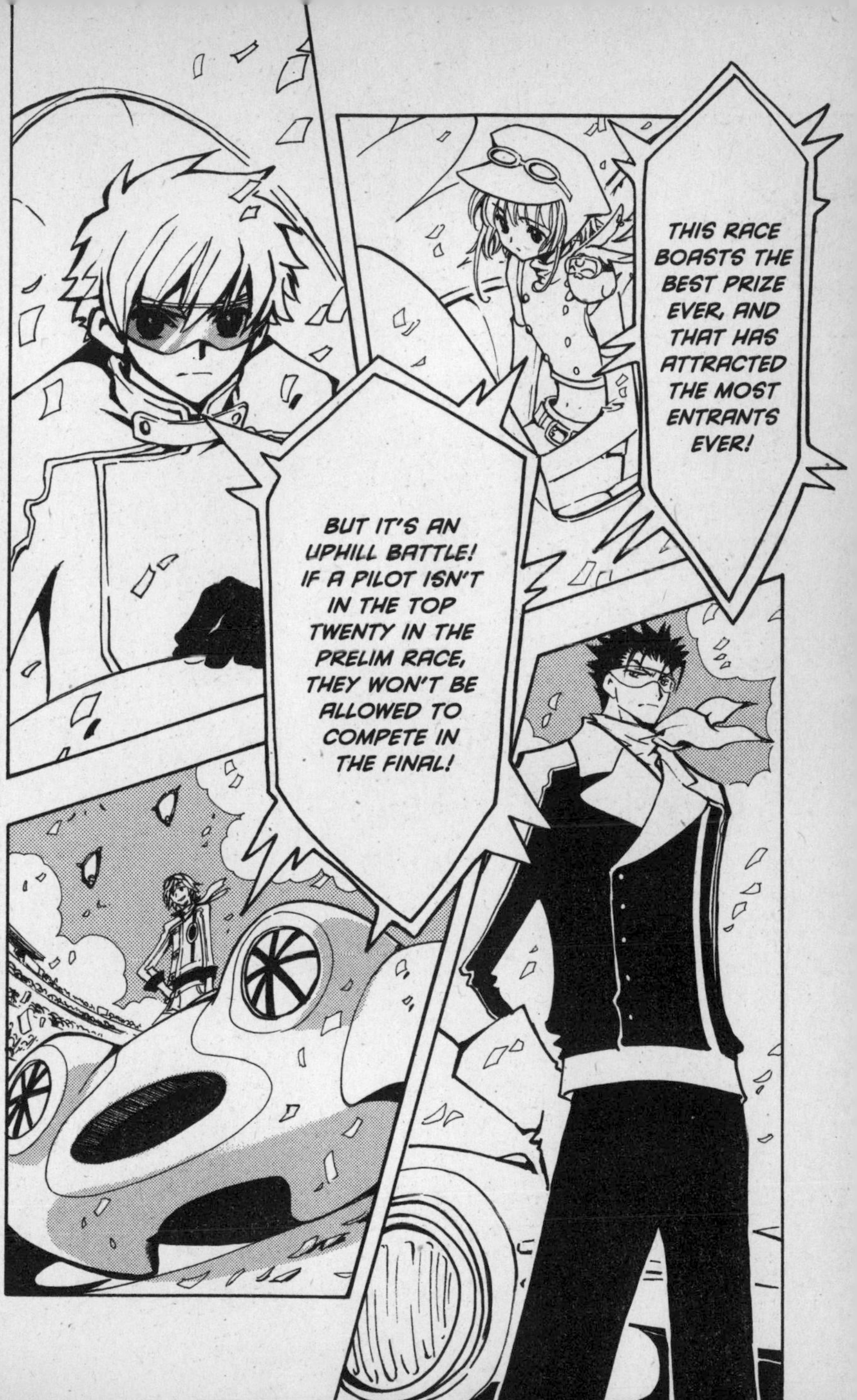
THIS RACE BOASTS THE BEST PRIZE EVER, AND THAT HAS ATTRACTED THE MOST ENTRANTS EVER!
BUT IT'S AN UPHILL BATTLE! IF A PILOT ISN'T IN THE TOP TWENTY IN THE PRELIM RACE, THEY WON'T BE ALLOWED TO COMPETE IN THE FINAL!

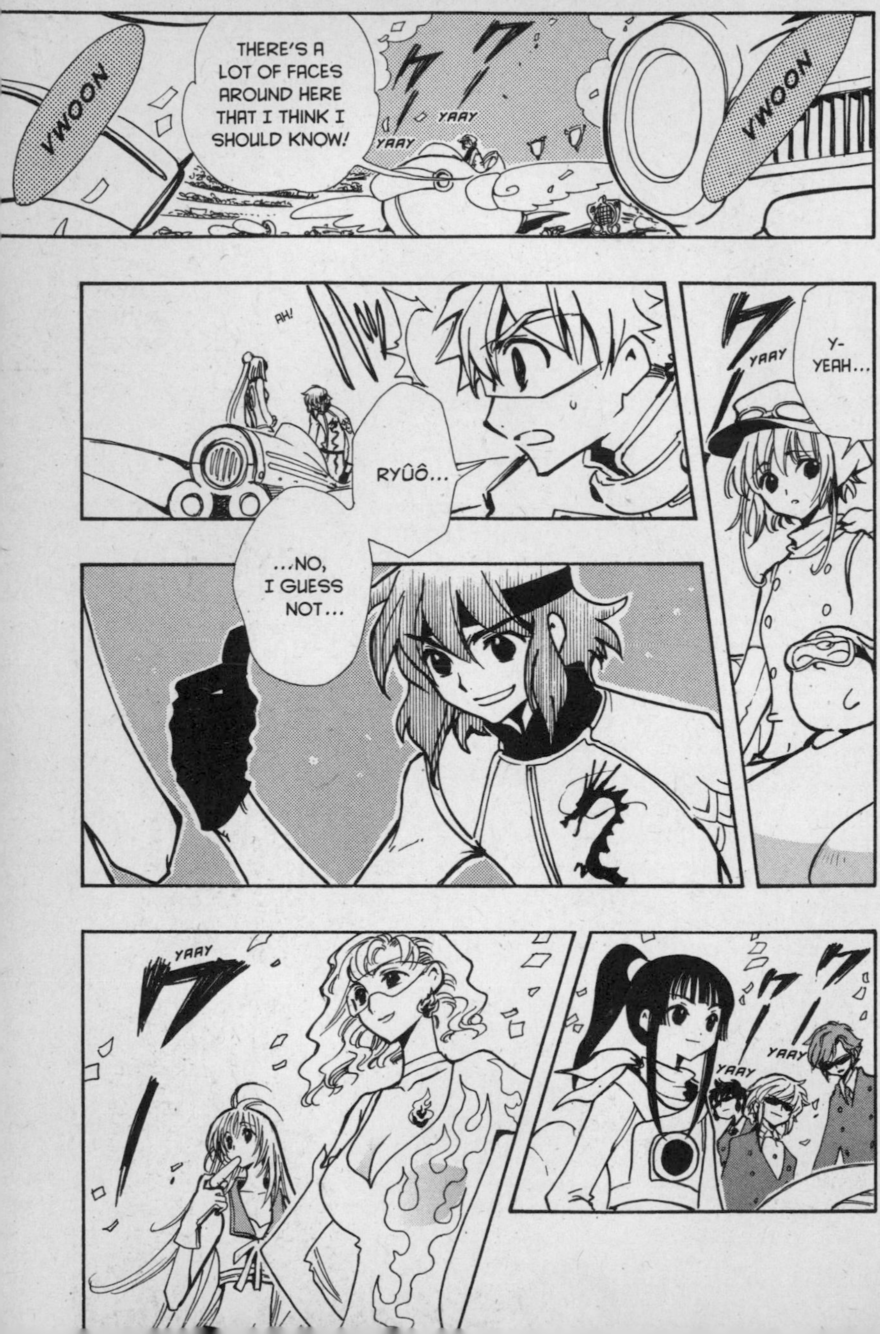
VWOON
YAAY
YAAY
THERE'S A LOT OF FACES AROUND HERE THAT I THINK I SHOULD KNOW!
VWOON
YAAY
Y-YEAH...
AH!
RYÛÔ...
...NO, I GUESS NOT...
YAAY
YAAY
YAAY

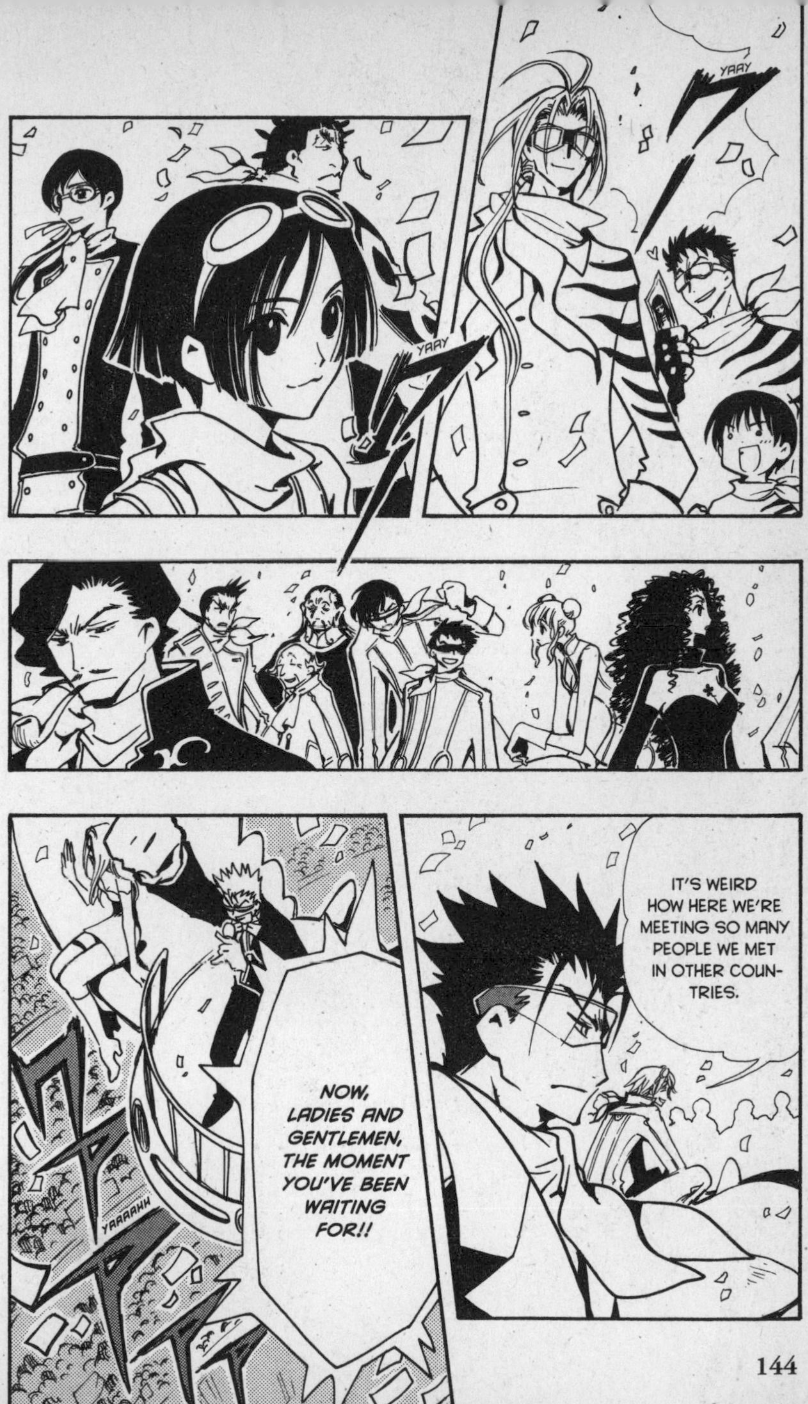
YAAY
YAAY
IT'S WEIRD HOW HERE WE'RE MEETING SO MANY PEOPLE WE MET IN OTHER COUN-TRIES.
NOW, LADIES AND GENTLEMEN, THE MOMENT YOU'VE BEEN WAITING FOR!!
YAAAAHH

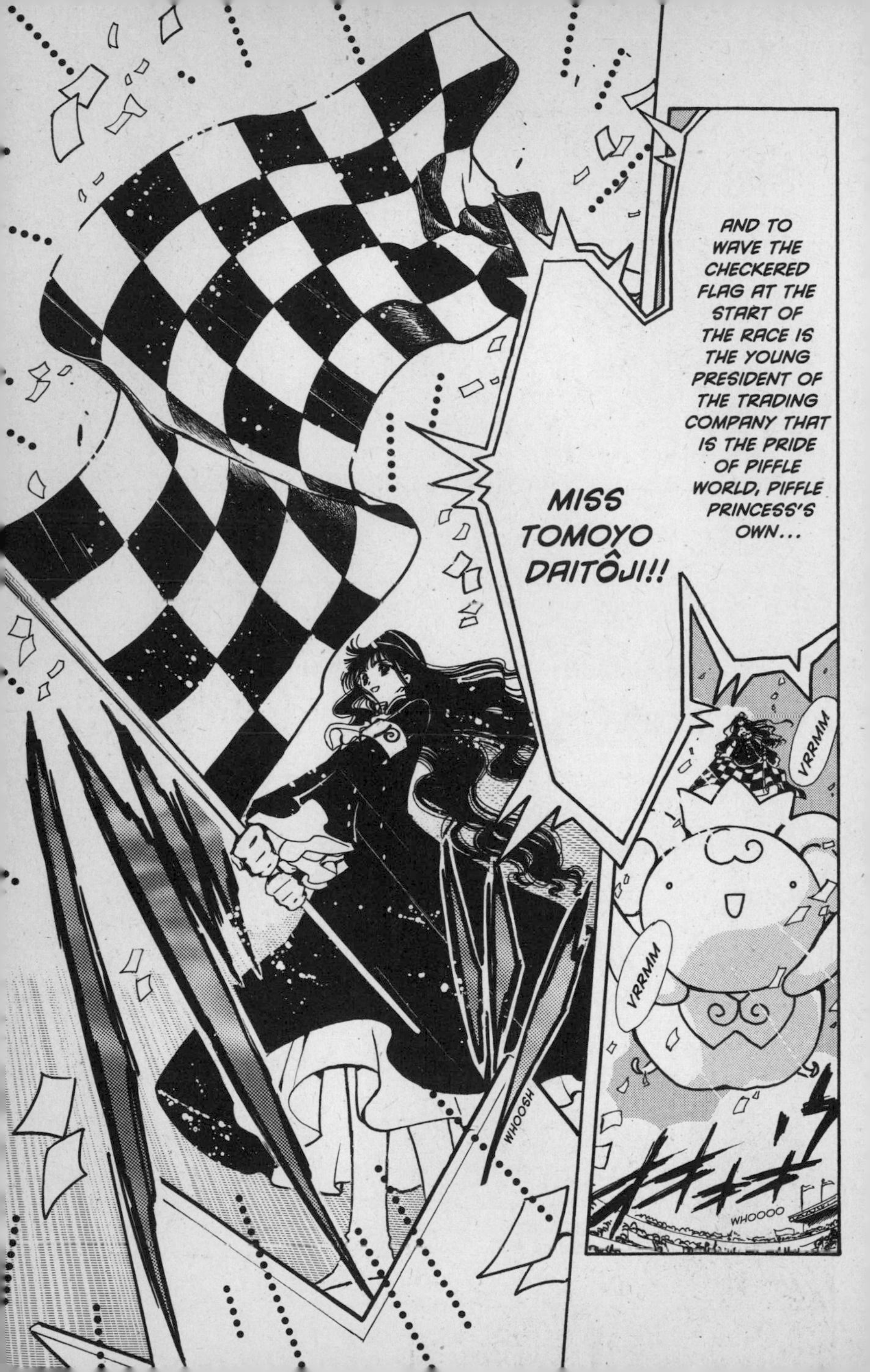
AND TO WAVE THE CHECKERED FLAG AT THE START OF THE RACE IS THE YOUNG PRESIDENT OF THE TRADING COMPANY THAT IS THE PRIDE OF PIFFLE WORLD, PIFFLE PRINCESS'S OWN...
VRRMM
VRRMM
WHOOOO
MISS TOMOYO DAITÔJI!!
WHOOSH

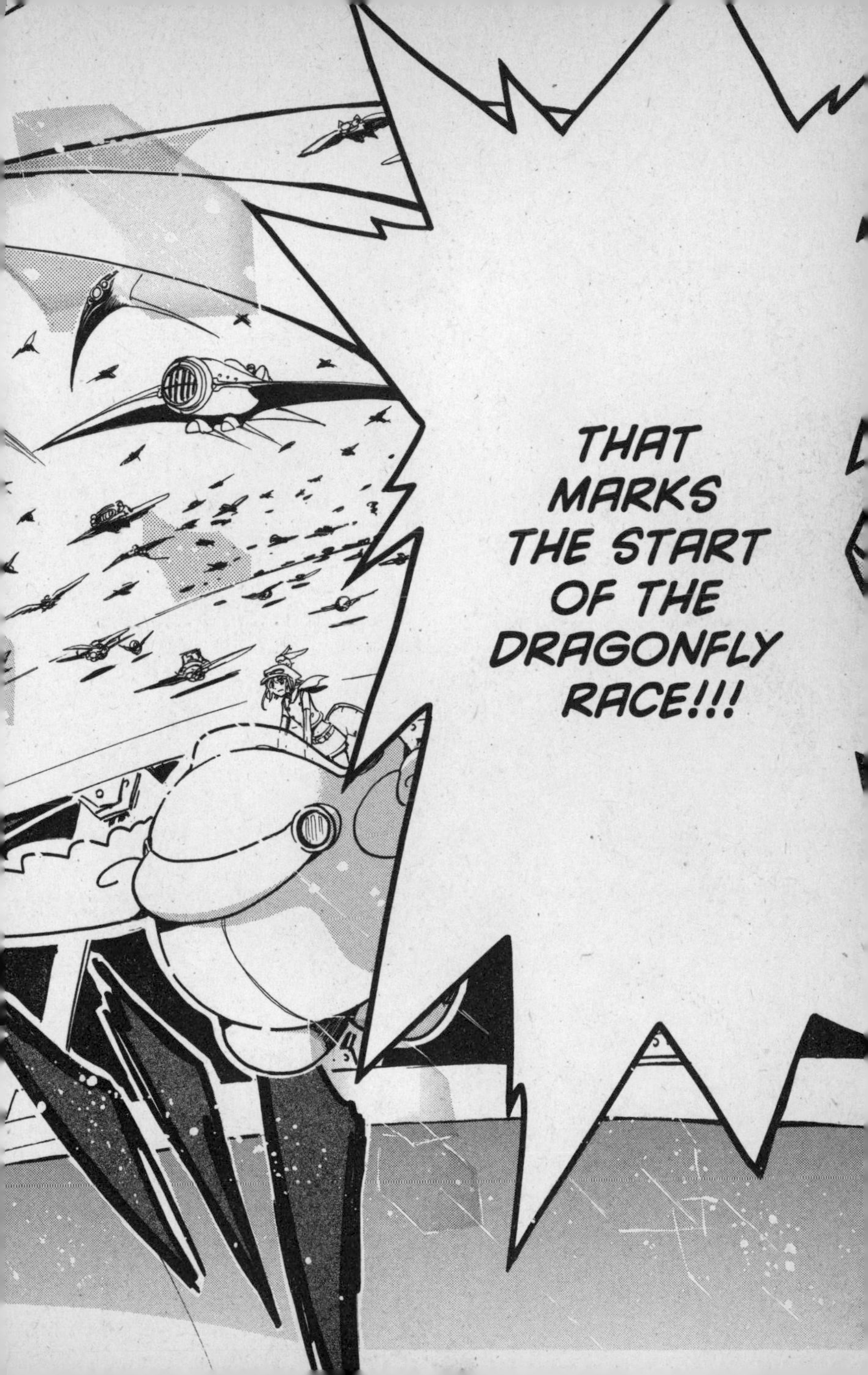
THAT MARKS THE START OF THE DRAGONFLY RACE!!!

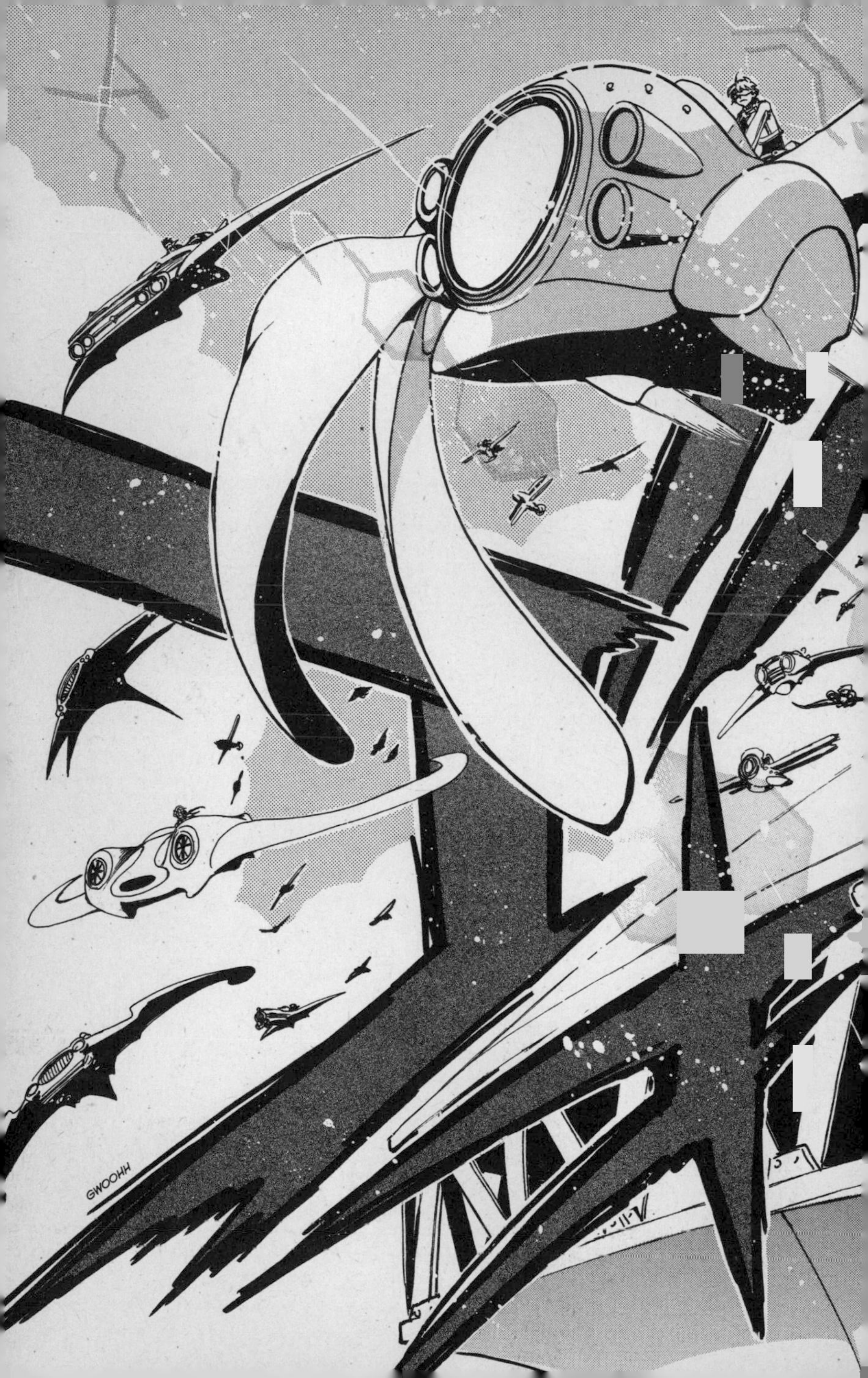
GWOOHH

ツバサ

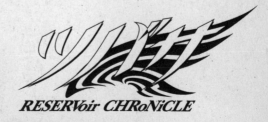

RESERVoir CHRoNiCLE

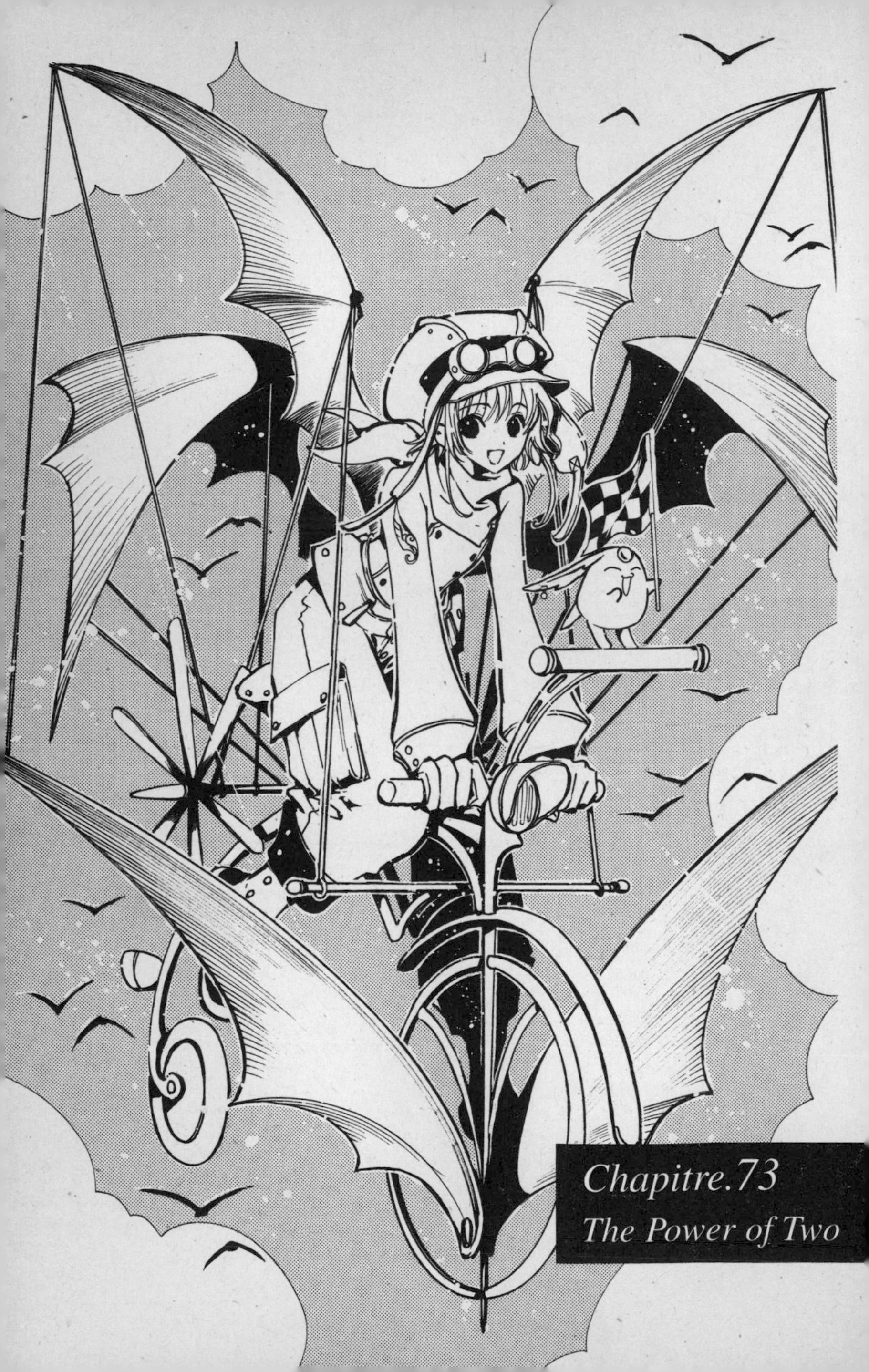
Chapitre.73
The Power of Two

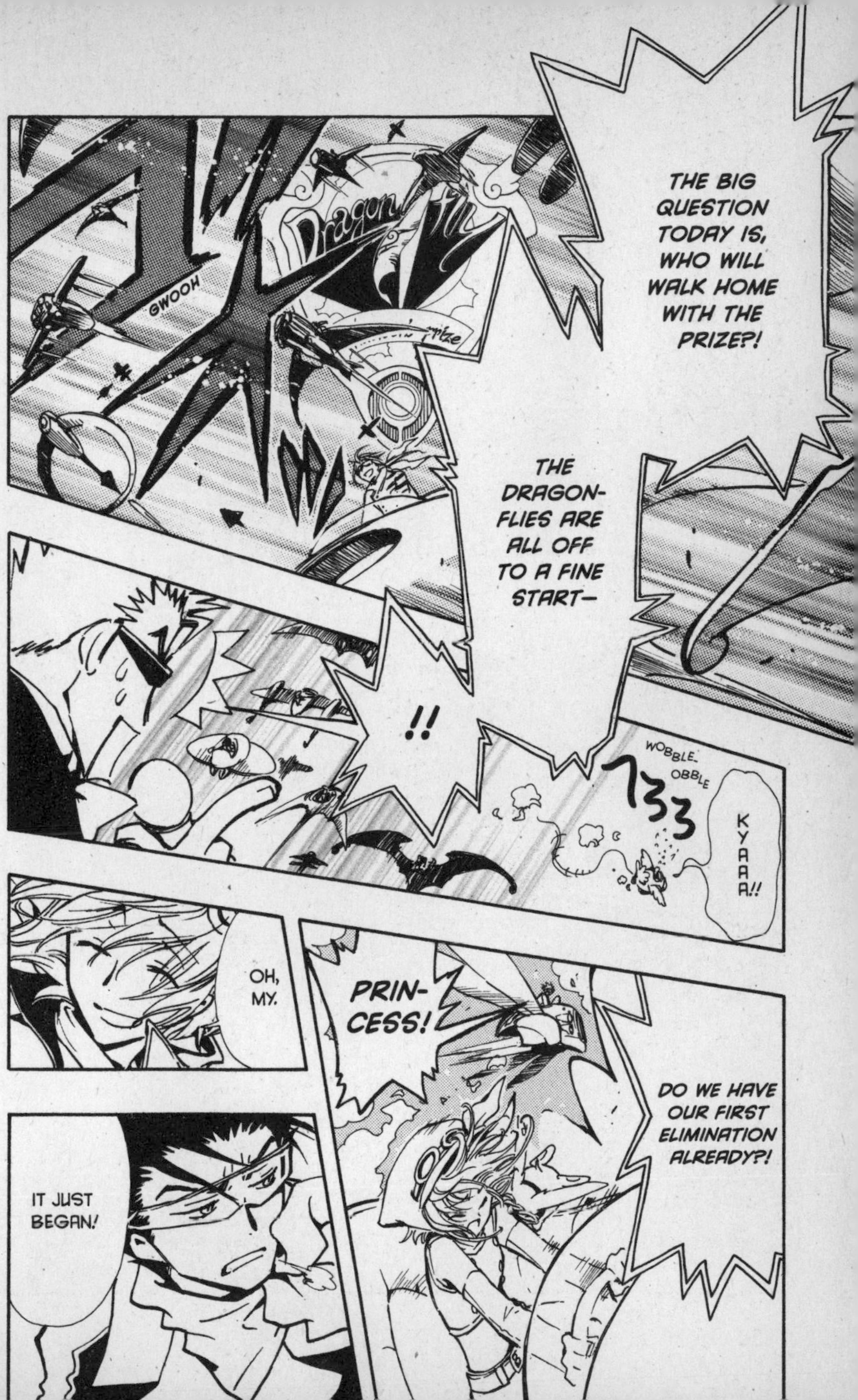
THE BIG QUESTION TODAY IS, WHO WILL WALK HOME WITH THE PRIZE?!
THE DRAGON-FLIES ARE ALL OFF TO A FINE START—
GWOOH
KYAAA!!
WOBBLE-OBBLE
!!
PRIN-CESS!
DO WE HAVE OUR FIRST ELIMINATION ALREADY?!
OH, MY.
IT JUST BEGAN!

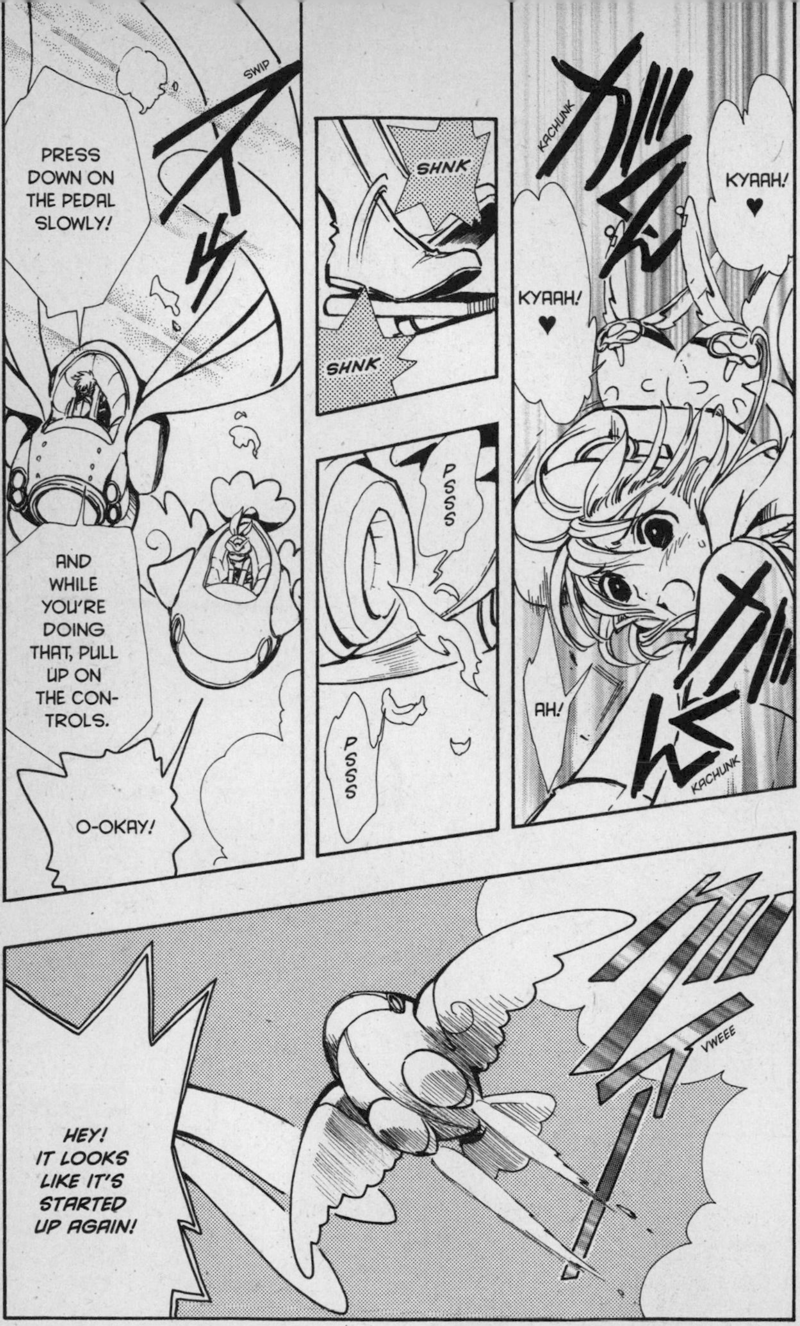
KYAAH! ♥
KACHUNK
KYAAH! ♥
AH!
KACHUNK
SHNK
SHNK
PSSS
PSSS
SWIP
PRESS DOWN ON THE PEDAL SLOWLY!
AND WHILE YOU'RE DOING THAT, PULL UP ON THE CON-TROLS.
O-OKAY!
VWEEE
HEY! IT LOOKS LIKE IT'S STARTED UP AGAIN!

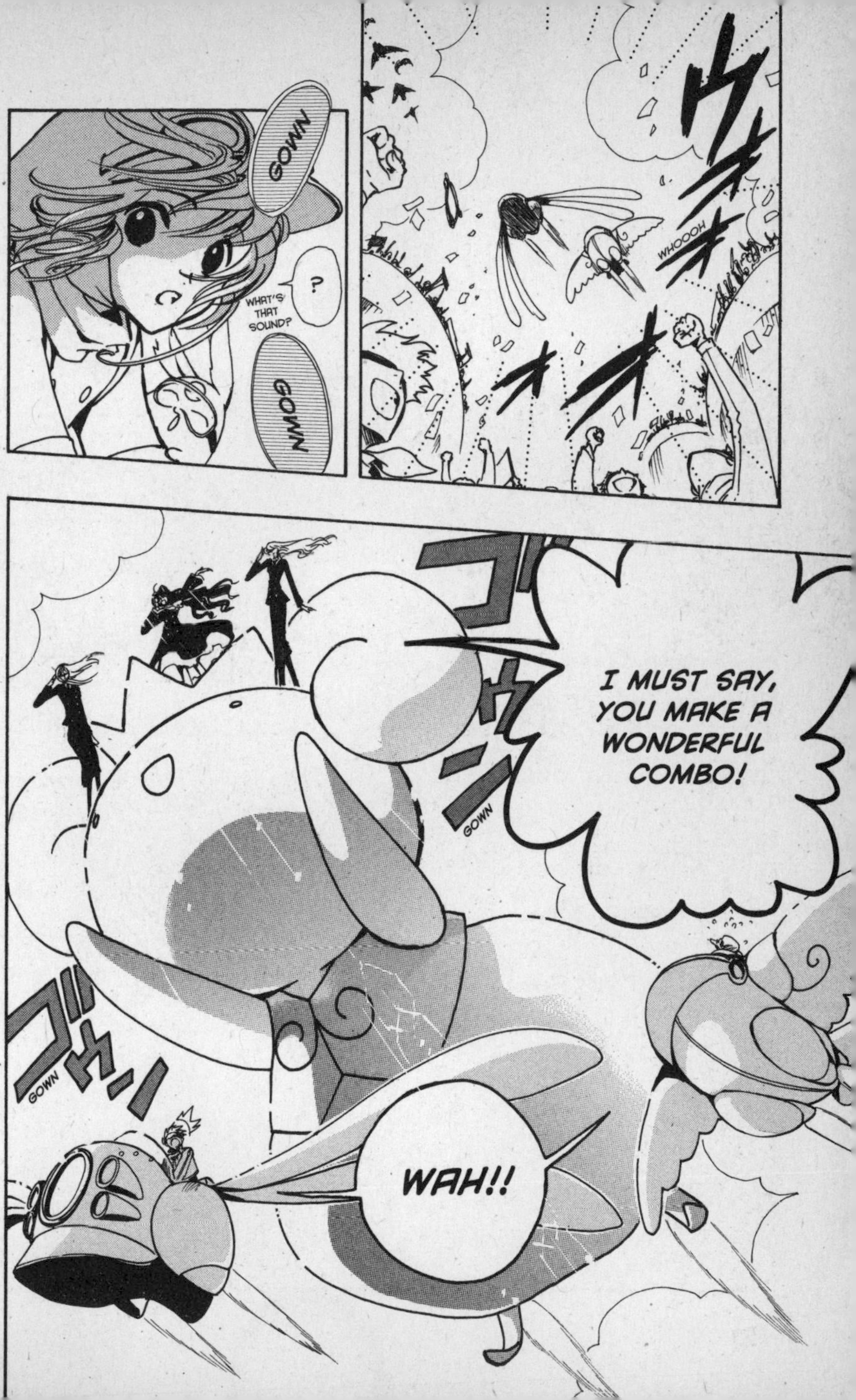
WHOOOH
GOWN
?
WHAT'S THAT SOUND?
GOWN
GOWN
I MUST SAY, YOU MAKE A WONDERFUL COMBO!
WAH!!
GOWN

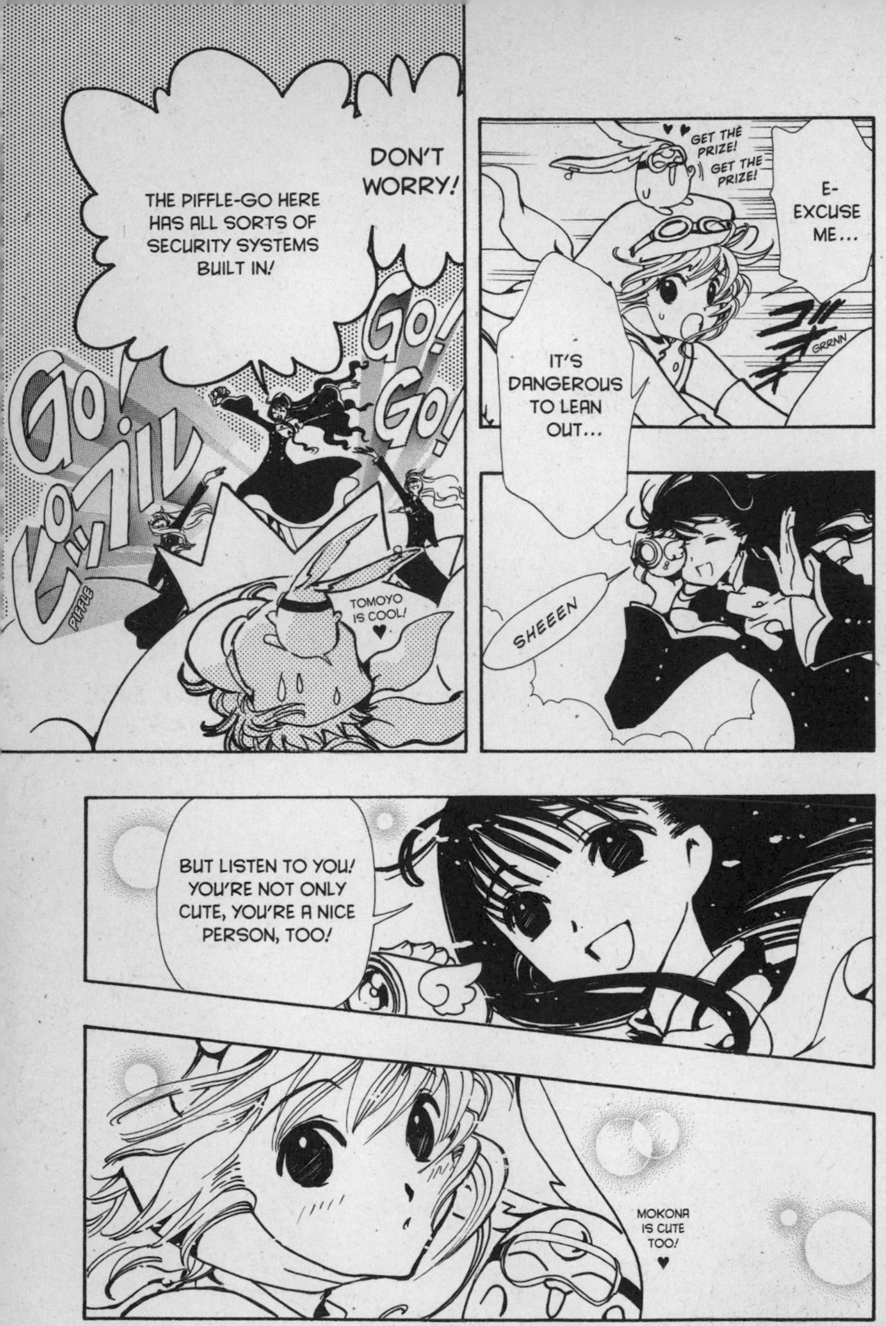
GET THE PRIZE!
GET THE PRIZE!
E- EXCUSE ME...
GRRNN
IT'S DANGEROUS TO LEAN OUT...
SHEEEN
DON'T WORRY!
THE PIFFLE-GO HERE HAS ALL SORTS OF SECURITY SYSTEMS BUILT IN!
GO! GO!
GO!
PIFFLE
TOMOYO IS COOL! ♥
BUT LISTEN TO YOU! YOU'RE NOT ONLY CUTE, YOU'RE A NICE PERSON, TOO!
MOKONA IS CUTE TOO! ♥

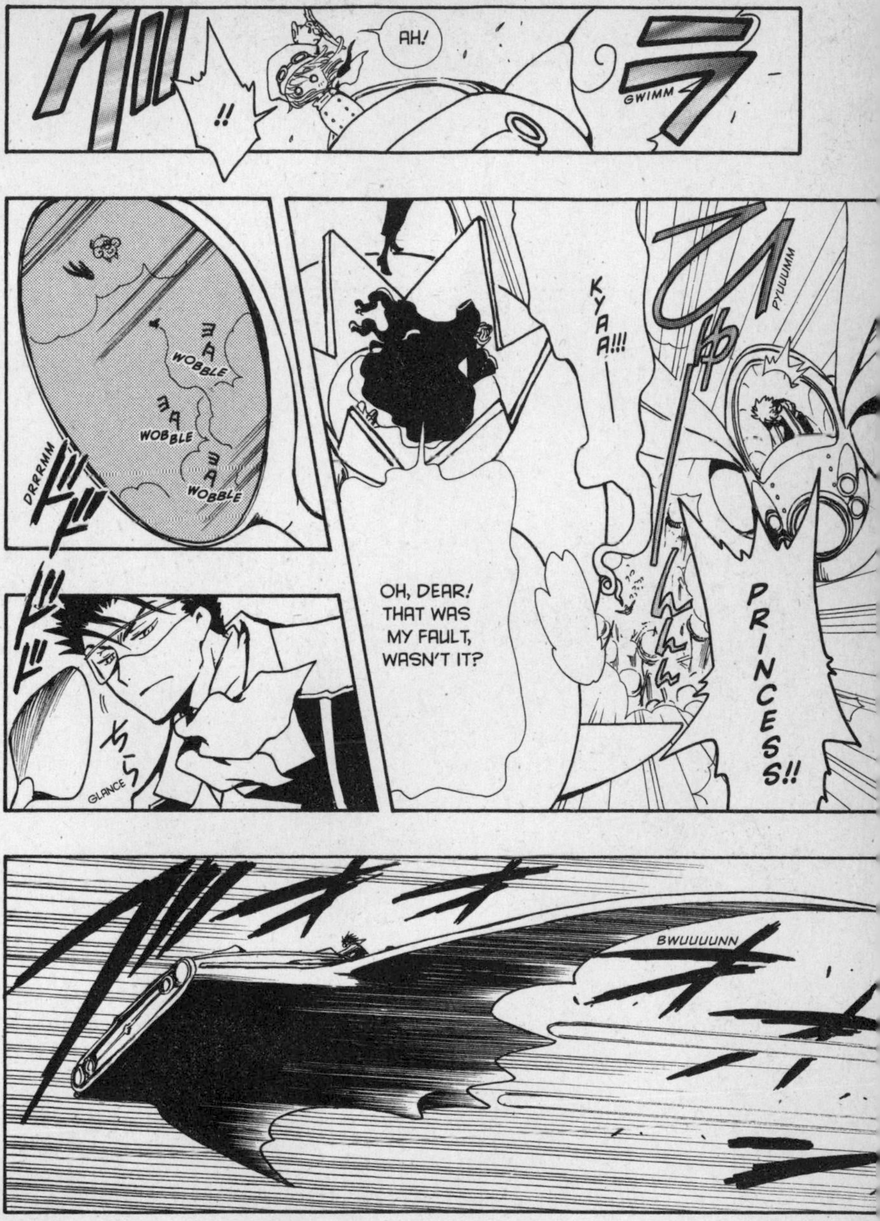
GWIMM
AH!
!!
PRINCESS!!
PYUUUMM
KYAA!!!
OH, DEAR! THAT WAS MY FAULT, WASN'T IT?
WOBBLE
WOBBLE
WOBBLE
DRRRMM
GLANCE
BWUUUUNN

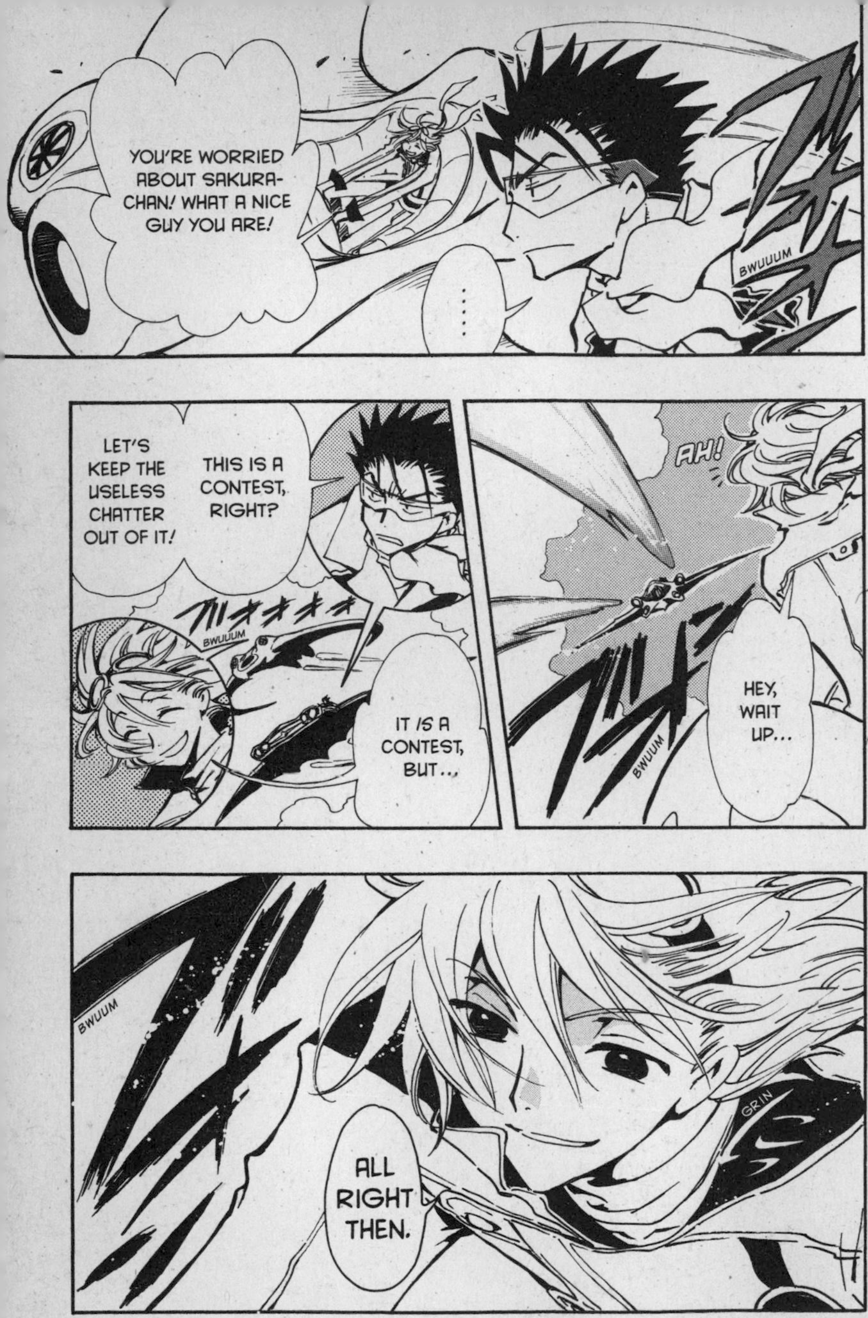

BWUUUM
YOU'RE WORRIED ABOUT SAKURA-CHAN! WHAT A NICE GUY YOU ARE!
......
AH!
HEY, WAIT UP...
BWUUUM
THIS IS A CONTEST, RIGHT?
LET'S KEEP THE USELESS CHATTER OUT OF IT!
BWUUUM
IT IS A CONTEST, BUT...
GRIN
ALL RIGHT THEN.
BWUUM

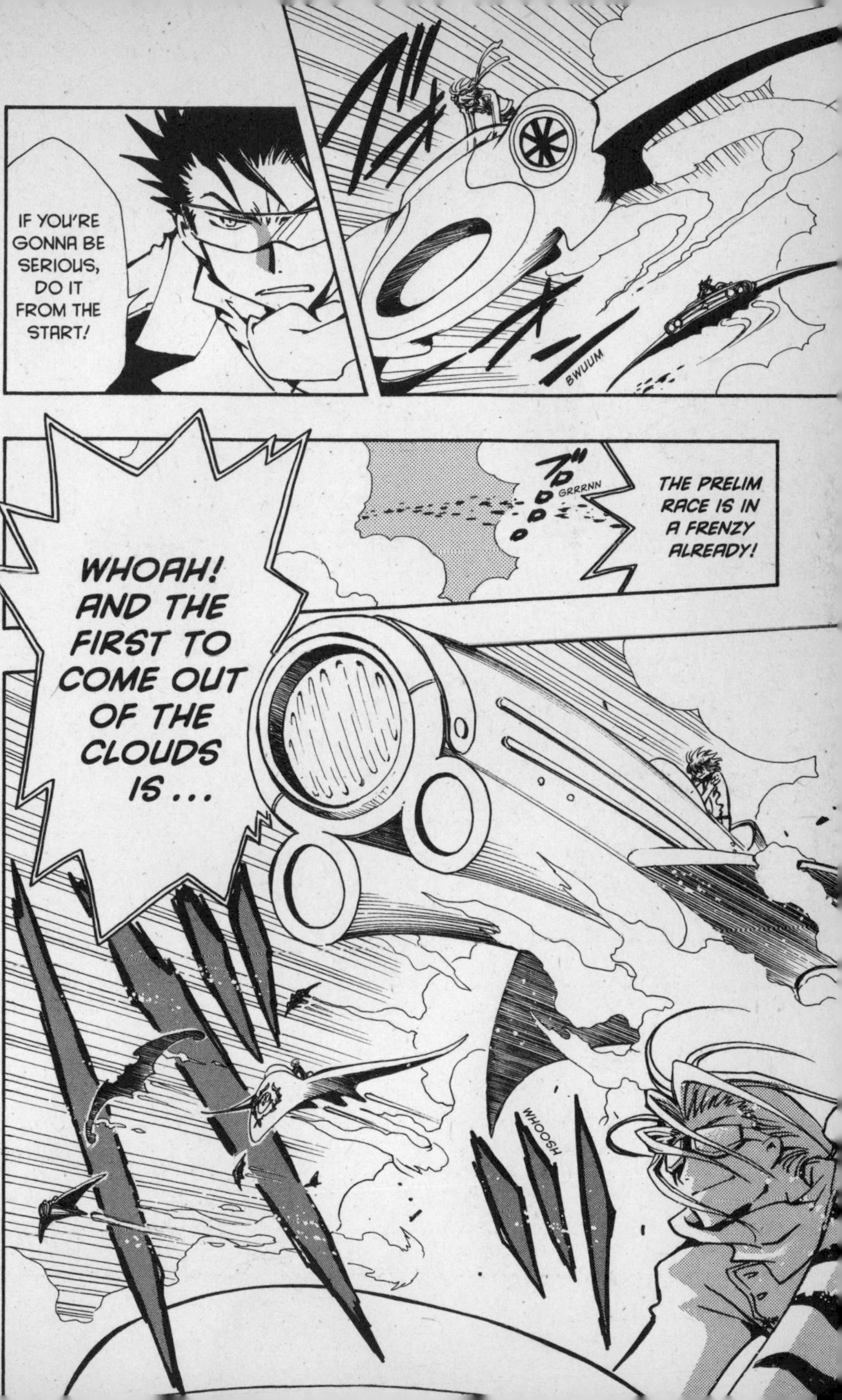
BWUUM
IF YOU'RE GONNA BE SERIOUS, DO IT FROM THE START!
GRRRNN
THE PRELIM RACE IS IN A FRENZY ALREADY!
WHOAH! AND THE FIRST TO COME OUT OF THE CLOUDS IS . . .
WHOOSH

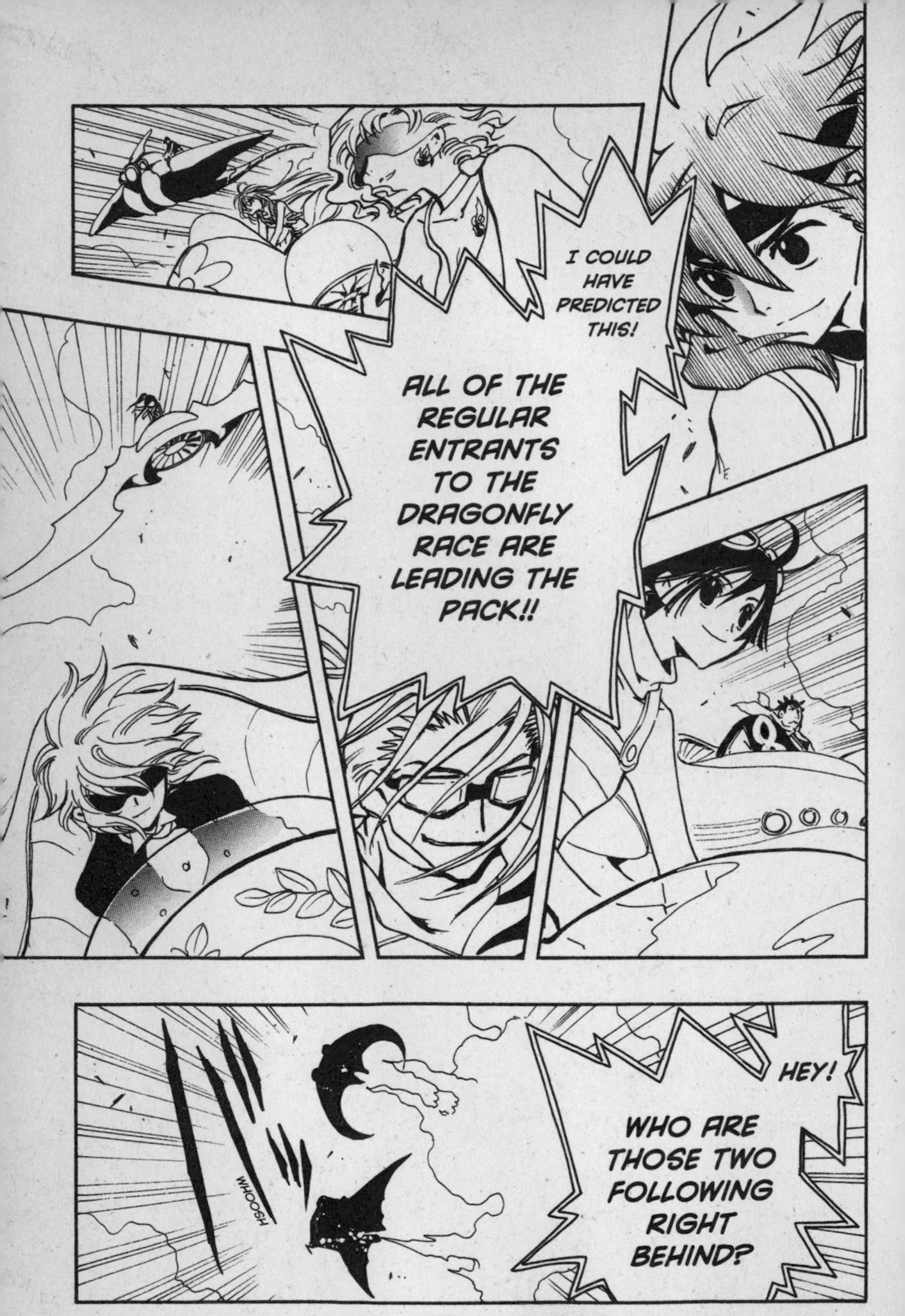
I COULD HAVE PREDICTED THIS!
ALL OF THE REGULAR ENTRANTS TO THE DRAGONFLY RACE ARE LEADING THE PACK!!
HEY!
WHO ARE THOSE TWO FOLLOWING RIGHT BEHIND?
WHOOSH

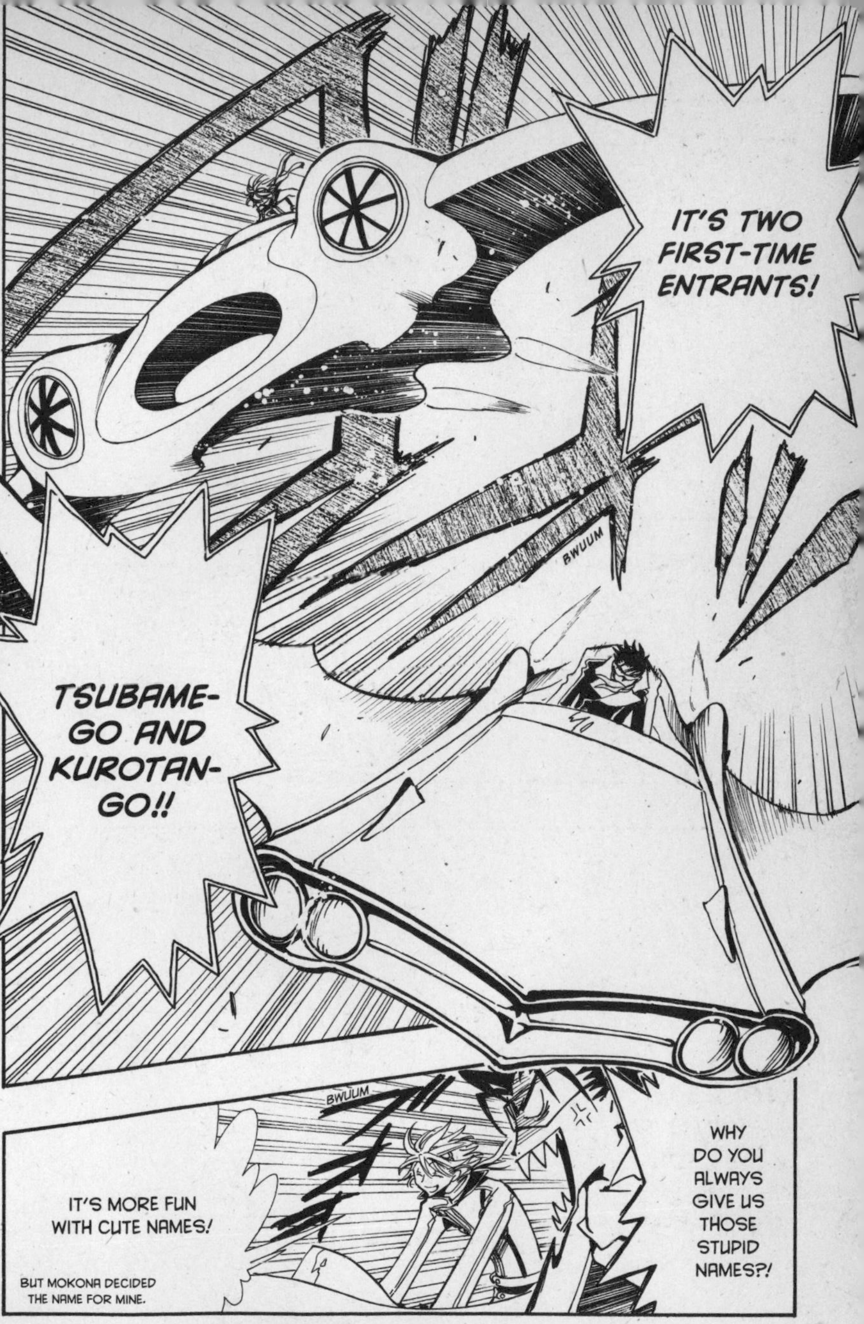
IT'S TWO FIRST-TIME ENTRANTS!
BWUUM
TSUBAME-GO AND KUROTAN-GO!!
BWUUM
WHY DO YOU ALWAYS GIVE US THOSE STUPID NAMES?!
IT'S MORE FUN WITH CUTE NAMES!
BUT MOKONA DECIDED THE NAME FOR MINE.

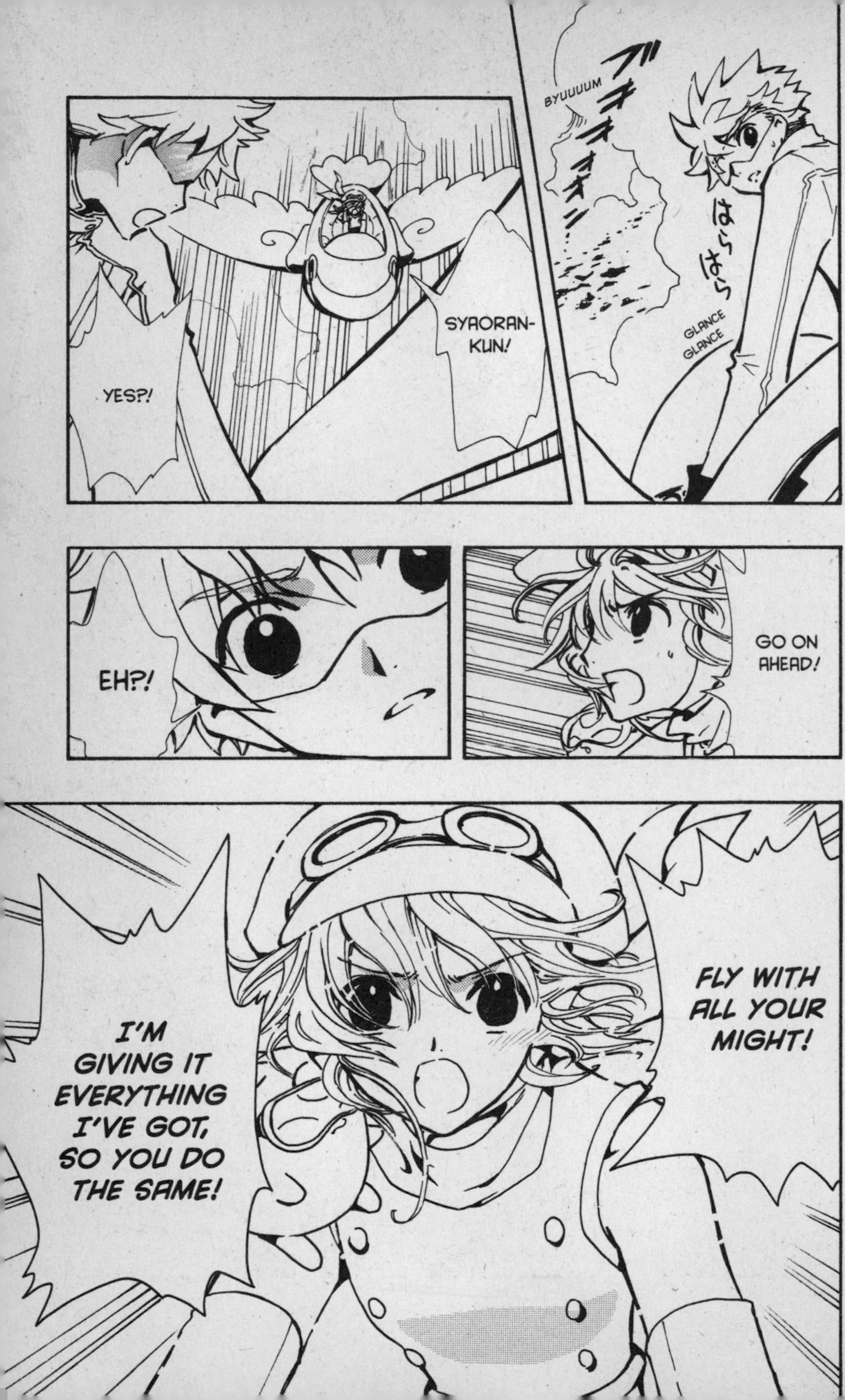
BYUUUUM
はらはら
GLANCE GLANCE
SYAORAN-KUN!
YES?!
GO ON AHEAD!
EH?!
FLY WITH ALL YOUR MIGHT!
I'M GIVING IT EVERYTHING I'VE GOT, SO YOU DO THE SAME!

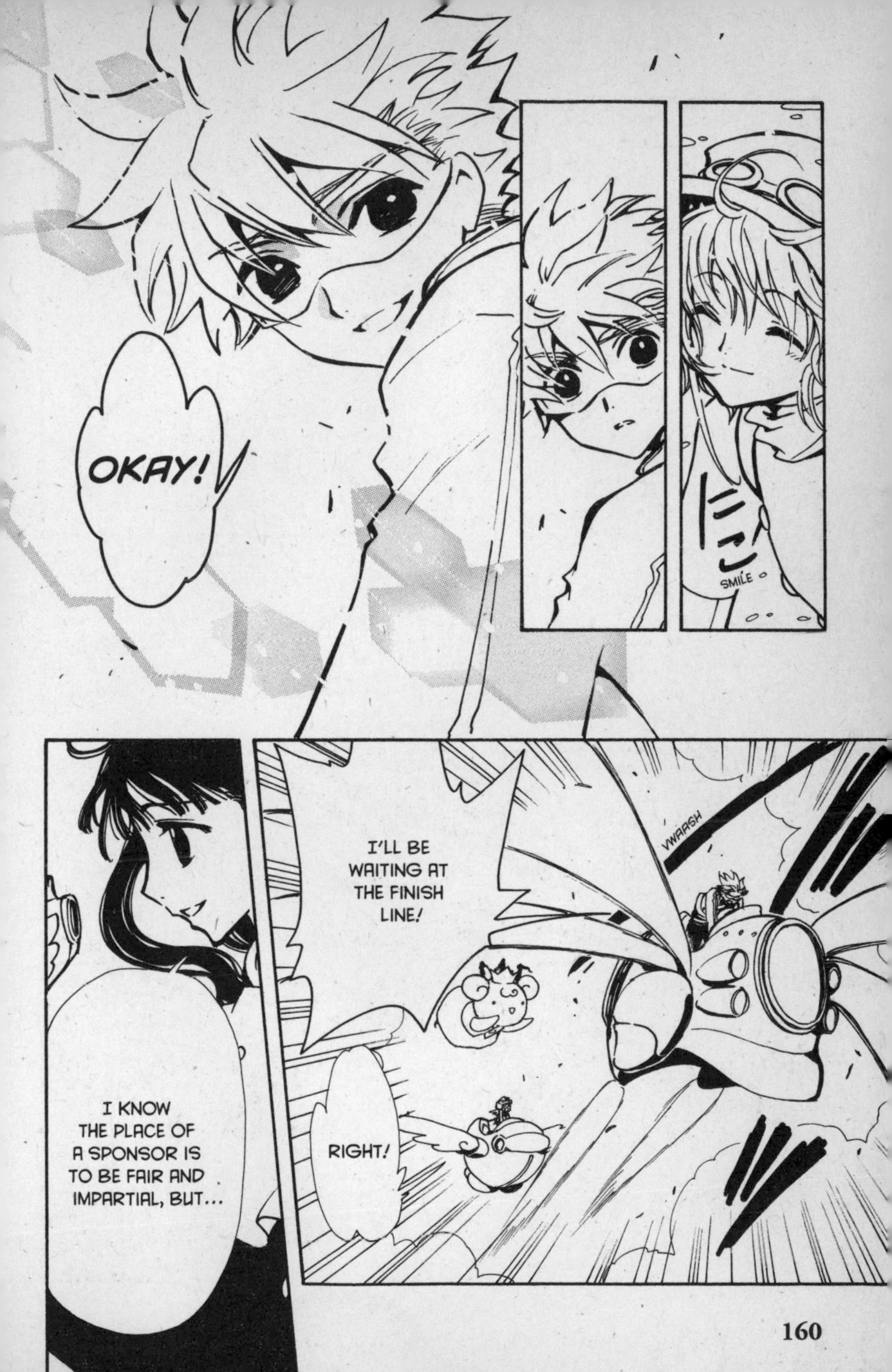
SMILE
OKAY!
I'LL BE WAITING AT THE FINISH LINE!
VWAASH
RIGHT!
I KNOW THE PLACE OF A SPONSOR IS TO BE FAIR AND IMPARTIAL, BUT...

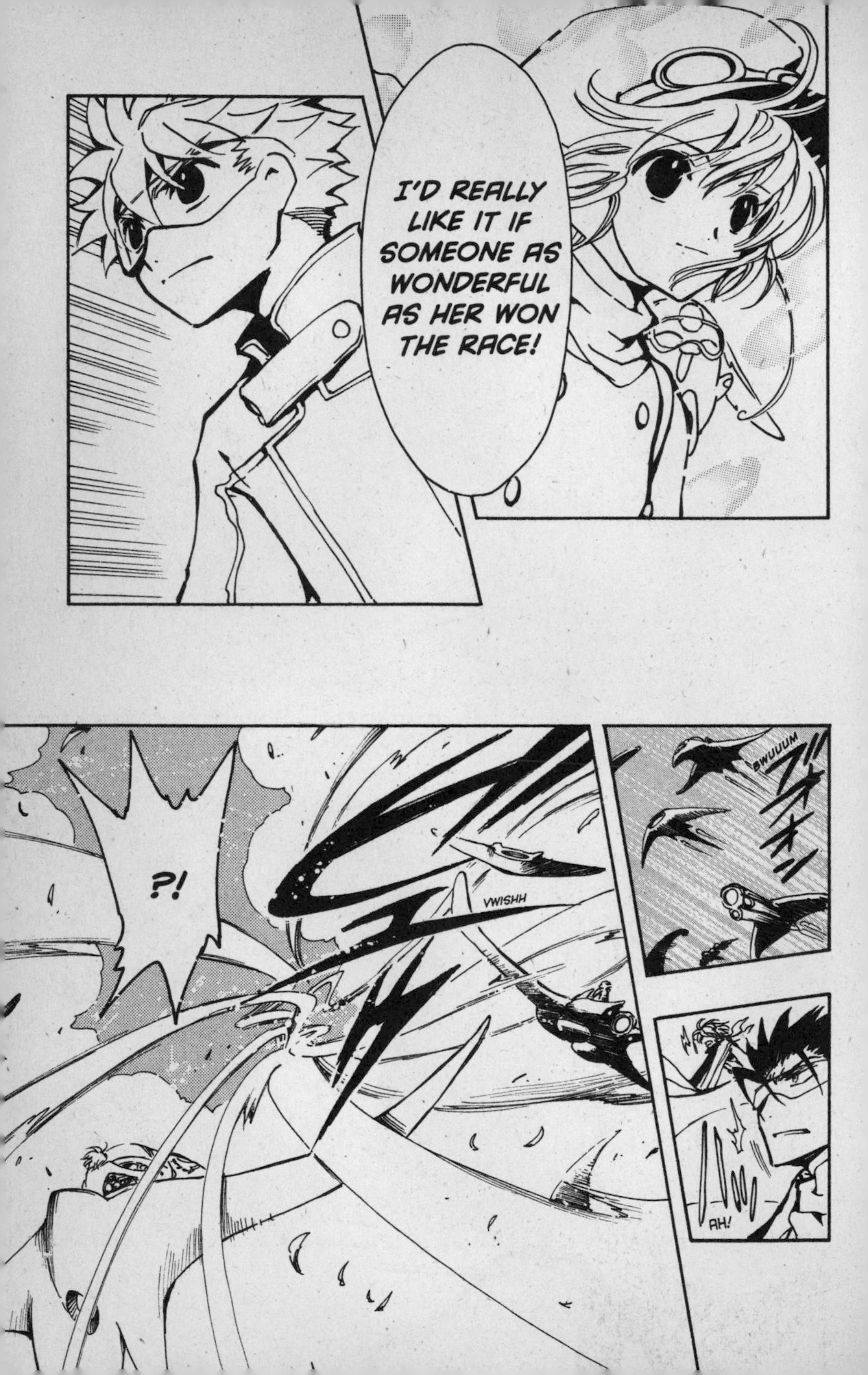
I'D REALLY LIKE IT IF SOMEONE AS WONDERFUL AS HER WON THE RACE!
BWUUUM
AH!
?!
VWISHH

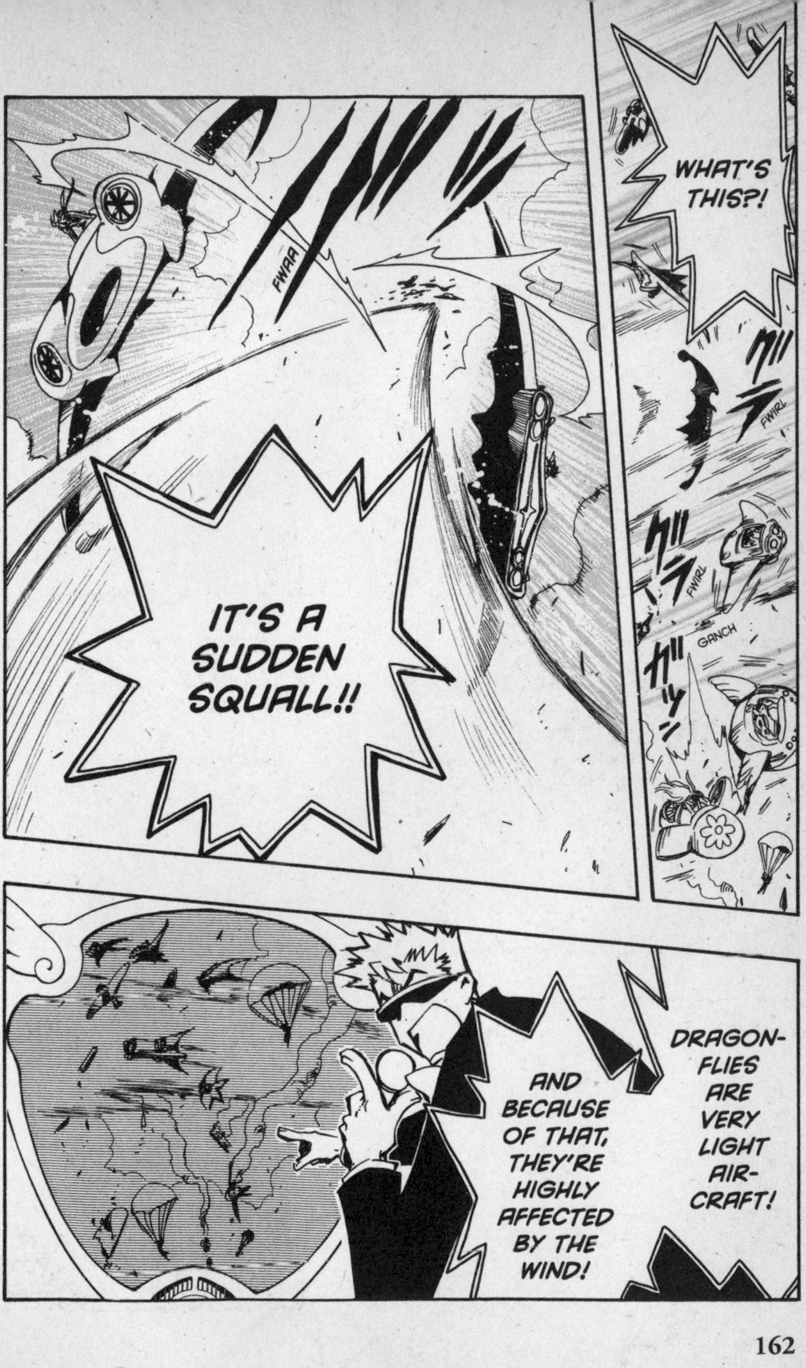

WHAT'S THIS?!
FWIRL
FWIRL
GANCH
FWAA
IT'S A SUDDEN SQUALL!!
DRAGON-FLIES ARE VERY LIGHT AIR-CRAFT!
AND BECAUSE OF THAT, THEY'RE HIGHLY AFFECTED BY THE WIND!

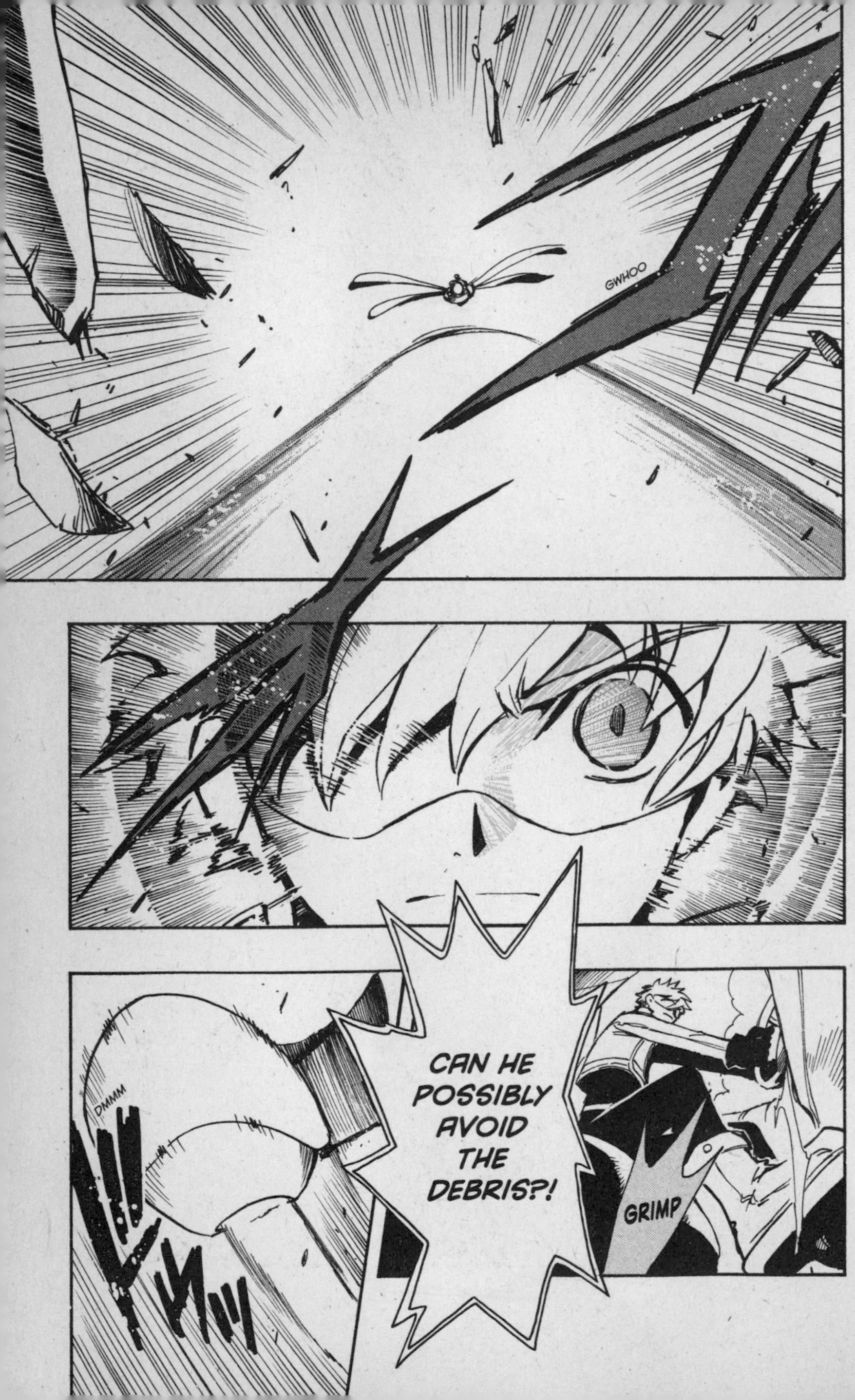
GWHOO
GRIMP
CAN HE POSSIBLY AVOID THE DEBRIS?!
DMMM

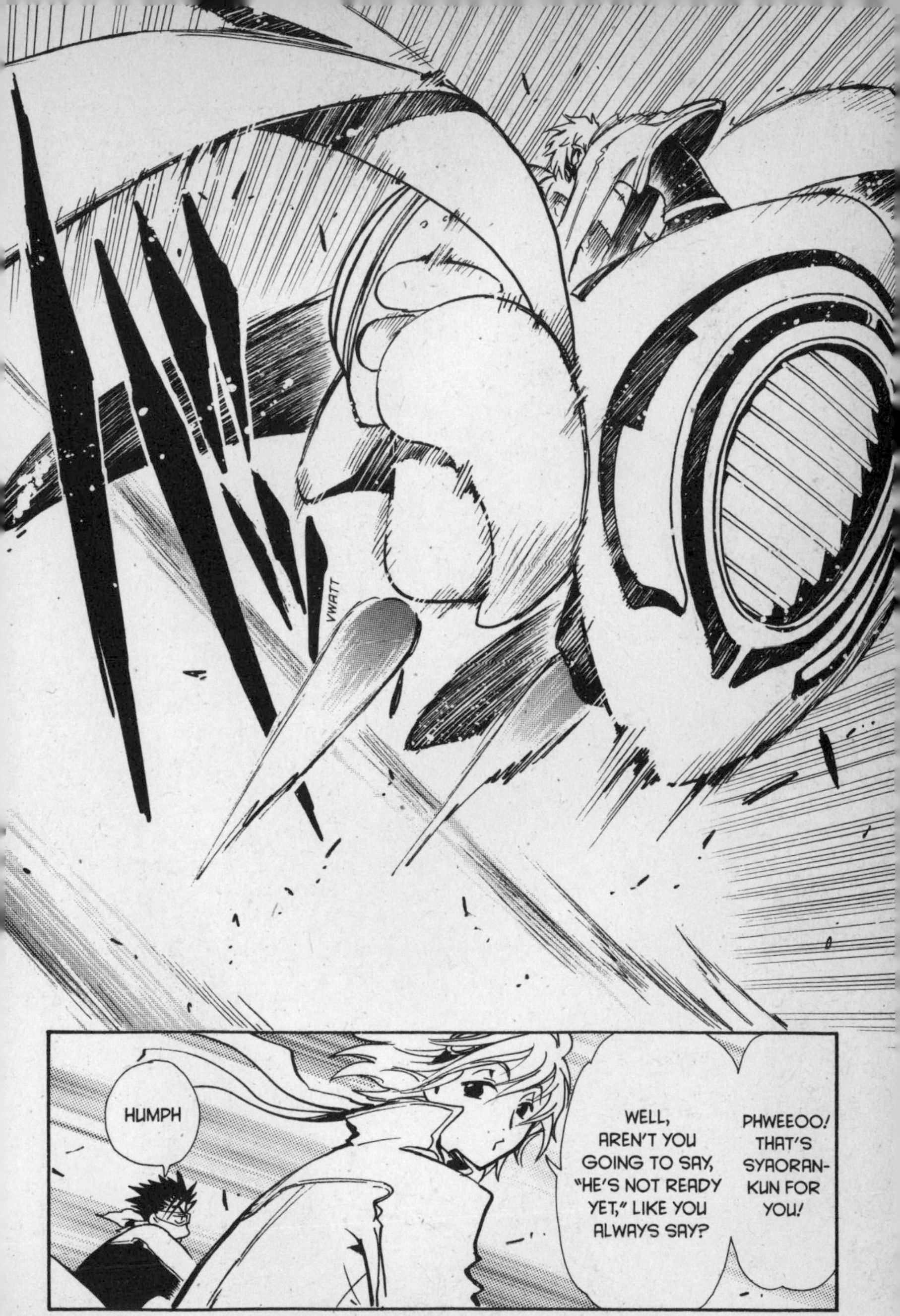
VWATT
PHWEEOO! THAT'S SYAORAN-KUN FOR YOU!
WELL, AREN'T YOU GOING TO SAY, "HE'S NOT READY YET," LIKE YOU ALWAYS SAY?
HUMPH

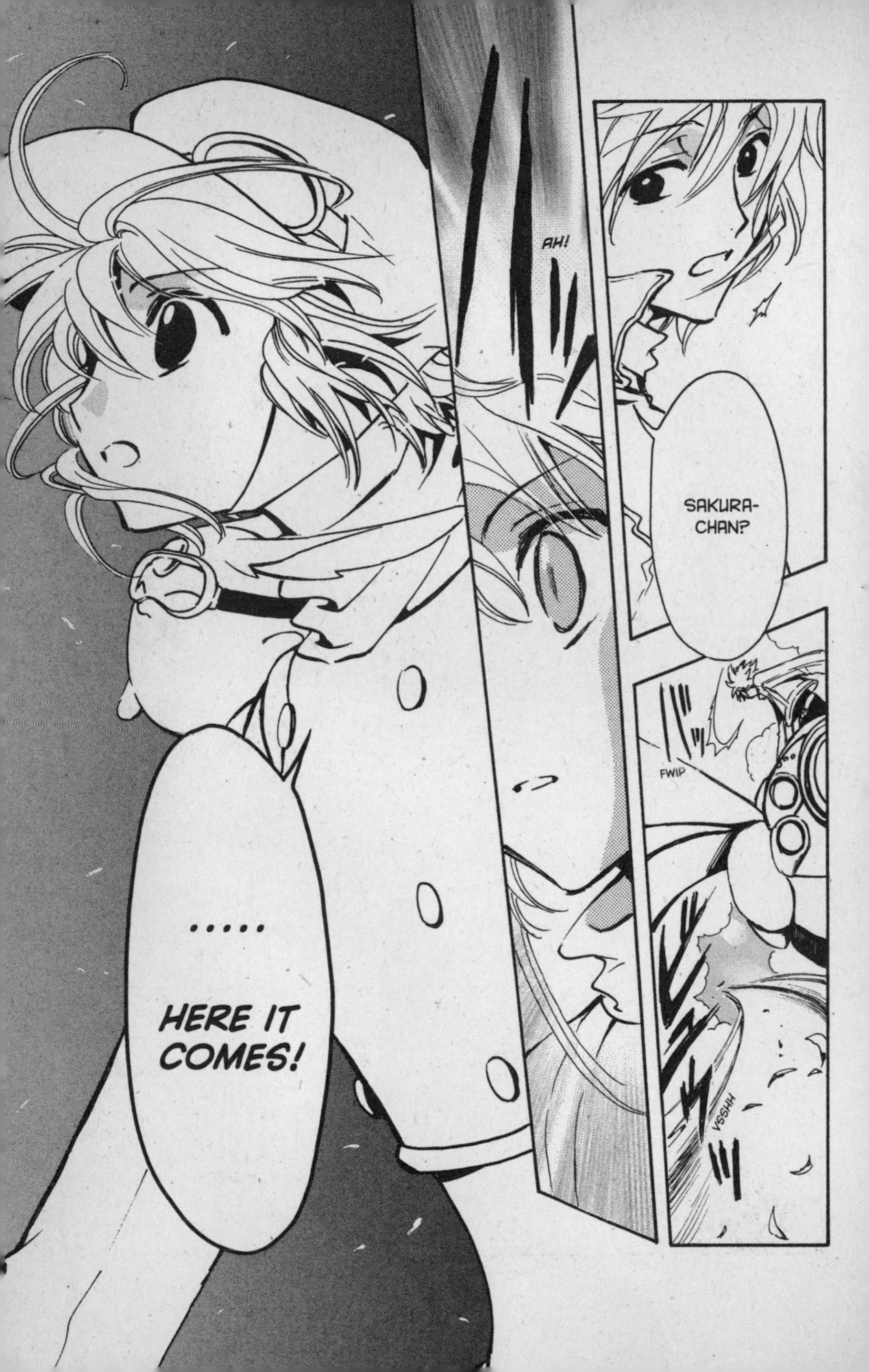
AH!
SAKURA-CHAN?
FWIP
VSSH
.....
HERE IT COMES!

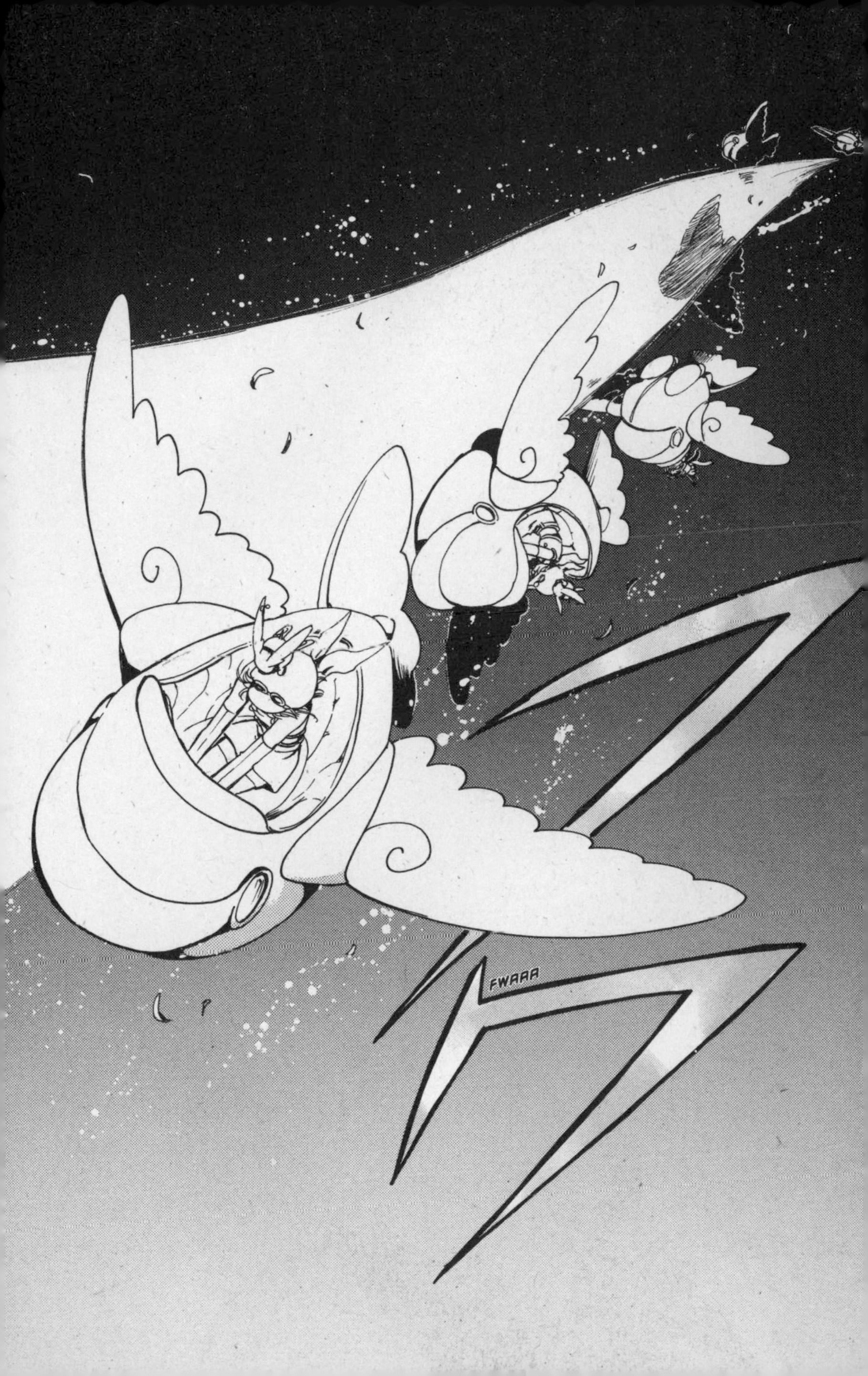
FWAAA

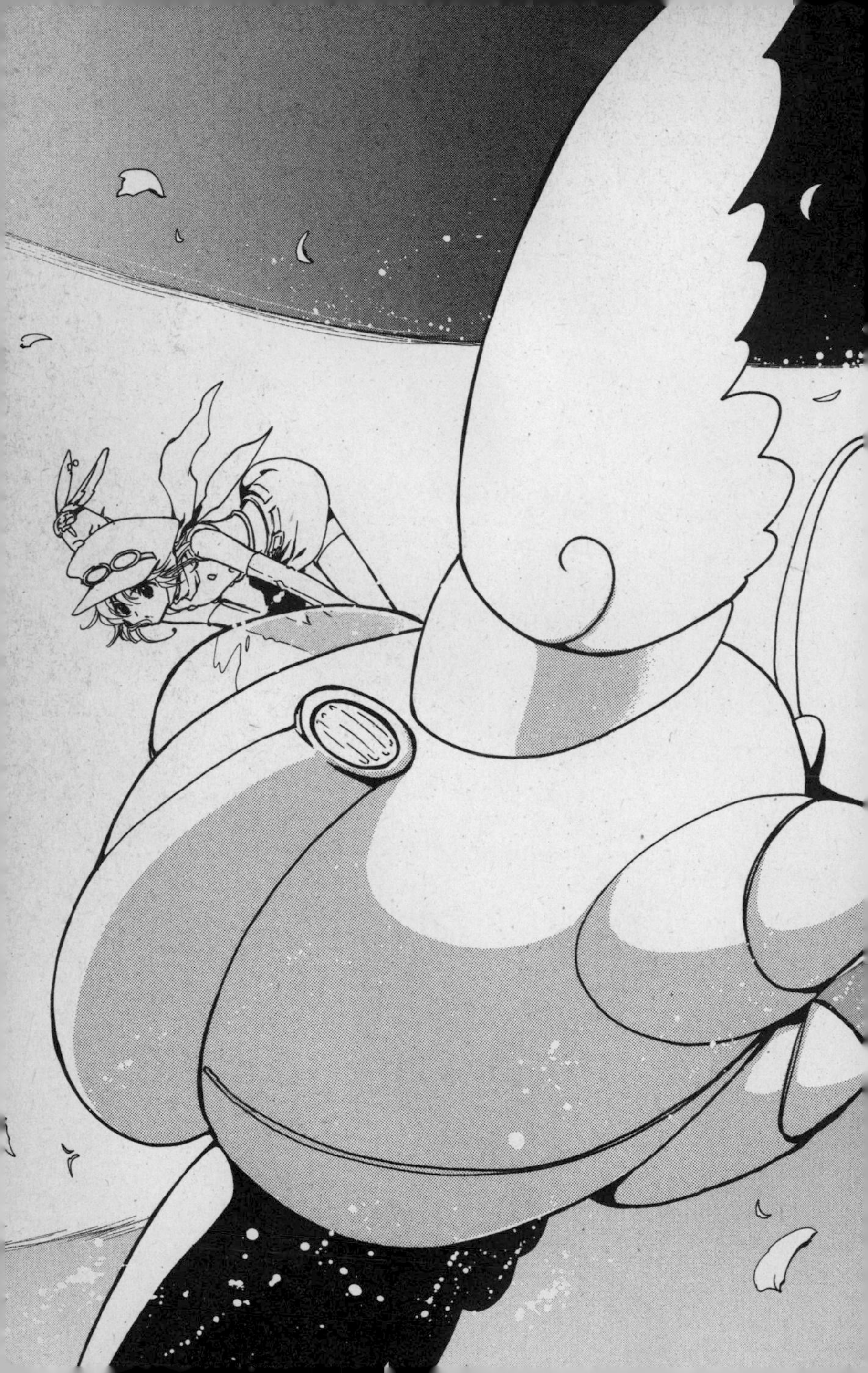

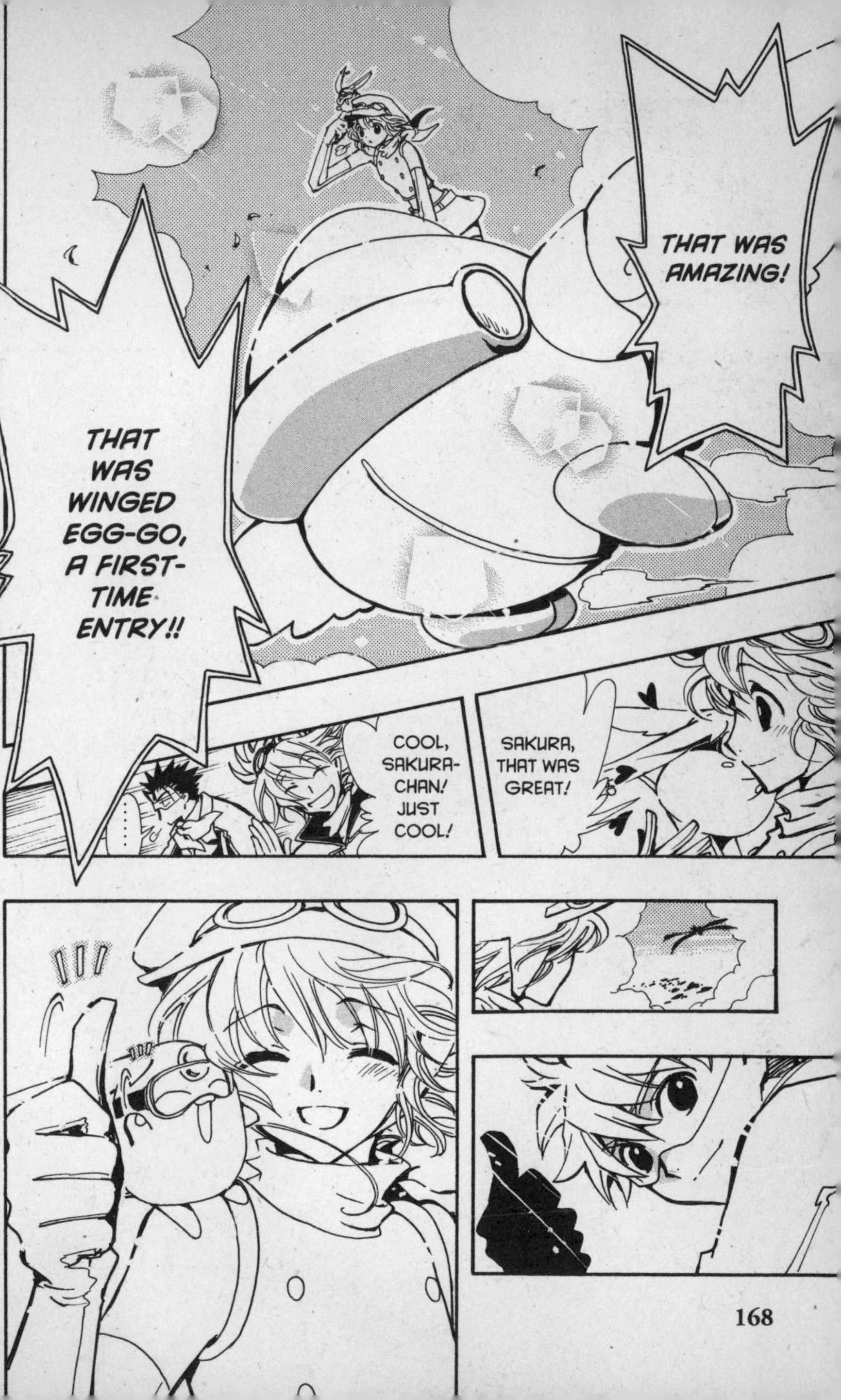
THAT WAS AMAZING!
THAT WAS WINGED EGG-GO, A FIRST-TIME ENTRY!!
SAKURA, THAT WAS GREAT!
COOL, SAKURA-CHAN! JUST COOL!

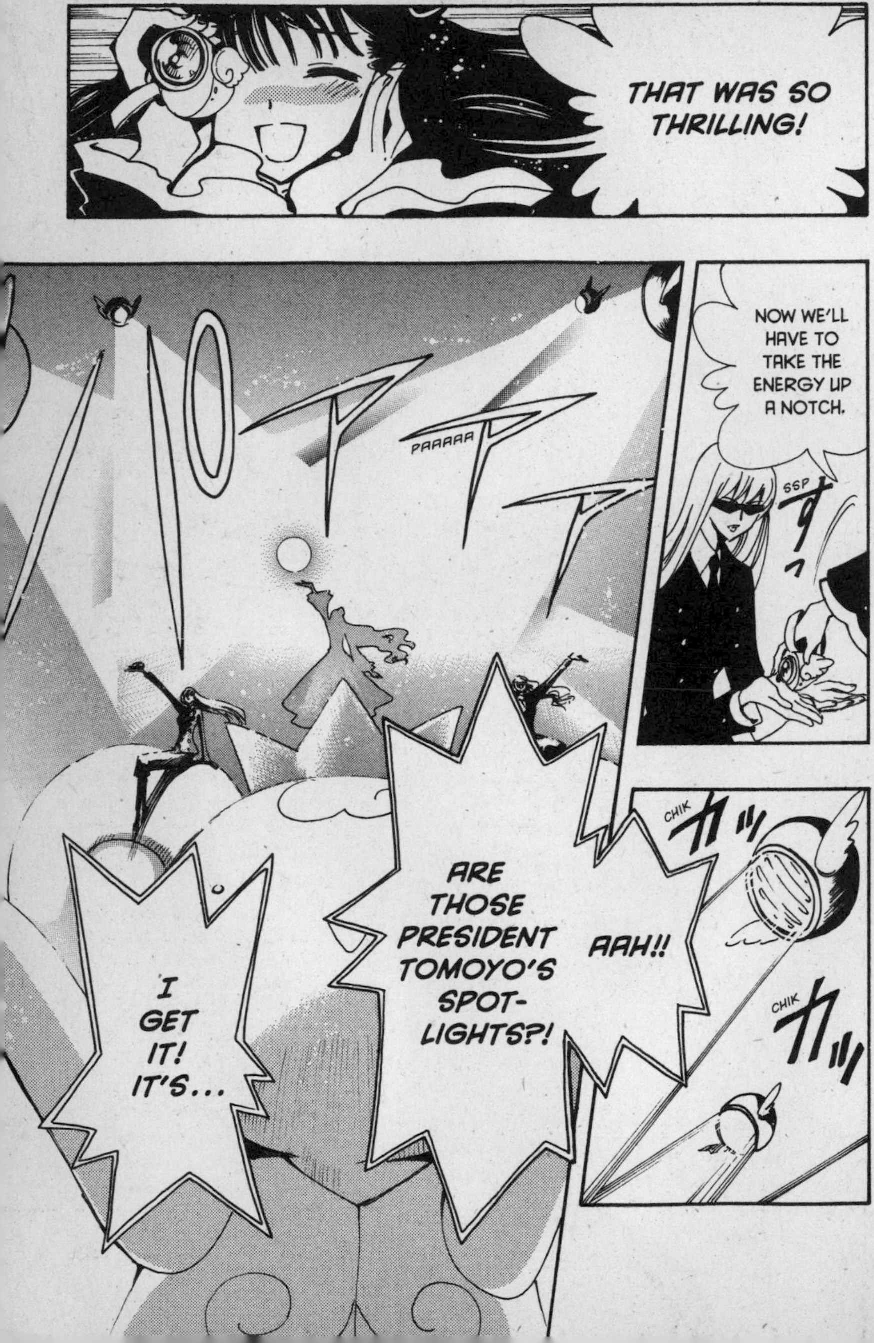
THAT WAS SO THRILLING!
NOW WE'LL HAVE TO TAKE THE ENERGY UP A NOTCH.
SSP
CHIK
CHIK
PAAAAA
AAH!!
ARE THOSE PRESIDENT TOMOYO'S SPOT-LIGHTS?!
I GET IT! IT'S...

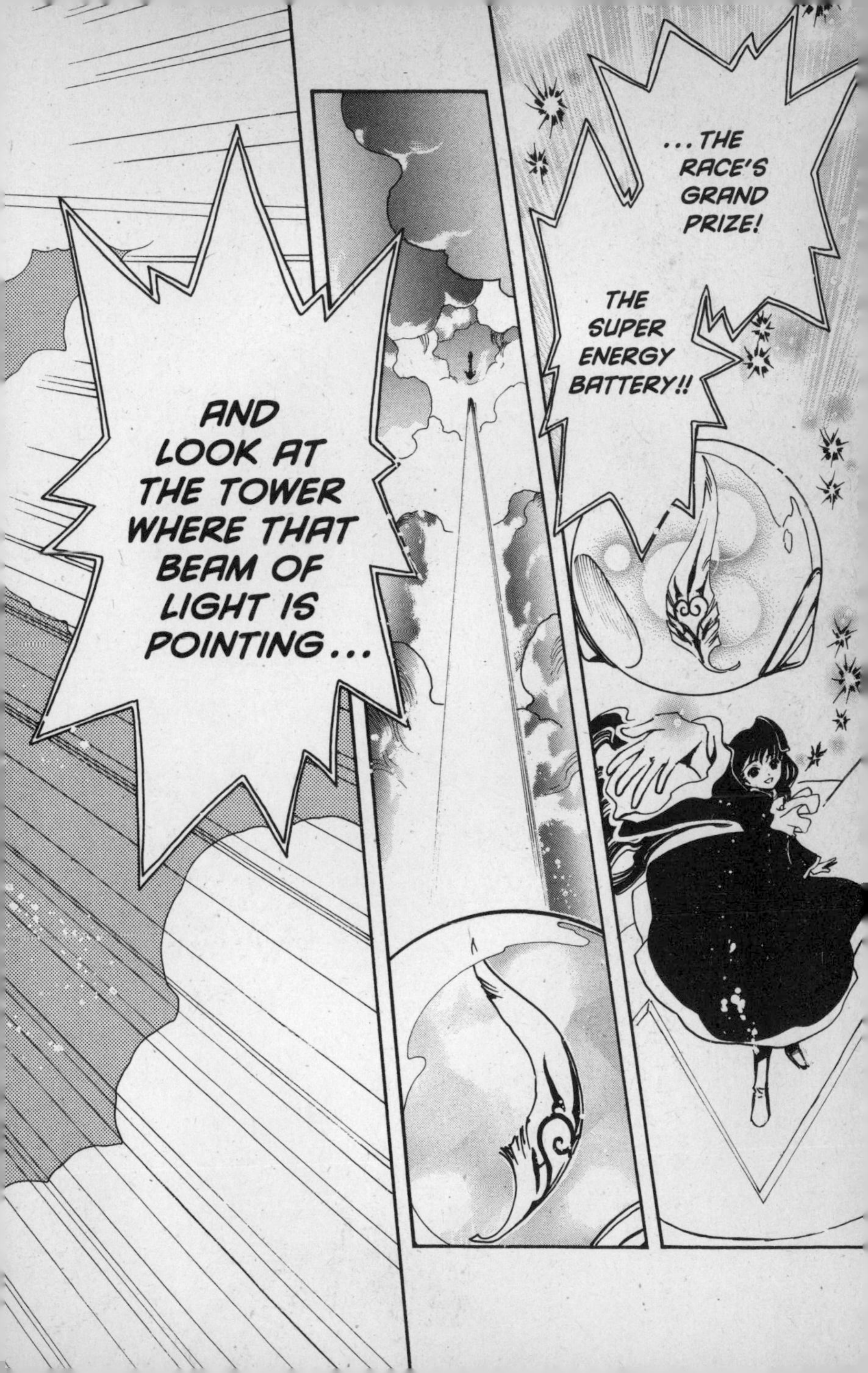
AND LOOK AT THE TOWER WHERE THAT BEAM OF LIGHT IS POINTING...
...THE RACE'S SUPER GRAND PRIZE!
THE SUPER ENERGY BATTERY!!

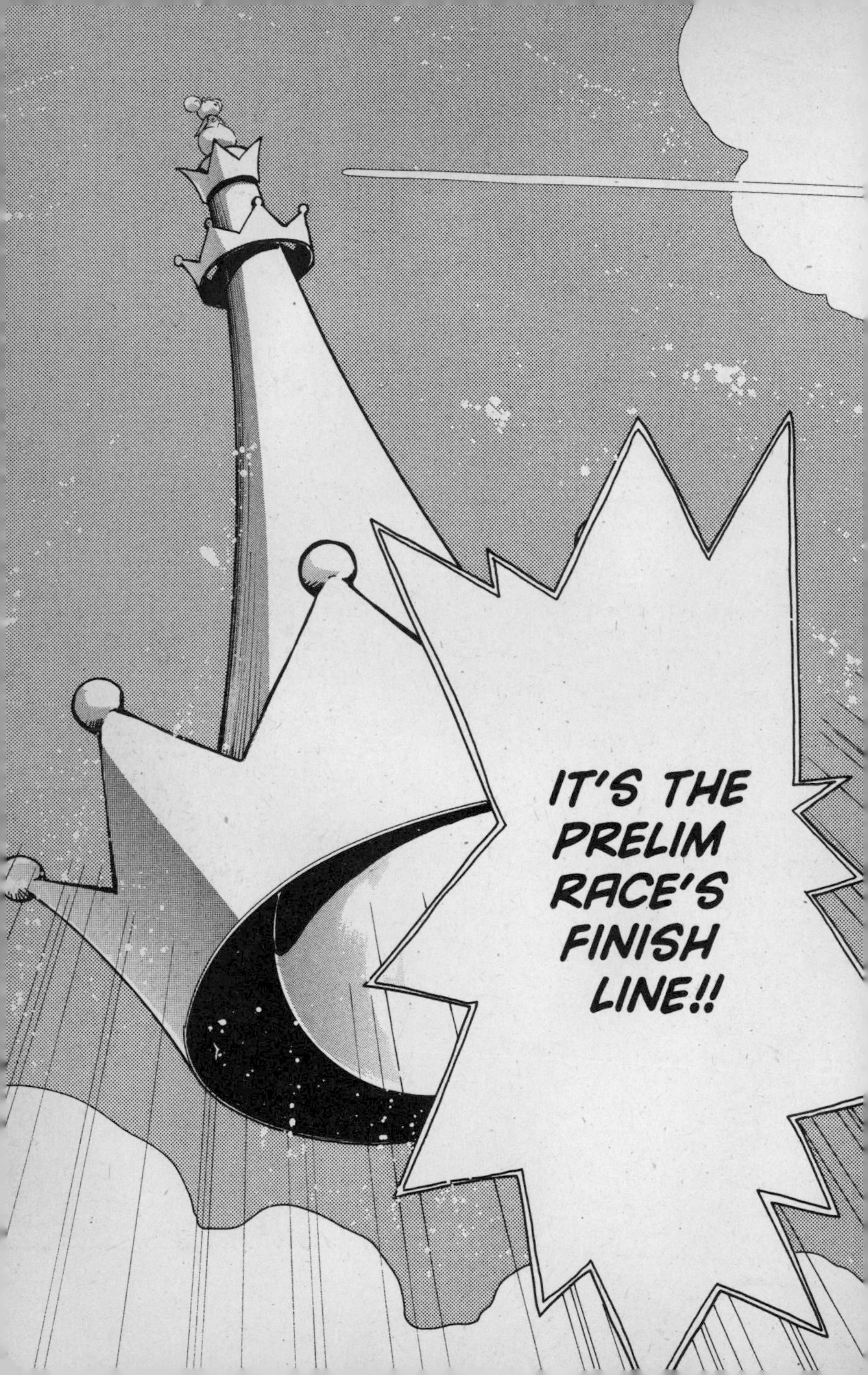
IT'S THE PRELIM RACE'S FINISH LINE!!

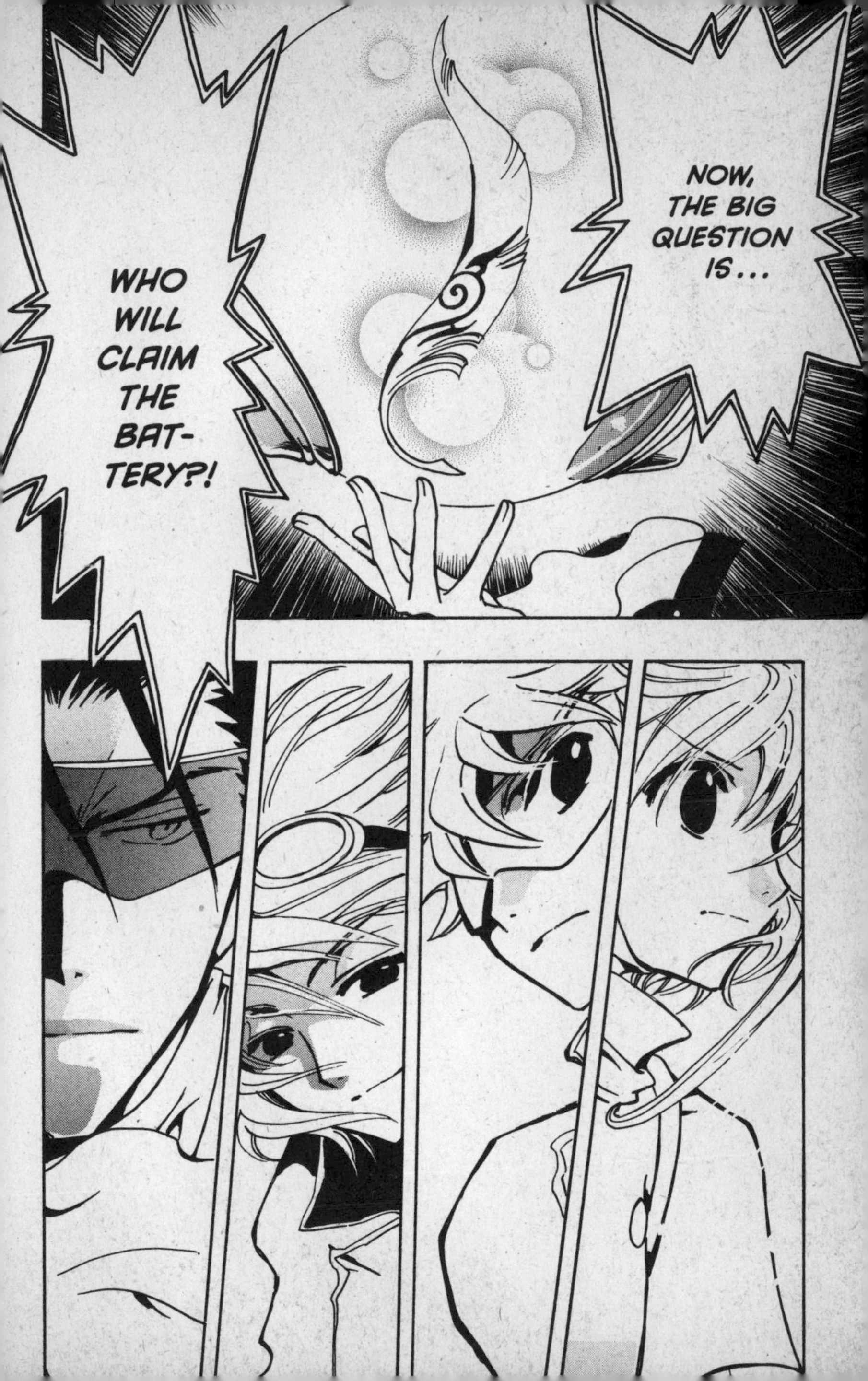
NOW, THE BIG QUESTION IS...
WHO WILL CLAIM THE BAT-TERY?!

To Be Continued

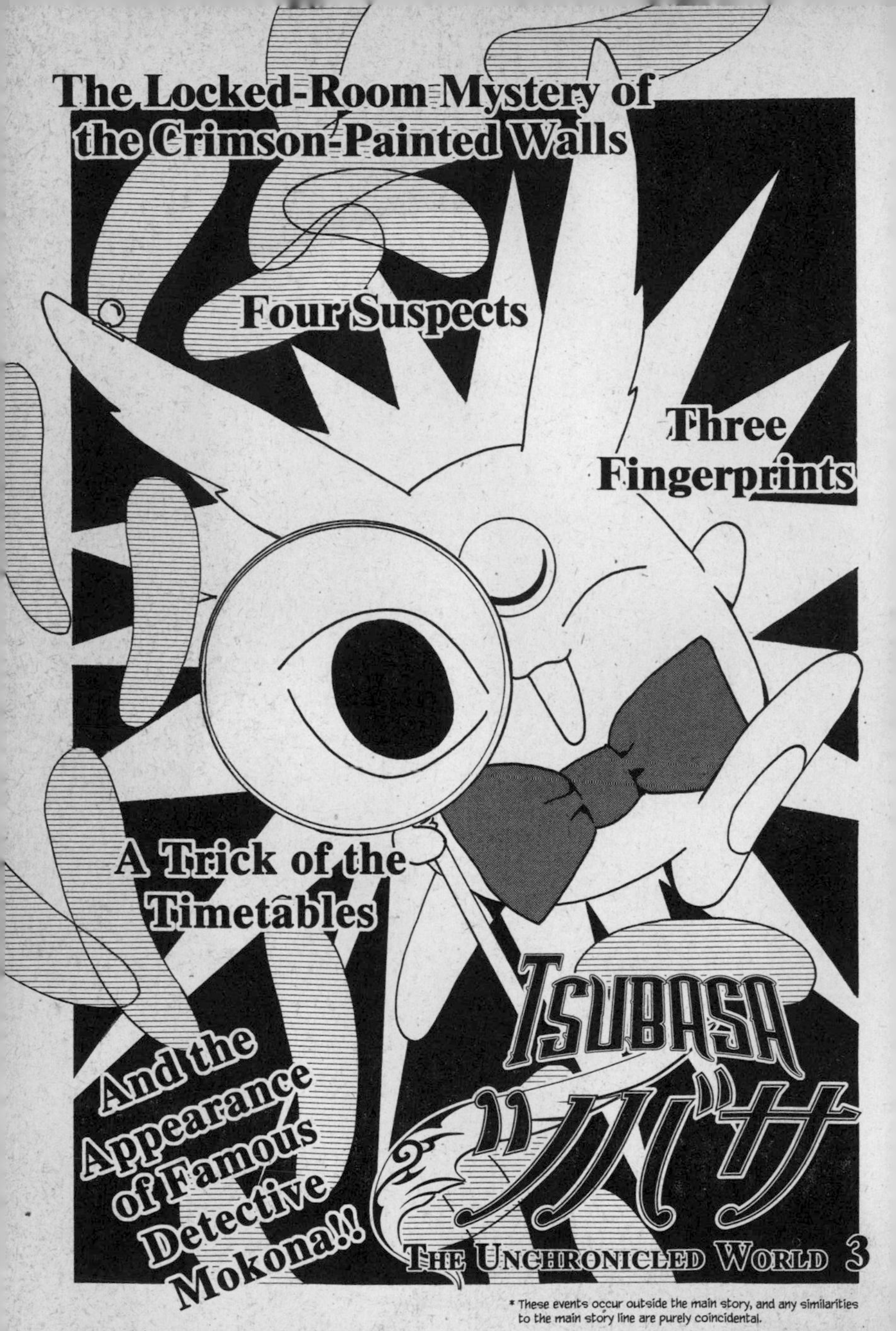
The Locked-Room Mystery of the Crimson-Painted Walls
Four Suspects
Three Fingerprints
A Trick of the Timetables
And the Appearance of Famous Detective Mokona!!
TSUBASA
ツバサ
THE UNCHRONICLED WORLD 3
* These events occur outside the main story, and any similarities to the main story line are purely coincidental.

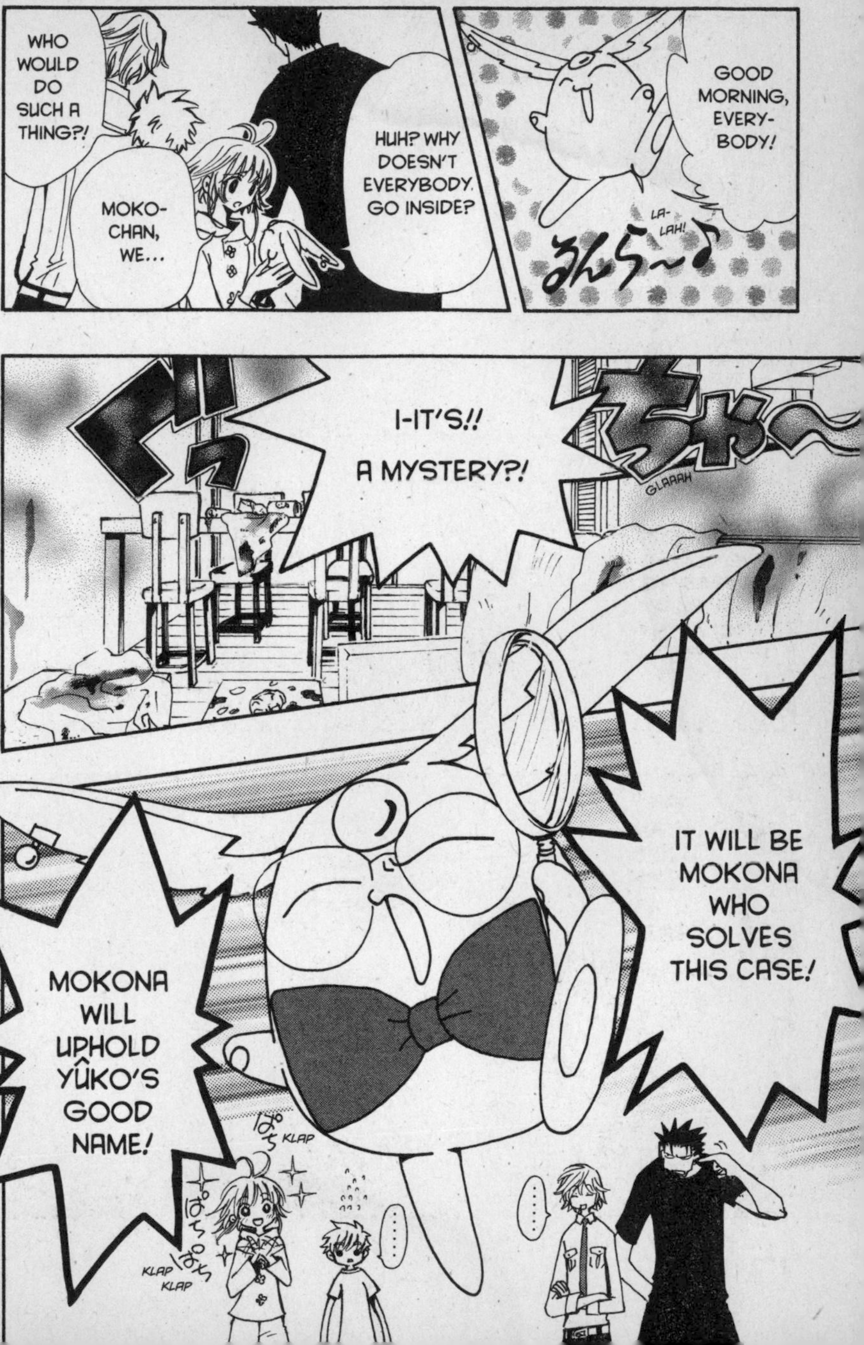
GOOD MORNING, EVERY-BODY!
LA-LAH!
HUH? WHY DOESN'T EVERYBODY GO INSIDE?
WHO WOULD DO SUCH A THING?!
MOKO-CHAN, WE...
GLAAAH
I-IT'S!!
A MYSTERY?!
IT WILL BE MOKONA WHO SOLVES THIS CASE!
MOKONA WILL UPHOLD YÛKO'S GOOD NAME!
KLAP
KLAP KLAP
……
……

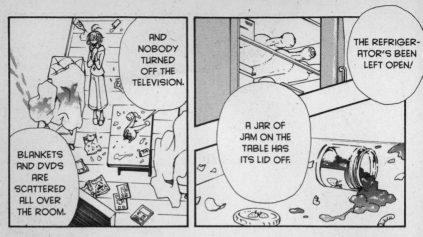

THE REFRIGERATOR'S BEEN LEFT OPEN!
A JAR OF JAM ON THE TABLE HAS ITS LID OFF.
AND NOBODY TURNED OFF THE TELEVISION.
BLANKETS AND DVDS ARE SCATTERED ALL OVER THE ROOM.
MOKO-CHAN, THERE'S EVEN JAM OVER HERE!
IT SEEMS THAT THE CULPRIT OPENED THE REFRIGERATOR, AND ATE JAM WHILE WATCHING TELEVISION...
ふ
HEH
IT'S MOKONA'S CONJECTURE THAT WHAT THE CULPRIT WATCHED...
...IS KUROGANE'S PRIZED DIRTY DVD.
WHO ARE YOU SAYING "PRIZED" THAT THING?!
I MEAN, I NEVER HEARD OF IT!
ANOTHER THING...
不思議の国の美幸ちゃん
MIYUKI-CHAN IN WONDERLAND

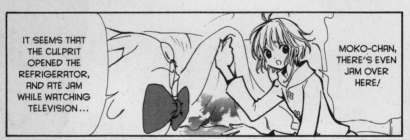

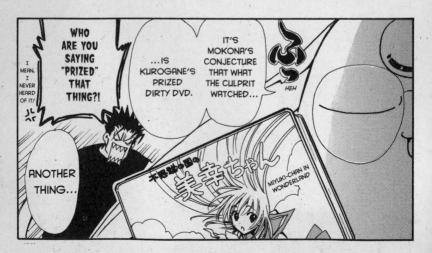

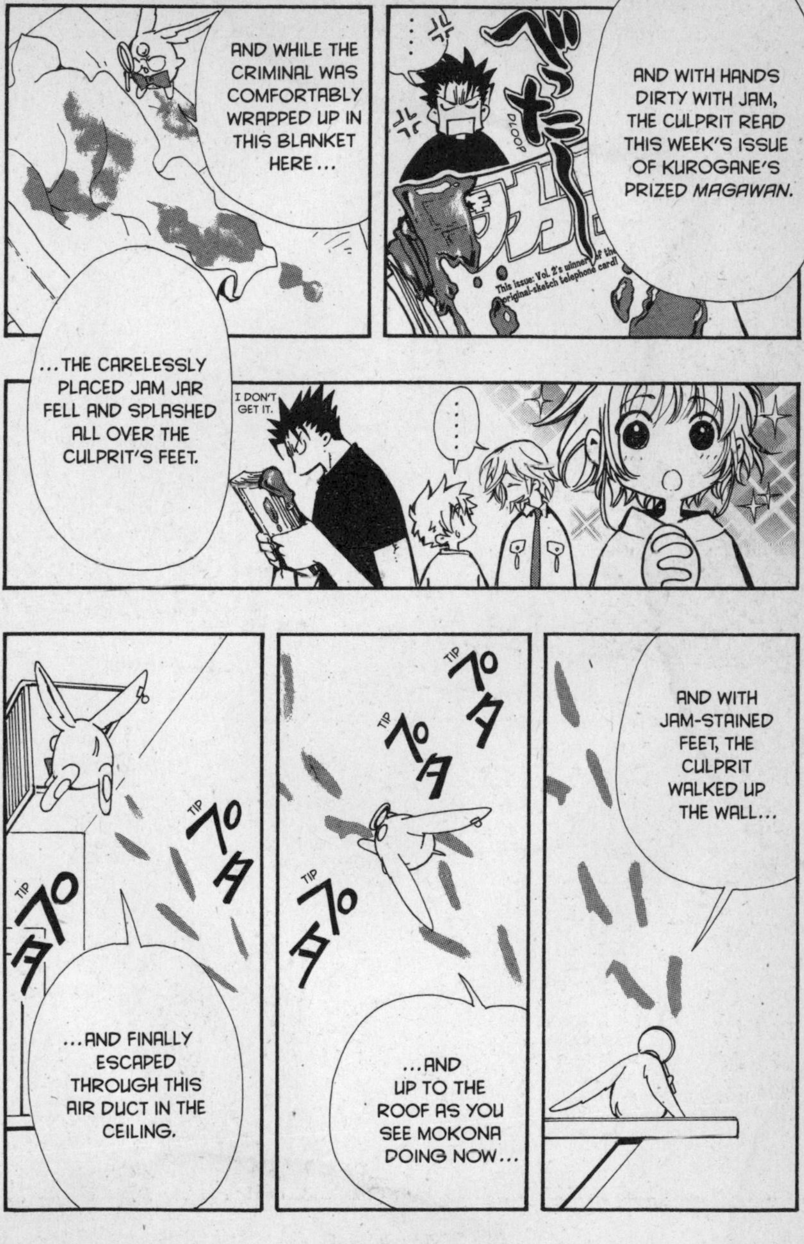

DLOOP
This issue: Vol. 2's winner of the original-sketch telephone card!
AND WITH HANDS DIRTY WITH JAM, THE CULPRIT READ THIS WEEK'S ISSUE OF KUROGANE'S PRIZED *MAGAWAN.*
AND WHILE THE CRIMINAL WAS COMFORTABLY WRAPPED UP IN THIS BLANKET HERE...
...THE CARELESSLY PLACED JAM JAR FELL AND SPLASHED ALL OVER THE CULPRIT'S FEET.
......
I DON'T GET IT.
AND WITH JAM-STAINED FEET, THE CULPRIT WALKED UP THE WALL...
TIP
TIP
TIP
...AND UP TO THE ROOF AS YOU SEE MOKONA DOING NOW...
TIP
TIP
...AND FINALLY ESCAPED THROUGH THIS AIR DUCT IN THE CEILING.

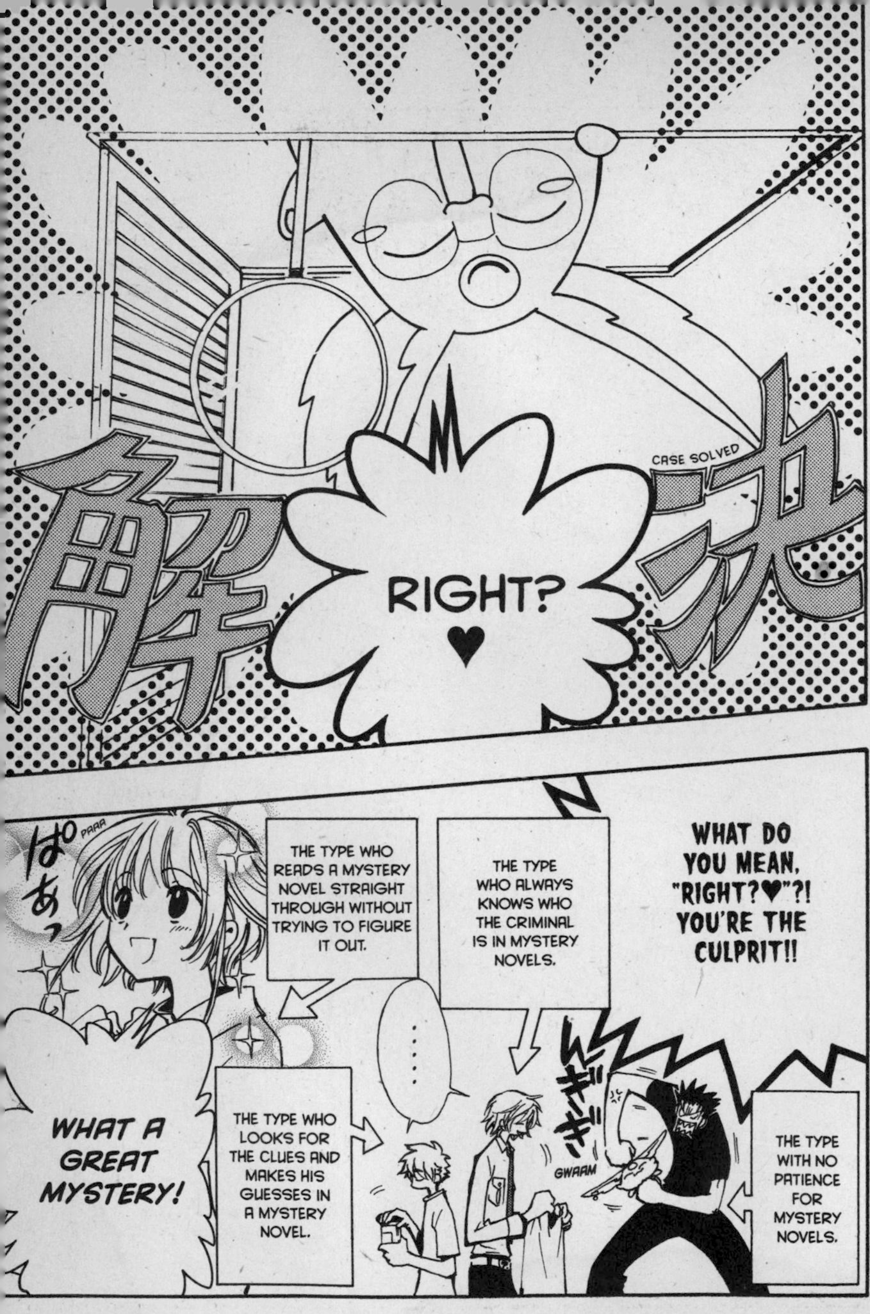
解決
CASE SOLVED
RIGHT? ♥
WHAT DO YOU MEAN, "RIGHT?♥"?! YOU'RE THE CULPRIT!!
THE TYPE WHO ALWAYS KNOWS WHO THE CRIMINAL IS IN MYSTERY NOVELS.
THE TYPE WHO READS A MYSTERY NOVEL STRAIGHT THROUGH WITHOUT TRYING TO FIGURE IT OUT.
ぱあっ
PAAA
THE TYPE WITH NO PATIENCE FOR MYSTERY NOVELS.
んぎぎ
GWAAM
……
THE TYPE WHO LOOKS FOR THE CLUES AND MAKES HIS GUESSES IN A MYSTERY NOVEL.
WHAT A GREAT MYSTERY!

★ The End ★

About the Creators

CLAMP is a group of four women who have become the most popular manga artists in America—Ageha Ohkawa, Mokona, Satsuki Igarashi, and Tsubaki Nekoi. They started out as doujinshi (fan comics) creators, but their skill and craft brought them to the attention of publishers very quickly. Their first work from a major publisher was *RG Veda*, but their first mass success was with *Magic Knight Rayearth*. From there, they went on to write many series, including *Cardcaptor Sakura* and *Chobits*, two of the most popular manga in the United States. Like many Japanese manga artists, they prefer to avoid the spotlight, and little is known about them personally.

CLAMP is currently publishing three series in Japan: *Tsubasa* and *xxxHOLiC* with Kodansha and *Gohou Drug* with Kadokawa.

Translation Notes

Japanese is a tricky language for most Westerners, and translation is often more art than science. For your edification and reading pleasure, here are notes on some of the places where we could have gone in a different direction in our translation of the work, or where a Japanese cultural reference is used.

A Special Honorific for the Country of Shura

The Country of Shura is based on the world of *RG Veda* (which in turn is based on Hindu mythology). Its citizens employ a special honorific which is used in the Japanese version of Tsubasa.

-ô: Taken from the *kanji* for king, the -ô honorific is reserved for the high gods/heroes who are the powerful rulers of their particular clans. The player character in the country of Ôto, Ryûô, was a character originated in *RG Veda*, and his name is made up of the kanji for dragon and king where the final ô sound is the same kind of honorific.

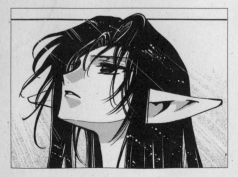

Ashura's Gender

The TokyoPop translation of *RG Veda* establishes Ashura as male. However the dialog of this book had no gendered pronouns or other indications of Ashura's gender. As it has done for Mokona Modoki, this translation has striven to keep the character's gender as ambiguous as in the original.

Jinja, page 58

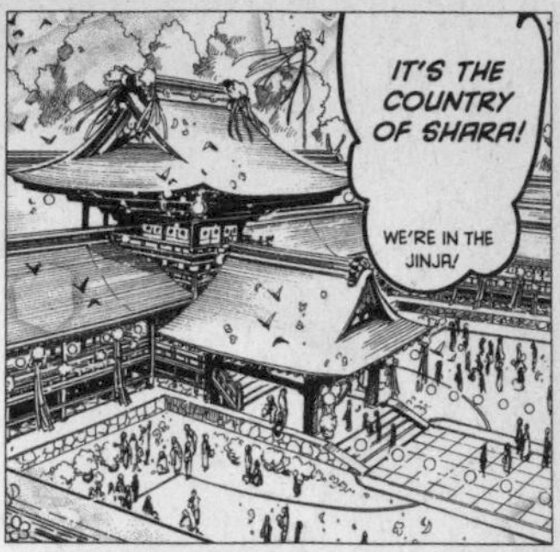
IT'S THE COUNTRY OF SHARA!
WE'RE IN THE JINJA!

The *Jin* part of *Jinja* is a kanji that sounds the same as the kanji for god but means army or troops. Therefore this word comes off sounding like the Japanese word for a Shinto shrine, *Jinja*, except that it's a shrine dedicated to the military arts.

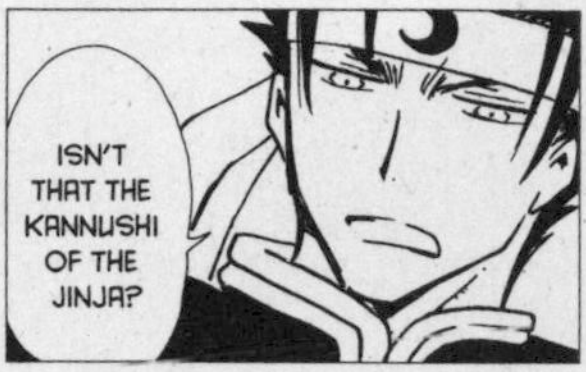
ISN'T THAT THE KANNUSHI OF THE JINJA?

Kannushi, page 62

The word means a Shinto priest and one who protects a shrine.

Cracking the saké cask (*Kagami-wari*), page 70

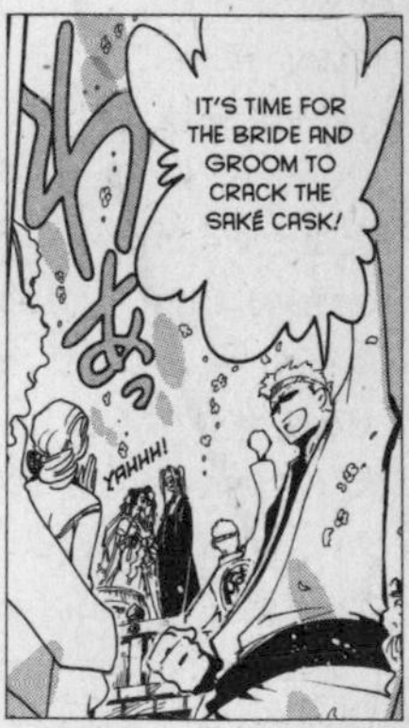
IT'S TIME FOR THE BRIDE AND GROOM TO CRACK THE SAKÉ CASK!
YAHHH!

This tradition is practiced not only at weddings, but at many types of celebrations. Saké is brought in to the proceedings in a large wooden container with a rough-hewn wooden lid. The main celebrants take a large wooden mallet and crack the boards of the lid apart, and that's when the saké is served to all of the guests. Sort of like the traditional popping of the cork.

Manju, page 78

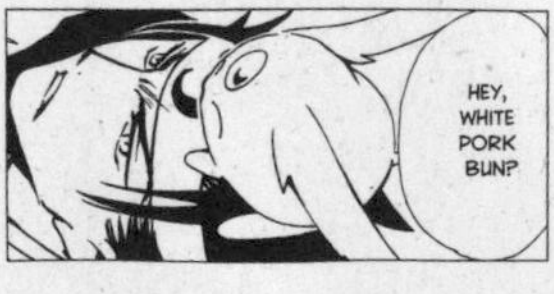
HEY, WHITE PORK BUN?

The same type of big, white, wheat-dough bun as *siu bao*, found in dim sum restaurants and sometimes sold steaming hot on chilly autumn days from street vendors in Yokohama's Chinatown. Yum . . .

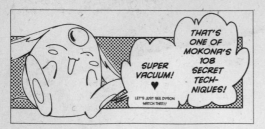

SUPER VACUUM! ♥

THAT'S ONE OF MOKONA'S 108 SECRET TECH-NIQUES!

LET'S JUST SEE DYSON MATCH THAT!!

Dyson, page 81

A maker of home cleaning products such as vacuum cleaners. Although Dyson is a Western manufacturer and Dyson products are available in North America, the brand hasn't penetrated the American popular culture as much as other brands of vacuum cleaners. So it would be like saying, "Let's see a Hoover try to match that!" in the U.S.A.

Piffle World, page 101

If you're a CLAMP fan, you've probably seen Piffle Princess products scattered throughout the various recent books by CLAMP, the most recent being the White Day gift that Kimihiro Watanuki gives to the Zashiki-Warashi in Volume 5 of xxxHOLiC. The heart and soul of Piffle Princess can be found in the CLAMP tournament manga *Angelic Layer*. Piffle World looks to be the ultimate evolution of the Piffle Princess store and line of products.

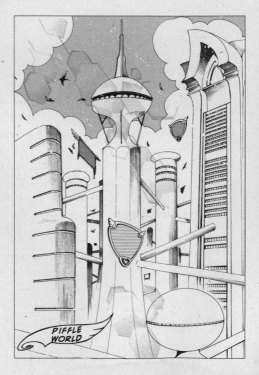

PIFFLE WORLD

Tea for the guests, page 122

Serving tea to one's guests is a time-honored tradition in Japan, and although servants are not necessarily included in the tradition, Fai and Syaoran are far too polite to allow the servants to stand in the hot sun without offering refreshments.

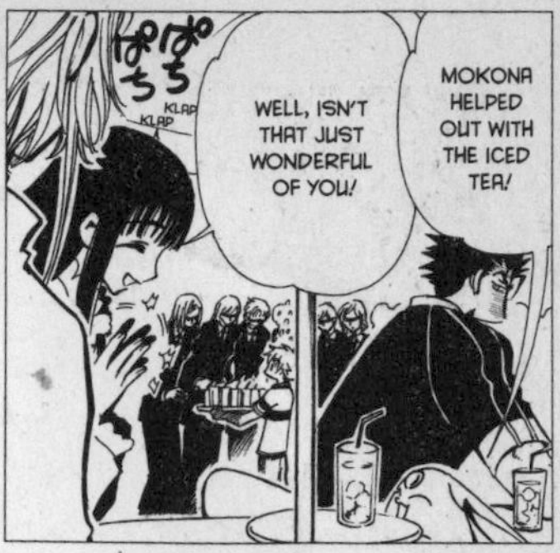
MOKONA HELPED OUT WITH THE ICED TEA!
WELL, ISN'T THAT JUST WONDERFUL OF YOU!
KLAP
KLAP

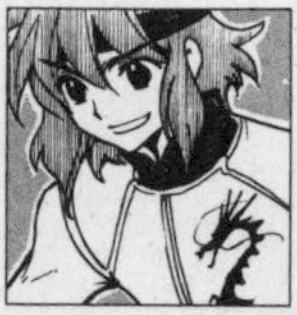

Ryûô's emblem, page 143

The dragon on Ryûô's flight suit stands for the first character in his name, *ryû*, which means dragon.

Piffle-go and the suffix for vehicles, page 153

Go is a Japanese suffix for certain types of machines and vehicles when those machines are given names. The original title for *Speed Racer* (*Maha Go-go, Go!*) was a pun based on that fact. It combined this suffix with the Japanese word for five (*go*) and the English word "go" to get Mach 5-go, Go! And the repetition of "go" in the original Japanese *Speed Racer* song is mirrored in the sound effect seen on panel three of this page.

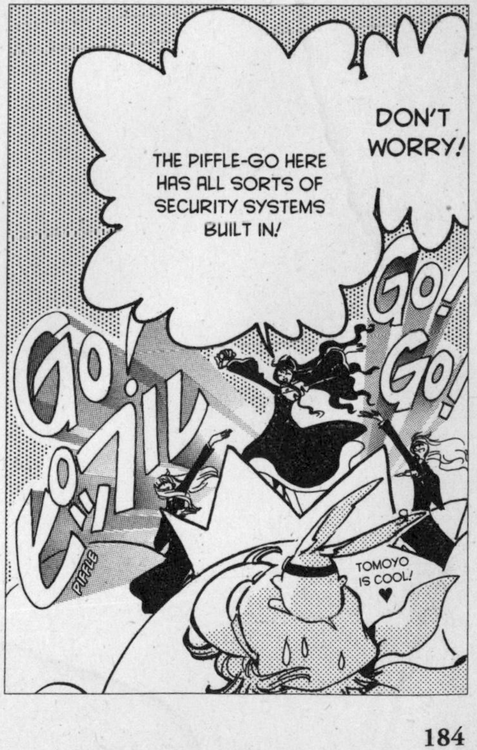
DON'T WORRY!
THE PIFFLE-GO HERE HAS ALL SORTS OF SECURITY SYSTEMS BUILT IN!
GO! GO!
GO!
TOMOYO IS COOL! ♥
PIFFLE

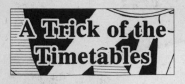

A Trick of the Timetables

Timetables, page 175

The most obvious similarity between England and Japan is that both are island nations. But a far more subtle similarity is their love for whodunit-style murder mysteries. And since both nations rely heavily on their train service, it is not uncommon for an average citizen of either country to carry around railway timetables on any particular outing. So mystery writers of both countries have devised whodunit novels where one of the major clues to solving the mystery is knowing exactly when a certain train stops at a certain station.

Watch for Volume 11 of Tsubasa, on sale October 31, 2006!

TOMARE!

[STOP!]

You're going the wrong way!

Manga is a completely
different type of reading
experience.

To start at the *beginning*,
go to the *end*!

That's right! Authentic manga is read the traditional Japanese way—from right to left. Exactly the *opposite* of how American books are read. It's easy to follow: Just go to the other end of the book, and read each page—and each panel—from right side to left side, starting at the top right. Now you're experiencing manga as it was meant to be.

FEB 08

CH